Customer Service
Skills for Success

Robert W. Lucas
Webster University, Orlando, Florida

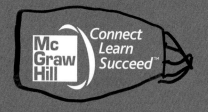

Mc
Graw
Hill

*Connect
Learn
Succeed*™

The McGraw-Hill Companies

Mc Graw Hill

Connect
Learn
Succeed™

CUSTOMER SERVICE: SKILLS FOR SUCCESS

Published by McGraw-Hill, a business unit of The McGraw-Hill Companies, Inc., 1221 Avenue of the Americas, New York, NY, 10020. Copyright © 2012 by Robert W. Lucas. All rights reserved. Previous editions © 1996, 2002, 2005, and 2009. No part of this publication may be reproduced or distributed in any form or by any means, or stored in a database or retrieval system, without the prior written consent of The McGraw-Hill Companies, Inc., including, but not limited to, in any network or other electronic storage or transmission, or broadcast for distance learning.

Some ancillaries, including electronic and print components, may not be available to customers outside the United States. Printed in the United States of America.

This book is printed on acid-free paper.

3 4 5 6 7 8 9 0 QDB/QDB 1 0 9 8 7 6 5 4 3 2

ISBN 978-0-07-339711-5
MHID 0-07-339711-3

Vice president/Editor in chief: *Elizabeth Haefele*
Vice president/Director of marketing: *Alice Harra*
Sponsoring editor: *Barbara Owca*
Director of development: *Sarah Wood*
Developmental editor: *Kristin Bradley*
Executive marketing manager: *Keari Green*
Lead digital product manager: *Damian Moshak*
Digital development editor: *Kevin White*
Director, Editing/Design/Production: *Jess Ann Kosic*
Lead project manager: *Susan Trentacosti*
Buyer II: *Debra R. Sylvester*
Senior designer: *Srdjan Savanovic*
Senior photo research coordinator: *Lori Hancock*
Photo researcher: *Pam Carley*
Cover design: *Eric Kass*
Interior design: *Ellen Pettengell*
Typeface: *10.5/13 New Aster LT Std*
Compositor: *Aptara, Inc.*
Printer: *Quad/Graphics*
Credits: The credits section for this book begins on page 388 and is considered an extension of the copyright page.

Library of Congress Cataloging-in-Publication Data

Lucas, Robert W.
   Customer service : skills for success / Robert W. Lucas.—5th ed.
     p. cm.—(Connect, learn, succeed)
   Includes index.
   ISBN-13: 978-0-07-339711-5 (alk. paper)
   ISBN-10: 0-07-339711-3 (alk. paper)
   1. Customer services. I. Title.
  HF5415.5.L83 2012
  658.8'12—dc22
                                                    2010048859

The Internet addresses listed in the text were accurate at the time of publication. The inclusion of a Web site does not indicate an endorsement by the author or McGraw-Hill, and McGraw-Hill does not guarantee the accuracy of the information presented at these sites.

www.mhhe.com

Personal Biography

Robert (Bob) W. Lucas holds dual roles as president of *Creative Presentation Resources*—a creative training and products company—and founding managing partner for *Global Performance Strategies*, LLC—an organization specializing in performance-based training, consulting services, and life-planning seminars.

Bob has extensive experience in human resources development, management, and customer service over the past three decades in a variety of organizational environments. This background gives him a real-world perspective on the application of theory he has studied and used for several decades. He is certified in a variety of programs from various national and international training organizations.

Bob focuses on assisting organizations and individuals in developing innovative and practical strategies for improved workplace performance. His areas of expertise include customer service, presentation skills, training and management program development, train-the-trainer, interpersonal communication, adult learning, and employee and organizational development.

Bob serves on the board of the Central Florida Chapter of the American Society for Training and Development (ASTD) and is the 2011 president.

In addition to giving regular presentations to various local and national groups and organizations, Bob serves as an adjunct faculty members for Webster University. In that position, he teaches organizational and interpersonal communication, diversity, and Introduction to Training and Development.

Listed in the *Who's Who in the World*, *Who's Who in America*, and *Who's Who in the South and Southeast* for a number of years, Bob is also an avid writer. Published works include *The Creative Training Idea Book*; *Inspired Tips and Techniques for Engaging and Effective Learning*; *The BIG Book of Flip Charts*; *How to Be a Great Call Center Representative*; *Customer Service Skills and Concepts for Success*; *Job Strategies for New Employees*; *Communicating One-to-One*; *Making the Most of Interpersonal Relationships*; *Coaching Skills: A Guide for Supervisors*; *Effective Interpersonal Skills*; *Training Skills for Supervisors*; and *Customer Service: Skills and Concepts for Business*. Additionally, he has been a contributing author for the *Annual: Developing Human Resources* series by Pfeiffer & Company since 1992 and to the HRHandbook by HRD Press. Bob's 20th book, *Please Every Customer: The Ultimate Guide to Delivering Stellar Service Across Cultures* through McGraw-Hill, will be published in 2011.

Bob has earned a Bachelor of Science degree in Law Enforcement from the University of Maryland and a Master of Arts degree with a focus in Human Resources Development from George Mason University in Fairfax, Virginia. He also completed a Master of Arts program in Management and Leadership at Webster University.

Brief Contents

Contents

Part Two Skills for Success   76

Part Three Building and Maintaining Relationships 182

Preface

New to This Edition

Chapter 1

- New chapter opening case study (Amica Insurance Company)
- New Think About It
- Updated research and statistics
- Updated discussion on Growth in the Service Sector
- New section on Global Economic Shifts
- New discussion of Mindsets in a Changing Economy
- Expanded coverage of Human Resources
- Addition of a Small Business Perspective section

Chapter 2

- New chapter opening case study (Ben & Jerry's Ice Cream)
- New Think About It
- Updated research and statistics
- Expanded discussion of Attitude in Service
- New explanation of Organizational Mentors
- Updated coverage of Service Strategy
- Addition of a Small Business Perspective section

Chapter 3

- New chapter opening case study (The Methodist Hospital System)
- New Think About It
- Updated research and statistics
- Revised and expanded section on Two-Way Communication
- New explanation of Using Eye Contact Effectively
- Updated information on Assertive versus Aggressive Behavior
- Addition of a Small Business Perspective section

Chapter 4

- Updated chapter opening case study (Starbucks)
- Updated Think About It
- Updated research and statistics
- New explanations of Spatial Cues
- Addition of a Small Business Perspective section

Chapter 5

- New chapter opening case study (The American Red Cross)
- New Think About It
- Updated research and statistics
- Expanded coverage of Biases
- New explanations for Faulty Assumptions
- New and expanded Ethical Dilemmas
- Addition of a Small Business Perspective section

Chapter 6

- New chapter opening case study (Orange County Clerk of Courts)
- New Think About It
- Updated research and statistics
- New Customer Service Tips
- Explanation of Determining Styles
- Addition of a Small Business Perspective section

Chapter 7

- New chapter opening case study (Heinz Ketchup)
- New Think About It
- Updated research and Statistics
- Tips for Staying Connected
- New and expanded Ethical Dilemmas
- Addition of a Small Business Perspective section

Chapter 8

- New chapter opening case study (Netflix)
- New Think About It
- Updated research and statistics
- New coverage of Technologies to Help the Hearing Impaired
- New and expanded Ethical Dilemmas
- Addition of a Small Business Perspective section

Chapter 9

- Updated chapter opening case study (Google)
- Updated Think About It
- Updated research and statistics
- Heavily expanded coverage to include Emerging Service Technologies
- New coverage on Customer Call Centers
- Inclusion of Twitter, Social Networking Sites, and Video Sharing Sites and their Impact on Customer Service
- New and expanded Ethical Dilemmas
- Addition of a Small Business Perspective section

Chapter 10

- New chapter opening case study (Stoner Inc.)
- New Think About It
- Updated research and statistics
- New discussion of Word of Mouth Advertising
- Discussion of Customer Service in the Context of the BP Oil Spill
- New information on Personalizing Your Approach
- Expanded coverage of the Benefits of Customer Relationship Management
- New discussion of the Role of Channel Partner Relationships on Customer Loyalty
- Addition of a Small Business Perspective section

Not the Same Old Customer Service Textbook

Customer Service: Skills for Success uses a variety of activities and example to gain and hold readers' interest while providing additional insights into the concepts and skills related to customer service.

The text begins with a macro view of what customer service involves today and provides projections for the future then focuses on specific skills and related topics.

The fifth edition of *Customer Service: Skills for Success* contains 10 chapters divided into three parts, plus the Appendix, Glossary, and Bibliography. These parts focus on different aspects of customer service: (1) The Profession, (2) Skills for Success, and (3) Building and Maintaining Relationships. Along with valuable ideas, guidance, and perspectives, readers will also encounter interviews of real-world service providers and case study scenarios and activities to help you apply concepts learned to real-world situations in order to challenge your thinking on the issues presented. For users of previous editions, you will note a streamlined approach where we have combined material from several previous chapters. If you need the chapters on Time and Stress Management, they can be found on our Web site, www.mhhe.com/customerservice, along with many new activities, case studies, and other support material.

Learning Outcomes

Each chapter starts with behavioral-based **Learning Outcomes** to direct your focus and to help you measure your end of chapter success in grasping the concepts presented. You will also find a **quote** from a famous person to prompt your thinking related to the chapter topic and the text focus. Throughout the book and in the Contents, the abbreviation LO indicates the Learning Outcome that appears to that section.

> **Learning Outcomes**
>
> **After completing this chapter, you will be able to:**
>
> **3-1** Explain the importance of effective communication in customer service.
> **3-2** Recognize the elements of effective two-way interpersonal communication.
> **3-3** Avoid language that could send a negative message and harm the customer-relationship.
> **3-4** Project a professional customer service image.
> **3-5** Provide feedback effectively.
> **3-6** Use assertive communication techniques to enhance service.
> **3-7** Identify key differences between assertive and aggressive behavior.

As you explore the chapter material, readers will find many helpful tools to enhance their learning experience and assist them in transferring their new knowledge to the workplace. These tools are outlined below.

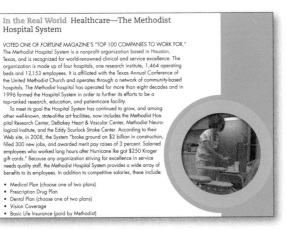

In the Real World Healthcare—The Methodist Hospital System

VOTED ONE OF *FORTUNE* MAGAZINE'S "TOP 100 COMPANIES TO WORK FOR," The Methodist Hospital System is a nonprofit organization based in Houston, Texas, and is recognized for world-renowned clinical and service excellence. The organization is made up of four hospitals, one research institute, 1,464 operating beds and 12,153 employees. It is affiliated with the Texas Annual Conference of the United Methodist Church and operates through a network of community-based hospitals. The Methodist hospital has operated for more than eight decades and in 1996 formed the Hospital System in order to further its efforts to be a top-ranked research, education, and patient-care facility.

To meet its goal the Hospital System has continued to grow, and among other well-known, state-of-the art facilities, now includes the Methodist Hospital Research Center, DeBakey Heart & Vascular Center, Methodist Neurological Institute, and the Eddy Scurlock Stroke Center. According to their Web site, in 2008, the System "broke ground on $2 billion in construction, filled 300 new jobs, and awarded merit pay raises of 3 percent. Salaried employees who worked long hours after Hurricane Ike got $250 Kroger gift cards." Because any organization striving for excellence in service needs quality staff, the Methodist Hospital System provides a wide array of benefits to its employees. In addition to competitive salaries, these include:

- Medical Plan (choose one of two plans)
- Prescription Drug Plan
- Dental Plan (choose one of two plans)
- Vision Coverage
- Basic Life Insurance (paid by Methodist)

In the Real World

In the Real World sections, placed at the beginning of many of the chapters, provide insights into customer service in a variety of well-known businesses, industries, and organizations. These candid snapshots provide an overview of how successful businesses provide products and services and succeed in a highly competitive global world.

Think About It

Think About It activities provide an opportunity for readers to reflect on the In the Real World scenarios that they just read, do an Internet search on those organizations, and then answer the questions provided. The goal of the activity is to cause readers to delve further into how the organization addresses customer service, and to relate it to their personal knowledge and what they read about service in the book. These activities can be done individually or as a group, where answers are shared.

Quick Preview

Pretests called **Quick Preview** are provided at the beginning of each chapter as a self-assessment of current skills and knowledge levels before even reading the first page. This allows readers to check their topic knowledge and primes them for specific content to watch for as they read the chapter. Answers to the questions are provided at the end of the chapter.

Work It Out

Work It Out activities throughout the chapters challenge readers' knowledge and provide an opportunity for individual and/or small group work on a specific topic or issue.

Summary and Review Questions

At the end of each chapter is a **Summary** and also **Review Questions**, which bring together the key elements and issues encountered in the chapter. These questions will test the readers' absorption level for the content they have read and highlight areas for remedial study to assure mastery of the chapter topic.

Search It Out

Search It Out activities at the end of chapters provide the opportunity to research chapter-related skills on the Internet. In each chapter, readers will explore the Internet to obtain a variety of customer service facts, figures, and related information associated with chapter content to use in group activities, presentations, or discussions. Visit the Web site especially designed by McGraw-Hill for *Customer Service: Skills for Success* at www.mhhe.com/customerservice.

Collaborative Learning Activity

Collaborative Learning Activities allow one or more readers to work together with the instructor and actually address a customer service issue in order to practice their skills, find answers to various questions, and reinforce their knowledge of the chapter topic.

Collaborative Learning Activity

Role-Playing to Improve Verbal Communication

Find a partner (or two) and use the following role-plays to improve your verbal communication skills. After reading the scenarios, pick the two for which you want to practice and receive the most feedback. Next, take a moment to think about how each of you will play your part and then have a two- or three-minute dialogue centering on the situation.

For the four scenarios, alternate roles with your partner(s): each of you should role-play twice, and each of you will be the debriefer twice. If possible, videotape or audiotape the conversation. This will allow each of you to see or hear how you seem when you interact with others. After the role-play, discuss how each of you felt about the way the other person han-

dry cleaning. He is upset because the garment is expensive and was to have been worn to a class reunion yesterday. When playing the customer, do not become calmed or satisfied until the service provider offers what you believe is a realistic solution or compensation. As the service provider, try to avoid "giving away the store" by quickly offering to replace the shirt or offering financial compensation.

Scenario 2
You are a member services representative in an automobile club that provides maps, trip information, towing and travel services, and a variety of travel-related products. A member has stopped by to find out whether she can get a replacement membership card and assistance in planning an upcoming vacation.

Face to Face

Face to Face exercises are customer service scenarios in which readers assume the role of a specified employee and use information provided to determine how they might handle a similar customer service issue if faced with it on the job.

Face to Face

Seeking Information from a Client

Background
LKM Graphics has been in business in Norfolk, Virginia, for almost five years. The company employs 17 full-time employees in its graphic design department, a part-time administrative assistant, and three interns from Old Dominion University's graphic arts program. During a typical week, LKM prints 300,000 to 400,000 documents for businesses in the surrounding Tidewater metropolitan area. Most clients have 15 or fewer employees, although there are two active and ongoing government contracts with the Naval Operations Base, which is nearby. The owner of LKM, Linda McLaroy, hired you three years ago when you graduated from the graphic arts program. You are now one of the senior graphics account managers with the company and supervise four other team members.

recent visit to Brickman Bakery, you met the new office manager, Sylvia Greco. You had been told by a friend who works at Brickman's that Sylvia is considering closing her account with LKM Graphics and moving it to a competitor. Before joining Brickman's last month, she had been employed by another organization in the area and had developed a strong relationship with your competitor. Since she is comfortable with the competitor's operation and has friends there, she wants to maintain the relationship. You've also heard through the grapevine that Sylvia prefers to work with your competitor's account representative.

Critical Thinking Questions
1. Since you don't have a relationship with Sylvia, what will you do to get off to a solid start during

Planning to Serve

Planning to Serve activities provide a roadmap for planning strategies and identifying techniques from the book that can be used to provide superior customer service in the future.

Planning to Serve

Using the content of this chapter as a guide, create a Personal Action Plan focused on improving your verbal communication skills when providing service to your customers. Begin by taking an objective assessment of your current verbal communication strengths and areas for improvement. Once you have identified areas that need improvement, set goals for improvement.

Start your assessment by listing as many strengths and areas for improvement as you are aware of. Share your list with other people who know you well to see

if they agree or can add items. Keep in mind that you will likely be more critical of yourself than will others. Additionally, you may be sending messages that you are not aware of because of the way you currently communicate. For those reasons, keep an open mind when considering their comments.

Once you have a list, choose two or three items that you think need the most work and can add the most value when interacting with others. List these items on a sheet of paper along with specific courses of action you will take for improvement, the name of

Quick Preview Answers

1. F	3. F	5. T	7. F	9. F	11. T
2. T	4. T	6. F	8. F	10. F	12. F

Ethical Dilemma Summary

Ethical Dilemma 3.1 Possible Answers
1. How would you react to or feel about your supervisor's position?
   Depending on how you were reared and the values that were reinforced to you (e.g., personal from your parents and/or religious) the supervisor's stance might be a real demotivator for you and could lead to loss of respect or other feelings toward him/her.

is at stake and could result in lost business (from the customer and anyone else he/she tells the story to).
2. Would this cause any change in your relationship with your supervisor? Why or why not?
   This is a personal decision that only you can make. In many cases, such behavior on the part of the supervisor could lead to suspicion (e.g., if he or she lies about this type of thing, what else

Quick Preview Answers and Ethical Dilemma Summary

These are the answers to the Quick Preview pretest at the beginning of the chapter, along with the possible answers to the Ethical Dilemma features throughout the chapter.

Appendix

Use the **Reader Satisfaction Survey** found in the **Appendix** at the end of the text to provide the author with feedback. For doing so, readers will receive a free publication on Interpersonal Communication.

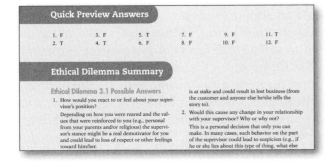

Appendix

Reader's Customer Service Survey

Name _____
Title _____
Organization/School _____
Address (where you want booklet mailed) _____

City/State/Zip _____
Phone ( ) _____

Customer feedback is crucial for delivering effective service and addressing specific needs. For us to make necessary additions, deletions,

The Customer Service Text that Gives You More

Student Resources

Online Learning Center (OLC)—Student Content: A separate section of the McGraw-Hill Web site has been reserved for students and instructors. This section contains online practice tests, additional learning exercises, and other World Wide Web links to stimulate your research efforts. Visit www.mhhe.com/customerservice.

Spanish Translations: Spanish-speaking readers can take advantage of the **Spanish Translations** of the glossary of key terms and online quizzes.

Student Study Guide: The **Student Study Guide** includes worksheets, practice tests, and supplemental learning materials so students can reinforce their learning of the chapter concepts. The Student Study Guide is organized by chapter and learning outcome to assist students in understanding each chapter's goals and objectives. This guide is available in both a print version or as part of the online enhanced cartridge.

Instructor Resources

Online Learning Center (OLC)—Instructor Content: The instructor's side of the **Online Learning Center (OLC)**, also at www.mhhe.com/customerservice, serves as a resource for instructors and has several features that support instructors in the creation of lessons. Included on the OLC are the Instructor's Manual (IM), which is organized by each chapter's learning outcomes and includes page references; PowerPoint slides that include additional instructor teaching notes; the Asset Map; and other valuable materials.

Instructor's Manual: The **Instructor's Manual** outlines course materials, additional in-class activities, and support for classroom use of the text. It has been organized by learning outcomes to give instructors not only a basic outline of the chapter, but to assist in all facets of instruction. For every question posed in the text, the IM provides a viable answer. The text page numbers provide easy reference for instructors. In addition, the Instructor's Manual guides instructors through the process of integrating supplementary materials into lessons and assignments. It also includes sample syllabi, video notes, and student success insights. Ultimately, this will be an instructor's greatest advantage in using all materials to reach all learners.

Test Bank: Every chapter provides a series of test questions, available in our **Test Bank.** Questions are organized by learning outcome and Bloom's Taxonomy. A Test Table aligns questions with the content and makes it easy for you to determine the questions you want to include on tests and quizzes.

Asset Map: We know that instructors' time is valuable. To help you prepare, we have created an **Asset Map.** The Asset Map identifies by chapter, learning outcome, and page number exactly which supplements are available for you to use. Visit our Web site at www.mhhe.com/customerservice to preview how the Asset Map can help!

PowerPoints: PowerPoint slides, created specifically for instructors, include additional teaching notes and are tied directly to learning outcomes. Each slide also includes a text page reference for your convenience.

Sample Syllabi: Six- and sixteen-week syllabi are provided in order to tailor content to different learning programs.

Customer Service DVD: These videos were created exclusively to accompany *Customer Service: Skills for Success*. Each video matches to chapter content to offer real-world examples of customer service theories.

Basis for Content

This book draws from my more than three plus decades of real-world experience in customer service environments, management, and human resource development. I have worked in sales, retail management, and service functions for a number of organizations; I am a performance consultant working with client organizations in many different industries; and I have been the president of my own e-commerce retail company—Creative Presentation Resources (www.presentationresources.net)—since 1994. I have taught at numerous colleges and universities through the Master's level for nearly two decades. I deal with customer issues and needs everyday, and know that the techniques described in this book work. While there are some research and theoretical sections in the chapters, much of the information is derived from personal experience, research, and reflections of actual customer service encounters experienced by others.

Whether you are new to the service profession and have no base of customer service knowledge, or are more experienced and wish to enhance your knowledge and skills, *Customer Service: Skills for Success* and accompanying ancillary materials can provide a catalyst for their success.

I am confident that this book will assist you reaching your goal to become a better service provider.

Bob Lucas

Acknowledgments

Throughout the years, my wife, friend, and life partner, M.J., and my mother, Rosie, have sacrificed much as I have dedicated time and effort to developing tools such as this book to help others grow. Their support and love have been an invaluable asset in helping me reach my goals and are much appreciated.

A special note of appreciation also goes to Alice Harra and Kristin Bradley, and the entire McGraw-Hill team, for their expert guidance and support. Their efforts were essential in helping to create this book and add many new features to enhance its value.

Preparing any project of the length and depth of this book requires much assistance. No one person can bring together all the necessary knowledge, expertise, and insights to capture the essence of a topic.

It is with deepest gratitude to all of the following experts who took the time to read through many draft pages of the manuscript for *Customer Service: Skills for Success* and provide valuable insights, guidance, and suggestions for improvement. Without them, the final product would have proven to be of far less value to its users.

Michael Discello, *Pittsburgh Technical Institute*

Scott Warman, *ECPI Technical College*

Toni R. Hartley, *Laurel Business Institute*

Richard S. Janowski, *The Butler Business School / The Sawyer School*

Barbara VanSyckle, *Jackson Community College*

Jorjia Clinger, *McCann School of Business and Technology*

Fran Green, *Everest University*

Gary M. Corona, *Florida State College at Jacksonville, Kent Campus*

Diane Lolli, *Cambridge College*

Joel Whitehouse, *McCann School of Business and Technology*

Gordie Dodson, *Remington College Cleveland East*

Special thanks also to the following educators who reviewed previous editions and offered suggestions, critique, and guidance in the refinement of the book content and format.

A. Murlene Asadi, *Scott Community College*

Blake Beck, *Idaho State University*

Claudia Browning, *Mesa Community College*

Gary Corona, *Florida Community College at Jacksonville*

Brenda Dupras, *The Saulter School*

Margaret A. Fisher, *Florida Community College at Jacksonville*

Matthew Graham, *Andover College*

Elizabeth D. Hall, *Tidewater Technical College*

Linda Harris, *Florida Metropolitan University*

DeAnn Hurtado, *Sinclair Community College*

Heidi Hutchins, *Gateway Community College*

Mark King, *Indiana Business College*

Lea Ann Kremer, *McCann School of Business & Technology*

Albert Mastromartino, *Sir Sanford Fleming College*

John Moonen, *Daytona Beach Community College*

Jacqueline Nicholson, *Holyoke Community College*

Shelly Rex, *York Technical Institute*

Paul Ricker, *Broward Community College—North Campus*

Judith Rozarie, *Gibbs College*

Dee Shields, *Indiana Business College*

Carl Stafford, *Manchester Community College*

Henry Tarbi, *Year Up*

Kathleen Wachter, *University of Mississippi*

Joyce Walsh-Portillo, *Broward Community College*

Michael Wierzbicki, *Scottsdale Community College*

Callie P. Williams, *Florida Community College at Jacksonville*

Richard Williams, *Nashville State Community College*

Customer Service
Skills for Success

Customer Service Interview
Larry Wilson
Director of Special Programs, Florida Safety Council

1 What are the personal qualities that you believe are essential for anyone working with customers in a service environment?

- Patience (*Check your temper, frustrations, prejudices, and attitudes at the door*)
- Understanding (*Understand that your customer may be frustrated, angry, unwilling to listen, or rude, but it is your job to turn his/her frown into a smile*)
- Empathy (*What would I want if I were in the customer's shoes*)
- Excellent communication skills (*Identify the customers' ability to communicate and never speak above them, speak in terms that they can understand*)
- Excellent listening skills (*Listen with your body as well as your ears. Maintain eye contact and block out all distractions while assisting your customers. To you, they are the only person in the world for those few minutes*)
- Outstanding knowledge of products/services (*Know everything about your products or services and believe in their usefulness in your customer's life. A lack of knowledge will impart a feeling of insecurity to your customer.*)
- Hospitable (*Treat any customer as if he or she has just walked into your own home. Introduce yourself to customers and let them know that they are welcome and wanted in your environment*)

2 What do you see as the most rewarding part of working with customers? Why?

The knowledge that you have made a difference in the lives of your customers. You may be the only true, warm, and understanding person that they will come in contact with that day or perhaps even that week. Through the services or products that you offer, you have the ability to improve the quality of their lives. Good customer service leaves you with the feeling that you have truly made a difference in someone's life.

3 What do you believe is the most challenging part of working with customers? Why?

The ability to identify and adjust to a customer's cultural customs or traditions. You must know the basics of other countries' social courtesies. For example, showing the sole of your shoe in front of someone from an Arabic country is considered very rude; therefore, you must keep your feet firmly on the ground while assisting them. In other words, do not cross your legs. If you are bilingual (English/Spanish), you must adjust the words that you use when speaking with customers from other countries, as some words that you may use could have a completely different meaning to the customer (perhaps they would consider a word to be vulgar) with whom you are speaking.

4 What changes have you seen in the customer service profession since you took your first service provider position? For example types of customers, their attitudes, people who work in the service industry, how technology is applied to provide service, etc.

The state of the economy has a direct reflection on the attitudes that one experiences with customers. During a downturn in the economy, customers are reluctant to spend as freely as when the economy is in an upward turn. This is also reflected in the customer's expectation of service. When money is tight, customers want and expect more service for the dollars that they spend.

In recent years, the Internet has vastly increased competition for customers. Twelve years ago, customers may have had only two or three sources from which to purchase their products or services; they now have an infinite number.

5 What future issues do you see evolving related to dealing with customers in your profession and why do you think these are important?

I foresee much more competition in our markets. This competition will most likely come from worldwide sources online. Therefore, the only resource that we will have available to combat this will be extraordinary customer service. When you cannot compete with the low prices available online, you must compensate by providing an enjoyable, first-rate personal experience that cannot be duplicated online. We must turn back the clock and return to the small town, relationship-based, "doing business with a friend" mentality.

6 What advice related to customer service do you have for anyone seeking a career in a customer service environment?

I would say that we all have careers in customer service, no matter what field we choose to enter. For the rest of our lives, whether we are physicians, attorneys, accountants, or perhaps clergy, we all will have customers. The difference will be whether we have internal customers or external customers. For example, an internal accountant's customers will be his/her fellow workers, who are dependent on him/her for their paychecks. There is simply no such thing as a job that does not involve customer service in one way or another. Therefore, my suggestion to anyone entering the workforce would be to take customer service classes. This is not a skill that comes naturally to most people. It is a learned skill, which with experience will serve them in all areas, both personal and professional, for the rest of their lives.

The Customer Service Profession

"Treat every customer as if they sign your paycheck, because they do."

—Unknown

● Learning Outcomes

After completing this chapter, you will be able to:

1-1 Define customer service.

1-2 Describe factors that have impacted the growth of the service sector in the United States.

1-3 Identify the socioeconomic and demographic changes that have influenced customer service.

1-4 Recognize the changes in consumer behavior that are impacting service.

1-5 List the six major components of a customer-focused environment.

1-6 Explain how some companies are addressing the changes impacting the service sector.

● Key Terms

business-to-business (B2B)
cottage industries
customer-focused organization
customer relationship management (CRM)
customer satisfaction
customer service
customer service environment
deliverables

delivery system
deregulation
downsizing
e-commerce
external customers
globalization
human resources
internal customers
learning organizations
networking
North American Free Trade Agreement (NAFTA)

offshoring
organizational culture
outsourcing
product
service economy
service industry
service recovery
service sector
Small Business Administration (SBA)
telecommuting

In the Real World Insurance–Amica Insurance Company

AMICA MUTUAL INSURANCE COMPANY OF AMERICA WAS FOUNDED IN Providence, Rhode Island, in 1907 by a visionary businessman (A.T. Vigneron) who saw an opportunity with the invention of the "horseless carriage" (automobile). Vigneron had two founding principles:

1. To seek out responsible policyholders.
2. Treat customers with respect by providing the best service possible.

As a result of these concepts, Amica is the oldest mutual insurer of automobiles in the United States today, with over <u>3,000</u> employees nationwide. It now provides homeowners, automobile, marine, and excess liability insurance and does business in all states, except Hawaii.

According to AMICA'S Web site, "From the start, the companies' mutual insurance model created a different kind of workplace. The focus at Amica was on policyholders and their interests, not stockholders. New employees were quickly trained in the 'Amica way' of providing efficient and respectful service. In addition, policyholders received dividends, which were first declared in 1908 and have been paid on most policies every year since."[1]

Apparently Amica's efforts have paid off because the company has been in business and has expanded operations over the past 100+ years. The Web site says that Amica strives to deliver "exceptional service to policyholders." An effect of efforts in this area is the receipt of the J.D. Power Award for service in the 2009 National Automobile Insurance Study. Amica was rated as one of the best insurance companies in the United States for the 10th year in a row. Additionally, Consumersearch.com (a Web site that rates and compares insurance companies) reports the following about Amica:

- Outstanding customer service
- Pays claims promptly
- Low prices

A major part of the Amica philosophy on servicing policyholders is the fact that it does not use intermediaries or agents to sell products. Unlike many insurance companies, if someone contacts the company by telephone, e-mail, or U.S. mail, Amica provides a representative who is empowered to answer questions rather than take information and have the prospective customer wait to speak to a particular person.

Go to www.amica.com and do an Internet search on Amica and its competitors. Look at the historical and other information about the organization related to services and products on the Amica Web site, as well as the company's mission statement. Also, compare Amica to competing insurance companies and look at www.jdpower.com to see how the organization is rated in service.

Think About It
Based on this organization's profile and what you found on the Internet, answer the following questions and be prepared to discuss your responses.

1. From a service perspective, how does this organization differ from other insurance companies you have dealt with or have heard about?
2. What do you believe are the strengths and weaknesses of this organization? Why?
3. How do you feel that Amica compares to some of its major competitors (e.g., Allstate, California State Automobile Association, GMAC, GEICO, State Farm, Allstate, Liberty Mutual, and Travelers)?
4. What role do you think the Amica mission statement plays in the way employees see their customers and handle service?
5. As a consumer, would you now consider using Amica for insurance services in the future? Why or why not?

Quick Preview

Before reviewing the content of the chapter, respond to the following statements by placing a "T" for true or an "F" for false on the rules. Use any questions you miss as a checklist of material to which you will pay particular attention as you read through the chapter. For those you get right, congratulate yourself, but review the sections they address in order to learn additional details about the topics.

_____ 1. The concept of customer service evolved from the practice of selling wares in small general stores, off the back of wagons, or out of the home.

_____ 2. The migration from other occupations to the service industry is a recent trend and started in the late 1970s.

_____ 3. One reason for the shift from a manufacturing to customer service–dominated society is more stringent government regulations.

_____ 4. As more women have entered the workforce, the demand for personal services has increased.

_____ 5. Advances in technology have created a need for more employees in manufacturing businesses.

_____ 6. Since the beginning of the twenty-first century, workers in the United States have more disposable income now than at any other time in history.

_____ 7. As a result of deregulation in a variety of industries, competition has slowed.

_____ 8. Quality customer service organizations recruit, select, and train qualified people.

_____ 9. Luckily, the recent recession had little impact on the service industry.

_____ 10. To determine whether delivery needs are being met, organizations must examine industry standards, customer expectations, capabilities, costs, and current and projected requirements.

_____ 11. There are two customer types with which service representatives must interact.

_____ 12. An organization's "culture" is what the customer experiences.

Answers to Quick Preview can be found at the end of the chapter.

LO 1-1 Defining Customer Service

Concept Customer-focused organizations determine and meet the needs of their internal and external customers. Their focus is to treat everyone with respect and as if they were special.

Many attempts have been made to define the term **customer service.** However, depending on an organization's focus, such as retailing, medical, dental, industry, manufacturing, or repair services, the goals of providing customer service may vary. In fact, we often use the term **service industry** as if it were a separate occupational field unto itself. In reality, most organizations provide some degree of customer service. For the purposes of this text, *customer service* is defined as the ability of knowledgeable, capable, and enthusiastic employees to deliver **products** and services to their internal and external customers in a manner that satisfies identified and unidentified needs and ultimately results in positive word-of-mouth publicity and return business. By doing these things, organizations can truly become **customer-focused organizations** (see Figure 1.1).

Many organizations specialize in providing only services. Examples of this category are associations, banks and credit unions, consulting firms, Internet service providers, utility companies, waste management services, county tax collectors, call centers, brokerage firms, laundries, plumbing and electrical companies, transportation companies, and medical or

customer service The ability of knowledgeable, capable, and enthusiastic employees to deliver products and services to their internal and external customers in a manner that satisfies identified and unidentified needs and ultimately results in positive word-of-mouth publicity and return business.

service industry A term used to describe businesses and organizations that are engaged primarily in service delivery. Service sector is a more accurate term, since many organizations provide some form of service to their customers even though they are primarily engaged in research, development, and manufacture of products.

product Something produced or an output by an individual or organization. In the service environment, products are created to satisfy customer needs or wants.

customer-focused organization A company that spends energy and effort on satisfying internal and external customers by first identifying customer needs, then establishing policies, procedures, and management and reward systems to support excellence in service delivery.

customer relationship management (CRM) Concept of identifying customer needs: understanding and influencing customer behavior through ongoing communication strategies in an effort to acquire, retain, and satisfy the customer. The ultimate goal is customer loyalty.

Some common characteristics for leading edge customer-focused organizations are:

- They have internal customers (for example, peers, co-workers, bosses, subordinates, people from other areas of their organization) and/or external customers (for example, vendors, suppliers, various telephone callers, walk-in customers, other organizations, others not from within the organization).

- Their focus is on determining and meeting the needs of customers while treating everyone with respect and as if they were special. Information, products, and services are easily accessible by customers. Policies are in place to allow employees to make decisions in order to better serve customers.

- Management and systems support and appropriately reward employee efforts to serve customers.

- Reevaluation and quantitative measurement of the way business is conducted is ongoing and results in necessary changes and upgrades to deliver timely quality service to the customer.

- Continual benchmarking or comparison with competitors and related organizations helps maintain an acute awareness and implementation of best service practices by the organization.

- The latest technology is used to connect with and provide service to customers, vendors, or suppliers and to support business operations.

- They build relationships through **customer relationship management (CRM)** programs.

Figure 1.1 **Customer-Focused Organizations**

Before distribution systems were modernized, peddlers went from house to house, particularly in rural areas, to deliver merchandise or services. Doctors often went to the sick person's home and made house visits. *How do these methods of delivery differ from those used today? Do you think the ones used today are better? Why or why not?*

dental facilities. Other organizations provide both products and services. Examples are businesses such as car dealerships, brick and mortar (physical buildings) and online retail stores and manufacturers that have support services for their products, public utilities, supermarkets, theaters, and restaurants.

No matter what type of organization you work in, it is crucial for you to remember that when dealing with customers, it is not about you. Your purpose and goal should be to assist customers in meeting their needs whenever possible. Be proactive and positive and strive to do the best you can by taking ownership of a customer contact situation. You have a vested interest to succeed since your success and that of your organization depends on it.

service sector Refers to organizations and individuals involved in delivering service as a primary product.

The term **service sector** as used by the Census Bureau and the Bureau of Labor Statistics in their reports and projections typically includes:

Transportation, communication, and utilities

Wholesale trade

Retail trade

Finance, insurance, and real estate

Other services (including businesses such as legal firms, barbershops and beauty salons, personal services, housekeeping, and accounting)

Federal government

State and local governments

In addition, there are people who are self-employed and provide various types of services to their customers and clients.

The Concept of Customer Service

The concept or practice of customer service is not new in the United States and other countries. Over the years, it has evolved from a meager beginning into a multibillion-dollar, worldwide endeavor. In the past when many people worked on farms, small artisans and business owners provided customer service to their neighbors. No multinational chain stores existed. Many small towns and villages had their own blacksmith, general store, boardinghouse (hotel), restaurant, tavern, barbershop, and similar service-oriented establishments owned and operated by people living in the town (often the place of business was also the residence of the owner). For people living in more rural areas, peddlers of kitchenware, medicine, and other goods made their way from one location to another to serve their customers and distribute various products. Further, to supplement their income, many people made and sold or bartered products from their homes in what came to be known as **cottage industries.** As trains, covered wagons, and stagecoaches began to cross the United States, they carried vendors and supplies in addition to providing transportation. During that whole era, customer service differed from what it is today by the fact that the owners and chief executive officers (CEOs) were also motivated frontline employees working face-to-face with their customers. They had a vested interest in providing good service and in succeeding.

When industry, manufacturing, and larger cities started to grow, the service industry really started to gain ground. In the late 1800s, as the mail services matured, companies such as Montgomery Ward and Sears Roebuck introduced the mail-order catalog to address the needs of customers. In rural areas, the population grew and expanded westward, and service providers followed.

Post–World War II Service

After World War II, there was a continuing rise in the number of people in the United States in service occupations. According to an article published by the Bureau of Labor Statistics, "At the conclusion of the war in 1945, the service industry accounted for only 10 percent of nonfarm employment, compared to 38 percent for manufacturing. In 1982 services surpassed manufacturing as the largest employer among major industry groups. From 2000–2010 virtually all nonfarm wage and salary employment growth was expected to be in the service-producing sector, accounting for a net increase of 8.9 million jobs."[2]

The Shift to Service

Today, businesses have changed dramatically as the economy has shifted from a dependence on manufacturing to a focus on providing timely quality service. The age of the **service economy** has been alive and strong for some time now. Tied to this trend has been the development of international quality standards by which effectiveness is measured in many multinational organizations. Many customer-centric organizations are adding the executive-level position of chief customer officer (CCO) to their hierarchy. CCOs are responsible for all operational functions that influence or relate to customer relations and add a new dimension to the customer service career path.

Because of the multinational nature of business in this century, many companies choose to use outsourcing and offshoring for certain job functions, one of which may be the customer service function. This will be discussed later in this chapter.

Customer Service Success Tip

Educate yourself on the service profession in general and your organization in particular by reading trade magazines, articles, newsletters, and books (e.g., CRM Magazine, Alexander Communications Group, or www.customerservicemanager.com). Focus on trends, improvements, and enhancements being made by organizations similar to yours, and on developing skills that add value to your organization.

cottage industries The term adopted in the early days of customer service when many people started small businesses in their homes or cottages and bartered products or services with neighbors.

service economy A term used to describe the trend in which businesses have shifted from primarily production and manufacturing to more service delivery. As part of this evolution, many organizations have developed specifically to provide services to customers.

Figure 1.2
From Pre–WW II
Occupations to
Service Occupations

Typical Former Occupations	Typical Service Occupations
Farmer	Salesperson
Ranch worker	Insurance agent
Machinist	Food service
Engineer	Administrative assistant
Steelworker	Flight attendant
Homemaker	Call center representative
Factory worker	Repair person
Miner	Travel professional
Tradesperson (for example, watchmaker)	Child care provider
Railroad worker	Security guard

As shown in Figure 1.2, since the end of World War II, people have moved from other occupations to join the rapidly growing ranks of service professionals.

LO 1-2 Growth of the Service Sector

Concept Technology has affected jobs in the following ways: quantity of jobs created, distribution of jobs, and quality of jobs. The service sector is projected to have the largest job growth.

According to the U.S. Bureau of Labor Statistics, there are employment demands in many occupations (see Figure 1.3). Service-providing sectors employment is expected to grow while most goods-producing occupations are expected to shrink. "Growth in the service sector is driven by increasing demand for information, wholesale and retail trade, health care and social assistance, and professional and business services. The push to keep businesses competitive and profitable will increase demand for services

Figure 1.3
Percent Change in Total
Employment by Major
Occupational Groups,
Projected 2004–2014

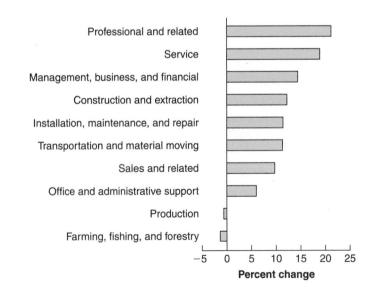

within professional and business services. Management, scientific, and technical consulting services; computer systems design and related services; and employment services are needed to develop and implement new technologies, ensure compliance with government regulations, provide computer security, and develop, improve, and maintain computer networks. The need to accommodate an aging population is spurring demand for health care and social assistance."[3]

The impact of these numbers can be seen as technology replaces many production line workers, and increasing numbers of service jobs are created. This comes about because, as greater numbers and greater varieties of goods are produced, more service people, salespeople, managers, and other professionals are needed to design and market service delivery systems that support those products. Technology-related service jobs such as those of database administrators, computer support specialists, computer scientists, computer engineers, and systems analysts are expected to continue to grow at a rapid pace.

Other data from the Bureau of Labor Statistics shows that growth will continue in service sectors:

- The Nation's employment is expected to increase from 150.9 million to 166.2 million over the coming decade, adding 15.3 million jobs. This average annual growth rate of 1.0 percent is slightly faster than the 0.7 percent seen between 1998 and 2008, largely because 2008 was a recession year during which employment in several sectors that, historically, had been growing actually declined. Nearly all of the 15.3 million job increase will be in the service-providing sector, led by gains in professional and business services and in health care and social assistance, which are projected to contribute a combined 8.2 million new jobs, more than half of all new jobs created in the nation. State and local government (which includes public hospitals and schools) and leisure and hospitality also will generate numerous jobs. These four sectors are among those exhibiting the fastest job growth.

- Manufacturing will continue its long-run decline, but at a slower pace than during 1998–2008. Businesses will continue to realize efficiencies by automating more production processes and streamlining their use of labor. Some industries are expected to decline because more production is taking place overseas and because import competition will reduce demand for many products manufactured in the United States. Among declining industries will be those in the textile, apparel, footwear, and leather and allied product subsectors, whose products are anticipated to face stiff competition from foreign manufacturers.[4]

Impact of the Economy

According to leading economists, today's economy is affecting jobs in three ways: (1) overall quantity of jobs created; (2) the distribution of jobs among industries, occupations, geographic areas, and organizations of different sizes; (3) the quality of jobs, measured by wages, job security, and opportunities for development.

Improving Service Quality

TAKE A MOMENT TO LIST SOME OF THE CHANGES RELATED TO SERVICE THAT YOU HAVE PERSONALLY WITNESSED IN THE BUSINESS WORLD DURING YOUR LIFETIME.

Are these changes for better or worse? Why do you believe this to be true? With these changes in mind, what do you—or would you—do to improve service quality as a customer service professional in your own chosen industry or position?

Quantity of Jobs Being Created

A variety of factors, including prevailing interest rates and consumer demand, typically cause companies to evaluate how many people they need and which jobs will be established or maintained. In addition, the advent of technology has brought with it the need for many new technical skills in the areas of computer hardware and software operation and maintenance. At the same time, technology has created an opportunity for organizations to transfer tasks previously performed by employees to automation.

"Projected employment growth is concentrated in the service-providing sector, continuing a long-term shift from the goods-producing sector of the economy. From 2008 to 2018, service-providing industries are projected to add 14.6 million jobs, or 96 percent of the increase in total employment. The two industry sectors expected to have the largest employment growth are professional and business services (4.2 million) and health care and social assistance (4.0 million) Goods-producing employment, as a whole, is expected to show virtually no growth."[5]

Even with projected growth in many service related industries, there are projected declines in the service sector. Figure 1.4 shows some of these projections.

Distribution of Jobs

Two parallel trends in job development are occurring. The first comes about from the need for employees to be able to have regular access to personal and professional networks and to engage in collaborative exchanges.

Today, many employees work from their homes all or part of the time. Telecommuting, as this is called, is used frequently by companies in large cities, such as Los Angeles, to decrease travel time. *Do you think you would need different skills or abilities to telecommute? Why or why not?*

	Employment		Change	
Industry	2008	2018	Number	Percent
Department stores	1,557	1,398	−159	−10.2%
Postal service	748	650	−98	−13.0
Newspaper publishers	326	245	−81	−24.8
Gasoline stations	843	769	−75	−8.9
Wired telecommunications carriers	666	593	−73	−11

Figure 1.4
Service-Related Industries with the Largest Wage and Salary Employment Declines, 2008–2018

Source: U.S. Bureau of Labor Statistics, Projections: 2008–2018 Summary. www.bls.gov/news.release/ecopro.nr0.htm.

This trend means that more jobs are likely to develop in major metropolitan areas, where ease of interaction with peers and suppliers, high customer density, and access to the most current business practices exist. Training and technology resources are also available in these areas. Access to technology resources helps ensure continued learning and growth of employees and also aids organizations in achieving their goals and objectives.

The second trend in job development arises from the ease of transmission and exchange of information by means of technology. It is called **telecommuting.** Employees can now work from their homes or satellite office location. Government agencies, technology-focused organizations, and many companies with large staffs in major metropolitan areas that experience traffic congestion (for example, Los Angeles, Boston, Chicago, and Washington, D.C.) often use telecommuting to eliminate the need for employees to travel to work each day. According to the U.S. Department of Labor, "on the days that they worked, 21 percent of employed persons did some or all of their work at home, and 86 percent did some or all of their work at their workplace. Men and women were about equally likely to do some or all of their work at home. Self-employed workers were more likely than wage and salary workers to have done some work at home—55 versus 17 percent"[6]

From an industry perspective, workers employed in professional and business services, in financial activities, and in education and health services are among the most likely to work at home. The telephone, fax, and computer make it possible to provide services from almost any remote location. For example, telephone sales and product support services can easily be handled from an employee's home if the right equipment is used. To do this, a customer calls a designated 800 number and a switching device at the company dispatches the call to an employee working at home. This is seamless to the customer, who receives the service needed and has no idea where the call was answered. This also makes it easier for many companies to outsource some functions, thus saving money by relocating those jobs to geographical areas worldwide where wages and benefits may be less competitive. You will learn more about technology in customer service in Chapter 9.

telecommuting A trend seen in many congested metropolitan areas and government offices. To reduce traffic, pollution, and save resources (e.g., rent, telephone, and technology systems) many organizations allow employees to set up home offices and from there electronically communicate and forward information to their corporate offices.

Customer Service Success Tip

Make yourself indispensable to your employer by building a strong internal network of associates within the organization in order to reduce your chances of layoff during **downsizing.** This will help you share information and resources and add to your personal power base because you will have information that co-workers potentially do not have. Also, become thoroughly educated on the products and services that your organization provides and continually volunteer ideas and assistance to improve the organization.

downsizing Term applied to the situation in which employees are terminated or empty positions are left unfilled once someone leaves an organization.

networking The active process of building relationships and sharing of resources.

Quality of Service Jobs

The last decade of the twentieth century saw increasing economic growth, low interest rates, and new job opportunities. Unemployment rates reached a historic low in 1999, then rose dramatically as the worst recession since the Great Depression resulted in unemployment rates from 6 to 14 percent or more in most states. As many people struggle to find meaningful employment, social and workplace demographics continue to shift and people move around in our mobile society, job security has been affected and it is likely that competition for desired jobs will continue to become much more intense.

Employees who obtain and maintain the better customer service jobs that provide good working conditions, security, and benefits will be better educated, trained, and prepared. They will also be the ones who understand and have tapped into the concept of professional networking. **Networking** is the active process of building relationships inside and outside the organization through meetings, interactions, and activities that lead to sound interpersonal relationships and sharing of resources. Practices such as joining and becoming actively involved in committees and boards of governors or directors will prove to be invaluable. Many good books have been published on the subject. The Internet (for example, Amazon.com, Barnes&Noble.com, and Borders.com) can provide such resources. Additionally, as you will read in Chapter 10, an abundance of technology (e.g., cell phones, PDAs, and computers) can allow access, organization, and storing of information and provide a gateway to social networking sites like Facebook and LinkedIn. All of this will enhance the job search process and provide valuable information and opportunities for those attempting to prepare and position themselves for key jobs in the service sector.

LO 1-3 Societal Factors Affecting Customer Service

Concept Many factors caused the economic shift from manufacturing to service. Increased technology, globalization of the economy, deregulation, and many government programs are a few factors. You will read about these and others in the following paragraphs.

The economies of America and many other countries are being dramatically changed by the forces that are shaping the world. Declining economic conditions, demographic shifts in population, constant technological change, globalization, deregulation of industries, geopolitical changes, increases in the number of white-collar workers, socioeconomic program development, and more women entering the workplace are some of the major shifts that continue to occur each year in the United States and around the world.

You may wonder what factors have impacted the service industry. Some of the more important elements are identified in the following sections.

Global Economic Shifts

Not since the 1980s have economic indicators (e.g., stock trades, home sales, purchases, international transactions, and construction) been in such turmoil worldwide. Many people have lost jobs, personal savings are dwindling, people are losing their homes, and spending is down greatly around the world. As the economy took a downward spiral in the latter part of the first decade on the twenty-first century, consumer confidence shifted, many organizations struggled to provide quality service levels with reduced staff, and budgets and revenue from products and services slipped for most organizations as consumers held onto precious cash. According a 2009 *AdMedia/The Harris Poll* of 2,066 people online, "four in five North Americans (79%) say they have made cuts over the past year in their personal spending due to the economy. One-third (32%) have made a lot of cuts while almost half (47%) have made some cuts."[7] All of this creates challenges for those in the service profession throughout all industries. As many consumers struggle to make ends meet financially, they often cut back on spending, have difficulty meeting their financial commitments, and have less expendable cash. The result is that service professionals are often faced with frustrated and angry people who have little patience for someone they see as representing an organization that they may or may not view favorably (e.g., financial institutions, tax and debt collectors, utility representatives, customer service representatives, and sales people).

Another important factor related to the changes in the economic environment that have occurred in recent years is that many companies have made dramatic shifts in the way they do business and attempt to attract and hold customers. The approach to customer service in many instances is no longer "business as usual." Instead of viewing it as something that should be done well, most organizations now see it as something that must be done.

Because of the financial meltdown that occurred during the high point of the recession, many organizations that have been household names for decades and had international presence have cut back severely on the size of their workforce and sold off or merged or closed operations. They have also have taken dramatic steps to attract and keep customers. Companies like Chrysler, General Motors (GM), Citigroup, Goldman Sachs, and American Express received funds through the Emergency Economic Stabilization Act of 2008 from the federal government in the United States in order to remain financially solvent. In addition, companies struggled (and still do in many instances) to find a balance between profitability and providing quality service. For example, at the end of 2009 GM announced that Pontiac and Saturn lines would be shut down. This move shocked and disappointed many customers loyal to those brands. At the same time, the announcements provided an opportunity for GM. The company's approach was to get creative in offering ways to attract more business. GM offered zero percent financing, offered more powerful warranties on vehicles, and gave significant discounts to dealers for excess inventory that carried the Pontiac and Saturn brand names. In effect, they sold brand new cars to dealers as fleet vehicles (meaning the cars were registered with the dealer as first purchaser). This in turn allowed those dealerships to sell cars at nearly half-off the original new car prices in order to entice customers to purchase. Customers benefited by getting a brand new car at a reduced price, GM unloaded costly inventory, and dealerships gained new patrons. It was a win-win situation for everyone.

Shifts in the Population and Labor Force

According to the U.S. Department of Labor, "The U.S. civilian noninstitutional population is expected to increase by 23.9 million over the 2004–14 period, at a slower rate of growth than during both the 1994–2004 and 1984–94 periods. Additionally the youth population, aged 16 to 24, will grow 2.9 percent over the 2004–14 period. As the baby boomers continue to age, the group aged 55 to 64 will increase by 36 percent or 10.4 million persons, more than any other group. The group aged 35 to 44 will decrease in size, reflecting the birth dearth following the baby boom generation.

"Continued growth will mean more consumers of goods and services, spurring demand for workers in a wide range of occupations and industries. The effects of population growth on various occupations will differ. The differences are partially accounted for by the age distribution of the future population."[8]

Since the size of the labor force is the most important factor related to the size and makeup of the available pool of workers, organizations that hire service representatives will have to make some adaptations in order to obtain quality candidates for open positions. The Bureau of Labor Statistics reports that figures will continue to shift based on race and ethnic origin, (see Figure 1.5) in the following ways between 2009–2018:

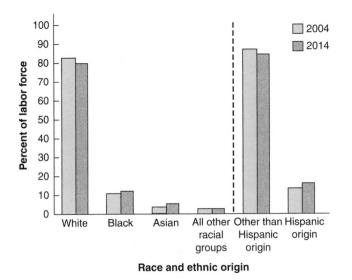

Figure 1.5 **Percent of Labor Force by Race and Ethnic Origin, 2011 and Projected 2018**

As a result of higher population growth—stemming from an increased number of births and increased immigration—and high labor force participation rates by Hispanics and Asians, the share of the workforce held by minorities is expected to increase significantly.

- The overall civilian labor force is projected to increase from slightly under 157 million to almost 167 million workers between 2011–2018
- The male labor force is projected to grow slightly under 4 million while the female workforce population is expected to grow to slightly over 4 million employees.
- The youth labor force, aged 16 to 24, is expected to continue its decline from approximately 22.5 million in 2011 to 21.1 million in 2018.
- The primary working age group, between 25 and 54 years old, is projected to change from 104.6 million in 2011 to 105.9 million in 2018.
- Workers 55 and older, on the other hand, will increase between the same period from 31.6 million to 39.8 million.[9] As a result of the size of the increase, this age group will compose nearly a quarter of the labor force by 2018. This phenomenon is often referred to as the graying of the workforce and will contribute to what many see as a future "brain drain" when masses of senior employees will take their expertise and exit the workforce, leaving huge voids in knowledge and talent in organizations that do not effectively plan for the inevitable result.

Increased Efficiency in Technology

The development and increased sophistication of machines and computers have caused an increase in production and quality. Two results of this trend have been an increased need for service organizations to take care of the technology and a decrease in manufacturing and blue-collar jobs.

An advantage of this change is that machines can work 24 hours, seven days a week with few lapses in quality, no need for breaks, and without increases in salary and benefits. This makes them extremely attractive to profit-minded business and corporate shareholders. Although technology can lead to the loss of some jobs, technological advances in the computer and telecommunications industry alone have created hundreds of service opportunities for people who monitor and run the machines and automated services. As you will read in Chapter 9, everything from 800 numbers and telemarketing to shopping and service via the Internet, television, and telephone has evolved and continues to expand.

A major factor driving implementation of technology-based service is that, according to the 2007 U.S. Census figures, "62.0 percent of U.S. households reported using Internet access in the home. This is up from 18 percent in 1997, the first year the bureau collected data on Internet use. Sixty-four percent of individuals 18 and over used the Internet from any location, eighty-two percent of households with Internet reported using a high-speed connection, and 17 percent used a dial-up connection . . . the percentage of 18- to 34-year-olds who accessed the Internet was more than

Customer Service Success Tip

Knowledge is power. Learn as much about as many software packages and pieces of equipment used by your organization as possible. Stay abreast of emerging technology trends in your industry. Volunteer to attend training and to work on committees tasked with identifying and implementing new service technology in your organization and professional organizations to which you belong.

For many customer service jobs, skill in using technology will increase your value as a source of information for current and future customers. *How can you keep abreast of changes in technology?*

globalization The term applied to an ongoing trend of information, knowledge, and resource sharing around the world. As a result of a more mobile society and easier access to transportation and technology, more people are traveling and accessing products and services form international sources than ever before.

business-to-business (B2B) Refers to a business-to-business customer service.

offshoring Refers to the relocation of business services from one country to another (e.g., services, production, and manufacturing).

outsourcing Refers to the practice of contracting with third-party companies or vendors outside the organization (usually in another country) to deliver products and services to customers or produce products.

double (seventy-three percent) that of people 65 and older (thirty-five percent). Among children 3 to 17, fifty-six percent used the Internet."[10]

The value of technology is that much of it can be used in remote locations. This allows employees to work independently from home (telecommuting). No longer do organizations have to have a brick-and-mortar workplace. Because of the affordability of current technology, which allows workers to do their jobs "virtually" instead of commuting to a common workplace, many customer-service–oriented jobs are done in a home or in remote locations (on laptops in Wi-Fi areas) instead of an office.

Globalization of the Economy

Beginning in the 1960s, when worldwide trade barriers started to come down, a variety of factors have contributed to expanded international cooperation and competition. This trend has been termed **globalization,** with many companies focusing on **business-to-business (B2B)** initiatives, as well as individual consumers. Since the 1960s, advances in technology, communication, and transportation have opened new markets and allowed decentralized worldwide access for production, sales, and service. To survive and hold onto current market share while opening new gateways, U.S. firms need to hone the service skills of their employees, strengthen their quality, enhance their use of technology and look for new ways of demonstrating that they can not only meet but exceed the expectations of customers. All of this means more competition and the evolution of new rules and procedures that they have not been able to obtain in the past. Sometimes the deciding factor for the customer on whether to purchase a foreign or domestic product will be the service you provide.

At some point, many companies make staffing and/or production decisions based on bottom-line figures. When this happens, companies can, because of recent changes in the law, take their production or call center functions "offshore" **(offshoring)** to other countries (Mexico, India, etc.). In doing so, companies save money on costs such as production, wages, and benefits. This is becoming more and more common in technology-oriented companies. Additionally, many organizations are also **outsourcing** job functions that have been traditionally handled internally (e.g., recruiting, payroll, benefits, training, marketing, and distribution) to third-party companies that specialize in these areas. An example of this occurred in 2010 when Walmart Stores Inc.

announced that it was cutting about 11,200 jobs at Sam's Club warehouses in order to turn over the task of in-store product demonstrations of items like food, electronics, and personal wellness products to an outside marketing company.

Deregulation of Many Industries

Over the years, we have witnessed the deregulation of a number of industries (e.g., airline, telephone, railroads, and the utility industries from the later 1970s to the early 2000s). **Deregulation** is the removal of government restrictions on an industry. The continuing deregulation of major U.S. public services has caused competition to flourish. However, deregulation has also brought major industry shakeups, sometimes leading to breakdowns in service quality in many companies and, in some instances, closure or restructuring of the company. An example of this was the breakup of AT&T ("Ma Bell") into many smaller communication companies ("Baby Bells").

These events have created opportunities for newly established companies to step in with improvements and innovations to close the gaps and better serve customers. For example, smaller low-cost carriers (e.g. Southwest Airlines, Air Tran, and Sky Blue) came into existence and provided cheaper fares to cities not traditionally covered by larger carries or where demand is not normally as great. They even challenged the traditional internationally known airlines (American, United, Continental, Northwest, US Air, and Delta) on traditional routes to larger cities in the United States.

Geopolitical Changes

Events such as oil embargoes, political unrest, and conflicts and wars involving various countries have reduced U.S. business access and competition within some areas of the world (for example, Cuba, Vietnam, Iran, and Venezuela) while some countries have free access in those areas. These circumstances not only limit access to product, manufacturing, and distribution channels, but also reduce the markets to which U.S. businesses can offer products and services. For example, every closed port or country border has a negative effect on travel industry professionals, such as reservationists, air transport and manufacturing employees, cruise operators, tour guides, and border-area retail businesses.

Other positive and negative historical changes have occurred that—like it or not—have affected the way companies do business and will continue to do so into the twenty-first century. The passage of the **North American Free Trade Agreement (NAFTA),** which was a trade agreement between the United States, Canada, and Mexico that eliminated a number of trade and investment barriers between the three countries. The agreement made it easier for many U.S.-based companies to relocate and send jobs across borders (offshoring) in order to find less expensive labor forces, increase profits, and avoid unions and federal taxes. Like many such political arrangements, there are pros and cons to this agreement that impact a number of industries.

deregulation Occurs when governments remove legislative or regulatory guidelines that inhibit and control an industry (e.g., transportation, natural gas, and telecommunications).

North American Free Trade Agreement (NAFTA) A trade agreement entered into by the United States, Canada, and Mexico to help, among other things, eliminate barriers to trade across barriers to trade, promote conditions of fair trade across borders, increase investment opportunities, and promote and protect intellectual property rights.

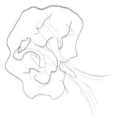

Further events, such as trade agreements with China and the thawing of relations with Vietnam in recent years have opened new political and economic doors. The shift in relations with Iran, Iraq, Afghanistan, and several other nations as the result of human rights violations, violence, terrorism, and military-related actions have created obstacles to international trade and commerce in a variety of ways in areas of the Middle East, Asia, and South America.

Geopolitical events such as these will lead to more multinational mergers and partnerships and a need for better understanding of diversity-related issues by all employees and managers. As a service provider, it is your responsibility to research these major world events and the cultures of others in order to better understand and relate to people with whom you come into contact in the workplace. Failure to do so can lead to breakdowns in service and relationships and ultimately the loss of business. From a personal standpoint, this could limit your ability to secure meaningful employment in the service industry and your opportunities (e.g., training, pay, enhanced benefits) in your organization.

With increased ease of transportation and communication, companies cannot afford to ignore international competitors. For years, North American firms viewed Japan as their chief economic and business rival. Now other countries are challenging Japan (e.g., Taiwan, South Korea, Vietnam, China, and India) and are becoming firmly entrenched in the marketplace. An example of this was the introduction of the South Korea–made KIA car line into the U.S. market in the 1990s. Initially, many people did not view that company as a significant economic threat and the car was sometimes called the "poor man's automobile." Kias were even compared to the ill-fated Russian Yugo that was manufactured in Yugoslavia in the mid-1980s and introduced into the U.S. market. That brand quickly faded from existence due to its terrible quality. To the surprise of many, Kia has begun to turn its reputation around and has built a series of vehicles that are starting to rival the quality of larger U.S. manufacturers. In 2008, they reported their 14th year of consecutive growth in market share.

Another geopolitical event that has impacted many organizations was the formation of the European Union. This alliance of neighboring countries formed an economic market made up of 27 states that subscribe to a standardized system of laws that ensure free movement of people, goods, services, and capital. The majority of member states adopted the euro as a common currency and accepted it at a standard exchange rate. They also eliminated the requirement for a passport from the people of member countries who travel throughout the Union. The last step has positive economic implications because it encourages more use of travel-related services.

Increase in the Number of White-Collar Workers

With the movement out of factories and mines and off the farm, more people find themselves working at a traditional nine-to-five office job or providing service on a variety of work shifts (telephone and technical support

TO HELP YOU RECOGNIZE THE IMPACT THIS GLOBAL TREND HAS ON YOU AND YOUR FAMILY AS CONSUMERS, THINK ABOUT ALL THE PRODUCTS YOU OWN (FOR EXAMPLE, CAR, CLOTHING, MICROWAVE OVEN, TELEVISION, COMPUTER, FAX MACHINE).

List five major products that you or your family members own, along with their country of origin (you can find this on the warranty plate along with the product's serial number, usually on the back or bottom of the product).

centers). This trend has led to the creation of new types of service occupations. Office workers need to have someone clean their clothes, spruce up their homes (inside and out), care for their children, do their shopping, run their errands, and feed their families. In effect, the service phenomenon has spawned its own service trend.

More Women Entering the Workforce

The fact that more women are in the workplace means that many of their traditional roles in society have shifted, out of necessity or convenience, to service providers such as cleaners, cooks, and child care providers. The tasks previously handled by the stay-at-home wife and mother are now being handled by the employees of various service companies.

The Department of Labor has published statistics showing that the number of women in the workplace, in all age groups, continues to grow more rapidly than the number of men. As a result, women's share of the workplace is projected to increase from about 71,700 in 2008 to approximately 78,200 in 2018.[11]

As women have become a larger part of the workforce, they have slowly seen their income levels rise compared to those of their male counterparts. "Women who usually worked full time had median earnings of $657 per week, or 80.9 percent of the $812 median for men. The female-to-male earnings ratios were higher among blacks (95.3 percent) and Hispanics (95.2 percent) than among whites (80.0 percent) or Asians (82.6 percent). Among women, weekly earnings were highest for those age 35 to 44 and age 45 to 54, $720 and $727, respectively."[12] The direct impact of this trend related to service is that many women often now have more disposable income as consumers than they did in the past.

A More Racially and Ethnically Diverse Population Is Entering the Workforce

As with the entrance of women into the workforce, the increase in numbers of people from different cultures entering the workforce will have a profound impact on the business environment. Not only are the members of this expanded worker category bringing with them new ideas, values,

A population made up of women, ethnically different people, older people, and those with other diverse characteristics, make a better understanding of various groups essential for service success. *How can you improve your own knowledge of different groups so that you can better serve?*

expectations, needs, and levels of knowledge, experience, and ability, but as consumers themselves, they bring a better understanding of the needs of the various groups that they represent.

"In 2008, 24.1 million persons, or 15.6 percent of the U.S. civilian labor force age 16 and over, were foreign born. Hispanics comprised 49.4 percent of the foreign-born labor force compared with 7.8 percent of the native-born labor force. Asians made up 22.4 percent of the foreign-born labor force compared with 1.3 percent of the native-born labor force.

Among the major race and ethnicity groups, labor force participation rates of foreign-born whites (60.3 percent) and Hispanics (70.7 percent) were down over the year. The rates for foreign-born blacks (73.2 percent) and Asians (68.2 percent) showed little change in 2008."[13]

You will explore these trends, and other diversity factors, further in Chapter 8.

More Older Workers Entering the Workforce

Think about the last time you went to a fast-food restaurant or a retail store like McDonald's, Wendy's, Burger King, Walmart, Big Kmart, or Target. Did you notice the number of people serving and assisting you who seemed to be older than people you usually see in those roles? This relatively new phenomenon is the result of a variety of social factors. The most significant factor is that the median age of people in the United States is rising because of the aging of the "baby boom" generation (those born between 1946 and 1964).

From a workplace perspective, this means that more of the people in this age group will stay in the workplace or return once they leave (see Figure 1.6). This may be caused by pure economic necessity, since many people may have not prepared adequately for retirement and cannot be certain that the Social Security system will support them. Some people return to the workplace for social reasons—they miss the work and/or the opportunity to interact with others and feel useful. Whatever the reason for the desire or willingness of older workers to reenter the workforce, many organizations have realized that they often have an admirable work ethic. Also, since there are not enough entry-level people in the traditional pool of younger workers (because of smaller birth rates during the 1970s), companies are actively recruiting older workers.

In 2018, baby-boomers will be age 54 to 72 years, and this age group will grow significantly over the 2008–2018 period. The civilian labor force will continue to age:

- The number of workers in the 55-and-older group is projected to grow by 43.0 percent.
- The 55-and-older age group is projected to gain share of the labor force, and is expected to make up nearly one-quarter of the labor force by 2018.
- Youths—those between the ages of 16 and 24—will decline in numbers, lose share of the labor force from 15.1 percent in 2004, and account for 12.7 percent of the labor force by 2018.
- Prime-age workers—those between the ages of 25 and 54—also will lose share of the labor force and account for 63.5 percent of the labor force by 2018.

Source: Employment Projections, 2008–2018, U.S. Bureau of labor Statistics, www.bls.gov/news.release/ecopro.nr0.htm

Figure 1.6

2008–2018 Employment Projections for the Civilian Workforce

> ✳ **Customer Service Success Tip**
>
> Diversity is here to stay. Network with people from different cultures; visit ethnic restaurants; travel to other countries; read books and articles about different countries; learn a second language; and explore research on the Internet about different cultures, gender issues, age groups, religions, ability issues, and other factors that each person brings to the workplace. All this will help you more effectively interact with and maximize the potential of others.

✳ Ethical Dilemma 1-1

With all the competition for customer service jobs in your organization, you are concerned that you might not be able to get a promotion that you feel you deserve. You have heard that there are three other employees for a job opening for which you want to apply. You know all three people and their work habits. Each has a "skeleton in the closet" related to performance issues in the past of which you are aware, but your supervisor is not. Your supervisor will be screening applicants soon.

1. Should you inform your supervisor of what you know to ensure that she makes an educated choice based on qualifications? Why or why not?

2. What could be the potential result of any action that you take about this issue?

See possible responses at the end of the chapter.

Growth of E-Commerce

The past two decades have been witness to unimagined use of the personal computer and the Internet by the average person. As an example of the impact of e-commerce, the retail trade sector (e.g., motor vehicle and parts, furniture, electronics, food, sporting goods, and mail order houses) had sales of nearly $4 billion in 2007. Nearly $127 million of that amount was in e-commerce sales.[14] Almost any product or service is available at the click of a mouse, press of a key, or voice command. Consumers regularly "surf the net" for values in products and services without ever leaving their homes or offices. For example, many people do business with others all over the world without ever meeting them face-to-face or even talking to them on the telephone. Entire business-to-business customer relationships occur every day between people who are strangers, but who provide key products and services to their customers electronically (e.g., computer programmers, book editors, graphic artists, and Web site designers). This new way of accessing goods and services through technology has been termed **e-commerce.**

e-commerce An entire spectrum of companies that market products and services on the Internet and through other technology, and the process of accessing them by consumers.

Armed with a password, site addresses, and credit cards, shoppers use this virtual marketplace to satisfy needs or wants that they likely did not know they had before logging onto their computer and connecting with the Internet. And, with so many options available for just a small investment of time, they can comparison-shop simply by changing screens. No wonder the twentieth century saw the establishment of more millionaires and billionaires than any of its predecessors. The creators and owners of the most innovative sites and products can provide products, services, and information worldwide without ever physically coming into contact with a customer, and yet can amass huge reserves of money. Examples of these success stories and popularity are eBay (an online auction service), Craig's List (an online listing of items for sale, services, personal announcements, local classifieds and forums for jobs, housing, and events), and Amazon. com (an online book and product seller and auction line), which have become household names and are used by millions of shoppers yearly.

LO 1-4 Consumer Behavior Shifts

Concept Americans are enjoying increasing amounts of leisure time and have more disposable income as they age. The income and wealth of people in other countries is also rising and they are pursuing life and leisure activities at a record pace.

Different Mindset

In the past, many consumers took a "money is no object" approach to shopping because, if they did not have cash readily available, they had several pieces of plastic in their wallet that allowed them to spend (often beyond their means). This was possible because financial institutions were doling out these instruments of commerce in a very haphazard manner to virtually all who looked like they could potentially repay what they spent. Unfortunately, that practice proved to be highly flawed. As a result, the financial institutions that let credit practices run rampant fell like proverbial dominos and took along the world's economy with them. In the aftermath of this economic carnage, many consumers have had a reality check and have learned that prudence is an important element of commerce. Plainly speaking, if you do not have the money, do not spend it!

A majority of consumers who formerly acted on impulse and bought whatever they desired, are now taking a very cautious approach. Initially, the shock of having credit severely curtailed or cut off totally by their banks and credit unions sent many people into panic mode. As jobs disappeared, savings and bank accounts dwindled and many people became homeless, a sense of panic spread throughout the United States and the world. Economic reports are now starting to show that people have begun to shift from a "cutting back" mentality to a slightly more optimistic "cautious spending" approach. Part of their new strategy is to reevaluate their paradigm or the way they look at products. Where they might have only gone for the nationally known brand or reputation in the past, they now evaluate and consider generic or store brands with comparable options and services offered by local providers. They are also being more conscientious about their spending. The sales advertisements and coupons that they overlooked in the past are often sought out and acted upon. Online, they frequent www.eBay.com and similar auction sites or product clearance sites like www.overstock.com. Sites like www.pricegrabber.com that allow online product and price comparison are also very popular.

Today's consumers are also looking to save money in other ways. Instead of jumping in their car and driving around to numerous stores to compare sale prices and products, they often sit at their computer and do their research and buying there. They also look to consolidate trips in order to save on the amount of gas they expend. This is why stores like Walmart and Target Super Stores have become so popular and powerful. One company that realized the impact of this shift in consumer mindset is Blockbuster. In the past few years, Blockbuster had to rethink its business and service model. A variety of factors led management to consider bankruptcy in 2008 before they decided on a plan to reinvent the way they did business. For years, they continued to add more stores yearly and bought up numerous smaller video rental competitors. With the advent of competitors like Netflix delivering videos to consumer mailboxes, and Redbox allowing people to rent videos out of a machine at Walmart and other locations, Blockbuster had to quickly retool its operations. In less than two years, the company dumped nearly 1,000 of its brick-and-mortar stores and began setting up its own video rental machines. It also began offering "Rent on Demand" video download services via its Web site in order to compete with Comcast and Time Warner Cable.

Expectation of Quality Service

Most customers expect that if they pay a fair dollar, in return they will receive a quality product or service. If their expectations are not met, customers simply call or visit a competing company where they can receive what they think they paid for. An even more powerful example of a new trend where consumers are getting what they want via technological means was highlighted in a 2007 article on www.trendwatching.com. When consumers or others band together to send a message online, the results can be powerful. The site dubbed the trend "crowd clout." An example of the full potential of such clout was seen in the efforts to get Barack Obama elected as the 44th president of the United States. Web sites such as www.moveon.org act as a rallying point for civic and political action. Another example of consumer clout was the initiatives put in place by government to shore up the electrical grid system following the 2003 blackout because of public and political outrage.

The expectation of quality service that most consumers have also creates a need for better-trained and better-educated customer service professionals. Not only do these professionals need up-to-date product information, but they also need to be abreast of current organizational policies and procedures, what the competition offers, and the latest techniques in customer service and satisfaction.

Customer Service Success Tip

If your goal is to ultimately have your own service-oriented business, start planning today. Take college courses on business-related topics, network with others in your industry through professional groups like the International Customer Service Association (ICSA), and conduct research on how to start a small business effectively through the Small Business Association.

Enhanced Consumer Preparation

Customers today are not only more highly educated than in the past, they are also well informed about the price, quality, and value of products and services. This has occurred in part through the advertising and publicity by companies competing for market share and by the activities of consumer information and advocacy groups that have surfaced. As Syms, a discount-clothing store, used to tout in its advertising, "An informed consumer is our best customer." That advertising campaign was based on the belief that if you shop around and compare quality and costs, you will come back to Syms. This type of strategy sends a message that "we have nothing to hide" and invites customer confidence.

Armed with knowledge about what they should receive for their money, consumers make it extremely difficult for less-than-reputable businesspeople to prosper or survive. With consumers now on the defensive and ready to fight back, all business owners find that they have to continually prove the worth of their products and services. They must provide **customer satisfaction** or face losing customers to competitors.

customer satisfaction The feeling of a person whose needs have been met by an organization.

customer service environment An environment made up of and influenced by various elements of an organization. Examples are delivery systems, human resources, service, products, and organizational culture start here.

LO 1-5   The Customer Service Environment

> **Concept** In this section the six components that make up a service environment and contribute to customer service delivery are discussed. Use these factors to ensure that a viable customer service environment is the responsibility of every employee of the organization—not just the customer service representatives.

Components of a Customer Service Environment

Let's take time to examine the six key components of a **customer service environment,** which will illustrate many factors that contribute to customer service delivery:

1. The customer
2. Organizational culture
3. Human resources
4. Products/deliverables
5. Delivery systems
6. Service

What goes into the making of quality customer service? This is discussed in the following sections.

The Customer

As shown in Figure 1.7, the key component in a customer-focused environment is the customer. All aspects of the service organization revolve around the customer. Without the customer, there is no reason for any organization to exist. And, since all employees have two types of customers with

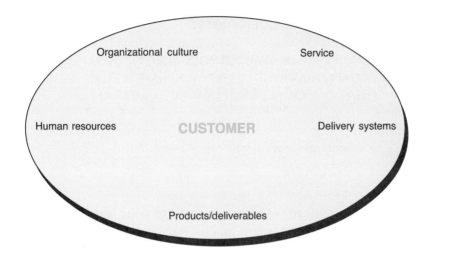

Figure 1.7
**Components of a
Customer-Focused
Environment**

whom they must interact, either internal or external, there must be a continuing consciousness of the need to provide exceptional, enthusiastic customer service. As Karl Albrecht and Ron Zemke say in their book *Service America*, "If you're not serving the customer, you'd better be serving someone who is." This is true because if you aren't providing stellar support and service to internal customers, external customers usually suffer.

External Customers

External customers may be current or potential customers or clients. They are the ones who actively seek out, research, and buy, rent, or lease products or services offered by your organization. This group can involve business customers who purchase your product to include with their own for resale. It can also involve an organization that acts as a franchise or distributor. Such an organization buys your products to resell or uses them to represent your company in its geographic area.

Internal Customers

Many people in the workplace will tell you that they do not have "customers." They are wrong. Anyone in an organization has customers. They may not be traditional customers who come to buy or use products or services. Instead, they are **internal customers** who are co-workers, employees of other departments or branches, and other people who work within the same organization. They also rely on others in their organization to provide services, information, and/or products that enable them to do their jobs.

Recognizing this formidable group of customers is important and crucial for on-the-job success. That is because, in the internal customer chain, an employee is sometimes a customer and at other times a supplier. At times, you may call a co-worker in another department for information. Later that same day, this co-worker may call you for a similar reason. Only when both parties are acutely aware of their role in this customer-supplier relationship can the organization effectively prosper and grow to full potential.

external customers Those people outside the organization who purchase or lease products and services. This group includes vendors, suppliers, people on the telephone, and others not from the organization.

internal customers People within the organization who either require support and service or provide information, products, and services to service providers. Such customers include peers, co-workers, bosses, subordinates, and people from other areas of the organization.

Who Are My Internal Customers?

TAKE A FEW MINUTES TO THINK ABOUT YOUR CURRENT ORGANIZATION OR SELECT ANY ORGANIZATION WITH WHICH YOU HAVE BEEN ASSOCIATED AND CREATE TWO LISTS: ONE OF YOUR INTERNAL CUSTOMERS AND ANOTHER OF YOUR SUPPLIERS.

Then compare your lists to see which customers also act as suppliers and help you better serve the external customers of your organization.

The important point to remember related to your internal customers is that you must take care of them, just as you do your external customers. They must be serviced effectively in order to allow them to provide exceptional service to their customers. Without the information, products, and services that you provide them, they do not have the tools needed to do their job.

Organizational Culture

organizational culture
Includes an element of an organization that a customer encounters.

human resources Refers to employees of an organization.

Without the mechanisms and atmosphere to support frontline service, the other components of the business environment cannot succeed. Put simply, **organizational culture** is what the customer experiences. This culture is made up of a collection of subcomponents, each of which contributes to the overall service environment. Typically, culture includes the dynamic nature of the organization and encompasses the values and beliefs that are important to the organization and its employees and managers. The experiences, attitudes, and norms cherished and upheld by employees and teams within the organization set the tone for the manner in which service is delivered and how service providers interact with both internal and external customers. The impact of culture on customer satisfaction is discussed further in Chapter 2.

Human Resources

To make the culture work, an organization must take great care in recruiting, selecting, training, and retaining qualified people—its **human resources.** That's why, when you apply (or applied) for a job as a customer service professional, a thorough screening process will be (or was) likely used to identify your skills, knowledge, and aptitudes. Without motivated, competent workers, any planning, policy, and procedure change or systems adaptation will not make a difference in customer service.

Many organizations go to great lengths to obtain and retain the "right" employees who possess the knowledge, skills, and competencies to professionally serve customers (see Figure 1.8). Employees who are skilled, motivated, and enthusiastic about providing service excellence are hard to find and are appreciated by employers and customers. As noted earlier, organizations now rely on all employees to provide service excellence to

Receptionist/Front Desk Clerk

Salary range: $7.60–$9.91 per hour (less than 1 year experience)

Employees performing this function in organizations have the primary role of meeting, greeting, and offering initial assistance to customers and visitors. This is a crucial role that starts setting the tone for how others view the organization. Whether in a doctor's or attorney's office, gym, car dealership, homeless shelter, or office building, these frontline service representatives are the standard bearer for an organization and should be adequately trained and empowered to assist those with whom they come into contact.

Customer Service (CS)/Member Support Clerk

Salary range: $6.88–$8.35 per hour (less than 1 year experience)

This is typically an entry-level position requiring strong organizational ability, an ability to follow instructions, listen, and manage time, and a desire to help. A key function is clerical support, which includes filing, researching information, typing, and similar assignments. Deal with customers via the telephone, e-mail, correspondence, and face-to-face.

Customer Service (CS) Representative/Member Counselor

Salary range: $8.66–$12.33 per hour (less than 1 year experience)

This position is an entry-level position into the customer service field (although many people have years of experience in the job). Since these employees interact directly with customers and potential customers, they need strong interpersonal (communication, conflict management, listening) skills as well as a desire to help others, a fondness for working with people, a knowledge of organizational products and services, and thorough understanding of what a CS representative does. Key functions include interacting face-to-face or over the telephone with customers, receiving and processing orders or requests for information and services, responding to customer inquiries, handling complaints, and performing associated customer contact assignments.

Data Entry/Order Clerk

Salary range: $9.00–$11.88 per hour (less than 1 year experience)

The data entry/order clerk is an entry-level position requiring knowledge of personal computers and software, ability to work on repetitive tasks for long periods of time, and an eye for accuracy. Key functions include verifying and batching orders received from customer service representatives for input by computer personnel. In organizations that have personal computer systems connected by networks, data entry/order clerks enter data and generate and maintain reports.

Senior Customer Service (CS) Representative/Member Counselor

Salary range: $12.16–$16.29 per hour (1–4 years experience)

This position is usually staffed by personnel with experience as a CS representative. A position like this one requires a person with a sound understanding of basic supervisory skills, since job duties may include providing feedback, training, and support and administering performance appraisals to other representatives or counselors.

Service Technician or Professional

Salary range varies by specialty. For example, an Auto Service Technician/Mechanic with less that 1 year experience can earn between $8.62–$14.48 per hour.

This group provides many different types of services and carries a variety of titles (for example, air-conditioning technologist, plumber, automotive specialist, office

Figure 1.8
Typical Titles and Functions Performed by Customer Service Personnel in Organizations

(continued)

Figure 1.8
(concluded)

equipment technician, law enforcement officer, firefighter, or sanitation worker). Each specialized area requires specific knowledge and skills.

Inbound/Outbound Telemarketing Specialist

Salary range: $7.72–$9.86 per hour

Customer service representatives may perform some or all of the functions of this job, but often specially hired or trained employees fill the position. They make and receive phone calls with the intent of promoting or selling company products or services. In many organizations these employees are full-time or part-time sales personnel whose job is to use the telephone to call customers or potential customers or receive orders or questions from customers. Employees in these positions need strong self-confidence because of the number of rejections to offers and irate calls they receive, sound verbal communication and listening skills, positive attitude, good knowledge of sales techniques, ability to handle people who are upset, and a desire to help others through identification and satisfaction of needs. Key functions include placing and/or receiving calls, responding to inquiries with product and service information, asking for and recording orders, and following up on leads and requests for information.

Help Desk Computer Analyst

Salary Average: $17.39 per hour (less than 1 year experience)

Typically responsible for providing hardware or software support via an automatic call distributor (ACD) system (see Chapter 9) or e-mail to callers in various geographic locations for their desktop PCs, laptops, and peripheral devices. They answer calls, log all incidents into their call-tracking database, and provide technical assistance.

Counter and Rental Clerk

Salary range: $7.94–$10.03 per hour (1–4 years experience)

These employees work in a variety of organizations receiving orders for services such as repairs, car and equipment rentals, dry cleaning, and storage. They are typically responsible for estimating costs, accepting payments, and, in some cases, completion of rental agreements.

Other Service-Related Functions

In addition to these positions, many organizations have supervisory, manager, director, and vice president positions in most of the job areas indicated or in the service area as a whole. The existence of higher-level positions provides opportunities for upward advancement and learning as experience is gained.

Note: Salaries vary greatly in any occupation and industry and are often dictated by an employee's experience, education, knowledge, initiative, and ability to quickly assume more responsibility or perform at a higher level. Salary examples shown here are from www.payscale.com. To get an idea of salaries for various types of service jobs in your area, visit www.monster.salary.com.

customers; however, they also maintain specially trained "elite" groups of employees who perform specific customer-related functions. Depending on their organization's focus, these individuals have a variety of titles (for example, a customer service representative in a retail organization might be called a *member counselor* in an association, but these employees often perform similar functions).

A challenge for many organizations is finding a way to attract and keep qualified employees. In years past, it was not unusual for someone to spend

Types of Service

TAKE A MINUTE TO THINK ABOUT CUSTOMER SERVICE.
In what ways do organizations typically provide service to external customers?

WORK IT OUT
1.4

an entire career with one or two employers. Times have changed for many reasons. One of the biggest is that there is often no loyalty toward the organization by employees or vice versa by the organization toward employees. One Bureau of Labor study found that "In January 2008, about 23 percent of all wage and salary workers age 16 and over had 12 months or less of tenure with their current employer. These short-tenured workers include new entrants and reentrants to the labor force, job losers who found new jobs during the previous year, and workers who had voluntarily changed employers during the previous year. Younger workers are more likely than older workers to be short-tenured employees. For example, among 20- to 24-year-old workers, about half had a year or less of tenure with their current employer. Among wage and salary workers age 55 to 64 and those age 65 and over, less than 10 percent had a year or less of tenure. . . . Among the major occupations, workers in management, professional, and related occupations had the highest median tenure (5.1 years) in January 2008. Within this group, employees with jobs in architecture and engineering occupations (6.4 years) and management occupations (6.0 years) had the longest tenure. Workers in service occupations, who are generally younger than persons employed in management, professional, and related occupations, had the lowest median tenure (2.8 years). Among employees working in service jobs, food service workers had the shortest median tenure, at 2.0 years."[15]

Deliverables

The fourth component of a service environment is the **deliverables** offered by an organization. A deliverable may be a tangible item manufactured or distributed by the company, such as a piece of furniture or a service available to the customer, such as pest extermination. In either case, there are two potential areas of customer satisfaction or dissatisfaction—quality and quantity. If your customers receive what they perceive as a quality product or service to the level that they expected, and in the time frame promised or viewed as acceptable, they will likely be happy. On the other hand, if customers believe that they were sold an inferior product or given an inferior service or one that does not match their expectations, they will likely be dissatisfied and could take their business elsewhere. They may also provide negative word-of-mouth advertising for the organization.

deliverables Products or services provided by an organization.

Attracting and Training Employees

THINK ABOUT ORGANIZATIONAL STRATEGIES AIMED AT RECRUITING AND TRAINING SERVICE EMPLOYEES.
What are some things you have heard or read about that companies are doing to attract, hire, and keep qualified employees?

Customer Service Success Tip

Visit the Salary Wizard section at www.monster.com to gain a better perspective of the scope of service jobs and salaries for the profession.

delivery system The method(s) used by an organization to provide services and products to its customers.

learning organizations A term used by Peter Senge in his book *The Fifth Discipline* to describe organizations that value knowledge, education, and employee training. They also learn from their competition, industry trends, and other sources, and they develop systems to support continued growth and development in order to remain competitive.

Delivery Systems

The fifth component of an effective service environment is the method(s) by which the product or service is delivered. In deciding on **delivery systems,** organizations examine the following factors.

Industry standards: How is the competition currently delivering? Are current organizational delivery standards in line with those of competitors?

Customer expectations: Do customers expect delivery to occur in a certain manner within a specified time frame? Are alternatives acceptable?

Capabilities: Do existing or available systems within the organization and industry allow for a variety of delivery methods?

Costs: Will providing a variety of techniques add real or perceived value at an acceptable cost? If there are additional costs, will consumers be willing to absorb them?

Current and projected requirements: Are existing methods of delivery, such as mail, phone, and face-to-face service meeting the needs of the customer and will they continue to do so in the future?

Service

Stated simply, service is the manner in which you and other employees treat your customers and each other as you deliver your company's deliverables. Effective use of the techniques and strategies outlined later in this book is required in order to satisfy the needs of your customers.

LO 1-6 Addressing the Changes

Concept All customer-based organizations must provide excellence in service and an environment in which customer needs are identified and satisfied.

With all the changes, developing strategies for providing premium service that will attract and hold loyal customers has become a priority for most organizations. All customer-based organizations have one focus in common—they must provide service excellence and an environment in which customer needs are identified and satisfied—or perish.

To this end, organizations must become **learning organizations,** a term made popular by author Peter Senge in his book *The Fifth Discipline.* Basically, a learning organization is one that uses knowledge as a basis for competitive advantage. This means providing ongoing training and development opportunities to employees so that they can gain and maintain cutting-edge skills and knowledge while projecting a positive can-do customer-focused attitude. A learning organization also ensures that there are systems that can adequately compensate and reward employees on the basis of their performance. In such an organization, systems and processes are continuously examined and updated. Learning from mistakes, and adapting accordingly, is crucial. In the past, organizations took a reactive approach to service by waiting for customers to ask for something or by trying to recover after a service breakdown. Often, a small customer service staff dealt with customer dissatisfaction or attempted to fix problems after they occurred. In today's economy, a proactive approach of anticipating customer needs is necessary and becoming common. To excel, organizations must train all employees to spot problems and deal with them before the customer becomes aware that they exist. Every employee must take personal responsibility for customer care. If a service breakdown does occur, managers in truly customer-focused organizations should empower employees at all levels to do whatever is necessary to satisfy the customer. For this to happen, management must educate and train staff members on the techniques and policies available to help serve the customer. They must then give employees the authority to act without asking first for management intervention in order to resolve customer issues. This concept, known as **service recovery,** is described in detail in Part Three, "Building and Maintaining Relationships."

Small Business Perspective

Customer service is equally or more important in small businesses because those organizations do not have the deep pockets possessed by their multinational competitors. Because of limited staff and resources, these organizations must excel at identifying and addressing the needs of current and potential customers. They must then depend on every employee to put forth 110 percent effort to help satisfy customer needs and expectations. Smaller companies do not have the luxury of a large human resource team to support employees. The owners must get creative to figure out ways to effectively train staff in order to provide them with the knowledge, skills, and attitudes needed to excel and to aid employee retention.

The law defines a small business as "one that is independently owned and operated and is not dominant in its field of operation." According to **Small Business Administration's (SBA)** Office of Advocacy, "The United States had 6.0 million small employers in 2006, representing 99.7% of the nation's employers and 50.2% of its private-sector employment."

Nationally, these small businesses make up more than 70 percent of all businesses. They may be run by one or more individuals, can range from home-based businesses to corner stores or construction contractors, and often are part-time ventures with owners operating more than one business at a time.

service recovery The process of righting a wrong or correcting something that has gone wrong involving provision of a product or service to a customer. The concept involves not only replacing defective products, but also going the extra step of providing compensation for the customer's inconvenience.

Small Business Administration (SBA) United States governmental agency established to assist small business owners.

The Center for Women's Business Research (CWBR) states that one in 11 adult women is an "entrepreneur," and that nearly half of all privately held U.S. businesses are 50 percent or more woman-owned. The CWBR also states that 10.6 million firms are at least half owned by women, and that "these firms employ 19.1 million people and generate nearly $2.5 trillion in sales. Between 1997 and 2004, the number of companies 50% or more women-owned increased at nearly twice the rate of all companies—as did employment rates."[16]

Impact on Service

Based on your experience and what you just read, answer the following questions.

1. What level of customer service have you experienced from small businesses in your local area? Explain.
2. In what ways have you seen service providers in small businesses excel from a service standpoint?
3. In what ways have you seen service providers in small businesses fail from a service standpoint?

Summary

As many organizations move toward a more quality-oriented, customer-focused environment, developing and fine-tuning policies, procedures, and systems to better identify customer needs and meet their expectations will be crucial. Through a concerted effort to perfect service delivery, organizations will be able to survive and compete in a global economy. More emphasis must be placed on finding out what the consumer expects and going beyond those expectations. Total customer satisfaction is not just a buzz phrase; it is a way of life that companies are adopting in order to gain and maintain market share. As a customer service professional, it is your job to help foster a customer-oriented service environment.

Review Questions

Either on your own or in discussion with someone else review what you have learned in this chapter by responding to the following questions:

1. What is service?
2. Describe some of the earliest forms of customer service.
3. What are some of the factors that have facilitated the shift to a service economy?
4. What have been some of the causes of the changing business environment in recent decades?
5. Describe the impact of a company's culture on its success in a customer-focused business environment.
6. What role does the human resources element of the customer service environment play in customer satisfaction?

7. What two factors related to an organization's products or deliverables can lead to customer satisfaction or dissatisfaction?

8. When organizations select a delivery method for products or services, where do they get information on the best approach to take?

9. What are the six key components of a customer service environment?

10. Why are many organizations changing to learning organizations?

Do it

Search It Out

Searching the Web for Salary and Related Information

To learn more about the history, background, and components of customer service occupations, select one of the topics below, log on to the Internet, and gather additional research data. One valuable site is the U.S. Department of Labor at http://stats.bls.gov. You can also type in the term "salaries" on a search engine to identify other sources of income information.

Report your findings to your work team members, peers, or students, depending on the setting in which you are using this book.

Research the projected salaries and benefits for customer service providers in your industry or in one that interests you.

Search for information on organizational behavior and organizational cultural and share your findings with the class. Discuss how behavior and culture impact service delivery.

Develop a bibliographic listing of books and other publications on topics introduced in this chapter. The resources should be less than five years old. You can do this by going to sites such as:

www.amazon.com
www.bn.com
www.glencoe.com/ps
www.mhprofessional.com

Find the Web sites of at least three companies that you believe have adopted a positive customer service attitude and are benefiting as a result. Select any issue raised in this chapter and research it further.

Note: A listing of Web sites for additional research on specific URLs is provided on the Customer Service Web site at www.mhhe.com/customerservice.

Collaborative Learning Activity

Emphasizing Education

Team up with several other people to form a discussion group. Spend some time talking about what you believe the role of schools is today and how well schools are preparing young people for the work world. Share specific personal examples from your own educational background or that of someone you know.

Face to Face

Getting Ready for New Employee Orientation at PackAll

Background

PackAll is a packing and storage company headquartered in Minneapolis, Minnesota, with franchises located in 21 cities throughout the United States. Since opening its first franchise in Minneapolis in 1987, the company has shown great market potential, ending its first year with a profit and growing every year since.

The primary services of the organization are packaging and preparing nonperishable items for shipment and mailing via parcel post. Air-conditioned spaces for short-term storage of personal items and post office boxes are also available to customers.

To ensure consistency of service at all locations, specific standards for employee training and service delivery have been developed and implemented. Before owners or operators can hang up their PackAll sign, they must sign an agreement to comply with standards and must successfully complete a rigorous eight-week management-training program. The program focuses on the key management and business skills necessary to run a successful business and educates employees on corporate philosophy and culture. In addition management offers tips for guiding employee development. At intervals of three and six months after opening their operation, owners or operators are required to participate in a retreat during which they share best practices, receive additional management training, and have an opportunity to ask questions in a structured setting.

Your Role

Today, you joined a PackAll franchise in Orlando, Florida, as a customer service representative. New-employee orientation will be held tomorrow. At that time, you will learn about the service culture, policies and procedures, techniques for handling customers, and specific job skills and requirements.

Before being hired, you were told that your primary duties would be to service customers, provide information about services offered, write up customer orders, collect payments, and package and label orders.

Critical Thinking Questions

1. What interpersonal skills do you currently have that will allow you to be successful in your new position?

2. What general questions about handling customers do you have for your supervisor?

3. If a customer asks for a service that PackAll does not provide, how will you handle the situation? Exactly what will you say?

Planning to Serve

Working alone or with others, creates a list of the major issues facing the service industry or your organization (if you are working) and which directly impact you. Also, list strategies that you can implement to personally address these issues.

To do this, draw a line down the center of a sheet of blank paper. On the left side write the word "Issues" and on the right side, the word "Strategies."

Here is an example of one issue with strategies to address it:

Issue	Strategies
Service industry is growing quickly.	Do Internet research to gather statistics on an occupation that I am currently in or in which I am interested. Identify geographic areas of opportunity, possible salary and benefits, and specific targeted employers.

Quick Preview Answers

1. F	3. F	5. T	7. T	9. F	11. T
2. T	4. F	6. T	8. T	10. T	

Ethical Dilemma Summary

Ethical Dilemma 1.1 Possible Answers

1. Should you inform your supervisor of what you know to ensure that she makes an educated choice based on qualifications? Why or why not?

   This is a touchy issue. If a candidate's performance (or lack of it) is affecting you, other employees, the organization, and customers, then you should probably approach your supervisor in a confidential manner to inform her of what is going on. The downside of taking such action is that your supervisor might question your timing and motives for doing so, especially since there are three different people involved and you have not come forward earlier.

2. What could be the potential result of any action that you take about this issue?

   In such situations, when you witness inappropriate activities or behavior of others that impacts the organization, you should discreetly point it out to them, and if necessary, to someone in charge. It is unwise to save such information for an opportune time in which you can use it in retaliation or to gain personally. This could affect how they, your supervisor, and peers view you and could impact trust in the future, thus negatively affecting your future opportunities. (See also customer service environment.)

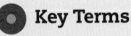
2

Contributing to the Service Culture

"Your earning ability today is largely dependent upon your knowledge, skill and your ability to combine that knowledge and skill in such a way that you contribute value for which customers are going to pay."

—Brian Tracy

Learning Outcomes

After completing this chapter, you will be able to:

2-1 Explain the elements of a service culture.

2-2 Define a service strategy.

2-3 Recognize customer-friendly systems.

2-4 Implement strategies for promoting a positive service culture.

2-5 Separate average companies from exceptional companies.

2-6 Identify what customers want.

Key Terms

attitudes
customer-centric
customer-friendly
  systems
employee expectations
employee roles

empowerment
feel, felt, found technique
mentees
mentors
mission
RUMBA

service culture
service delivery systems
service measurement
service philosophy
what customers want

In the Real World Retail—Ben & Jerry's Ice Cream

BEN & JERRY'S HOMEMADE, INC. IS ONE OF THE TWENTIETH CENTURY'S fabled success stories. The company was founded in 1978 by two childhood friends—Ben Cohen and Jerry Greenfield. The two met in gym class on Long Island in 1963 and have been lifelong friends since.

Being children of the 60s, both Ben and Jerry concluded that college was a wise decision. This epiphany was driven in no small part by the fact that Vietnam was at a high point and the military draft was in full swing.

The two conducted extensive, yet rudimentary, research. Among other things, they visited libraries, stood on the corner and counted foot traffic, and brainstormed a lot. With their newly acquired knowledge, they decided to open an ice cream store. This decision was based on the realization that it was a simple business that did not require large amounts of start-up capital or experience. Also, Jerry had worked in his college cafeteria scooping ice cream, while Ben had several jobs driving an ice cream truck and managing freezer boxes for an ice cream company (counting product and loading/unloading trucks). With such in-depth experience, the two were destined to succeed in the ice cream business.

After searching for a location, facility, and equipment for their new enterprise, they settled on a rundown gas station building in Burlington, Vermont. Realizing that they had much to learn about the ice cream industry and would need more investment capital to get their business off to a sound start, they sought additional industry knowledge. Before they applied for a small business loan, they decided to enroll in a correspondence course on ice cream making from Penn State University. Since they could not afford the tuition ($5 dollars), they split the cost and sent in one fee, then, jointly completed the mail-in materials.

From the beginning, Ben & Jerry's embodied the 60s "for the people" philosophy. Their free-wheeling, let-it-all-hang-out personas helped them succeed by endearing them to their local customers. They capitalized on the image that they were just two guys trying to make it in the business world. By developing a "people's ice cream" concept and using high-quality, locally produced ingredients, they built a loyal customer base. They also used low-cost, unorthodox marketing strategies, which continue to this day. For example, they priced their ice cream so the ordinary person could afford it (originally 52¢ per cone). Next, they started a free outdoor movie festival where they projected movies onto the outside wall of their store in the summer. They also started a tradition in which anyone can get a free ice cream cone on Ben & Jerry's anniversary date. The latter promotion is still in effect and each year they give away nearly half a million free cones nationwide.

The business philosophy of Ben & Jerry's is summed up in its Mission Statement, which comprises three parts, a Social Mission, a Product Mission, and an Economic Mission. (www.benjerry.com/activism/mission-statement/). As a result of Ben & Jerry's philosophy, the organization's community involvement and philanthropy through its Ben & Jerry's Foundation have brought international recognition over the years. In 1988, the company was awarded the Corporate Giving award for donating 7.5 percent of its pretax profits to nonprofit organizations. Also in that year, Ben Cohen and Jerry Greenfield were named Small Business Persons of the Year and received their award from President Reagan at the White House. From the beginning of their operation, Ben & Jerry's emphasis has been on quality products, affordable pricing, and local supporting the local community. These factors have served the company well and gave a sound base for what has become a multimillion dollar, international organization.

To get to the point that they are today, Ben and Jerry have used many unique marketing strategies and used an approach that business should be fun and "real." From scraggy beards, jeans, and pith helmets, the two have strived not to be the typical corporate executives in a traditional work environment. As in the beginning, employees at Ben & Jerry's still enjoy a casual working environment where fun and activities are commonplace.

Some of the unusual marketing approaches used by Ben & Jerry's include:

- Outdoor movie festival with free ice cream.
- Free ice cream cones for mothers on Mother's Day.
- Carnival-like performances by Ben and Jerry in which Ben (aka Habeeni-Ben-Coheeni) is carried aloft on a board, dressed in a bed sheet. Once on a stage, he assumes a trancelike state in which his body becomes rigid and he is suspended between two wooden chairs. At that point, Jerry places a cinder-block on Ben's stomach and proceeds to smash it with a sledgehammer.
- The Cowmobile (an RV) that travels around the country to major locations and events distributing free ice cream samples.
- Pictures of Ben and Jerry appear on their packaging with the phrase, "two real guys."
- Sponsorship of the Newport Folk Festival in Newport, Rhode Island.
- Elvis Day celebration (on Elvis Presley's birthday).
- Products with unusual and memorable names (e.g., Cherry Garcia, Zsa Zsa Gaboreo, Rainforest Crunch, Norieggnog, and Peace Pops).
- Currently, they are conducting the One Sweet Whirled Campus Tour of 20 colleges and universities. The intent of the initiative is to raise the awareness of young people about global warming and the need to reduce CO_2 release.

In 2000, Ben & Jerry's was acquired by British-Dutch multinational food giant Unilever. Although the founders are still engaged with the company, they do not hold any board or management position and are not involved in day-to-day management of the company. Their efforts are more focused on the promotional aspects, "waving the flag" and speaking at events and staying involved in philanthropic ventures.

Ben & Jerry's franchises and PartnerShops can be found in 27 different countries with nearly 500 in North America (United States and Canada). The latter types of franchises are ones in which Ben & Jerry's provides special incentives to qualified nonprofit organizations that open ice cream scoop shops. They are part of Ben & Jerry's social initiative to help nonprofit organizations generate revenue and to provide training in the food industry to otherwise unemployable young people.

Think About It

Visit the Internet and library to learn more about the Ben and Jerry's organization. Based on what you learn and read above, answer the following questions and be prepared to discuss your responses in class.

1. Do you have personal experience with this company? If so, describe your impressions.
2. How does this organization differ from other similar successful companies of which you are aware?
3. How is this organization similar to other successful companies of which you are aware?
4. What does Ben & Jerry's do that encourages customer support and loyalty?
5. Does the organization do anything that might cause a negative impression in the mind of customers? Explain.
6. Would you want to work for this company? Why or why not?

Quick Preview

Before reviewing the chapter content, respond to the following questions by placing a "T" for true or an "F" for false on the rules. Use any questions you miss as a checklist of material to which you will pay particular attention as you read through the chapter. For those you get right, congratulate yourself, but review the sections they address in order to learn additional details about the topic.

_____ 1. Service cultures include such things as policies and procedures.

_____ 2. To remain competitive, organizations must continually monitor and evaluate their systems.

_____ 3. Advertising, service delivery, and complaint resolution are examples of customer-friendly systems.

_____ 4. To better face daily challenges and opportunities in the workplace, you should strive to increase your knowledge, build your skills, and improve your attitude.

_____ 5. Some of the tools used by organizations to measure service culture include employee focus groups, mystery shoppers, and customer lotteries.

_____ 6. By determining the added value and results for me (AVARFM), you can develop. more personal commitment to service excellence.

_____ 7. Use of "they" language to refer to management when dealing with customers helps demonstrate your commitment to your organization and its culture.

_____ 8. Communicating openly and effectively is one technique for working more closely with customers.

_____ 9. Even though you depend on vendors and suppliers, they are not your customers.

_____ 10. Business etiquette dictates that you should return all telephone calls within four hours.

_____ 11. Your job of serving a customer should end at the conclusion of a transaction so that you can switch your attention to new customers.

_____ 12. Customers want value for their money and effective, efficient service.

Answers to Quick Preview can be found at the end of the chapter.

LO 2-1 Defining a Service Culture

Concept Many elements contribute to a service culture.

What is a **service culture** in an organization? The answer is that it is different for each organization. No two organizations operate in the same manner, have the same focus, or provide management that accomplishes the same results. Among other things, a culture includes the values, beliefs, norms, rituals, and practices of a group or organization. Any policy, procedure, action, or inaction on the part of your organization contributes to the service culture. Other elements may be specific to your organization or industry. A key point to remember about service culture is that you play a key role in communicating the culture of your organization to your customers. You may communicate through your appearance, your interaction with customers, and your knowledge, skill, and **attitude.** The latter element is crucial in your success and that of your organization. As a service provider, if you take a job just to have a paycheck without buying into the service culture and supporting the goals of the organization, both you and the organization will lose. For you to be successful in the service industry (or any other for that matter) you must take ownership of your roles and responsibilities and show commitment to doing the best you can every day that you go to work. Even further, you must project a positive attitude when you are not at work as well. Think about the number of times you have heard friends "bad mouth" their boss, organization, products, and services. Did their attitude toward their job inspire you to want to patronize their workplace or apply for a job there? What you do or say around others in any environment sends a powerful message about you, your level of professionalism and your organization. If you cannot support your employer; quit and find a job where you can. To do less is being unfair to yourself and your organization. Remember that if the organization loses money because of poor word-of-mouth publicity (things you and others say about it), there will be fewer customers. This will result in lowered revenue and money available to provide employee salary increases and benefits.

Culture also encompasses your products and services, and the physical appearance of the organization's facility, equipment, or any other aspect of the organization with which the customer comes into contact. Unfortunately, many companies are top-down–oriented (with upper management at the top of their hierarchy and customers as a final element or afterthought) or product-centered and view customers from the standpoint of what company products or services they use (Figure 2.1). Successful organizations are customer-centered or **customer-centric** and focus on individual needs (Figure 2.2).

An organization's service culture is made up of many facets, each of which affects the customer and helps determine the success or failure of customer service initiatives (Figure 2.3). Too often, organizations overpromise and underdeliver because their cultural and internal systems (*infrastructure*) do not have the ability to support customer service initiatives.

service culture A service environment made up of various factors, including the values, beliefs, norms, rituals and practices of a group or organization.

attitudes Emotional responses to people, ideas, and objects. They are based on values, differ between individuals and cultures, and affect the way people deal with various issues and situations.

customer-centric A term used to describe service providers and organizations that put their customers first and spend time, effort, and money identifying and focusing on the needs of current and potential customers. Efforts are focused on building long-term relationships and customer loyalty rather than simply selling a product or service and moving on to the next customer.

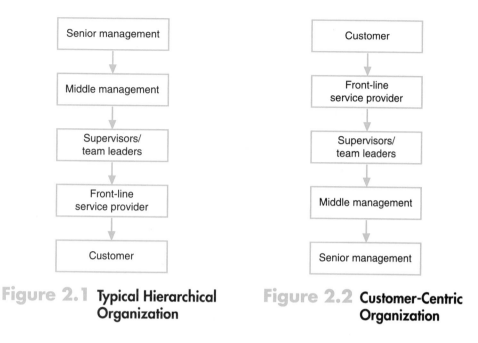

Figure 2.1 **Typical Hierarchical Organization**

Figure 2.2 **Customer-Centric Organization**

For example, suppose that management has the marketing department develop a slick piece of literature describing all the benefits of a new product or service provided by a new corporate partner. Then a special 800 number or Web site is set up to handle customer responses, but no additional staff is hired to handle the customer calls or current service providers are not given adequate information or training to do their job. The project is likely doomed to fail because adequate service support has not been planned and implemented.

In the past, organizations were continually making changes to their product and service lines to try to attract and hold customers. Often this has been their primary approach to customer satisfaction. Now, many major organizations have become more customer-centric and stress relationships with customers. They realize that it is cheaper, and smarter, to keep current customers rather than subscribe to a revolving door approach of continually trying to attract new customers to replace the ones that they lost to competitors. Advertising campaigns often reflect this new awareness as companies try to communicate that they are focused on their customers. The following are some familiar slogans used by companies in their promotional materials:

"Like a good neighbor"—State Farm Insurance

"When you're here, you're family"—Olive Garden Restaurants

"You're in good hands"—Allstate Insurance Company

"It's your store"—Albertsons Grocery Stores

"We'll leave the light on for you." Motel 6

"Think what we can do for you." Bank of America

Figure 2.3
Elements of a Service Culture

Many elements define a successful organization. Some of the more common are shown here.

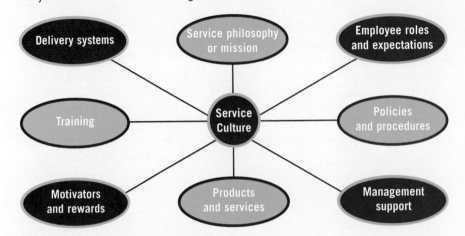

Service philosophy or mission: The direction or vision of an organization that supports day-to-day interactions with the customer.

Employee roles and expectations: The specific communications or measures that indicate what is expected of employees in customer interactions and that define how employee service performance will be evaluated.

Delivery systems: The way an organization delivers its products and services.

Policies and procedures: The guidelines that establish how various situations or transactions will be handled.

Products and services: The materials, products, and services that are state of the art, competitively priced, and meet the needs of customers.

Management support: The availability of management to answer questions and assist front-line employees in customer interactions when necessary. Also, the level of management involvement and enthusiasm in coaching and mentoring professional development.

Motivators and rewards: Monetary rewards, material items, or feedback that prompts employees to continue to deliver service and perform at a high level of effectiveness and efficiency.

Training: Instruction or information provided through a variety of techniques that teach knowledge or skills, or attempt to influence employee attitude toward excellent service delivery.

Service Philosophy or Mission

mission The direction or focus of an organization that supports day-to-day interactions with customers.

service philosophy The approach that an organization takes to providing service and addressing the needs of customers.

Generally, an organization's approach to business, its **mission** or its **service philosophy,** is driven from the top of the organization. Upper management, including members of the board of directors, when appropriate, sets the vision or tone and direction of the organization. Without a clearly planned and communicated vision, the service ethic ends at the highest levels. This is often a stumbling block where many organizations falter because of indecision or dissension at the upper echelons.

Leadership, real and perceived, is crucial to service success. In successful organizations, members of upper management make themselves clearly visible to frontline employees and are in tune with customer needs and expectations.

Although it is wonderful when organizations go to the trouble of developing and hanging a nicely framed formal mission or philosophy statement on the wall, if it is not a functional way of life for employees, it serves little purpose.

Employee Roles and Expectations

In addition to some of the job responsibilities of service providers described in Chapter 1, many tasks and responsibilities are assigned to frontline service providers. Depending on your job, the size and type of your organization, and the industry involved, the **employee roles** and **employee expectations** may be similar from one organization to another, and yet they may be performed in a variety of different ways. Such roles and expectations are normally included in your job description and in your performance goals. They are updated as necessary during your tenure on the job. Where goals are concerned, you are typically measured against them during a performance period and subsequently rewarded or not rewarded, depending on your performance and your organization's policy.

RUMBA

For you and your organization to be successful in providing superior service to your external and internal customers, your roles and expectations must be clearly defined and communicated in terms of the following characteristics, sometimes referred to as **RUMBA** (**R**ealistic, **U**nderstandable, **M**easurable, **B**elievable, **A**ttainable).

Realistic   Your behavior and responsibilities must be in line with the reality of your particular workplace and customer base. Although it is possible to transfer a standard of performance from one organization, and even industry, to another, modifications may be necessary to fit your specific situation. For example, is it realistic that all customer calls must be handled within a specified time period? Many managers set specific goals in terms of "talk time" for their customer service representatives. Can every angry customer be calmed and handled in a two- to three-minute time frame? If not, then a standard such as this sets up employees for failure.

After a performance goal has been set for you, evaluate it fairly and objectively for a period of time (possibly 30 days). This allows time for a variety of opportunities to apply it. At the end of the specified trial period, if you think the goal is unrealistic, go to your supervisor or team leader and discuss modifying it. In preparation for this discussion, think of at least two viable alternatives to the goals. Also, recognize that performance goals are often driven by organizational goals that may be passed down from upper management. Although they might be modified, it may take some time for the change to come about, so be patient. Ultimately, if the goal cannot

employee roles Task assignments that service providers assume.

employee expectations Perceptions about positive and negative aspects of the workplace.

RUMBA An acronym for five criteria (realistic, understandable, measurable, believable, and attainable) used to establish and measure employee performance goals.

Customer Service Success Tip

Meet with your supervisor to discuss your organization's service philosophy and mission statement and what your role is related to helping accomplish this. If there are policies or other standards in place that make your job difficult or impossible to successfully achieve, propose and discuss possible alternatives. Make sure that you have researched the options that you plan to propose and have examples of situations and organizations in which they have been successful. Also, approach the discussion from a positive, proactive approach rather than from an emotional, negative one in which you appear to be simply complaining or making excuses for performance that is not meeting current standards.

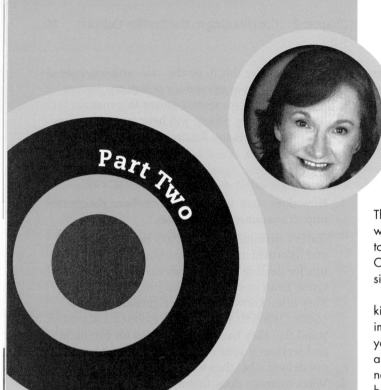

Customer Service Interview
Ruth Sprous
Webster University, Orlando, Florida

1 What are the personal qualities that you believe are essential for anyone working with customers in a service environment?

There are numerous qualities that come in handy when working with customers in any industry. The job of a customer representative really demands the ability to multitask. Often, interruptions from phone calls and people can easily sidetrack you from the task at hand.

As a customer service representative, you will have all kinds of questions and situations presented to you. A very important asset is to have good listening skills, which allows you to hear a question or problem in total. You should also know your limits, meaning that you know when you need to refer to someone else who will be better able to handle or correct a problem or question. Other important characteristics or qualities include:

Be willing to help others by trying to be a customer pleaser and put customers in a good frame of mind.

Display a calm attitude is important since providing service can get pretty hectic sometimes.

Learn about nonconfrontational verbal skills and be prepared to use them because you never know when you might need such a skill to defuse a situation or keep one from escalating.

Of course, having a respectful attitude of all races and ethnicities is expected.

2 What do you see as the most rewarding part of working with customers? Why?

It can be very satisfying knowing that you have helped someone, saved them time or whatever, and that they appreciate your efforts.

As a front-line representative of your company, you provide a valuable contribution to the organization when you do your job well. The job allows one an opportunity to meet and talk with a wide variety of people, both external customers and internal (other employees) ones who often get to know you even when you don't work with them directly.

3 What do you believe is the most challenging part of working with customers? Why?

For me, the most challenging part of the job is dealing with irate or dissatisfied customers. It is easy to lose patience or become annoyed with a customer's complaints. Responding with a cool head instead of reacting to the customer's dissatisfaction is challenging. It is important to determine exactly what the problem is since they may not have received correct information. Also, juggling many phone calls and having people drop by can sometimes be frustrating and leave you breathless, particularly on busy days. When this happens, I just keep in mind that I need to do a mental pep talk and remind myself that not every day is like this. You will have days of down time.

4 **What changes have you seen in the customer service profession since you took your first service provider position? For example: types of customers, their attitudes, people who work in the service industry, how technology is applied to provide service, etc.**

People today have many responsibilities and tight schedules, often making time a premium. They may be less patient and be demanding because of their own frustrations. As a result, they forget things, have more expectations and may be unrealistic. In other words, consider seeing the person as not trying to make your life difficult. They have a reason for being there. Try viewing them as people needing help and remind yourself how appreciative you might be if you were in their place. People want and expect professionalism and don't appreciate getting a runaround. Their time is valuable.

Additionally, today's customers are able to take advantage of the increased amount of online services that companies make available. Being able to deal directly with an organization at their leisure and from the convenience of home suits a lot of customers in this technology-loving world.

5 **What future issues do you see evolving related to dealing with customers in your profession and why do you think these are important?**

While the customer appreciates the benefits of online service, nothing replaces the human contact in certain situations.

Another point is that business today is truly global, and many countries remain a magnet for those people seeking better business and educational opportunities. As a result, a service representative often has to deal with customers who speak other languages. If you experience that situation and persevere, you eventually "develop an ear" and are able to understand other accents.

6 **What advice related to customer service do you have for anyone seeking a career in a customer service environment?**

There are four things that I believe are important if you plan to succeed in any service-related profession:
1. Know your product. Have information at your fingertips so you can relay accurate information.
2. Make notes and organize them around you. For instance, I work for a university and I keep a list of the courses that require prerequisites so as not to mistakenly register a student that has not taken the prerequisite course. Also, sometimes students will call asking how to request a transcript. I keep a sticky on my computer of the steps to take on the university Web site to request one online.
3. Be detail-oriented.
4. Stay updated on company policies and calendar events.
5. Open communication lines spread harmony throughout the team and the customer representative plays a big part in that function. Communicate information to co-workers.

Verbal Communication Skills

People don't want to communicate with an organization or a computer. They want to talk to a real, live, responsive, responsible person who will listen and help them get satisfaction.

—Theo Michelson, State Farm Insurance

Learning Outcomes

After completing this chapter, you will be able to:

3-1 Explain the importance of effective communication in customer service.

3-2 Recognize the elements of effective two-way interpersonal communication.

3-3 Avoid language that could send a negative message and harm the customer-relationship.

3-4 Project a professional customer service image.

3-5 Provide feedback effectively.

3-6 Use assertive communication techniques to enhance service.

3-7 Identify key differences between assertive and aggressive behavior.

Key Terms

assertiveness	global terms	rapport
channel	"I" or "we" messages	receiver
conflict	message	sender
decoding	noise	small talk
encoding	nonverbal feedback	two-way
feedback	paraphrase	communication
filters	pet peeves	verbal feedback

In the Real World Healthcare—The Methodist Hospital System

VOTED ONE OF *FORTUNE* MAGAZINE'S "TOP 100 COMPANIES TO WORK FOR," The Methodist Hospital System is a nonprofit organization based in Houston, Texas, and is recognized for world-renowned clinical and service excellence. The organization is made up of four hospitals, one research institute, 1,464 operating beds and 12,153 employees. It is affiliated with the Texas Annual Conference of the United Methodist Church and operates through a network of community-based hospitals. The Methodist hospital has operated for more than eight decades and in 1996 formed the Hospital System in order to further its efforts to be a top-ranked research, education, and patient-care facility.

To meet its goal the Hospital System has continued to grow, and among other well-known, state-of-the art facilities, now includes the Methodist Hospital Research Center, DeBakey Heart & Vascular Center, Methodist Neurological Institute, and the Eddy Scurlock Stroke Center. According to their Web site, in 2008, the System "broke ground on $2 billion in construction, filled 300 new jobs, and awarded merit pay raises of 3 percent. Salaried employees who worked long hours after Hurricane Ike got $250 Kroger gift cards." Because any organization striving for excellence in service needs quality staff, the Methodist Hospital System provides a wide array of benefits to its employees. In addition to competitive salaries, these include:

- Medical Plan (choose one of two plans)
- Prescription Drug Plan
- Dental Plan (choose one of two plans)
- Vision Coverage
- Basic Life Insurance (paid by Methodist)
- Basic Accidental Death and Dismemberment Insurance (paid by Methodist)
- Optional Life Insurance (employee and/or dependent)
- Voluntary Accidental Death and Dismemberment Insurance (employee and/or dependent)
- Short-Term Disability (paid by Methodist)
- Long-Term Disability (paid by Methodist)
- Workers' Compensation (paid by Methodist)
- 403(b) Tax-Sheltered Annuity with employer matching
- Defined Contribution Plan–Methodist makes contribution
- Savings Bond

The organization's mission statement, found on its Web site, emphasizes the spiritual nature of the organization and the fact that its focus is "To provide high quality, cost-effective health care that delivers the best value to the people we serve in a spiritual environment of caring in association with internationally recognized teaching and research." Each employee is expected to exhibit the organization's values of integrity, compassion, accountability, respect, and excellence.

In conjunction with its core values and mission statement, the organization gives back to the community in many ways that relate to a focus on effective communication and relationship- building inside and outside the organization. Through several programs the System provides opportunities for underprivileged children and their families to attend Houston Astros and Houston Texans baseball and football games. The organization also sponsors the Volunteer Circle of excellence, which encourages people in the community to donate time and talents to help teens, volunteer in the hospital, help students and patients, and network with various other community-based volunteer initiatives to help out in many other ways. It also offers a Speaker's Bureau where organizations can request experts on various medical topics to come in to speak to groups and employees.

Think About It

Do an Internet search of Methodist Hospital System to gather additional information about the organization. Try to find examples of community connections, employees' support programs, and customer service initiatives. Once you have the information, answer the following questions and be prepared to discuss the organization in class.

1. How does the Methodist Hospital System compare to organizations of which you are aware? Explain.
2. What indications do you have that Methodist is committed to quality service?
3. In what ways does this organization portray one that is committed to service excellence?
4. What do you think about Methodist's commitment to its employees? Explain.
5. Based on what you discovered on the Internet, do you believe that the organization will reach its goal of top-ranked research, education, and patient-care facility? Explain.
6. Would you want to be a patient at this hospital? Why or why not?
7. Would you want to work for Methodist? Why or why not?

Quick Preview

Before reviewing the chapter content, respond to the following questions by placing a "T" for true or an "F" for false on the rules. Use any questions you miss as a checklist of material to which you will pay particular attention as you read through the chapter. For those you get right, congratulate yourself, but review the sections they address in order to learn additional details about the topic.

_____ 1. Feedback is not an important element in the two-way communication model.

_____ 2. Customers appreciate your integrity, and they trust you more when you use language such as "I'm sorry" or "I was wrong" when you make a mistake.

_____ 3. Phrases such as "I'll try" or "I'm not sure" send a reassuring message that you're going to help solve a customer's problem.

_____ 4. When you use agreement or acknowledgment statements, customers can vent without their emotions escalating.

_____ 5. You should attempt to make a positive impression by focusing on the customer and his or her needs during your initial and subsequent contacts.

_____ 6. Having one prepared greeting and closing statement to use with all customers is a good practice.

_____ **7.** When you are not certain of an answer, it is a good idea to express an opinion or speculate when something will occur if a customer asks.

_____ **8.** An acceptable response to a customer's question about why something cannot be done is "Our policy does not allow . . . "

_____ **9.** You should delay feedback whenever possible unless you're communicating in writing.

_____ **10.** The appearance of your workplace has little effect on customer satisfaction as long as you are professional and help solve problems.

_____ **11.** Assertive communication means expressing your opinions positively and in a manner that helps the customers recognize that you are confident and have the authority to assist them.

_____ **12.** Assertiveness is another word for "aggressiveness."

Answers to Quick Preview can be found at the end of the chapter.

LO 3-1 The Importance of Effective Communication

Concept You represent your organization, and customers will respond according to you and your actions.

As a customer service professional, you have the power to make or break the organization. You are the front line in delivering quality service to your customers. Your appearance, actions or inactions, and ability to communicate say volumes about the organization and its focus on customer satisfaction. Additionally, in order to be successful you need knowledge and skill in communicating verbally, nonverbally, across genders and cultures and with a variety of personality types. For all these reasons, you should continually work to enhance your knowledge and skills, strive to project a professional image, and go out of your way to make a customer's visit or conversation with you a pleasant and successful one.

Two key elements in making your interactions with customers successful are to recognize how you tend to communicate and understanding how the communication process works. The easiest way to find out how you communicate is to ask those who know you best. Unfortunately, many people are leery about requesting feedback because of what they might hear. Conversely, most people have difficulty giving useful feedback because they either never learned how to do it or are uncomfortable doing it. In any event, try it. Ask a variety of people for their feedback because each person will likely have a different perspective.

LO 3-2 Ensuring Two-Way Communication

Concept Two-way communication involves a sender and a receiver, who each contribute to the communication process. Part of the communication process is deciding which is the best channel to ensure clear message delivery.

Customer Service Success Tip

In addition to any specifics you would like to learn for yourself, ask the following questions of those with whom you interact regularly:

Do I tend to smile when I speak?

What other body cues (nonverbal signals) do I use regularly when I speak?

What mannerisms do I typically use when speaking?

How would you categorize my overall presence when I speak (confident, uncertain, timid, relaxed)? Why do you perceive that?

What "pet" words or phrases do I use regularly?

When I speak, how does my tone sound (assertive, attacking, calming, friendly, persuasive)? What examples of this can you provide?

When I am frustrated or irritated how do you know it?

Figure 3.1

Interpersonal Communication Model

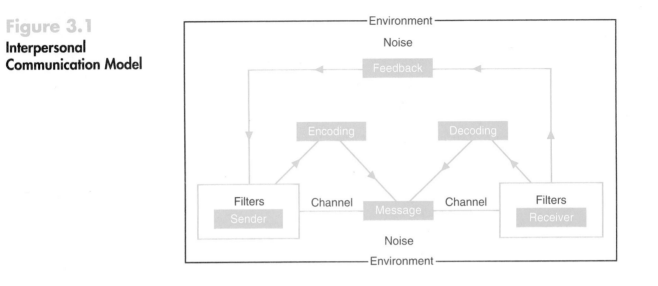

two-way communication
An active process in which two individuals apply all the elements of interpersonal communication (e.g., listening, feedback, positive language) in order to effectively exchange information and ideas.

As a customer service professional, you are responsible for ensuring that a meaningful exchange of information takes place. By accepting this responsibility, you can perform your job more efficiently, generate goodwill and customer loyalty for the organization, and provide service excellence. To facilitate this, you should be aware of all the elements of **two-way communication** and the importance of each. Figure 3.1 shows a communication model that clarifies the process.

Two-way communication is the foundation of effective customer service. *How can you be sure that you are listening to the customer?*

Interpersonal Communication Model

Environment. The environment (office, store, and group or individual setting) in which you send or receive messages affects the effectiveness of your message. For example, in a busy business environment, you are likely to be making an effort to meet deadlines, serve all customers, or create a positive experience for each customer. In such an environment, you or others may take shortcuts in communicating and send what might be perceived as curt or abrupt verbal and nonverbal messages. This could potentially cause a service breakdown. The key to success in such instances is to take a deep breath when things get hectic, remember to use a calm and professional tone, and to think before speaking or responding nonverbally.

Sender. You take on the role of **sender** as you initiate a message with your customer. Conversely, when customers respond, they assume that role. As the sender, you have a responsibility for thinking of the message that you want the customer to receive, then using words and nonverbal cues that effectively convey that message.

Receiver. Initially, you may be the **receiver** of your customer's message; however, once you offer feedback, you switch to the sender role. As the receiver, you must effectively listen in order to receive and effectively comprehend what the customer has said. If unsure, you should either paraphrase (repeat the customer's message in your own words) or ask questions that will clarify the meaning for you.

Message. The **message** is the idea or concept that you or your customer wishes to convey. Often our messages get lost in the delivery. Because we choose inappropriate words or nonverbal cues, the customer misinterprets or does not understand our intended point. This can lead to a breakdown in communication and service. In order to prevent this from occurring, it is important to think before speaking. Consider factors such as the customer's gender, age, culture, experience and knowledge level, ability to hear, and any other factor that might affect the way in which the customer might receive and analyze your message. Then, formulate a message that is clear and concise and communicates your intended meaning.

Channel. The method you choose to transmit your message (over the phone, in person, by fax, by e-mail, or by other means) is the **channel.** In an ideal world, it is typically best to communicate face to face, with a secondary preference being over the telephone. Through these two channels, you and your customer are able to hear words, inflections, tone, and other voice qualities that impact message meaning or in the case of face to face, see the nonverbal cues that accompany the words. When you revert to written communication there is the potential for misunderstanding of words, lost opportunity to supplement the words with verbal and nonverbal cues, and the potential feeling of the message being impersonal.

sender One of the two primary elements of a two-way conversation.

receiver One of the two primary elements of a two-way conversation. Gathers the sender's message and decides how to react to it.

message A communication delivered through speech or signals, or in writing.

channel Term used to describe the method through which people communicate messages. Examples are face to face, telephone, e-mail, written correspondence, and facsimile.

encoding The stage in the interpersonal communication process in which the sender decides what message will be sent and how it will be transmitted along with considerations about the receiver.

decoding The stage in the interpersonal communication process in which messages received are analyzed by a receiver in an effort to determine the sender's intent.

feedback The stage of the interpersonal communication process in which a receiver responds to a sender's message.

filters Psychological barriers in the form of personal experiences, lessons learned, societal beliefs, and values through which people process and compare information received to determining its significance.

noise Refers to physiological or psychological factors (physical characteristics, level of attention, message clarity, loudness of message, or environmental factors) that interfere with the accurate reception of information.

Encoding. **Encoding** occurs as you evaluate what must be done to effectively put your message into a format that your customer will understand (language, symbols, and gestures are a few options). Failing to correctly determine your customer's ability to decode your message could lead to confusion and misunderstanding. As mentioned under the "message" section above, you must consider many personal factors about your recipient in order to ensure that she gets the message that you intend.

Decoding. **Decoding** occurs as you or your customer converts messages received into familiar ideas by interpreting or assigning meaning. Depending on how well the message was encoded or whether personal filters (e.g., gender, background, age, language, or cultural differences) interfere, the received message may not be the one you originally sent. This can lead to a service breakdown and potential conflict.

Feedback. Unless a response is given to messages received, there is no way to determine whether the intended message was received. **Feedback** is one of the most crucial elements of the two-way communication process. Without it, you have a monologue. Feedback typically comes in the form of nonverbal reactions or verbal responses or questions during face-to-face or telephonic communication. When you are using e-mail, texting, or other written formats, you have to wait for a response. In such instances (or when no response is forthcoming) it is a good idea to clarify receipt and proper understanding of your original message based on the type of feedback that you receive. Never assume that someone got and interpreted your message the way you intended. Read the response well before leaping to any potential negative conclusions. There have been too many instances in which people have sent an inappropriate emotional response, which they later regretted, because they initially misinterpreted feedback they received.

Filters. **Filters** are factors that distort or affect the messages you receive. They include, among other things, your attitude, interests, biases, expectations, experiences, education, beliefs and values, background, culture, and gender. These factors can cloud our perception and judgment and can sometimes result in communication and service breakdowns. Consider your own filters when sending or interpreting messages.

Noise. **Noise** consists of physiological factors (e.g., health or physical characteristics and abilities) or psychological factors (e.g., level of attention, mood, mental health, or emotional condition) that interfere with the accurate reception of information. It can also include environmental factors (e.g., external sounds or room acoustics) that inhibit communication and listening.

LO 3-3 Avoiding Negative Communication

Concept Use positive words or phrases, rather than emphasize the negative.

You can squelch customer loyalty and raise customer frustration in a number of ways when communicating. Your choice of words or phrasing can often lead either to satisfaction or to confrontation, or it can destroy a customer-provider relationship. Customers do not want to hear what you can't do; they want to hear how you're going to help satisfy their needs or expectations. Focus your message on how you can work with the customer to accomplish needs satisfaction. Don't use vague or weak terminology. Instead of "I'm not sure . . . " or "I'll try . . . ", say "Let me get that answer for you . . . " or "I can do . . .."

Another pitfall to watch out for is the use of **global terms** (all-encompassing or inclusive expressions such as *always*, *never*, *everyone*, *all*). If your customer can give just one example for which your statement is not true, your credibility comes into question and you might go on the defensive. Suppose you say, "We always return calls in four hours," yet the customer has personally experienced a situation when that did not happen. Your statement is now false. Instead, phrase statements to indicate possible variances such as, "We attempt to return all calls within four hours" or "Our objective is to return calls within four hours." Be careful, too, about "verbal finger pointing," especially if your customer is already upset. This tactic involves the use of the word you, as in "You were supposed to call back to remind me" or "You didn't follow the directions I gave you." This is like pointing your finger at someone or using a patronizing tone to belittle them. People are likely to react powerfully and negatively to this type of treatment. See Figure 3.2.

global terms Potentially inflammatory words or phrases used in conversation. They tend to inappropriately generalize behavior or group people or incidents together (e.g., always, never, everyone, everything, all the time).

Figure 3.2
Words and Phrases That Damage Customer Relationships

Here are some words and phrases that can lead to trouble with your customers. Avoid or limit their use.

You don't understand.	You aren't listening to me.
You'll have to . . .	Listen to me.
You don't see my point.	I never said . . .
Hold on (or hang on) a second.	In my opinion . . .
I (we, you) can't . . .	What's your problem?
Our policy says (or prohibits) . . .	The word *problem*.
That's not my job (or responsibility).	Do you understand?
You're not being reasonable.	Are you aware . . .
You must (or should) . . .	The word *no*.
The word *but*.	Global terms (*always, never, nobody*).
What you need to do is . . .	Endearment terms (*honey, sweetie, sugar* and *baby*).
Why don't you . . . ?	Profanity or vulgarity.
I don't know.	Technical or industry-specific jargon
You're wrong or mistaken.	

LO 3-4 Communicating Positively

Concept A positive approach can produce positive results.

Just as you can turn customers off with your word choice, you can also win them over. Figure 3.3 contains some tips.

Plan Your Messages

You should think out everything from your greeting to your closing statements before you come into contact with a customer. Know what you want and need to say, avoid unnecessary details or discussion, and be prepared to answer questions about the organization, its products and services, and the customer's order.

Focus on the Customer as a Person

Strive to let customers know that you recognize them as individuals and appreciate their time, effort, patience, trust, and business. This is important. To deliver quality service effectively, you must deal with the human being before you deal with his or her needs or business concerns.

For example, if someone has waited in a line or on hold for service, as soon as this person steps up or you come back on the line, smile warmly, thank him or her for being patient, apologize for the wait, and ask what you can do to assist him or her. Often in such situations the service provider says something like "Next" (sounds canned and not customer-focused) or "Can I help the next person?" (better, but still goes straight to business without an apology or without recognizing the customer's inconvenience or wait). On the phone the service provider goes straight to, "This is Jean, how may I help you?" (with no recognition of the customer's inconvenience).

Another opportunity to focus on the customer occurs at the end of a transaction or call. If your organization does not have a standard parting comment to use with customers, simply smile and say something like,

Figure 3.3
Words and Phrases that Build Customer Relationships

Some phrases can assist you in strengthening relationships with your customers. Such language reinforces your integrity and encourages customers to trust you. How do you or could you use these words? Which ones do you use the most?

Please.	May I . . . ?
Thank you.	Have you considered . . .
I can or will . . .	I'm sorry (I apologize) for . . .
How may I help?	However, and, or yet (instead of but).
I was wrong.	It's my (our) fault.
I understand (appreciate) how you feel.	Would you mind . . .
Situation, issue, concern (instead of problem).	What do you think?
Often, many times, some (instead of global terms).	I appreciate . . .
You're right.	Use of customer's name.

"Mr. Rinaldi, thank you for coming to (or calling) ABC Corporation. Please come back (or call) again." The key is that you must sound sincere. You may even want to modify your parting statement for subsequent customers so that it sounds more personal—and so the next person in line doesn't hear you parrot the same words with each customer.

Offer assistance. Even if a problem or question is not in your area of responsibility, offer to help get answers, information, or assistance. Your customer will likely appreciate the fact that you went out of your way to help.

Be prepared. Know as much as possible about the organization, its products and services, your job, and as appropriate, the customer. Also, make sure that you have all the tools necessary to serve the customer, take notes, and do your job in a professional manner. This allows you to deliver quality information and service while better satisfying customer needs and expectations.

Provide factual information. Don't express opinions or speculate why something did or didn't, or will or will not, occur. State only what you are sure of or can substantiate. For example, if you are not sure when a delivery will take place or when a coworker who handles certain functions will return, say so, but offer to find the answer or handle the situation yourself. Don't raise customer expectations by saying, "This should be delivered by 7:30 tomorrow morning," or "Sue should be back from lunch in 10 minutes." If neither event occurs, the customer is likely to be irritated.

Be helpful. If you cannot do something or don't have a product or service, admit it but be prepared to offer an alternative. Do not try to "dance around" an issue in an effort to respond in a manner that you feel the customer expects. Most people will spot this tentative behavior, and your credibility will suffer as a result. Do not insult your customer's intelligence by taking this approach. You and the organization will lose in the long run.

Accept responsibility. Take responsibility for what you do or say and, if necessary, for actions taken by someone else that failed to satisfy the customer. Don't blame others or hide behind "they said" or "policy says" excuses. When something goes wrong, take responsibility and work to resolve the problem positively and quickly. If you don't have the authority needed, get someone who does, rather than refer the customer to someone else.

Take appropriate action. You should go to great lengths to satisfy the customer. Sometimes this may mean bending the rules a bit. In such cases, it may be easier to ask forgiveness from your supervisor than to explain why you lost the organization a good customer. If a request really cannot be honored because it is too extreme (a customer demands a free $100 item because he or she had to return one that did not work properly), explain why that specific request cannot be fulfilled and then negotiate and offer alternatives. In Chapter 7 you will find some suggestions for appropriate service recovery strategies.

Customer Service Success Tip

Look for ways to celebrate your customers and make them feel special and valued. For example, congratulate them on special events of which you are aware (e.g., weddings or anniversaries, birthdays, birth of children, graduation from school, and other successes). This will return dividends of increased customer satisfaction, higher levels of customer trust in the organization, and reduced stress for you because you will have fewer instances of unhappy customers with whom you have to deal.

Analyzing Your Verbal Communication Skills

TO HELP YOU DETERMINE HOW YOU SOUND TO OTHERS, TRY A BIT OF OBJECTIVE SELF-ANALYSIS.

To do this, place a cassette recorder nearby, either at home or in the office, and leave it on for about 45 minutes to an hour while you interact with other people. Then play the cassette to hear what your voice sounds like when you communicate verbally with others. Be especially alert for verbal cues that send a negative message or seem to be misinterpreted by the other people involved. Also, listen carefully to the manner in which others respond to you. Do their words or voice tone seem different from what you expected? Did they seem to respond to your comments in a way that shows confusion, frustration, or irritation because of what you said or how you said it? If you answer yes to these questions, and this occurs several times on the tape, go back to the people involved in the conversation and ask them to help you interpret what's on the tape. You may find that your communication style is doing more to hurt than help in gathering information and building relationships with others.

Greet Customers Warmly and Sincerely

If appropriate, shake hands, smile often, and offer a sincere welcome, not the canned "Welcome to . . . ." Instead, use whatever your organizational policy dictates, such as, "Good morning/afternoon, welcome to . . . . My name is . . . . How may I assist (or help) you?"

Even on the telephone you should smile and verbally "shake your customer's hand," because your smile can definitely be heard in your voice. Be conscious of the need to sound approachable and receptive.

> **Customer Service Success Tip**
>
> When the telephone rings, mentally "shift gears" before answering. Stop doing other tasks, clear your head of other thoughts, focus on the telephone, then cheerfully and professionally answer the call.

Use Customer-Focused Language

A mistake by many service providers is to communicate as if they are the important element of a transaction. In reality, it is the customer upon whom a message should be focused. The following examples show the difference in focus:

Provider-Centered

- As soon as I have time . . .
- I'll send out a form that we need you to complete and sign.
- Let me explain the benefits of this product.

Customer-Centered

- I'll take care of that right away.
- To make sure that we have all the information needed to ensure you the best service, once you get the form, please complete and sign it.
- As a savvy consumer, you'll appreciate the benefits of this product. May I explain?

Make Customers Feel Welcome

Most people like to feel as if they belong, to be recognized as special, and to be seen as individuals. Know the customer's name when possible. Use it in greeting him or her, several times throughout the conversation, and when closing the encounter. Try to avoid using negative-sounding "you" messages as a primary means of addressing your customer. For example, instead of "You'll need to fill out this form before I can process your refund," try "Mr. Renaldi, can you please provide some information on this form while I start processing your refund? That way, we'll have you out of here quickly." The latter approach makes it sound as if you recognize customers as being important, respect their time, and are not dictating to them. This can often mean the difference between a smile from your customer and a confrontation and demand to speak to a supervisor.

Many companies go out of their way to send the message of "family." For example, the Saturn automobile company advertisements tout that customers become part of the "Saturn family" once they buy a car from the company. Similarly, CarMax and several other national automobile chains go to great lengths to make the customer feel welcome and special. For example, they drape a huge ribbon over a newly purchased vehicle in a well-lit garage, available sales representatives gather with the customer to congratulate him or her on being part of the "family," and photographs are taken of this "special moment."

Listen Carefully and Respond Appropriately

Listening is the key element of two-way verbal communication. The manner in which you listen and respond often determines the direction of the conversation. When customers feel that they are not being listened to, their attitude and emotions can quickly change from amiable to confrontational. If necessary, review Chapter 5 for specific suggestions on effective listening.

Be Specific

Whenever you have to answer questions, especially details relating to costs, delivery dates, warranties, and other important areas of customer interest, give complete and accurate details. If you leave something out, possibly because you believe it isn't important, you can bet that the customer may feel it was important, and will be upset.

Examples

If deliveries are free, but only within a 50-mile radius, make sure that you tell the customer about the mileage policy. (The customer may live 51 miles away!) If a customer calls to ask for the price of an item and your quote does not include tax, shipping, and handling, say so. Give the total cost, so that there are no surprises when the customer drives to the store to make the purchase or orders from your Web site and ends up paying more.

Use Positive "I" or "We" Messages

In addition to avoiding the "you" statements mentioned earlier, focus on what "I" or "we" can do for or with the customer. In addressing the customer, state the specific service approaches you will take, for example, "I'll handle this personally," as opposed to "I'll do my best" or "I'll try." Expressions like "I'll handle this personally" sound proactive and positive. **"I" or "we" messages** go a long way in subtly letting the customer know that you have the knowledge, confidence, and authority to help out.

Use "Small Talk"

Look for opportunities to communicate on a personal level or to compliment your customer. If you promptly establish a professional relationship with your customers, they are less likely to attack you verbally or complain. Listen to what they say. Look for specific things that you have in common. For example, suppose your customer mentions that she has just returned form Altoona, Pennsylvania, where she visited relatives. If you grew up in or near Altoona, comment about this and ask questions. By bonding with the customer, you show that you recognize the customer as more than a nameless face or a prospective sale.

One thing to keep in mind about **small talk** is that you must listen to your customer's words and tone. If it is obvious he or she is impatient or in a hurry, skip the small talk and focus on efficiently providing service.

"I" or "we" messages Messages that are potentially less offensive than the word "you," which is like nonverbal finger-pointing when emotions are high.

small talk Dialogue used to enhance relationships, show civility, and build rapport.

Use Simple Language

Many interpersonal impartation decompositions can be ascribed to one singular customer service professional fallacy—that all customers can discern the significance of the employee's vernacular. Simply stated: *Many customer service professionals fail to use language their customers can understand.*

When dealing with customers, especially if you are selling or servicing in a technical field, use terms and explanations that are easily understood. Watch the customer's nonverbal body language for signs of confusion or frustration as you speak, and frequently ask for feedback and questions.

If you are on the telephone, listen for sounds of confusion or pauses that may indicate that the customer either did not understand something you said or has a question.

Paraphrase

To ensure that you get the message the customer intended to communicate, take time to ask for feedback. Do this by repeating to the customer the message you

Look for opportunities to communicate in a friendly atmosphere. *Do you think a friendly conversation can facilitate working through a conflict or problem?*

heard, but in your own words—**paraphrase.** An example would be, "If I understand the problem, Mrs. Hawthorne, you bought this item on June 28 as a present for your son. When he tried to assemble it, two parts were missing. Is that correct?"

paraphrase The practice of a message receiver giving back in his or her own words what he believes a sender said.

Ask Positively Phrased Questions

Sometimes the simplest things can cause problems, especially if someone is already irritated. To avoid creating a negative situation or escalating customer emotions, choose the wording of your questions carefully. Consider these two specific techniques.

The first is to find a way to rephrase any question that you would normally start with "Why?" The reason is that this word cannot be inflected in a way that doesn't come across as potentially abrasive, intrusive, or meddlesome. As with many experiences you have, the origin of negative feelings toward the word likely stem from childhood. Remember when you wanted to do something as a child and were told no? The word that probably came out of your mouth (in a whiney voice) was "Why?" This was a verbal challenge to the person who was telling you that you couldn't do something. And the response you probably heard was "Because I said so" or "Because I'm the mommy (or daddy), that's why." Most likely, you didn't like that type of response then, and neither did your customers when they were children. The result of this early experience is that when we hear the word why, it can sound like a challenge and can prompt a negative emotional reaction. To prevent this from occurring, try rewording your "Why" questions.

Examples

Instead of	**Try**
Why do you feel that way?	What makes you feel that way?
Why don't you like . . . ?	What is it that you don't like about . . . ?
Why do you need that feature?	How is that feature going to be beneficial to you?
Why do you want that color?	What other colors have you considered?

The second technique to consider regarding question phrasing is to ask questions that do not create or add to a negative impression. This is especially important if you have a customer who is already saying negative things about you, your product, or service, or the company. By asking questions that start with a negative word and trying to lead customers to an answer, you can be subtly adding fuel to an emotional fire.

For example, suppose your customer is upset because he ordered window blinds through the mail and did not get the color he wanted. He has called you to complain. You have asked a few questions to determine the color scheme of the room in which the blinds will be installed. You say, "Based on what you have told me, don't you think the color you received would work just as well?" Your customer now launches into a tirade. He probably thinks that you were not listening to him, were not concerned about his needs, and presumed you could lead him to another decision.

Here are some more examples of questions that could cause communication breakdowns, along with some suggested alternatives.

Examples

Instead of	Try
Don't you think . . . ?	What do you think . . . ?
Wouldn't this work as well?	How do you think this would work?
Couldn't we do . . . instead?	Could we try . . . instead?
Aren't you going to make a deposit?	What amount would you like to deposit?
Don't you have two pennies?	Do you have two pennies?
Shouldn't you try this for a week before we replace the part again?	How do you feel about trying it for a week to see how it works before we replace the part again?

Ask Permission

Get customer approval before taking action that was not previously approved or discussed, such as putting a telephone caller on hold or interrupting. By doing so, you can raise the customers to a position of authority, boost their self-esteem, and empower them (to say yes or no). They'll likely appreciate all three. You'll learn more about telephone etiquette and effective usage in Chapter 9.

Agree with Customers

Like most other people, customers like to hear that they are right. This is especially true when a mistake has been made or something goes wrong. When a customer has a complaint or is upset because a product and/or service does not live up to expectations, acknowledge the emotion he or she is feeling and then move on and help resolve the issue. Defusing by acknowledgment is a powerful tool.

However, listen carefully for the level of emotion. If the customer is very angry, you may want to choose your words carefully. For example, suppose you have a customer who has called or returned to your store on four occasions to address a single problem with a product. She has been inconvenienced, has not gotten satisfaction in the previous encounters, and has spent extra time in an effort to correct the problem. When she calls or arrives, her voice tone and volume are elevated and she is demanding that you get a supervisor. In this situation, your best approach probably is to let her vent and describe the problem without interrupting, apologize as often as appropriate, and do everything you can to resolve the issue fairly (assuming that she has a legitimate complaint). You would not want to use a statement that could further enflame her.

Although phrases such as, "You sound upset Ms. O'Malley," or "I can understand how you feel" can help diffuse some tense situations, they can come across as patronizing and insincere when someone is really angry (such as in the above example). Instead of using such terminology, try looking for something she is saying that you can agree with. Also, remember that when customers get angry, raise their voices, and say certain things, they are not typically angry with you—they are frustrated and angry with the organization and/or system. Try not to become defensive or sound irritated, since this will likely only escalate the customer's emotions.

For example, suppose Ms. O'Malley says something like, "You people are a bunch of idiots. I've been coming in here for years and I always have problems. Why don't you hire someone with brains to serve your customers?" The normal human response would be to retaliate. However, think back on what happened when you were a child at the playground. When someone pushed you or called you a name and you responded with name-calling or pushed back, emotions escalated until someone either struck out or ran away crying. No one won. The relationship was damaged, possibly irreparably.

In the case of Ms. O'Malley, if you strike back with similar comments, neither of you will win. Moreover, you will likely lose a valued customer who will tell her story to many friends—and you will have to explain to your boss why you acted the way you did. Instead, try a defusing technique in which you seek something to agree upon. For example, you might reply, "I know this is frustrating, especially when it seems we haven't done a good job solving your problem." After this, assuming she doesn't launch back in with another tirade, you might then offer, "Let me help you take care of this right now." If she does verbally attack again, let her vent and then try another calm agreement response, followed by a second offer to assist. The key is to remain professional and in control of your emotions so that you can find a suitable resolution to the issue.

The value in this approach is that in letting Ms. O'Malley vent, you are discovering her emotions and possibly the history of the problem by listening actively. If you need more information, you can ask questions once you have defused her emotions and she calms down a bit. Typically, if you remain calm and objective and look for minor things with which you can agree, the customer will back off. Also, the customer may likely start to see that she is the one out of control and that you are being professional while trying to help her. If the customer truly wants the problem to be solved, she soon realizes that cooperation with you is necessary.

In many cases, if you resolve the customer's problem professionally, the customer will often apologize for his or her actions and words.

My Pet Peeves

TAKE A FEW MINUTES TO THINK ABOUT IRRITATING BEHAVIORS THAT SERVICE
PROVIDERS HAVE EXHIBITED WHEN HELPING YOU IN THE PAST.
Make a list of these behaviors and strive not to exhibit similar ones, since your customers
will likely also be irritated by them. After you create your list, compare it with others in
the class.

As an alternative, your instructor may form groups of four or five learners and do
this as a group activity.

rapport The silent bond
built between two people as
a result of sharing of common
interests and issues and demonstration of a win-win, I care
attitude.

pet peeves Refers to factors, people, or situations that
personally irritate or frustrate
a service provider and which,
left unchecked, can create a
breakdown in effective service.

Elicit Customer Feedback and Participation

Make customers feel as if they are a part of the conversation by asking
questions. Ask opinions, find out how they feel about what you're doing or
saying, and get them involved by building **rapport** through ongoing dialogue. Acknowledge their ideas, suggestions, or information with statements such as, "That's a good idea (or suggestion or decision)." This will
foster a feeling that the two of you are working together to solve a problem. The beauty of such an approach is that if the customer comes up
with an idea and you follow through on it, he or she feels a sense of ownership and is less likely to complain later or feel bad if things don't work
out as planned.

Close the Transaction Professionally

Instead of some parroted response used for each customer like, "Have a
nice day," offer a sincere "Thank you" and encourage the customer to
return in the future. Remember, part of a service culture is building
customer loyalty.

Address Pet Peeves

Most people have something that bothers them about how others communicate or behave. These "hot buttons," or **pet peeves,** can lead to customer
relationship breakdowns if you are not aware of what your pet peeves are
and how you come across to others. By identifying and acknowledging
your potential irritants, you can begin to modify your behavior in order to
prevent problems with customers. You may also be able to avoid situations
in which such behaviors are present or might manifest themselves and
cause problems for you.

Your customers also likely have a list of things that they dislike about
service providers. If you exhibit one of their pet peeves while serving them,
you could find yourself opposite a disgruntled person who is not afraid to
voice his or her displeasure. They may even escalate their complaint to
your supervisor or elsewhere.

Some typical behaviors that service providers exhibit, and that might bother customers, include:

Disinterest in serving

Excessive wait times

Unprofessional service provider appearance

Lack of cleanliness (environment or service provider)

Abruptly putting someone on telephone hold without their permission

Failing to answer telephone within four rings

Eating or chewing while dealing with a customer

Lack of knowledge or authority

Poor quality of service

Condescension (taking an air of superiority to the customer)

Rudeness or overfamiliarity (using first names without permission)

LO 3-5 Providing Feedback

Concept Your feedback could affect the relationship you have or are building with your customers. The effect may be positive or negative, depending on the content and delivery.

Feedback is a response to messages a listener receives. This response may be transmitted verbally (with words) or nonverbally (through actions or inaction). Depending on the content and delivery, your feedback could positively or negatively influence your relationships with your customers. Figure 3.4 offers some tips on providing feedback effectively, and the two types of feedback are discussed in the following sections.

Here are 10 tips for effectively providing feedback:

1. When appropriate, give feedback immediately when communicating face to face or over the telephone.

2. Communicate in a clear, concise manner.

3. Remain objective and unemotional when providing feedback.

4. Make sure that your feedback is accurate before you provide it.

5. Use verbal and nonverbal messages that are in congruence (agree with each other).

6. Verify the customer's meaning before providing feedback.

7. Make sure that your feedback is appropriate to the customer's original message (active listening helps in getting the original message).

8. Strive to clarify feedback when the customer seems unclear of your intention.

9. Avoid overly critical feedback or negative language (as described in this chapter).

10. Do not provide feedback if it could damage the customer-provider relationship.

Figure 3.4
Guidelines for Providing Positive Feedback

Feeling Special

THINK OF TIMES WHEN YOU HAVE BEEN PUT ON HOLD OR STOOD IN A LINE.

1. How did the service provider address you when it was your turn for service?
2. Did you feel special or did you feel like the next in a long line of bodies being processed? Why?
3. When the service provider simply picked up the phone and offered to assist you or shouted "Next" while you waited in line, what thoughts went through your mind about the provider and the organization?
4. What could service providers do or say to eliminate negative customer feelings in such situations?

Verbal Feedback

The words you choose when providing feedback to your customers are crucial to interpretation and understanding. Before providing feedback, you should take into consideration the knowledge and skill level of your customer(s). This is part of the "encoding" discussed earlier in the "Interpersonal Communication Model" discussed earlier in this chapter. Failure to consider the customer could result in breakdowns in understanding. For example, if you choose words that are not likely to be part of your customer's vocabulary, because of the customer's education and/or experience, your message may be confusing. Also, if you use acronyms or technical terms (jargon or words unfamiliar to the customer), the meaning of the message could get lost. When providing **verbal feedback,** you should also be conscious of how your customer is receiving your information. If the customer's body language or nonverbal cues (gestures, facial expressions) or words indicate misunderstanding, you should pause, and take any corrective action necessary to clear up the confusion.

Nonverbal Feedback

Nonverbal feedback will be explored in depth in Chapter 4. Here are a few ways in which feedback can be given nonverbally.

Manage Body Language

The ways in which you sit, stand, gesture, position your body (face-to-face or at an angle), or use facial expressions can all send positive or negative messages.

Use Eye Contact Effectively

In addition to greeting the customer, make regular eye contact (normally no longer than three to five seconds at a time) and assume a positive

verbal feedback The response given to a sender's message that allows both the sender and receiver to know that a message was received correctly.

nonverbal feedback Messages sent to someone through other than spoken means. Examples are gestures, appearance, and facial expressions.

approachable posture throughout your interaction with a customer. Also, be careful about giving customers the "evil eye" or showing your displeasure with them through your eyes when emotions are high or you are struggling with a difficult situation. More discussion on the topics of eye contact and nonverbal communication appears in Chapter 4.

Use Positive Facial Expressions

Over the years various sources have reported that it take more muscles to frown than to smile. With that in mind, spend more time (and less facial energy) projecting a pleasant, positive image with your face, rather than one that might send a negative message to your customers. Since customer service is about building relationships with customers and people generally prefer to be around someone who is happy rather than unhappy, be conscious of the power of your face. Smile often, even if you are having a bad day. The bottom line is that your customers really do not care what kind of day you are having. They do care about how you communicate with and treat them.

LO 3-6 Dealing Assertively with Customers

> **Concept** Express ideas simply without weakening your position.

Your level of **assertiveness** is directly tied to your style of behavior and your culture. Some people are direct and to the point; others are calm and laid back or come across as being passive or nonassertive. Neither style is better or worse than the other. What is important is to be able to recognize which style to call upon in various situations. You will explore behavioral styles in detail in Chapter 6.

Generally, assertive communication deals with expressing ideas positively and with confidence. An example would be to stand or sit erect, make direct eye contact, smile, listen empathetically, and then calmly and firmly nod and explain what you can do to assist the customer. This approach is sometimes a challenge for people entering a new culture. In such instances because of cultural beliefs or because they do not want to potentially offend, they tend to be less assertive in sharing ideas, giving feedback, or asking questions that may seem to challenge or discredit what someone else has said. The key to being effective, if you are from a different culture and find yourself in such situations, is to listen effectively and to give carefully thought out candid responses. Planning ahead by researching the cultures of customers with whom you interact can better prepare you for such inevitable contacts. In this multicultural world it is not a question of if, but when, you will meet someone with different cultural values.

Figure 3.5 lists several examples of nonassertive and assertive language and behaviors. Additional resources are listed in the Bibliography.

Customer Service Success Tip

To check your perception of nonverbal cues received from others so that you can respond appropriately, use the following process:

1. Identify the behavior observed.
   Example: "Mr. Warlinkowski, when I said that it would be seven to ten days before we could get your new sofa delivered to your home, your facial expression changed to what appeared to be one of concern."

2. Offer one or two interpretations.
   Example: "I wasn't sure whether you were indicating that the time frame doesn't work for you, or whether something else went through your mind."

3. Ask for clarification.
   Example: "Which was it?"

By asking for clarification, you reduce the chance of causing customer dissatisfaction. You also send a message that you are paying attention to the customer.

assertiveness Involves projecting a presence that is assured, confident, and capable without seeming to be aggressive or arrogant.

Perceptions Are Reality

TO EMPHASIZE THAT DIFFERENT PEOPLE OFTEN HAVE DIFFERENT PERCEPTIONS OF WHAT THEY SEE, AND THE IMPORTANCE OF APPEARANCE, LOOK AT THE PHOTOGRAPHS OF THE PEOPLE BELOW.

Honestly describe your reactions to and perceptions of each as asked below. Once finished, compare your responses to those of fellow students.

After viewing each photo, answer the following questions:

1. What are your perceptions?
2. Explain why you have these perceptions.
3. How might your perception affect your ability to effectively serve this person?

The following list contains examples of nonassertive and assertive language and behaviors, along with tips for increasing your assertiveness.

Figure 3.5
Nonassertive and Assertive Behaviors

Nonassertive	Assertive
• Poor eye contact while speaking.	• Look customer in the eye as you speak.
• Weak ("limp fish") handshake.	• Grasp firmly without crushing (web of your hand against web of the other person's hand).
• Use of verbal paralanguage (ah, um, you know).	• Stop, gather thoughts, speak.
• Apologetic in words and tone.	• Apologize if you make a mistake (I'm sorry, please forgive me), then take control and move on with the conversation.
• Soft, subdued tone.	• Increase volume, sound firm and convincing.
• Finger-pointing; blaming others.	• Take responsibility; resolve the problem.
• Nervous gestures, fidgeting.	• Hold something; grasp a table or chair; fold your hands as you talk.
• Indecisive or unsure.	• Know your products and services. If possible, prepare a list of points, comments, or questions before calling or meeting with your customer(s).
• Rambling speech, not really stating a specific question or information	• Think, plan, and then speak

LO 3-7 Assertive versus Aggressive Service

Concept Assertive service is good for solving problems; aggressive service may escalate them.

Do not confuse assertive with aggressive service. Why is the distinction so important in customer service? What's the difference? The answer: Assertiveness can assist in solving problems; aggression can escalate and cause relationship breakdowns. Asserting yourself means that you project an image of confidence, are self-assured, and state what you believe to be true in a self-confident manner. Some ways in which assertiveness might be demonstrated when dealing with customers include:

• Interact in a mature manner with customers who may be offensive, defensive, aggressive, hostile, blaming, attacking, or otherwise unreceptive to what you are trying to explain to them. Do not become defensive or confrontational.

• Use appropriate eye contact. Make positive eye contact as you speak. In Western cultures this is expected in order to demonstrate truthfulness, confidence, and friendliness. Maintain intermittent eye contact as you smile. Avoid squinting or glaring.

• Listen openly and use affirmative acknowledgements of what the customer is saying (e.g., "I understand what you are saying" or Uh huh").

- Use an open body posture if you are face to face (e.g., uncross your arms and keep hands off your hips). Stand or sit erectly, but not rigidly. Occasionally lean forward to emphasize key points. Use open gestures with arms and hands. Gesture with open palms, as opposed to pointing.

- Avoid blaming or judging or your customer. Simply give your views or explain what you can do to help remedy the situation. Express your feelings when it's appropriate, after you have allowed your customer to vent or state her issue or provide feedback.

- Use "I" statements, where you let customers know how you feel about the situation or something the customer said. Acknowledge that your message comes from your frame of reference and your perceptions (I feel that this situation is the result of . . ." or "In my opinion, the issue has been caused by . . .." You can also demonstrate ownership of a situation with statements such as, "I don't agree with what I just heard you say" (as compared to "You're wrong"). Blaming statements, such as the latter, or "You" statements are like verbal fingerpointing and can irritate and escalate emotions. This will likely foster resentment and resistance rather than understanding and cooperation.

- Ask for feedback and then listen carefully to the other person. For example, "Am I being clear?" "Does that make sense?" or "How do you see this situation?" Asking for feedback can indicate that you are open to dialogue and invite the customer's views or thoughts rather than try to control the situation or conversation. Through discussion, you can correct any misperceptions either of you have.

- Learn to say no to unreasonable requests in a confident, yet nonthreatening manner. Use the word "no" and offer an explanation if you choose to.

- When appropriate, paraphrase the customer's point of view. This will let him know that you hear and understand his point or request.

- You don't have to say "I'm sorry" every time anything goes wrong. Of course if something occurred and it was your fault, you should apologize and try to make it right immediately. Many women sometimes tend to put themselves down by saying things like "I'm only a doing my job" or "I just work here." There's no need to apologize to customers for what might be viewed by some of them as a job that lacks stature. Everything you do has an importance of its own. Without you, customers would not be able to transact their business effectively with your organization.

- Strive for win-win solutions. Work toward mutual understanding and the attainment of resolutions that allow the organization and the customer to succeed. Try to identify a "win-win" solution in handling customer problems or service breakdowns. Some service providers take a "You win and I lose" passive approach where they give up things unnecessarily to appease the customer without first attempting to negotiate an acceptable alternative. The "You lose and I lose" solution is a total passive solution where both you and the customer give up. In this instance, the customer goes away and you lose business for your organization. On the other hand, a "You lose and I win" solution is an aggressive solution where you ignore the customer's needs in order to get your way.

Your goal should be to achieve an assertive "You win and I win" solution where both you and the customer retain respect for one another and both parties gain something from the compromise.

Aggression involves hostile or offensive behavior, often in the form of a verbal or even physical attack. Aggressive people send messages verbally and nonverbally that imply that they are superior, or in charge. They often do this through behavior and language that is manipulative, judgmental, or domineering. An assertive person states (verbally and nonverbally), "Here's my position. What's your reaction to that?" An aggressive person sends the message, "Here is my position. Take it or leave it."

Aggressive behavior can lead to relationship failure. When someone verbally attacks another, the chances of emotions escalating and relationships failing increase significantly.

Obviously, the two modes of dealing with customers create very different service experiences. The manner in which you nonverbally or verbally approach, address, and interact with customers may label you as either assertive or aggressive. Consider the following interactions between a customer and a service provider:

Assertive Behavior Example

Customer (returning an item of merchandise): Excuse me, I received this sweater as a present and I'd like to return it.

Service Provider (smiling): Is there something wrong with it?

Customer (still smiling): Oh no. I just don't need another sweater.

Service Provider (still smiling): Do you have a receipt?

Customer (not smiling): No. As I said, it was a gift.

Service Provider (handing over a form): That's all right. To help me process your refund a bit faster for you, could you please provide a bit of information and sign this form?

Customer (not smiling): Does this mean I have to get out of line and then wait again? I've already been in line for 10 minutes.

Service Provider (smiling): Well, rather than delay the line, if you could step over to that table to fill out the form, and then bring it back to me, I'll take care of you. You won't have to wait in line again.

Customer (smiling): Okay, thanks.

In this example, the service provider is trying to assure the customer through words and body language that he or she is there to assist the customer.

Improving Feedback Skills

TO STRENGTHEN YOUR ABILITY TO PROVIDE FEEDBACK, WORK WITH TWO OTHER PEOPLE (ONE PARTNER AND ONE OBSERVER) TO PRACTICE YOUR SKILL IN DELIVERING FEEDBACK.

Select a topic for discussion (e.g., a vacation, career goals, or positive or negative customer experiences).

Spend 10 minutes talking about your selected topic with your partner.

During the conversation, you and your partner should use verbal and nonverbal feedback.

At the end of the 10 minutes, ask your partner, and then the observer, the following questions.

1. How did I do in providing appropriate verbal feedback? Give examples.

2. How well did I interpret verbal and nonverbal messages? Give examples.

3. What questions did I ask to clarify comments or feedback provided? Give examples.

4. What could I have done to improve my feedback?

Aggressive Service Example

Customer (returning an item of merchandise): Excuse me, I received this sweater as a present and I'd like to return it.

Service Provider (not smiling): What's wrong with it?

Customer (smiling): Oh nothing, I just don't need another sweater.

Service Provider (still not smiling): Do you have a receipt?

Customer (not smiling): No. As I said, it was a gift.

Service Provider (handing over a form): Well, our policy requires that you'll have to fill out this form since you don't have a receipt.

Customer (not smiling): Does that mean I have to get out of line and then wait again? I've already been in line for 10 minutes.

Service Provider (not smiling): The line's getting shorter. It shouldn't take long. Next . . ..

In this example, the service provider is not doing well on service delivery, nor is he or she projecting a positive image. The nonverbal and verbal messages convey an almost hostile attitude. This type of behavior can easily escalate into an unnecessary confrontation.

Responding to Conflict

Conflict should be viewed as neither positive nor negative. Instead, it is an opportunity to identify differences that may need to be addressed when dealing with your internal and external customers. It is not unusual for you to experience conflict when dealing with someone else. In fact, it is normal

conflict Involves incompatible or opposing views and can result when a customer's needs, desires, or demands do not match service provider or organizational policies, procedures, and abilities.

Figure 3.6
Forms of Conflict

Conflict typically results when you and someone else disagree about something. The following are examples of five forms of conflict that might occur in your organization.

- *Between individuals.* You and your supervisor (or another employee) disagree on the way a customer situation should be handled.
- *Between an individual and a group.* You disagree about a new customer procedure created by your work team.
- *Between an individual and an organization.* A dissatisfied customer feels that your organization is not providing quality products or services.
- *Between organizational groups.* Your department has goals (for example, the way customer orders or call handling procedures are processed) that create additional requirements or responsibilities for members of another department.
- *Between organizations.* Your organization is targeting the same customers to sell a new product similar to one that an affiliate organization markets to that group.

and beneficial as long as you stay focused on the issue rather than personalizing and internalizing the conflict. When you focus on the individual, or vice versa, conflict can escalate and can ultimately do irreparable damage to the relationship. Figure 3.6 describes various forms of conflict.

Causes of Conflict

There are many causes of conflict. The following are some common ones.

Conflicting values and beliefs. These sometime create situations in which the perceptions of an issue or its impact vary. Since values and beliefs have been learned over long periods of time and are often taken personally at face value, individuals get very defensive when their foundations are challenged. For example, you have been taught that stealing is not only illegal, but also morally wrong. One of your co-workers regularly takes pens, paper, and other administrative supplies home for his child to take to school. His logic is that "they (the organization) are a big company and can afford it." You disagree.

Personal style differences. As you will read in Chapter 6, each person is different and requires special consideration and a unique approach in interactions. For example, your supervisor has a high D style, is very focused, and typically wants to know only the bottom line in any conversation. You have a high E style and find it difficult to share information without providing a lot of details in a highly emotional fashion. When the two of you speak, this can lead to conflict unless one or both of you are aware of the other's style and are willing to adapt your communication style.

Differing perceptions. People often witness or view an incident or issue differently. This can cause disagreement, frustration, and a multitude of other emotional feelings. For example, an employee (Sue) tells you that she is upset because a deadline was missed because another employee (Fred) did not effectively manage his time. Fred later commented to you that your supervisor pulled him off the project in

Ethical Dilemma 3.2 Possible Answers

1. Would you intervene? If so why or why not?

   This is a touchy situation because you do not want to usurp your co-worker or make it appear that there are differing standards of service provided within the organization. At the same time, your organization's reputation for effectiveness, efficiency, and customer service are all at stake and all employees represent and impact that reputation.

   Since it seems that neither your organization nor the customer is at fault in this situation, you may want to intervene in order to deliver quality customer service and to prevent an emotional exchange between the customer and co-worker.

2. If you decide to intervene, what would you say or do? Why?

   You might say something like the following to the customer. "I'm sure my co-worker is going to handle this, but since she had to step away, let me get your copy rather than keep you waiting and cause further inconvenience." By getting the copy, you have satisfied the customer, who has already waited two weeks and now had to make a trip to the office to get resolution of the issue. You have also potentially salvaged the organization's reputation and prevented any type of confrontation between the customer and your co-worker.

   Of course, you will likely now have to explain to your co-worker why you intervened and gave a "free" copy. In that discussion, it is important to put your explanation in terms of how your efforts helped the coworker and sped up service to all customers, since the situation was resolved and the customer left satisfied without becoming emotional. Also, stress that it seemed that neither the organization nor customer was at fault and that you felt it important to deliver a high quality of service to the customer.

   Note: To prevent possible future repeats of this type of situation, you may want to bring it up globally (without naming your co-worker or pointing fingers) in your next staff meeting. Try to get some guidance on handling similar situations in the future.

Summa

Providing serv
can lead to cu
and your orga
and in a posit
your likelihoo
tion is needed,
elicit useful cu

Review

1. What are
   service pro
   the custon

2. What elem
   tion mode
   in a custor

3. What are
   words or
   relationsh

4. What are
   for ensuri

Nonverbal Communication Skills

chapter

4

The most important thing in communication is hearing what isn't said.

—Peter F. Drucker

Learning Outcomes

After completing this chapter, you will be able to:

4-1 Define nonverbal communication.

4-2 Recognize various nonverbal cues and their effect on customers.

4-3 Explain the effect that gender has on communication.

4-4 Describe the effect of culture on nonverbal communication.

4-5 Identify unproductive behaviors.

4-6 Use a variety of nonverbal communication strategies.

4-7 Demonstrate specific customer-focused nonverbal behavior.

Key Terms

appearance and grooming

articulation, enunciation, or pronunciation

body language

clusters of nonverbal behavior

emotional messages of color

environmental cues

etiquette and manners

gender communication

hygiene

impact of culture

inflection

interferences

miscellaneous cues

nonverbal messages

paralanguage

pauses

perception checking

pitch

posture

proxemics

pupilometrics

rate of speech

semantics

silence

spatial cues

time allocation

verbal fillers

vocal cues

voice quality

volume

In the Real World Retail—Starbucks Corporation

FOUNDED IN 1971 IN SEATTLE, WASHINGTON, STARBUCKS BEGAN TRADING on NSADAQ in 1985 as Starbucks Corporation with a goal of becoming the leading retailer and brand of coffee in each of its target markets. For a number of years, it was on track to dominate the world market with company stores throughout the United States and overseas. Like any company, it has stumbled occasionally and made bad business decisions. Today, the company continues to operate with favorable customer support even though the economic crisis that impacted the world during the first decade of this century caused it to retrench. An additional challenge came in the form of competition from McDonald's and others offering cheaper coffee products. These took away a portion of Starbuck's market share as consumers have become more cost conscious in recent years. As a result of these events (and others) Starbuck's closed over 800 stores worldwide as it has restructured and reconsidered its business model.

A secret to Starbucks' early success and expansion is the way that the company has addressed the needs of its customer markets. The format of the Starbucks stores can be varied from a full-size coffee shop to a small kiosk, with the differences being the array and amount of products stocked and offered. In addition to coffee drinks sold in its stores, the company offers a variety of branded products, such as ice cream and ice cream bars, bottled chilled coffee drinks, and a variety of teas through its wholly owned subsidiary Tazo Tea Company. Starbucks continues to think outside the box and over the years has signed licensing agreements with hotel chains, airports, food service companies, warehouse clubs, supermarkets, and a number of other venues that carry its products.

In the latter part of the first decade of the twenty-first century, Starbucks embarked on the redesign of its stores. The company wanted to reflect the character of each store's surrounding neighborhood and help to reduce environmental impacts. The intent was to enhance their customers' in-store experience and have a positive impact on the community and environment. To do this, Starbucks uses local craftsmen and materials for renovations and tries to incorporate recycled and reused materials and elements where possible. Nonverbally, its message is that "we are a part of this community and want to build a relationship with you (the customer)."

Starbucks takes an approach to business that is not only focused on profit, but also on the customer experience and sharing and giving back to the community. The company has set 2015 as a target date for a number of initiatives. One of the company's primary goals is to make a more positive impact on the world. The organization has a goal of having 100 percent of its coffee responsibly grown and ethically traded. To accomplish this, it is partnering with coffee farmers in various countries, like Costa Rica and Africa, to grow coffee that is of a better quality with minimal impact on the planet. They are also working with Conservation International to achieve this goal. Another goal is to give back to the communities in which Starbucks has a presence. According to Starbucks' Web site, "our partners and customers in the United States and Canada volunteered 245,000 hours of service in 2008." They have a goal of pushing that number to 1 million hours of community service by 2015. A fourth

114

initiative is to encourage at least 50,000 young social entrepreneurs to get actively engaged in their communities and to work to solve community issues.

Service and treatment of employees are two cornerstones of any successful company. Employees refer to one another as "partners." The Starbucks guiding principles from its mission statement, relating to creating a great work environment where people are treated with respect and dignity and developing enthusiastically satisfied customers, have helped form a culture that is prospering. It has also led to an environment that earned Starbucks a ranking of Number 24 on *Fortune* magazine's 100 Best Companies to work for in 2009 and as Number 65 of the 100 Best Corporate Citizens by *Business Ethics* magazine. Obviously, Starbucks' approach to business and dealing with customers and employees is working. Through its efforts, it continues to send a message of progression, support for employees and customers, and dedication to giving back to those the company serves.

Do a general Internet search and visit www.starbucks.com to research this organization. Find articles about the company and look at its annual report, values/mission, and other historical information about the organization on the Web site. Look for positive as well as negative information on the company.

Think About It

Think about what you read about Starbucks Corporation and answer the following questions. Your instructor may have you work together and share ideas in a group.

1. Have you been a customer of Starbucks or known anyone who has? What has been your experience or what have you heard about the company?
2. Do you believe Starbucks is truly customer-centric? Why or why not?
3. What do you believe are some of the driving forces behind the Starbucks success? Why?
4. If you were going to start a coffee-based business tomorrow, would you model after Starbucks Corporation? Why or why not?
5. What do you think about the company's approach to employees, community and the environment and the overall message they are sending about the organization? Explain.
6. Would you want to work for this organization? Why or why not?

Quick Preview

Before reviewing the chapter content, respond to the following questions by placing a "T" for true or an "F" for false on the rules. Use any questions you miss as a checklist of material to which you will pay particular attention as you read through the chapter. For those you get right, congratulate yourself, but review the sections they address in order to learn additional details about the topic.

_____ 1. It is possible for you to not send nonverbal messages

_____ 2. By becoming knowledgeable about body language, you can use the cues you observe to accurately predict the meaning of someone's message.

_____ 3. By leaning toward or away from people as they speak, you can better communicate your level of interest in what they are saying.

_____ **4.** Smiling may mean that someone agrees with what you say. Smiling may also mean that the person is listening.

_____ **5.** The use of open, flowing gestures could encourage listening and help illustrate key points.

_____ **6.** Taking the time to polish your shoes and clean and press your clothing can help in presenting a positive personal image.

_____ **7.** Vocal qualities have little effect on the way others perceive you.

_____ **8.** Pauses in your oral message delivery can nonverbally say, "Think about what I just said" or "It's your turn to speak."

_____ **9.** The words you use can distort message meaning.

_____ **10.** Spatial preferences are the same throughout the world.

_____ **11.** People often draw inferences about you on basis of the appearance of your office.

_____ **12.** The amount of time you allocate for meetings with people could nonverbally communicate your feelings about the importance of those people.

Answers to Quick Preview can be found at the end of the chapter.

LO 4-1 What Is Nonverbal Communication?

Concept Nonverbal messages can contradict or override verbal messages. When in doubt, people tend to believe nonverbal messages.

The study of messages sent via nonverbal means has fascinated people for decades. The general public became aware of this subject when books like *Body Language*[1] and several others were published over four decades ago. In *Body Language*, Julius Fast defined various postures, movements, and gestures by ascribing unspoken messages that they might send to someone observing them (for example, defensiveness or accessibility). Since then, hundreds of articles, books, and research studies have explored the topic and expanded the knowledge on the subject.

To be successful in the service profession, you must be aware that you constantly send **nonverbal messages** to others and that it is impossible for you to not communicate. Through this awareness, you can increase your effectiveness in customer encounters or anywhere you come into contact with another person. A significant fact to remember is that, according to a classic research study on how feelings are transmitted between two people during communication, nonverbal signals can contradict or override verbal messages.[2] This is especially true when emotions are high. In a classic and often-referenced study, Dr. Albert Mehrabian found that in communication between two people, 55 percent of message meaning (feelings) is extracted from nonverbal (facial and other body cues), 38 percent is taken from vocal cues, and 7 percent is received from the actual words used. (The various cues will be discussed in more detail later in this chapter.) Do not think that this means that your words are not important; they are just typically overridden by

nonverbal messages
Consist of such things as movements, gestures, body positions, vocal qualities, and a variety of unspoken signals sent by people, often in conjunction with verbal messages.

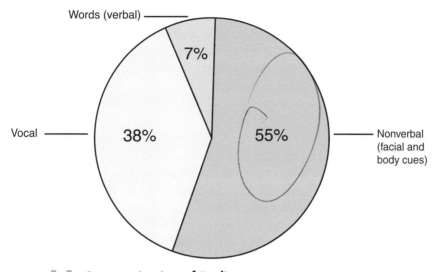

Figure 4.1 **Communication of Feelings**

nonverbal cues. When in doubt about your message meaning, people tend to believe the nonverbal (facial, body, and vocal) parts. Figure 4.1 illustrates the importance of the different types of cues.

Although nonverbal cues carry powerful messages, you should remember that there is considerable room for misinterpretation of the cues used by different people. Based on personality type, cultural and educational background, environment in which people have been reared, and many other factors, they may send and receive nonverbal cues differently from the way you would. The skill of recognizing, assigning meaning, and responding appropriately to nonverbal messages is not exact. Human behavior is too unpredictable and the interpretation of nonverbal cues is too subjective for accuracy of interpretation to occur with consistency.

LO 4-2 The Scope of Nonverbal Behavior

Concept Background, culture, physical conditions, communication ability, and many other factors influence whether and how well people use body cues.

In addition to verbal and written messages, you continually provide nonverbal cues that tell a lot about your personality, attitude, and willingness and ability to assist customers. Customers receive and interpret the messages you send, just as you receive and interpret their messages.

Body Language

By recognizing, understanding, and reacting appropriately to the body language of others, as well as using positive body language yourself, you will communicate with your customers more effectively. The key to "reading" **body language** is to realize that your interpretations should be used only as an indicator of the customer's true message meaning. This is because

> **Customer Service Success Tip**
>
> Ask a number of your friends (or customers with whom you have good rapport) if there are nonverbal cues that you use that stand out in their mind or even irritate them in order to get a better understanding of nonverbal cues that you might be using excessively or inappropriately. Based on their response, make necessary modifications in your nonverbal communication behavior.

body language Nonverbal communication cues that send powerful messages through gestures, vocal qualities, manner of dress, grooming, and many other cues.

background, culture, physical condition, communication ability, and many other factors influence whether and how well people use body cues. Placing too much importance on nonverbal cues could lead to miscommunication and possibly a service breakdown. Some typical forms of body language are discussed in the following sections.

Eye Contact

It has been said that the eyes are "the windows to the soul." Eye contact is very powerful. This is why criminal investigators are often taught to observe eye movement in order to determine whether a suspect is being truthful or not. In most Western cultures, the typical period of time that is comfortable for holding eye contact is 5 to 10 seconds; then an occasional glance away is normal. Looking away in many cultures can often send a message of disinterest, or dishonesty, or lack of confidence. If either the length or the frequency of eye contact differs from the "norm," many people might think that you are being rude or offensive. They might also interpret your behavior as an attempt to exert power or as flirting. Additionally, looking down before answering questions, glancing away continually as your customer talks, blinking excessively, and other such eye movements can create a negative impression. In any case, your customer might become uncomfortable and may react in an undesirable manner (for example, becoming upset or ending the conversation) if you use eye contact in what they perceive as an inappropriate manner. As with all other aspects of workplace interaction in a multicultural environment, do not forget that cultural values and practices often influence the way in which people communicate and interpret message signals.

Just as you send messages with your eyes, your customer's eye contact can also send meaningful messages to you. A customer's lack of direct eye contact with you could send a variety of messages, such as lack of interest, confidence or trust, or dishonesty, depending on how you interpret those cues. For example, if you are watching a customer shop and notice a quick loss of eye contact each time you try to engage the customer visually, the customer might be nervous because he or she is shoplifting, or the customer simply might not want your attention and assistance.

Another aspect of nonverbal communication has to do with the size of the pupils. Much research has been done on the correlation between a person's interest in an item or object being viewed and the size of the person's pupils. Typically, when a customer is interested in an item, his or her pupils will dilate (grow larger). This fact can be parlayed into increased sales and customer satisfaction because an astute and experienced salesperson can watch for dilation as a customer looks over merchandise. For example, even if a customer displays only mild interest in an item after asking the price, and then moves on to another, the salesperson who has observed the customer's interest as revealed by dilation of the pupils might be able to influence the customer's buying decision. As with all nonverbal communication, if you are using this technique, remember that there is room for misinterpreting a cue. According to research on **pupilometrics** (the study of pupil reaction to stimuli), other factors, such as drugs or a person's physical attraction to someone can also cause dilation. To avoid misinterpreting a customer's intent, listen carefully to tone of voice and observe other nonverbal signals so that you do not appear to be pushy or take the wrong action in dealing with a customer.

Posture

Posture (or stance) involves the way you position your body. Various terms describe posture (for example, formal, rigid, relaxed, slouched, awkward, sensual, and defensive). By sitting or standing in an erect manner, or leaning forward or away as you speak with customers, you can send a variety of messages. By standing or sitting with an erect posture, walking confidently, or assuming a relaxed, open posture, you might appear to be attentive, confident, assertive, and ready to assist your customer. On the other hand, slouching in your seat, standing with slumped shoulders, keeping your arms crossed while speaking to someone, shuffling or not picking up your feet when walking, or averting eye contact can possibly signal that you are unsure of yourself, are being deceitful, or just have a poor or indifferent customer service attitude.

In addition, your nonverbal behavior when listening to a customer speak can affect his or her feedback and reaction to you. For example, if you lean forward and smile as the customer speaks, you can signal that you are interested in what is being said and that you are listening intently. Leaning away could send the opposite message.

Facial Expressions

The face is capable of making many expressions. Your face can signal excitement, happiness, sadness, boredom, concern, dismay, and dozens of other emotions. By being aware of the power of your expressions and using positive ones, such as smiling, you can initiate and sustain relationships with others. In fact, smiling seems to be one of the few nonverbal cues that has a universal meaning of friendship or acceptance. Smiling typically expresses a mood of friendship, cheerfulness, pleasure, relaxation, and comfort with a situation. Even so, like any other nonverbal cue, you have to be cautious of "reading into" the intent of someone's cue because some people smile to mask nervousness, embarrassment, or deceit.

In some situations, smiling (yours and a customer's) may even lead to problems. For example, suppose that you are a male receptionist working

Nonverbal cues such as eye contact, proximity, smiling, and gesturing send powerful messages. *What cues do you regularly send that impact the way customers perceive you and your organization?*

pupilometrics The study of pupil reaction to stimuli.

posture Refers to how one sits or stands in order to project various nonverbal messages.

Facial Expressions

TAKE A FEW MINUTES TO LOOK AT EACH OF THE FACES SHOWN BELOW.
Write the emotion that you believe each image portrays and then compare your
response to others. Did each person have the same reaction to each nonverbal cue?

at a walk-in care clinic. A male patient from the Middle East and his wife
step up to your desk. You smile and greet the husband, and then turn your
attention to the wife and do likewise, possibly adding, "That's a very pretty
dress you have on?" She smiles and giggles as she looks away in an embarrassed effort to avoid eye contact. At this point, you notice that the husband looks very displeased. A cultural element may be involved. Although
your intention was to express friendliness and openness and to compliment the wife, because of his cultural attitudes, the husband may interpret
your words and smiling as flirtatious and insulting.

Don't think that this means you should ignore the wives of your customers.
Rather, be conscious of cultural and personal differences that people may
have, and take your cue from the customer. As the world grows smaller, it is
more crucial than ever that you expand your knowledge of different cultural
attitudes and recognize that your ways are not the ways of everyone.

Nodding of the Head

Nodding of the head is often used (and overused) by many people to signal
agreement or to indicate that they are listening to a speaker during a
conversation.

You must be careful when you are using this technique, and when you
are watching others who are doing so, to occasionally pause to ask a question for clarification. Stop and ask for or provide feedback through a para-
phrased message. A question such as, "So what do you think of what I just
said?" will quickly tell you whether the other person is listening and understands your meaning. The answer will also make it clear if the other person is simply politely smiling and nodding—but not understanding. The
latter sometimes happens when there are cultural differences or when
someone speaks a native language other than yours.

If you are a woman, be careful not to overuse the nodding technique. Some research has shown that many North American women often nod and smile more than men during a conversation. Doing so excessively might damage your credibility or effectiveness, especially when you are speaking to a man. The interpretation may be that you agree or that you have no opinion, whether you do or not.

Although nodding your head generally signals agreement, if you nod without a verbal acknowledgment or **paralanguage** (a vocal effect such as "uh huh, I see, hmmm"), a missed or misinterpreted cue could result. For example, suppose that you want to signal to a customer that you are listening to and understand her request. You may nod slowly, vocalize an occasional "I see" or "Uh-huh," and smile as she speaks. She might interpret this to mean that you are following her meaning and are nonverbally signaling acceptance of it. But if she is stating something contrary to your organization's policy or outside your level of authority, she might misinterpret your signals thinking that you *agree* with her, not that you are merely signaling *understanding*. Later, she might be upset, saying something like, "Well, earlier you nodded agreement when I said I wanted a replacement."

paralanguage Consists of voice qualities (e.g., pitch, rate, tone, or other vocal qualities) or noises and vocalizations (e.g., "Hmmm" or "Ahhh") made as someone speaks, which let a speaker know that his or her message is being listened to and followed.

❋ Ethical Dilemma 4.1

You joined the Federal Emergency Management Agency (FEMA) several months before the catastrophic Hurricane Katrina made landfall along the Gulf coast from Florida to Texas. At the time, you worked in an Agency office in Pearl, Mississippi. Within months after the disaster, you were transferred to Baton Rouge, Louisiana, where you could work with partner emergency management agencies to assist in processing victim claims and help set up low-cost loans and grants to get businesses back into operation in the New Orleans area. After arriving at the office, you set about identifying key resources and communicating with flood victims. There are 25 other specialists performing similar tasks. The work hours are long and stressful but the job is fulfilling and you really enjoy the opportunity to make a difference in the lives of people whom you are helping get their life back together.

Recently, you were in the corner of the break room, partly hidden by a vending machines as you read a book, when two other employees came in and stood by the coffee machine. From their conversation it was obvious that they were friends and you later found out that they were sisters-in-law. The two were discussing the amount of money that they dealt with every day and one made a comment to the other that there is really no sound paper trail to track the money. She went on to tell the other woman, "We could very easily 'create' some victims on paper and funnel money to ourselves. Nobody would even notice." The second woman agreed; they laughed and then left the room. As a result of what you heard, you started paying more attention to the two, since one of your jobs was to coordinate claims from the office and track the total amount of money being spent. Within months you noticed that the claims for replacement equipment and rentals from these two increased significantly over the previous quarter compared to those of other representatives in the office.

1. Do you think that these women are doing anything illegal? Explain.

2. Should you take any type of action at this point, based on what you know? If so, what?

3. What are possible consequences if you do take action? Explain.

Gestures

The use of the head, hands, arms, and shoulders to accentuate verbal messages adds color, excitement, and enthusiasm to your communication. Using physical movements naturally during a conversation with a customer may help make a point or result in added credibility.

Typically, such movements are designed to gain and hold attention (for example, waving a hand to attract the attention of someone), clarify or describe further (for example, holding up one finger to indicate the number 1), or emphasize a point (for example, pointing a finger while angrily making a point verbally).

Open, flowing gestures (gesturing with arms, palms open and upward, out and away from the body) encourage listening and help explain messages to customers. On the other hand, closed, restrained movements (tightly crossed arms, clinched fists, hands in pockets, hands or fingers intertwined and held below waist level or behind the back) could send a message of coolness, insecurity, or disinterest.

The key is to make gestures seem natural. If you do not normally use gestures when communicating, you may want to practice in front of a mirror until you feel relaxed and the gestures complement your verbal messages without distracting. Figure 4.2 summarizes positive and negative communication behaviors discussed in this chapter.

Vocal Cues

vocal cues Qualities of the voice that send powerful nonverbal messages. Examples are rate, pitch, volume, and tone.

Vocal cues, that is, pitch, volume (loudness), rate, quality, and articulation, and other attributes of verbal communication, can send nonverbal messages to customers.

Pitch

Changes in voice tone (either higher or lower) add vocal variety to messages and can dramatically affect interpretation of meaning. These changes are

Figure 4.2
Positive and Negative Nonverbal Communication Behaviors

Positive	Negative
Brief eye contact (3 to 5 seconds)	Yawning
Eyes wide open	Frowning or sneering
Smiling	Attending to matters other than the customer
Facing the customer	Manipulating items impatiently
Nodding affirmatively	Leaning away from customer as he or she speaks
Expressive hand gestures	Subdued or minimal hand gestures
Open body stance	Crossed arms
Listening actively	Staring blankly or coolly at customer
Remaining silent as customer speaks	Interrupting
Gesturing with open hand	Pointing finger or object at customer
Maintaining professional appearance	Casual unkempt appearance
Clean, organized work area	Disorganized, cluttered work space

referred to as inflection or **pitch** of the voice or tone. **Inflection** is the "vocal punctuation" in oral message delivery. For example, a raised inflection occurs at the end of a question and indicates a vocal "question mark." Some people have a bad habit of raising inflection inappropriately at the end of a statement. This practice can confuse listeners for they hear the vocal question mark, but they realize that the words were actually a statement. To rectify this communication error, be sure that your inflection normally falls at the end of sentence statements. Another technique is to use a vocal "comma" in the form of a brief pause as you speak.

Simple nonverbal cues like smiling at a customer send powerful messages that a service provider is customer-focused. *How do you feel when a service provider smiles at you?*

Volume

The range in which vocal messages are delivered is referred to as the degree of loudness or **volume.** Be aware of the volume of your voice, for changes in volume can indicate emotion and may send a negative message to your customer. For example, if a communication exchange with a customer becomes emotionally charged, your voice may rise in volume, indicating that you are angry or upset. This may escalate emotions and possibly lead to a relationship breakdown.

Depending on surrounding noise or your customers' ability to hear properly, you may have to raise or lower your volume as you speak. Be careful to listen to customer comments, especially on the telephone. If the customer keeps asking you to speak up, check the position of the mouthpiece in relation to your mouth, adjust outgoing volume (if your equipment allows this), and try to eliminate background noise, or simply speak up. On the other hand, if he or she is saying, "You don't have to shout," adjust your voice volume or the positioning of the mouthpiece accordingly or lower your voice.

Rate of Speech

Rate of speech varies for many people. This is often a result of the person's communication abilities, the region of the United States in which he or she was reared, or his or her country of origin. An average rate of speech for most adults in a workplace setting in Western cultures is 125 to 150 words per minute (wpm). You should recognize this because, as we discussed in Chapter 3, speed of delivery can affect whether your message is received and interpreted correctly. Speech that is either too fast or too slow can be distracting and cause loss of message effectiveness.

Voice Quality

Message interpretation is often affected by the sound or quality of your voice.

pitch Refers to the change in tone of the voice as one speaks. This quality is also called **inflection** and adds vocal variety and punctuation to verbal messages.

volume Refers to loudness or softness of the voice when speaking.

rate of speech Refers to the number of words spoken per minute. Some research studies have found that the average rate of speech for adults in Western cultures is approximately 125–150 words per minute (wpm).

Gesture Practice

TO SEE WHAT YOU LOOK LIKE WHEN YOU GESTURE AND COMMUNICATE NONVERBALLY, STAND IN FRONT OF A MIRROR OR VIDEOTAPE YOURSELF AS YOU PRACTICE EXPRESSING NONVERBAL CUES THAT DEMONSTRATE THE FOLLOWING EMOTIONS.

Once in class, pair up with another student and each of you select four emotions from the list. take turns and demonstrate each emotion without telling the other person the intended message. after each attempt discuss how your partner interpreted the emotion and what message you were actually trying to send. if the two differed, discuss why that might be the case and the potential impact on customer service.

1. Sadness
2. Frustration
3. Disgust
4. Happiness
5. Love

6. Fear
7. Anger
8. Excitement
9. Boredom
10. Frustration

voice quality Refers to the sound of one's voice. Terms often attributed to voice quality are raspy, nasal, hoarse, and gravelly.

articulation, enunciation, or pronunciation Refers to the manner or clarity in which verbal messages are delivered.

The variations in your **voice quality** can help encourage customers to listen (if your voice sounds pleasant and is accompanied by a smile) or discourage them (if it is harsh-sounding), depending on their perception of how your voice sounds. Some terms that describe unpleasant voice quality are *raspy, nasal, hoarse,* and *gravelly*. Such qualities can be a problem because others are less likely to listen to or interact with you if your voice quality is irritating. If you have been told, or you recognize, that your voice exhibits one or more of these characteristics and know that it is not a physiological issue, you may want to meet with a speech coach who specializes in helping improve vocal presentation of messages. Most local colleges and universities that have speech programs can supply the name of an expert, possibly someone on their staff. By taking the initiative to improve your voice quality, you can enhance your customer service image.

Articulation

Articulation, enunciation, or pronunciation of words refers to the clarity of your word usage. If you tend to slur words ("Whadju say?" "I hafta go whitja") or cut off endings (goin', doin', gettin', bein') you can distort meaning or frustrate listeners. This is especially true when communicating with customers who do not speak English well and with customers who view speech ability as indicative of educational achievement or your ability to assist them effectively. If you have a problem articulating well, practice by gripping a pencil horizontally between your teeth, reading sentences aloud, and forcing yourself to enunciate each word clearly. Over time, you will find that you slow down and form words more precisely.

Pauses

Pauses in communication can be either positive or negative depending on how you use them. From a positive standpoint, they can be used to allow a customer to reflect on what you just said, to verbally punctuate a point made or a sentence (through intonation and inflection in the voice), or to indicate that you are waiting for a response. On the negative side, you can irritate someone through the use of too many vocal pauses or **interferences.** The latter can be audible sounds ("uh," "er," "um," "uh-huh") and are often used when you have doubts or are unsure of what you are saying, not being truthful, or nervous. They are sometimes called **verbal fillers.** Interferences can also be external noises that make hearing difficult.

Silence

Silence is a form of tacit communication that can be used in a number of ways, some more productive than others. Many people have trouble dealing with silence in a conversation. This is unfortunate, because silence is a good way to show respect or show that you are listening to the customer while he or she speaks. It is also a simple way to indicate that the other person should say something or contribute some information after you have asked a question. You can also indicate agreement or comprehension by using body language and paralanguage, as discussed earlier. On the negative side, you can indicate defiance or indifference by coupling your silence with some of the nonverbal behaviors listed in Figure 4.2. Obviously, this can damage the customer-provider relationship.

Semantics

Semantics has to do with choice of words. Although not nonverbal in nature, semantics is a crucial element of message delivery and interpretation. You can add to or detract from effective communication depending on the words you use and how you use them. Keep in mind what you read earlier about the Mehrabian study and the fact that 7 percent of message meaning comes from the words you choose to use.

If you use a lot of jargon (technical or industry-related terms) or complex words that customers may not understand because of their background, education, culture, or experience, you run the risk of irritating, frustrating, or dissatisfying them and thus damaging the customer-provider relationship.

Appearance and Grooming

The way you look and present yourself physically (hygiene and grooming) and your manner of dress (clothes clean, pressed, well-maintained, and professionally worn and shoes shined) send a message of either professionalism or indifference. Even though you provide attentive, quality service, the customer will typically form an opinion of you and your organization within 30 seconds based on your appearance and that of your

Customer Service Success Tip

Sit up straight when speaking, since doing so reduces constriction and opens up your throat (larynx) to reduce muffling and improve voice quality.

pauses A verbal technique of delaying response in order to allow time to process information received, think of a response, or gain attention.

interferences Noises that can interfere with messages being effectively communicated between two people.

verbal fillers Verbal sounds, words, or utterances that break silence but add little to a converstion. Examples are uh, um, ah, and you know.

silence Technique used to gain attention when speking, to allow thought, or to process information received.

semantics The scientific study of relationships between signs, symbols, and words and their meaning.

Adding Emphasis to Words

TO PRACTICE HOW CHANGES IN YOUR VOCAL QUALITY AFFECT THE MEANING OF YOUR MESSAGE, TRY THIS ACTIVITY.

Pair up with someone. Take turns verbally delivering the following sentences one at a time. Each time, place the vocal emphasis on the word in boldface type. Following the delivery of each sentence, stop and discuss how you perceived the meaning based on your partner's enunciation and intonation of the key word in the sentence. Also, discuss the impact that you believe such emphasis could have on a customer interaction.

I said I'd do it.

I **said** I'd do it.

I said **I'd** do it.

I said I'd **do** it.

I said I'd do **it**.

work space. This opinion may make the difference in whether the customer will continue to patronize your organization or go to a competitor. For example, your clothing, grooming, and choice of jewelry or other accessories could send a negative message to some people. It is crucial to be able to distinguish between what is appropriate for the workplace and what is inappropriate for a business setting. A good starting point in determining this is to ask your supervisor about the organization's dress policy and adhere to it.

Through your **appearance and grooming** habits, you project an image of yourself and the organization. Good personal hygiene and attention to your appearance are crucial in a customer environment. Remember, customers do not have to return if they find you or your peers offensive in any manner. And without customers, you do not have a job.

Hygiene

Effective **hygiene** (regular washing and combing of hair, bathing, brushing teeth, use of mouthwash and deodorant, washing hands, and cleaning and trimming fingernails) is basic to successful customer service. This is true even when you work with tools and equipment, or in other skilled trades in which you get dirty easily.

Most customers accept that some jobs are going to result in more dirt and grime than others. However, they often have a negative feeling about someone who does not take pride in his or her personal appearance and/or hygiene. Such people are often perceived as inconsiderate, lazy, or simply dirty. If you failed to wash your hair, bathe or shave prior to reporting to work, you could be offensive in appearance to customers and co-workers (you might even have an unpleasant odor) even if you work in a job that requires manual labor. The latter is no excuse for poor hygiene. Think about the times you have encountered such service providers. What was your reaction to them personally? Failing to adhere to these basic commonsense suggestions could result in people avoiding you or complaining about you.

appearance and grooming Nonverbal characteristics exhibited by service providers that can send a variety of messages that range from being a professional to having a negative attitude.

hygiene The healthy maintenance of the body through such practices as regular bathing, washing of hair, brushing of teeth, cleaning of fingernails, and using commercial products to eliminate or mask odors.

Naturally, this would reduce your effectiveness on the job and lower customer satisfaction.

A number of grooming trends have been prompted by many Hollywood actors. One is for men to appear with a one- or two-day beard stubble. While this may look sexy in movies, it has little place in most professional work environments. Likewise, many studies show that prominent tattoos and visible piercings are becoming more commonplace. Still, in many instances they can not only raise some eyebrows, but also can cause a negative customer reaction based on stereotypes of people who have such things. Often, these reactions are from older customers, for example, older baby boomers. Since this group is one of the largest market forces in many countries, their views should be considered if you want to be a successful service provider. Covering tattoos or not wearing body jewelry while at work is a simple "fix" to prevent negative reactions from some customers.

Although good hygiene and grooming are important, going to an extreme through excessive or bizarre use of makeup, hair coloring, cologne, or perfume can create a negative impression and may even cause people to avoid you. This is especially true of people who have allergies or respiratory problems, think conservatively, or people with whom you work in confined spaces.

Clothing and Accessories

For a number of years, casual dress, "dress-down days," and business casual have been buzz words in many organizations in North America as management tried to adapt to the changing values of today's workforce. For example, many hi-tech and graphic work environments often have employees in jeans, t-shirts, and sandals. This trend toward being a bit too lax is now starting to slowly reverse in many companies because some employees have taken the concept of "casual" to an extreme. As a result, they have begun to negatively affect the workplace and the opinions that many customers have of some organizations. In an economy where every customer counts, organizations are definitely looking for ways to attract and keep this precious commodity. Part of that is rethinking the image that is being presented to the public.

Customer Service Success Tip

Have a candid conversation with your supervisor and ask him or her to give you constructive feedback on how he or she perceives your typical appearance and style of dress in the workplace. If possible, make any adjustments your supervisor recommends.

Work clothing does not have to be expensive, but should be well-maintained and appropriate to your work setting. No matter what type of clothing is designated in your organization, clean and pressed clothing, as well as polished shoes (where appropriate), help to project a positive, professional image. Certain types of clothing and accessories are acceptable in the work environment, but others are inappropriate. If your organization does not have a policy outlining dress standards, always check with your supervisor before wearing something that might deviate from the standards observed by other employees or might create an unfavorable image to the public. For example, very high heels and miniskirts, or jeans, bare midriffs, T-shirts, pants with holes or tattered cuffs, or that hang low on the hips, and tennis shoes, might be appropriate for a date or social outing, but they may not be appropriate in most workplaces. They could actually

Being aware of how people may react to violations of their space is necessary for those in customer service. Depending on the circumstances, there might be misperceptions of intentions and harassment claims.

proxemics Relates to the invisible barrier surrounding people in which they feel comfortable interacting with others. This zone varies depending on the level of relationship a person has with someone else.

spatial cues Nonverbal messages sent on the basis of how close or far someone stands from another person.

be distracting or cause customer disapproval and/or complaints and lost business to your organization.

If you are in doubt about appropriate attire, many publications and videos are available on the subject of selecting the right clothing, jewelry, eyeglasses, and accessories. Check with your company's human resources department, your local public library, or the Internet for more information.

Spatial Cues

Each culture (Figure 4.3) has its own **proxemics** or **spatial cues** (zones or distances in which interpersonal interactions take place) for various situations. When you violate co-workers spatial preference based on their culture, their comfort level is likely to decrease, and they may become visibly anxious, move away, and/or become defensive or offended.

Each culture has unwritten rules about contact and interpersonal proximity of which you should be aware and respect when dealing with people from a given culture. In the United States and many Western cultures, studies have resulted in definitions of approximate comfort zones. These may vary, for example, when someone has immigrated to a Western environment and still retains some of his or her own culture's practices related to space.

Intimate Distance (0 to 18 inches)

Typically this distance is reserved for your family and intimate relationships. Most people will feel uncomfortable when a service provider intrudes into this space uninvited.

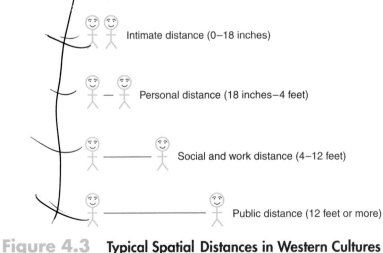

Figure 4.3   Typical Spatial Distances in Western Cultures

Personal Distance (18 inches to 4 feet)

This distance is used when close friends or business colleagues, with whom you have established a level of comfort and trust, are together. It might also occur if you have established a long-term customer relationship that has blossomed into a semifriendship. In such a situation, you and the customer may sometimes exchange personal information (about vacation plans, children, and so forth) and feel comfortable standing or sitting closer to one another than would normally be the case.

Social and Work Distance (4 to 12 feet)

Usually the distance range in face-to-face customer service situations. It is also typically maintained at casual business events and during business transactions.

Public Distance (12 or more feet)

This distance range is likely to be maintained at large gatherings, activities, or presentations where most people do not know one another, or where the interactions are formal in nature.

An important thing to remember about spatial distances in the service environment is how others might perceive your actions. For example, suppose you have an intimate or friendly spatial relationship with a co-worker or with someone who regularly comes into your place of business. Outside the workplace, you and this person might typically engage in interactions from zero to four feet (joking around, touching, kissing, and holding hands). However, if you exhibited similar behavior in the workplace, you could create a feeling of discomfort in others, especially customers or other people who do not know you. Even if they are aware of your relationship with this person, the workplace is not the appropriate place for such behavior. Any touching should be restricted to standard business practices (e.g., a firm business handshake). In fact, touching other than this can lead to claims of a hostile work environment and could lead to a lawsuit according to numerous federal and state laws in the United States.

> **✳ Customer Service Success Tip**
>
> The bottom line regarding touch in the workplace is keep it professional (e.g., firm handshake) or do not touch others. Respect the personal space preferences and norms of others.

Environmental Cues

The **environmental cues** of the surroundings in which you work or service customers also send messages. For example, if your work area looks dirty or disorganized, with tools, pencils, files, and papers scattered about, outdated or inappropriate information or items tacked to a bulletin board, or if there are stacks of boxes, papers stapled or taped to walls, and trash or clutter visible, customers may perceive that you and the organization have a lackadaisical attitude or approach to business. This perception may cause customers to question your ability and commitment to serve. Granted, in some professions keeping a work area clean all the time is difficult (service station, construction site office, manufacturing environment). However, that is no excuse for giving up on cleanliness and organization of your area.

environmental cues Any aspect of the workplace with which a customer comes into contact. Such things as the general appearance of an area, clutter, unsightly or offensive items, or general disorganization contribute to the perception of an environment.

If each employee takes responsibility for cleaning his or her area, cleaning becomes a routine event during work hours and no one has to get stuck with the job of doing cleaning tasks at a specific time. Also, by straightening and cleaning up after a task or project, the chance that an external customer may react negatively to the work area is reduced or eliminated.

To help reduce negative perceptions, organize and clean your area regularly, put things away and out of sight once you have used them (calculators, extra pencils, order forms, extra paper for the printer or copier, tools and equipment, supplies). Also, clean your equipment and desk area regularly (telephone mouthpiece, computer monitor and keyboard, cash register and/or calculator key surface, tools). In particular, all should do their part in cleaning common areas (break rooms or departmental refrigerators) so that co-workers (your internal customers) do not have to pick up a mess that you created. This often causes resentment and can affect the perception that others have of you.

It is also important to remove any potentially offensive items (photos of or calendars displaying scantily clad men or women; cartoons that have ethnic, racial, sexual, or otherwise offensive messages or that target a particular group; literature, posters, or objects that support specific political or religious views; or any item that could be unpleasant or offensive to view). These items have no place in a professional setting. In addition to sending a negative message to external customers who might see them, failure to remove such material might result in legal liability for you and your organization and create a hostile work environment.

Customer Service Success Tip

Strive to create a work environment that sends a positive message and will not cause offense or negative perceptions in others. Simple things like emptying your waste can, organizing items in your work area neatly, and cleaning spills or dusting the area can help send a positive message to customers entering the area.

Miscellaneous Cues

Other factors, such as the **miscellaneous cues** discussed in the following sections, can affect customer perception or feelings about you or your organization.

miscellaneous cues Refers to factors used to send messages that impact a customer's perception or feelings about a service provider of organization. Examples are personal habits, etiquette, and manners.

Personal Habits

If you have annoying or distracting habits, you could send negative messages to your customer. For example, eating, smoking, drinking, or chewing food or gum while servicing customers can lead to negative impressions about you and your organization. Any of the following habits can lead to relationship breakdowns:

Touching the customer (other than a professional handshake upon greeting and at the conclusion of a transaction, if appropriate).

Scratching or touching certain parts of your body typically viewed as personal.

Using pet phrases or speech patterns excessively ("Cool," "You know," "Groovy," "Am I right?" "Awesome," "Solid," "Whatever").

Talking endlessly without letting the customer speak.

Talking about personal problems.

Complaining about your job, employer, co-workers, or other customers.

Spatial Perceptions

PAIR UP WITH SOMEONE AND STAND FACING HIM OR HER FROM ACROSS THE ROOM.

Start a conversation about any topic (for example, how you feel about the concepts addressed in this chapter or how you feel about the activity in which you are participating) and slowly begin to move toward one another. As you do so, think about your feelings related to the distance at which you are communicating. Keep moving until you are approximately one inch from your partner. At that point, start slowly backing away, again thinking about your feelings. When you get back to your side of the room, have a seat and answer these questions:

1. How did you feel when you were communicating from the opposite side of the room (what were your thoughts)?
2. At what distance (moving forward or back) did you feel most comfortable? Why?
3. Did you feel uncomfortable at any point? Why or why not?
4. How can you use the information learned from this activity in the customer service environment?

 **Ethical Dilemma 4.2**

Suppose that you are a receptionist in a hospital emergency room waiting area and an older homeless male who is dirty, with cutoff jeans, sandals and a t-shirt with holes in it comes up to your desk. He has a dirty bloody rag wrapped around his hand and complains that he has cut himself with a rusty can lid. You greet him without a smile, hand him a clipboard with paperwork, and tell him to have a seat and complete the forms. At the same time that the indigent patient arrived, a well-dressed older woman wearing a suit arrives with a small crying girl and states that the child fell out of a tree and hurt her shoulder. You greet her warmly with a smile and proceed to engage her in conversation and assist attentively. Meanwhile the injured homeless patient waits to have a question answered about his paperwork. This certainly could tell the male patient that he is not welcome or respected.

1. How do you think you would feel if you were the homeless patient? Why?
2. Why do you think you might have used different standards of service for the two patients?
3. Do you think this approach to service is appropriate? Why or why not?
4. What could you have done differently/better to improve the service delivery in this situation?
5. How do you think other waiting patients might react to the difference in service that you provided?
6. What is the likely impact of the service delivery outlined in this situation?

Customer Service Success Tip

To determine if you have any annoying or potentially distracting personal habits that could cause relationship issues, ask someone who knows you well to be alert to gestures, movements, habits, or phrases that you repeat or use often. Once identified, make a conscious effort to reduce or eliminate the habits.

Time Allocation and Attention

Some organizations have standards for servicing customers within a specific time frame (for example, returning phone calls within four hours), but these **time allocations** should be targets because customer transactions cannot all be resolved in a specified period of time. The key is to be efficient and effective in your efforts. Continually reevaluate your work habits and patterns to see whether you can accomplish tasks in a more timely fashion. The amount of time you spend with customers often sends subliminal messages of how you perceive their importance. If your organization has service standards that dictate how much time to spend with customers and it is adversely affecting your ability to provide quality service, consider discussing your concerns in a positive manner with your supervisor or manager. Make realistic suggestions for change. If nothing else, taking the opportunity to do this can open up communication between the two of you. You might also learn the logic behind such a policy in the event that you do not already know.

Follow-Through

Follow-through, or lack of it, sends a very powerful nonverbal message to customers. If you tell a customer you will do something, it is critical to your relationship that you do so. If you can't meet agreed-upon terms or time frames, get back to the customer and renegotiate. Otherwise, you may lose the customer's trust. For example, suppose you assure a customer that an item that is out of stock will arrive by Wednesday. On Tuesday, you find out that the shipment is delayed. If you fail to inform the customer, you may lose the sale and the customer. Also, the customer may view you and your organization negatively and then share that perception with others.

Proper Etiquette and Manners

People appreciate receiving appropriate respect and prefer dealing with others who have good **etiquette and manners.** Many books and seminars address the dos and don'ts of servicing and working with customers. Tied to nonverbal messages, the polite things you do (saying "please" and "thank you," asking permission, or acknowledging contributions) go far in establishing and building relationships. Such language sends an unspoken message of that says, "I care" or "I respect you." In addition, behavior that affects your customer's perception of you can also affect your interaction and ability to provide service (interrupting others as they speak, talking with food in your mouth, pointing with your finger, or other items, such as using a fork or resting elbows on the table while eating lunch with a customer). Many good books are available on business manners and dining etiquette if you are unsure of yourself.

Color

Although color is not as important as some other factors related to nonverbal communication in the customer service environment, the way in which you use various colors in decorating a work space and in your clothing can

time allocation Amount of attention given to a person or project.

etiquette and manners Includes the acceptable rules, manners, and ceremonies for an organization, profession, or society.

Red	Stimulates and evokes excitement, passion, power, energy, anger, intensity. Can also indicate "stop," negativity, financial trouble, or shortage.	
Yellow	Indicates caution, warmth, mellowness, positive meaning, optimism, and cheerfulness. Yellow can also stimulate thinking and visualizing.	
Dark blue	Depending on shade, can relax, soothe, indicate maturity, and evoke trust and tranquility or peace.	
Light blue	Projects a cool, youthful, or masculine image.	
Purple	Projects assertiveness or boldness and youthfulness. Has a contemporary "feel." Often used as a sign of royalty, richness, spirituality, or power.	
Orange	Can indicate high energy or enthusiasm. Is an emotional color and sometimes stimulates positive thinking.	
Brown	An earth tone that creates a feeling of security, wholesomeness, strength, support, and lack of pretentiousness.	
Green	Can bring to mind nature, productivity, positive image, moving forward or "go," comforting, growth, or financial success or prosperity. Also, can give a feeling of balance.	
Gold and silver	Prestige, status, wealth, elegance, or conservatism.	
Pink	Signal projects a youthful, feminine, or warm image.	
White	Contains all the colors of the color spectrum. Typically used to indicate purity, cleanliness, honesty, and wholesomeness. Is visually relaxing.	
Black	Lack of color. Creates sense of independence, completeness, and solidarity. Often used to indicate financial success, death, or seriousness of situation.	

Figure 4.4
The Emotional Messages of Color Emotion or Message

have an emotional impact. You should at least consider the colors you choose when dressing for work. Much research has been done by marketing and communication experts to determine which colors evoke the most positive reactions from customers. In various studies involving the reaction people had to colors, some clear patterns evolved. Figure 4.4 lists various colors and the possible **emotional messages of color** they can send.

LO4-3 The Role of Gender in Nonverbal Communication

Concept   Research indicates that boys and girls and men and women behave differently. Young children are sometimes treated differently by their parents because of their gender preference (either male or female may be the preferred gender, no matter the gender of the parent).

Much has been discovered and written about differences in **gender communication** and interactions with others. For example, some researchers have found that females are more comfortable being in close physical proximity with other females than males are being close to other males. Although similarities exist between the ways in which males and females

emotional messages of color Research-based use of color to send nonverbal messages through advertisements and other elements of the organization.

gender communication Term used to refer to communication between genders.

Gender Communication

TO GET A BETTER IDEA OF HOW MALES AND FEMALES COMMUNICATE AND
INTERACT DIFFERENTLY, GO TO A LIBRARY OR TO THE INTERNET AND GATHER
INFORMATION ON THE TOPIC.

Look specifically for information on the following topics:

Brain differences between men and women and the impact of these differences on
communication and relationships.

Differences in nonverbal cues used by men and women.

Base for the communication differences in the workplace or business world between
men and women.

relate to one another, there are distinct differences in behavior, beginning
in childhood and carrying through into adulthood.

In the book *The Difference*, Judy Mann[3] hypothesizes that boys and girls
are different in many ways, are acculturated to act and behave differently,
and have some real biological differences that account for their actions
(and inactions), which are examined from a number of perspectives. The
book discusses various studies that have found that boys and girls typically
learn to interact with each other, and with members of their own gender, in
different ways. Girls generally tend to learn more nurturing and relationship skills early, whereas boys approach life from a more aggressive, competitive stance. Girls often search for more "relationship" messages during
an interaction and strive to develop a collaborative approach; boys typically
focus on competitiveness or "bottom-line" responses in which there is a
distinct winner. Obviously, these differences in approaches to relationship
building can have an impact in the customer service environment, where
people of all walks of life come together based on cultural differences.

The lessons learned early in life usually carry over into the workplace and
affect customer interactions. If you fail to recognize the differences between
the sexes and do not develop the skills necessary to interact with both men
and women, you could experience some breakdowns in communication and
ultimately in the customer-provider relationship.

The basis for gender differences is the fact that the brains of males and
females develop at different rates and focus on different priorities throughout
life. Women often tend to be more bilateral in the use of their brain (they can
switch readily between the left [analytical, logical, factual, facts-and-figures
oriented] and right [emotional, creative, artistic, romantic, and expressive of
feelings] brain hemispheres in various situations). Men, on the other hand,
tend to be more lateral in their thinking. This means that they typically favor
either the left hemisphere or the right hemisphere. This results in a difference in the way each gender communicates, relates to others, perceives, and
deals with various situations. Figure 4.5 lists some basic behavioral differences between females and males. Keep in mind that behavioral preferences
(discussed in Chapter 6) will influence how people communicate.

	Females	Males
Body	Claim small areas of personal space (e.g., cross legs at knees or ankles).	Claim large areas of personal space (e.g., use figure-four leg cross).
	Cross arms and legs frequently.	Use relaxed arm and leg posture (e.g., over arm of a chair).
	Sit or stand close to same sex.	Sit or stand away from same sex but closer to females.
	Use subdued gestures.	Use dramatic gestures.
	Touch more (both sexes).	Touch males less, females more.
	Nod frequently to indicate receptiveness.	Nod occasionally to indicate agreement.
	Glance casually at watch.	Glance dramatically at watch (e.g., with arm fully extended and retracted to raise sleeve).
	Hug and possibly kiss both sexes upon greeting.	Hug and possibly kiss females upon greeting.
	Use high inflection at end of statements (sounds like a question).	Use subdued vocal inflection.
Vocal	Speak at faster rate.	Speak at slower rate.
	Express more emotion.	Express less emotion.
	Use more polite "requesting" language (e.g., "Would you please?")	Use more "command" language (e.g., "Get me the . . .)
	Focus on relationship messages.	Focus on business messages.
	Use vocal variety.	Often use monotone.
	Interrupt less, more tolerant of interruptions.	Interrupt more, but tolerate interruptions less.
	Maintain eye contact.	Glance away frequently.
	Smile frequently.	Smile infrequently (with strangers).
Facial	Use expressive facial movements.	Show little variation in facial expression.
	Focus more on details.	Focus less on details.
	Are more emotional in problem solving.	Are analytical in problem solving, (e.g., try to find cause and fix problem).
Behavior	View verbal rejection as personal.	Do not dwell on verbal rejection.
	Apologize after disagreements.	Apologize less after disagreements.
	Hold grudges longer.	Do not hold grudges.
	Commonly display personal objects in the workplace.	Commonly display items symbolizing achievement.
	Use bright colors in clothing and decorations.	Use more subdued colors in clothing and decorations.
Environmental	Use patterns in clothing and decoration.	Use few patterns in clothing.

Figure 4.5

In North America men and women differ in their approach to relationships. Here are some general behavioral differences that are seen in many men and women.

LO4-4 The Impact of Culture on Nonverbal Communication

Concept To be successful in a global economy, you need to be familiar with the many cultures, habits, values, and beliefs of a wide variety of people.

impact of culture Refers to the outcome of people from various countries or backgrounds coming into contact with one another and potentially experiencing misunderstandings or relationship breakdowns.

As you read in Chapter 1, and will again in Chapter 8, cultural diversity is having a significant impact on the world and the customer service environment. The number of service providers and customers with varied backgrounds is growing at a rapid pace. This trend provides a tremendous opportunity for expanding your personal knowledge and interaction with people from cultures you might not otherwise encounter. However, with this opportunity comes challenge. If you are to understand and serve people who might be different from you, you must first become aware that they are also very similar to you. In addition, if you are to be successful in interacting with a wide variety of people, you will need to understand the **impact of culture** by learning about many cultures, habits, values, and beliefs from around the world. The Internet is a fertile source for such information. Take advantage of it, or visit your local library to check out books on different countries and their people. Join the National Geographic Society, and you will receive its monthly magazine, which highlights different cultures and people from around the globe.[4]

To become more skilled at dealing with people from other cultures, develop an action plan of things to learn and explore. At a minimum, familiarize yourself with common nonverbal cues that differ dramatically from one culture to another. Specifically, look for cues that might be perceived as negative in some cultures so that you can avoid them. Learn to recognize the different views and approaches to matters such as time, distance, touching, eye contact, and use of colors so that you will not inadvertently violate someone's personal space or cause offense.

LO4-5 Negative Nonverbal Behaviors

Concept You should be aware of habits or mannerisms that can send annoying or negative messages to customers.

Many people develop unproductive nonverbal behaviors without even realizing it. These may be nervous habits or mannerisms carried to excess (scratching, pulling an ear, or playing with hair). In a customer environment, you should try to minimize such actions because they might send a negative or annoying message to your customers. An easy way to discover whether you have such behaviors is to ask people who know you well to observe you for a period of time and tell you about anything they observe that could be a problem. Following are some more common behaviors that can annoy people and cause relationship breakdowns or comments about you and your organization.

Unprofessional Handshake

Hundreds of years ago, a handshake was used in many cultures to determine whether a person was holding a weapon. Later, a firm handshake became a show of commitment, of one's word, or of "manhood."

Today, in Western cultures and many others in which the Western way of doing business has been adopted, both men and women in the workplace are expected to convey greeting and/or commitment with a firm handshake. Failure to shake hands appropriately (palm-to-palm), with a couple of firm pumps up and down, can lead to an impression that you are weak or lack confidence or that you do not respect the other person. The grip should not be overly loose or overly firm. An overly firm handshake has its own problems. You may inadvertently injure a person who has specific medical issues (arthritis) with an overly powerful handshake. This type of handshake can be just as much a turn-off as a limp or clammy handshake.

When doing business in other countries or with people from other cultures, it is often helpful to know about their traditional forms of greetings so that you can greet people appropriately, depending on where you are serving them.

One mistake that some people make in a business setting is to carry informal forms of greetings over to the workplace. For example, while it may be appropriate for you to greet friends and peers with a "high five," slap of the palm of the hand, knuckle bump, or to grip their hand with fingers curled and a brief hug or chest press, this is not appropriate in a professional environment with a customer. In order to project a positive professional protocol, use the traditional handshake when in the workplace.

Fidgeting

Using some mannerisms can indicate to a customer that you are anxious, annoyed, or distracted, and should therefore be avoided, if possible. Such signals can also indicate that you are nervous or lack confidence. Cues such as playing with or putting hair in your mouth, tugging at clothing, hand-wringing, throat-clearing, playing with items as you speak (pencil, pen, or other object), biting or licking your lips, or drumming your fingers or tapping a surface with a pencil or other object can all send a potentially annoying and/or negative message.

Pointing a Finger or Other Object

For many people this is viewed as a very accusatory mannerism and can lead to anger or violence on the part of your customer. If you must gesture toward a customer, do so with an open flat hand (palm up) in a casual manner. The result is a less threatening gesture that almost invites comment or feedback, because it looks as if you are offering the customer an opportunity to speak.

Our nonverbal cues tell others a great deal about us, particularly when we display unproductive behaviors. *What are some possible reasons for the behaviors being displayed in this photo?*

Raising Eyebrow

This mannerism is sometimes called the *editorial eyebrow* because some television broadcasters raise their eyebrow. With the editorial eyebrow, only one eyebrow is arched, usually in response to something that the person has heard. This mannerism often signals skepticism or doubt about what you have heard. It can be viewed as questioning the customer's honesty.

Peering Over Glasses

This gesture might be associated with a professor, teacher, or someone who is in a position of authority looking down on a student or subordinate. For that reason, customers may not react positively if you peer over your glasses at them. Typical nonverbal messages that this cue might send are displeasure, condescension, scrutiny, or disbelief.

Crossing Arms or Putting Hands on Hips

Typically viewed as a closed or defiant posture, crossing your arms or putting your hands in your hips may send a negative message to your customer and cause a confrontation. People often view this gesture as demonstrating a closed mind, resistance, or opposition.

Holding Hands Near Mouth

By holding your hands near your mouth, you will muffle your voice or distort your message. If someone is hearing-impaired or speaks English as a second language and relies partly on reading your lips, this person will be unable to understand your message. Also, placing your hands over or in front of your mouth can send messages of doubt or uncertainty, or can suggest that you are hiding something.

LO4-6 Strategies for Improving Nonverbal Communication

Concept Nonverbal cues are all around us. Vocal and visual cues related to customers' feelings or needs are important and may mean the difference between a successful or unsuccessful customer service experience.

The four strategies discussed in this section will help improve your nonverbal communication skills if you practice them and try to understand the behavior of others.

Seek Out Nonverbal Cues

Too often, service providers miss important vocal and visual clues related to customer feelings or needs because they are distracted doing other things or not being attentive. These missed opportunities can often mean the difference between successful and unsuccessful customer experiences. Train yourself to look for nonverbal cues by becoming a "student of human nature."

Nonverbal cues are all around you, if you simply open your eyes and mind to them. Start spending time watching people in public places (at supermarkets, malls, airports, bus stops, school, or wherever you have the chance). Watch the behavior of others you see, and the behavior of the people with whom they are interacting. Try to interpret the results of each behavior. However, keep in mind that human nature is not exact and that many factors affect the nonverbal cues used by yourself and others (culture, gender, environment, and many more). Be aware that you may be viewing through your own filters or biases, so evaluate carefully. Also, look at **clusters of nonverbal behavior,** and the language accompanying them instead of interpreting individual signals. These clusters might be a combination of positive (smiling, open body posture, friendly touching) or negative (crossed arms, looking away as someone talks, or angry facial expressions or gestures). Evaluating clusters can help you gain a more accurate view of what is going on in a communication exchange.

From your observations, objectively evaluate what works and what doesn't, and then modify your behavior accordingly to mimic the positive things you learn.

Confirm Your Perceptions

Let others know that you have received and interpreted their nonverbal cues. Ask for clarification by **perception checking** (see Chapter 6), if necessary. This involves stating the behavior observed, giving one or two possible interpretations, and then asking for clarification of message meaning.

For example, suppose that you are explaining the features of a piece of office equipment to a customer and he reacts with a quizzical look. You might respond with a statement such as, "You seem astonished by what I just said. I'm not sure whether you were surprised by something I said or whether I was unclear in my explanation. What questions do you have?" Notice in this exchange, that the focus of the error is on the service provider (I) rather than the customer (you). It also does not include a potentially accusatory question of "What did you not understand?" This type of question potentially implies that the customer is not smart enough to grasp what you were saying and can be especially pointed if the person primarily speaks another language. By taking this approach, you focus on the customer's behavior and also provide an opportunity for her to gain additional necessary information.

clusters of nonverbal behavior Groupings of nonverbal behaviors that indicate a possible negative intent (e.g., crossed arms, closed body posturing, frowning, or turning away) while other behaviors (smiling, open gestures with arms and hands, and friendly touching) indicate positive message intent.

perception checking The process of clarifying a nonverbal cue that was received by stating what behavior was observed, giving one or two possible interpretations, then asking the message sender for clarification.

Seek Clarifying Feedback

In many instances you need feedback in order to adjust your behavior. You may be sending cues you do not mean to send or to which others may react negatively. Assume that you are on a cross-functional work team with members of various departments in your organization and have been in a meeting to discuss ideas for creating a new work process. During a heated discussion of ideas, you excuse yourself briefly to get a drink of water in order to take a prescribed pill. Later, a teammate mentions that others commented about your frustration level and the fact that you bolted out of the room. To determine what behaviors led to the team's reaction, you might ask yourself something like, "What did I do that made people perceive that I was upset?" If you later find out why people viewed your behavior the way they did, you can offer an explanation in your next team meeting and avoid exhibiting similar behaviors in the future.

Another example might be to ask a co-worker whether the clothing you have on seems too formal for a presentation you will give later in the day. Keep in mind, though, that some people will not give you honest, open feedback. Instead, they tell you what they think you want to hear or what they think will not hurt your feelings. For this reason, it is usually best to elicit information from a variety of sources before making any behavioral changes, or deciding not to make them.

Analyze Your Interpretations of Nonverbal Cues

One way to ensure that you are accurately evaluating nonverbal cues given by a variety of people is to analyze your own perceptions, stereotypes, and biases. The way you view certain situations or groups of people might negatively affect your ability to provide professional and effective customer service to all your customers. This is especially true of customers in the groups toward which you feel a bias. Without realizing it, you may send negative nonverbal cues that could cause a relationship breakdown and lead to a dissatisfied customer.

You will explore interactions with various groups and relationship-building strategies in more detail in Chapter 8.

LO4-7 Customer-Focused Behavior

Concept Being customer-focused in your behavior may help you solve a customer's problem or eliminate the opportunity for a problem to develop. The nonverbal cues discussed in this section can help you stay customer-focused.

The nonverbal behavior you exhibit in the presence of a customer can send powerful messages. You should constantly remind yourself of advice you may have heard often: "Be nice to people." One way you can indicate that you intend to be nice is to send customer-focused messages regularly and enthusiastically through your nonverbal cues. Figure 4.6 lists some important benefits of customer-focused behavior. It gives some simple ways to accomplish this when you are dealing with internal and external customers.

Figure 4.6
Courtesy Pays

Because of the competitive nature of business, organizations and customer service professionals should strive to pull ahead of the competition in any positive way possible. Simple courteous nonverbal behavior can be one way to beat the service quality levels of other companies. Why should you be courteous?

Image Is Enhanced. First impressions are often lasting impressions. A more professional impression is created when you and the organizational culture are customer-focused. When your customers feel comfortable about you and the image projected, they are more likely to develop a higher level of trust and willingness to be more tolerant when things do go wrong occasionally.

Customer Loyalty Increases. People often return to organizations where they feel welcome, serviced properly, and respected. In Chapter 10, you will explore specific strategies for increasing customer loyalty.

Word-of-Mouth Advertising Increases. Sending regular positive nonverbal messages can help create a feeling of satisfaction and rapport. When customers are satisfied and feel comfortable with you and your organization, they typically tell three to five other people. This increases your customer base while holding down formal advertising costs (newspapers and other publications, television, and radio).

Complaints Are Reduced. When people are treated fairly and courteously, they are less likely to complain. If they do complain, their complaints are generally directed to a lower level (below supervisory level) and are generally expressed with low levels of anger. Simple things like smiling or attentive actions can help customers relax and feel appreciated.

Employee Morale and Esteem Increase. If employees feel that they are doing a good job and get positive customer and management feedback, they will probably feel better about themselves. This increased level of self-esteem affects the quality of service delivered. Keep in mind your role in helping peers feel appreciated. They are often your internal customers and expect the same consideration and treatment that your external customers expect.

Financial Losses Decrease. When customers are satisfied, they are less likely to desert to competitors, file lawsuits, steal, and be abusive toward employees (who might ultimately resign), and spread negative stories about employees and the organization. Building good rapport through communication can help in this area.

Employee–Customer Communication Improves. By treating customers in a professional, courteous manner, you encourage them to freely approach and talk to you. Needs, expectations, and satisfaction levels can then be more easily determined.

Stand Up, If Appropriate

If you are seated when a customer arrives or approaches you, stand up and greet him or her. Use the customer's name if you know it and extend a handshake. This shows that you respect the person as an equal and are eager to assist her or him.

Act Promptly

The speed with which you recognize and assist customers, gather information, or respond to customers tells them what you think of their importance. If your service to the customer will take longer than planned or will be delayed, notify the customer, tell him or her the reason, and offer service alternatives if they are appropriate and available.

2. What personal example can you think of where an employee of a small organization sent you or someone you observed an inappropriate nonverbal message. What was the result?

3. If you worked for a small business, what type of situations might require a sound knowledge of nonverbal cues when dealing with customers? Explain.

Summary

Once you become aware of the potential and scope of nonverbal communication, it can be one of the most important ways you have of sharing information and messages with customers. Limitless messages can be conveyed through a look, a gesture, a posture, or a vocal intonation. To be sure that the messages received are the ones you intended to send, be vigilant about what you say and do and how you communicate. Also, watch carefully the responses of your customers. Keep in mind that gender, culture, and a host of other factors affect the way you and your customers interpret received nonverbal cues.

To avoid distorting customer messages, or sending inappropriate messages yourself, keep these two points in mind: (1) Use a nonverbal cue you receive from others as an indicator and not as an absolute message. Analyze the cue in conjunction with the verbal message to more accurately assess the meaning of the message. (2) Continually seek to improve your understanding of nonverbal signals.

One final point: Remember that you are constantly sending nonverbal messages. Be certain that they complement your verbal communication and say to the customer, "I'm here to serve you."

Review Questions

1. What are six categories of nonverbal cues?

2. What are some of the voice qualities that can affect message meaning?

3. What are some examples of inappropriate workplace attire?

4. How can grooming affect your relationship with customers?

5. What are the four spatial distances observed in Western cultures, and for which people or situations are each typically reserved?

6. What are some of the miscellaneous nonverbal cues that can affect your effectiveness in a customer environment?

7. What are some ways in which men and women differ in their nonverbal communication?

8. What are some examples of unproductive communication?

9. List four strategies for improving nonverbal communication.

10. What are five examples of customer-focused behavior?

Search It Out

Use the Internet to Further Your Knowledge of Nonverbal Communication

Now that you have learned some of the basics of nonverbal communication and the impact it can have on

your customer relationships, use the Internet to explore the topic further.

1. Select two topics from the following list, check out as many reputable sites as you can find, and

prepare a report of at least two pages in length to present to your peers.

Body language

Nonverbal cues

Gender communication

Spatial distances

The impact of color on people

The role of vocal cues in nonverbal communication

Professional appearance and grooming for the workplace

The impact of culture on nonverbal cues

2. Go online and research communication differences between men and women. Use your new knowledge of how males and females differ to improve your service by structuring your communication and approach to their preferences; however, remember that each person is unique, so service customers individually.

Collaborative Learning Activity

Focus on Your Speech Patterns

Set up a recording device. Then pair up with someone to discuss what you believe are the benefits of understanding and using nonverbal cues for building customer relations (spend at least 5 minutes presenting your ideas). Your partner should then present his or her views to you. Once both of you have presented your ideas, listen to the recording with your partner and focus on your speech patterns.

1. Are you using appropriate verbal cues in your relationships with others? In what ways?

2. Do you use silence effectively? If so, how?

3. How did you sound in regard to the following?

Rate

Pitch

Volume

Articulation

4. Once you've identified positive and negative areas in your communication, set up an action plan for improvement by targeting the following:

Area(s) for improvement

Target improvement date

Resources needed to improve (assistance of others, training, training materials)

Support person(s)—who will coach or encourage you toward improvement?

Face to Face

Handling Customer Complaints at Central Petroleum National Bank
Background

Central Petroleum National Bank is one of the largest financial institutions in the Dallas–Fort Worth, Texas, area. With revenues of more than $200 million and investment holdings all over the world, the bank does business with many individuals and organizations in the region and other parts of Texas. The bank has 17 branch offices in addition to the home office in downtown Dallas.

Your Role

As one of the 125 employees of Central Petroleum's Western Branch Office, you provide customer service and establish new checking and savings accounts.

On Tuesday, a new customer, Mr. Gomez, came in to open an account. He stated that he was moving his money, over $200,000, from an account at a competing bank because of poor service. As you spoke with Mr. Gomez, one of your established patrons, Mrs. Wyatt, came into the office. As she signed in, you looked over, smiled, nodded, and held up one finger to indicate that you'd be with her momentarily. She smiled in return as she went to sit in the waiting area. As you were finishing the paperwork with Mr. Gomez, his teenage son came in and joined him. The son had been working at a summer job and had saved several hundred dollars. He also wished to establish a checking account. He placed his money on your desk and asked what he needed to do. He stated that he was on his lunch break and had only 20 more minutes to fill out the necessary forms. By then, you noticed that Mrs. Wyatt was looking at her watch and glancing frequently in your direction. Shortly thereafter, she left abruptly.

When you arrived at work the next day, the branch vice president called you into her office to tell you that she had received a complaint letter from Mrs. Wyatt concerning your lack of customer service and uncaring attitude.

Critical Thinking Questions

1. What did you do right in this situation?
2. What could you have done differently?
3. Do you believe that Mrs. Wyatt was justified in her perception of the situation? Explain.
4. Could Mrs. Wyatt have misinterpreted your nonverbal messages? Explain.

Planning to Serve

Based on the content of this chapter, create a personal action plan focused on improving your nonverbal service to customers. Begin by taking an objective assessment of your current nonverbal skill strengths and areas for improvement. Once you have identified deficit areas, set goals for improvement.

Start your assessment by listing as many strengths and areas for improvement as you are aware of. Share your list with other people who know you well to see if they agree or can add additional items. Keep in mind that you will likely be more critical of yourself than other people will. Additionally, you may be sending nonverbal signals that you are not aware of. For those reasons, keep an open mind when considering their comments.

Once you have a list, choose two or three items that you think need the most work and can add the most value when interacting with others. List these items on a sheet of paper along with specific courses of action you will take for improvement, the name of someone you will enlist to provide feedback on your behavior, and a specific date by which you want to see improvement. Related to the last, keep in mind that it takes on average 21 to 30 days to see behavioral change; therefore, set a date that is at least in this range.

Nonverbal Communication Strengths	Areas for Improvement

Top Three Items	Who Will Help	Date for Change
1.		
2.		
3.		

Quick Preview Answers

1. F	3. T	5. T	7. F	9. T	11. T
2. F	4. T	6. T	8. T	10. F	12. T

Ethical Dilemma Summary

Ethical Dilemma 4.1 Possible Answers

1. Do you think that these women are doing anything illegal? Explain.

   While you have no concrete proof at this point that the women are doing anything illegal, the circumstantial evidence of their conversation and the increased volume of their claims should be a red flag or indication that something might be wrong. Since pointing a finger at them and identifying them as criminals can result in damage to their reputation, firing, and arrest, you should gather more information before alerting your supervisor to the situation. Certainly you should not discuss it with anyone else who does not need to know in order to provide you with additional documentation or validation. This is how rumors get started. Remember that at this point all you have are suspicions.

2. Should you take any action at this point, based on what you know? If so, what?

   It is not illegal for people to joke about criminal activity. Many people have done so in the past without ever intending to act upon their comments. If you do anything to implicate them and nothing is wrong, you could end up with a defamation of character lawsuit or worse.

   Your first step is to determine if all the claims being submitted are factual and that the money is being received by actual hurricane victims. If you have a system for cross-referencing and verifying that each claim is for a real victim, do whatever you can to determine validity of claims. This might mean checking computer files, background information gathered on claimants, and other sources or checking with claimants to see if they received checks. Just be careful about taking the last action unless your normal job requires that, since the victims are working with their assigned representative (one of the women) and are likely to mention your contact to them at some point. This could cause your co-workers to wonder why you are calling their claimant and they are likely to ask that question of you. Should you determine that all the claims are valid, you might continue to monitor the situation, but do nothing further.

   If it becomes evident that there is something wrong, immediately approach your supervisor to explain what you heard and share the data that you have gathered. He or she should then take action to bring it to the attention of proper authorities.

3. What are the possible consequences if you take action? Explain.

   Should criminal activity be occurring, the two women will likely be questioned, arrested, and potentially fired from their job, if they are found guilty in court. However, you should also be aware that in the real world, even if they are arrested, they will likely get bail and get out of jail before their trial. That means that they might potentially retaliate against you, your supervisor, and the agency. Unfortunately, workplace violence is a serious threat in today's world. Even so, you have a responsibility to your employer, claimants and the federal government to report any illegal activity. Failure to do so means that criminals are free to steal your tax dollars while they take needed funds away from needy victims of the hurricane.

Ethical Dilemma 4.2 Possible Answers

1. How do you think you would feel if you were the homeless patient? Why?

   He likely feels that there is a double standard that the receptionist views him as less important because he has no assets or resources, and that the quality and degree of service that he will receive, if any, will be inferior to that of other patients. This is likely due to his financial standing and social status level and the perception that the receptionist might have of such people.

2. Why do you think the receptionist used different standards of service for the two patients?

   He possibly has preconceived ideas about homeless people and negative stereotypes (e.g., they are lazy, drug/alcohol abusers, etc.). Also, that the hospital will not recoup its costs for treatment from the homeless man.

3. What could the receptionist have done differently/better to improve the service delivery in this situation?

   Attempt to avoid stereotypes about homeless people, treat the homeless man with more respect and as a customer who was not homeless, and use more positive nonverbal signals when dealing with all customers.

4. What is the likely impact of the service delivery outlined in this situation?

   The homeless person will likely have a negative impression about the receptionist and medical facility, he may possibly have lowered self-esteem as a result of his treatment, stereotypes might be reinforced with other patients, and possible legal action might result, especially if the homeless man has complications due to lack of or inferior treatment.

Listening to the Customer

The most basic of all human needs is the need to understand and be understood. The best way to understand people is to listen to them.

—Ralph Nichols

Learning Outcomes

After completing this chapter, you will be able to:

5-1 Describe why listening is important to customer service.

5-2 Define the four steps in the listening process.

5-3 List the characteristics of a good listener.

5-4 Recognize the causes of listening breakdown.

5-5 Develop strategies to improve your listening ability.

5-6 Use information-gathering techniques learned to better serve customers.

KEY TERMS

attending
biases
circadian rhythm
closed-end questions
comprehending or
  assigning meaning
congruence
customer needs
employee assistance
  programs (EAPs)

external obstacles
faulty assumptions
hearing
information overload
lag time
listening
listening gap
memory
objections

open-end questions
personal obstacles
psychological distracters
recognition
responding
service recovery
thought speed

In the Real World Nonprofit—The American Red Cross

THE AMERICAN RED CROSS IS AN INDEPENDENT, VOLUNTEER-LED ORGANIZATION, financially supported by voluntary public contributions and cost-reimbursement charges. It was formed in Washington, DC, in 1881 by a nurse named Clara Barton. Upon her return from a trip in Europe she, and a group of acquaintances, campaigned to establish an arm of the Swiss-inspired International Red Cross. Among other things, the organization has offered first aid, water safety, cardiopulmonary resuscitation (CPR), and public health nursing programs throughout the years. Its volunteers have assisted in fighting epidemics, educating the public on health-related issues (e.g., AIDS and swine flu epidemic), responding to natural catastrophes (e.g., Hurricanes Charley and Katrina), and terrorist attacks on New York, the Pentagon, and outside of Shanksville, Pennsylvania. Volunteers and staff members from the organization have provided assistance and services to the United States, its allies, veterans, and civilians in every world conflict in which the United States has participated. Following World War II the organization introduced the first nationwide blood bank, which today provides over 50 percent of the blood and blood products in the United States.

The Red Cross has been synonymous with helping people since its inception. It works with over 175 other relief organizations with over 97 million volunteers throughout the world to coordinate assistance in time of need. These volunteers help victims of more than 67,000 disasters annually. By actively partnering with other organizations and governments, being alert to worldwide events and listening to the needs of people in crisis situations, the organization has been a pillar of support for millions of people in times of catastrophe since its inception. For example, following the disastrous earthquake of the coast of Indonesia in 2006 and Haiti in 2010, the Red Cross helped coordinate and distribute millions of dollars in aid and provided volunteers to help in the aftermath.

As in any volunteer organization, the challenge is often gaining and sustaining support and being able to gather adequate funding for all the monumental humanitarian projects that continue to come to the organization. In fact, as of 2009, the organization had a debt of over $600 million.

Think About It

Before answering the following questions, do an Internet search to find out more about the American Red Cross. Visit www.redcross.org and any other site where you might find credible information.

1. Have you or anyone you have known ever been personally helped by the Red Cross or one of its programs (e.g., blood donated, financial assistance, assistance following a fire or natural disaster)? Explain.

2. From a service perspective, what types of skills do you think would be important for volunteers and staff members of this organization? Explain.
3. What role do you think listening plays for volunteers and employees of the Red Cross and its affiliated organizations? Explain.
4. Based on what you know about the Red Cross, how does the organization compare or differ service-wise from other nonprofits with which you are familiar? Explain?
5. Would you consider volunteering or working for this organization? Why or why not?

Quick Preview

Before reviewing the chapter content, respond to the following questions by placing a "T" for true or an "F" for false on the rules. Use any questions you miss as a checklist of material to which you will pay particular attention as you read through the chapter. For those you get right, congratulate yourself, but review the sections they address in order to learn additional details about the topic.

_____ 1. Listening is a passive process similar to hearing.

_____ 2. Listening is a learned process.

_____ 3. During the comprehending stage of the listening process, messages received are compared and matched to memorized data in order to attach meaning to the messages.

_____ 4. The two categories of obstacles that contribute to listening breakdowns are personal and professional.

_____ 5. Biases sometimes get in the way of effective customer service.

_____ 6. A customer's inability to communicate ideas effectively can be an obstacle to effective listening.

_____ 7. A faulty assumption arises when you react to or make a decision about a customer's message on the basis of your past experiences or encounters.

_____ 8. A customer's refusal to deal with you, coupled with a request to be served by someone else, could indicate that you are viewed as a poor listener.

_____ 9. Many people can listen effectively to several people at one time.

_____ 10. By showing a willingness to listen and eliminate distractions, you can encourage meaningful customer dialogue.

_____ 11. Two types of questions that are effective for gathering information are reflective and direct.

_____ 12. Open-end questions elicit more information than closed-end questions do because they allow customers to provide what they feel is necessary to answer your question.

Answers to Quick Preview can be found at the end of the chapter.

LO 5-1 Why Is Listening So Important?

Concept To be a better customer service professional, it is necessary to improve your listening skills.

Listening effectively is the primary means that many customer service professionals use to determine the needs of their customers. Many times, these needs are not communicated to you directly but through inferences, indirect comments, or nonverbal signals. A skilled listener will pick up on a customer's words and these cues and conduct follow-up questioning or probe deeper to determine the real need.

Most people take the listening skill for granted. They incorrectly assume that anyone can listen effectively. Unfortunately, this is untrue. Many people are complacent about listening and only go through the motions of listening. According to Andrew Wolvin and Carolyn Coakley in their book *Listening*, one survey found that three-fourths (74.3 percent) of 129 managers surveyed perceived themselves to be passive or detached listeners.

In a classic study on listening conducted by Dr. Ralph G. Nichols, who is sometimes called the *father of listening*, data revealed that the average white-collar worker in the United States typically has only about a 25 percent efficiency rate when listening. This means that 75 percent of the message is lost. Think about what such a loss in message reception could mean in an organization if the poor listening skills of customer service professionals led to a loss of 75 percent of customer opportunities. Figure 5.1 gives you some idea of the impact of this loss.

> **✳ Customer Service Success Tip**
>
> Stop doing other tasks and focus on what your customers are saying in order to increase your listening efficiency. Ask clarifying questions where appropriate.

Figure 5.1

Missed Opportunities (Based on a 25 Percent Efficiency Rate)

Opportunities	Action Taken	Impact
100 customers a day, each with a $10 order	25 orders were filled successfully	Loss of $750 per day ($273,750 per year)
1,000 customers went to a store in one day	250 were serviced properly	750 were dissatisfied
1,000,000 members were eligible for membership renewal in an association	250,000 returned their application after receiving a reminder call	750,000 members were lost

LO 5-2 What Is Listening?

Concept Listening is a learned process, not a physical one.

listening An active, learned process consisting of four phases—receiving/hearing the message, attending, comprehending/assigning meaning, and responding.

Listening is your primary means of gathering information from a customer or any other person. True listening is an active learned process, as opposed to hearing, which is the physical action of gathering sound waves through the ear canal. When you listen actively, you go through a process consisting of various phases—hearing or receiving the message, attending,

Implied Messages

TO HELP REINFORCE THE CONCEPT THAT MANY CUSTOMER MESSAGES ARE IMPLIED RATHER THAN ACTUALLY SPOKEN TO SERVICE PROVIDERS, FORM A GROUP WITH TWO OTHER STUDENTS AND ROLE-PLAY THE FOLLOWING SCENARIOS. Choose one in which you play the customer, one in which you play the service provider, and one in which you are the observer.

When you are the customer, simply state your issue or need in a way that does not ask the service provider to do something. Also, do not suggest a solution to the problem or issue. Let the person playing the provider role figure out your need and offer one or more solutions.

At the end of each scenario, you and your teammates should take time to answer the following questions:

1. What unspoken need was the customer sending to the service provider?
2. How well did the service provider do in identifying the customer's issue or need?
3. Specifically, what did the service provider do or say to address the customer's need or issue?
4. What could the service provider have done differently to improve service or satisfy the customer?

Possible answers to these scenarios can be found at www.mhhe.com/customerservice.

Scenario 1

A customer has a mortgage payment due on the first day of each month. In the past, payday was on the 10th and 25th; however, he/she started a new job and now gets paid on the 15th and 30th of each month.

Scenario 2

You work in a customer care center as a call center representative. A customer contacts you because he/she just placed an order on your company's Web site but forgot to enter a coupon code for free shipping that he/she received in the mail last week. His/her credit card had already been charged for the shipping when the order was sent.

Scenario 3

A customer moved into her/his newly built house in February and subsequently requested the cable company (your organization) to install cable service to the home. The installers came out with a backhoe, dug a trench, and installed the cable. It is now June and service has been fine until the customer turned on her/his lawn sprinkler system. The water pressure dropped immediately and upon investigation soggy ground was found where the cable company dug to install the cable months ago.

Figure 5.4
Listening Self-Assessment

To prepare yourself for effective customer interactions and to quickly assess how good your listening skills are, take a few moments to take the following assessment. Depending on your responses, you may need to develop a listening improvement plan using some of the strategies in this chapter and available from other sources.
Place a check mark in the appropriate column.

	Always	Sometimes	Never

1. When someone speaks to me, I stop what I am doing to focus on what they are saying.
2. I listen to people even if I disagree with what they are saying.
3. When I am unsure of someone's meaning, I ask for clarification.
4. I avoid daydreaming when listening to others.
5. I focus on main ideas, not details, when someone speaks to me.
6. While listening, I am also conscious of nonverbal cues sent by the speaker.
7. I consciously block out noise when someone speaks to me.
8. I paraphrase the messages I receive in order to ensure I understood the speaker's meaning.
9. I wait until I have received a person's entire message before forming my response.
10. When receiving negative feedback (e.g., a customer complaint), I listen with an open mind.

Rating key: Always = 5   Sometimes = 3   Never = 0
Add your total score. If you rated:

40–50	Your listening is excellent
26–39	Your listening is above average
15–25	Your listening likely falls into the range identified by Dr. Nichols' study (included in this chapter)
Below 15	You have a serious listening problem and should seek additional training or resources to improve.

✳ Customer Service Success Tip

Take time to slow down and actively listen to customers in order to make them feel important and allow you to better identify and meet their needs. This is important because many people spend time thinking about what they will say next rather than listening to what is being said. If you do this, your customer-provider relationship could suffer.

LO 5-3 Characteristics of a Good Listener

Concept   Listening will improve as you "learn" in the customer's shoes.

Successful listening is essential to service excellence. Like any other skill, listening is a learned behavior that some people learn better than others. Some common characteristics possessed by most effective listeners are discussed in the following sections. The characteristics of effective and ineffective listeners are summarized in Figure 5.5.

Empathy. By putting yourself in the customer's place and trying to relate to the customer's needs, wants, and concerns, you can often reduce

Many factors can indicate an effective or ineffective listener. Over the years, researchers have assigned the following characteristics to effective and ineffective listeners:

Effective Listeners	Ineffective Listeners
Focused	Inattentive
Responsive	Uncaring
Alert	Distracted
Understanding	Unconcerned
Caring	Insensitive
Empathetic	Smug/conceited
Unemotional	Emotionally involved
Interested	Self-centered
Patient	Judgmental
Cautious	Disorganized
Open	Defensive

Figure 5.5
Characteristics of Effective and Ineffective Listeners

the risk of poor service. Some customer service professionals neglect the customer's need for compassion, especially when the customer is dissatisfied. Such negligence tends to magnify or compound the effect of the initial poor service the customer received.

Understanding. The ability to listen as customers verbalize their needs, and to ensure that you understand them, is essential in properly servicing the customer. Too often, you hear people say, "I understand what you mean," when it is obvious that they have no clue as to the level of emotion being felt. When this happens while a customer is upset or angry, the results could be flared tempers, loss of business, bad publicity, and at the far end of the continuum, acts of violence. Some techniques for demonstrating understanding will be covered later in this chapter.

Patience. Patience is especially important when a language barrier or speech disability is part of the situation. Your job is to take extra care to determine the customer's needs and then respond appropriately. In some cases, you may have to resort to the use of an interpreter or written communication in order to determine the customer's needs.

Attentiveness. By focusing your attention on the customer, you can better interpret his or her

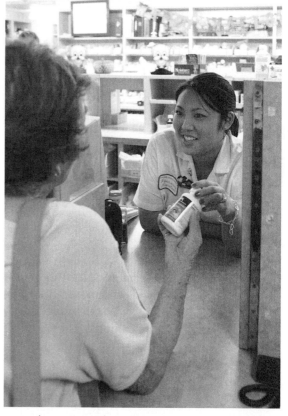

Active listening involves complete attention, a readiness and willingness to take action, and an open mind to evaluate customers and determine their needs. *What should customer service professionals do to achieve these goals of active listening?*

message and satisfy his or her needs. Attentiveness is often displayed through nonverbal cues (nodding or cocking of the head to one side or the other, smiling, or using paralanguage), which were discussed in detail in Chapter 4. When you are reading, talking on the phone to someone while servicing your customer, or doing some other task while "listening" to your customer, you are not really focusing. In fact your absorption rate will fall into the 25 percent category discussed earlier.

Objectivity. In dealings with customers, try to avoid subjective opinions or judgments. If you have a preconceived idea about customers, their concerns or questions, the environment, or anything related to the customers, you could mishandle the situation. Listen openly and avoid making assumptions. Allow customers to describe their needs, wants, or concerns, and then analyze them fairly before taking appropriate action.

LO 5-4 Causes of Listening Breakdown

Concept Poor customer service may result from a breakdown of the listening process.

Many factors contribute to ineffective listening. Some are internal, but others are external and you cannot control them. The key is to recognize actual and potential factors that can cause ineffective listening and strive to eliminate them. The factors discussed in the following sections are some of the most common.

Personal Obstacles

personal obstacles Factors that can limit performance or success in life. Examples are disabilities, lack of education, and biases.

biases Beliefs or opinions that a person has about an individual or group. Often based on unreasonable distortions of prejudice.

As a listener, you may have individual characteristics or qualities that get in the way of listening effectively to the customer. Some of these **personal obstacles** are discussed in the following sections.

Biases

Your opinions or beliefs about a specific person, group, situation, or issue can sometimes cloud your ability to listen objectively to what is being said. These **biases** may result in preconceived and sometimes incorrect assumptions. They can also lead to service breakdown, complaints, and angry or lost customers.

Often personal biases are a result of things learned earlier in life and not even recognized on a conscious level. Everyone has such biases to some degree because children repeat what they hear from caregivers, television, and other sources. Unfortunately, some of the things they hear are negative stereotypes about individuals or groups of people. Repeating such comments helps lock them into memory and as adults we have these memory tapes continually playing in the back of our subconscious mind. This is why many people who do not consider themselves as racist or biased against other people whom they perceive to be different, will sometimes shout or use slurs or derogatory comments based on race or some other aspect of a person (e.g., weight, color, dialect, or physical condition) in emotional situations. For example, someone cuts them off in traffic, bumps into them in a crowded store, or acts in a way that the person believes is "typical" of "those" people. In such instances we are reacting to the mental "tape" or memories in our head (Think about how you reacted to the photographs in Work It Out 3.4).

As a service provider, it is crucial that you never allow such biases to impact the way you listen to or deal with others. Often we see this occur when a service provider has an emotional exchange with a customer and after the customer leaves or hangs up the phone, the provider makes a derogatory comment (to him- or herself) or to a co-worker that is overheard by others. This portrays the provider in a negative light and potentially degrades the reputation of the organization, especially if another customer hears the comment.

Psychological Distracters

Your psychological state can impede effective listening. **Psychological distracters,** such as being angry or upset, or simply not wanting to deal with a particular person or situation, may negatively affect your listening. Think about a time when you had a negative call or encounter with a customer or someone else and you became frustrated or angry. Did your mood, and possibly your voice tone, change as a result? Did that emotion then carry over and affect another person later?

Often when people become upset, time is needed to cool off before they deal with someone else. If you do not cool off, the chance that you will raise your voice or become frustrated with the next person you encounter is increased greatly. And, if this second encounter escalates because of the person's reaction to a negative tone or attitude, you might respond inappropriately. Thus, a vicious cycle is started. You get angry at a person, your tone carries over to a second, who in turn gets upset with your tone, your emotions escalate, and you carry that mood to a third person, and so on. All of this lessens your ability to listen and serve customers effectively.

psychological distracters
Refers to mental factors that can cause a shift in focus in interacting with others. Examples are state of health and personal issues.

Physical Condition

Another internal factor that can contribute to or detract from effective listening is your state of wellness and fitness. When you are ill, fatigued, in poor physical condition, or just not feeling well, listening can suffer. Because of the hectic pace of today's world, the prevalence and easy access of television, and the belief by many people that they "need" to check their e-mail, text, or voice messages immediately when communication arrives, we are a world of tired people. All of this can cause problems when trying to effectively listen to others or function effectively each day.[1]

29% of North Americans fall asleep or become very sleepy at work

36% drive drowsy or fall asleep while driving

14% report having to miss family events, work functions, and leisure activities in the past month due to sleepiness

circadian rhythm The physiological 24-hour cycle associated with the earth's rotation that affects metabolic and sleep patterns in humans as day displaces night.

We often hear that a good diet and exercise are essential to good health. They are also crucial for effective listening. Try not to skip meals when you are working, stay away from foods high in sugar content, and get some form of regular exercise. These all affect physical condition. Try something as simple as using the stairs rather than the elevator or escalator. Another option is a brisk walk at lunchtime. All of these can help you maintain your "edge" so that you will be better prepared for a variety of customer encounters.

Circadian Rhythm

All people have a natural 24-hour biological pattern (**circadian rhythm**) by which they function. The physiological cycle is associated with the earth's rotation. It affects metabolic and sleep patterns in humans as day replaces night. This "clock" often establishes the body's peak performance periods. Some people are said to be morning people; their best performance typically occurs early in the day. They often wake early, "hit the ground running," and continue until after lunch, when the natural rhythm or energy level in their body begins to slow down. For such people afternoons are often a struggle. They may not do their best thinking or perform physically at peak during that point in the day. According to the National Sleep Foundation, "The circadian rhythm dips and rises at different times of the day, so adults' strongest sleep drive generally occurs between 2:00–4:00 A.M. and in the afternoon between 1:00–3:00 P.M., although there is some variation depending on whether you are a 'morning person' or 'evening person.' The sleepiness we experience during these circadian dips will be less intense if we have had sufficient sleep, and more intense when we are sleep deprived."[2]

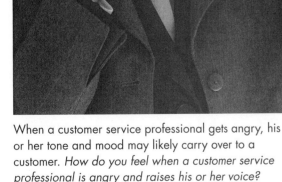

When a customer service professional gets angry, his or her tone and mood may likely carry over to a customer. *How do you feel when a customer service professional is angry and raises his or her voice?*

Personal Habits

TAKE A FEW MINUTES TO THINK ABOUT YOUR PERSONAL NUTRITIONAL (E.G., HOW MANY MEALS A DAY YOU EAT, SNACKS, QUANTITIES AND WHEN YOU EAT) AND EXERCISE (E.G., HOW OFTEN, DURATION AND TYPE OF EXERCISE) HABITS, SINCE THESE CAN AFFECT ATTENTION SPAN AND YOUR ABILITY TO LISTEN EFFECTIVELY; THEN CREATE A LIST OF THE ONES THAT ARE POSITIVE AND NEGATIVE.

Evening people often have just the opposite pattern of energy. They struggle to get up or perform in the morning; however, during the afternoon and in the evening they are just hitting their stride. They often stay awake and work or engage in other activities until the early hours of the next day, when the morning people have been sound asleep for hours. From a listening standpoint, you should recognize your own natural body pattern so that you can deal with the most important listening and other activities during your peak period if possible. For example, if you are a morning person, you may want to ask your boss to assign you to customer contact or to handling problem situations early in the day. At that time, you are likely to be most alert and productive, less stressed, and less apt to become frustrated or irritated by abusive or offensive behavior by others.

Preoccupation

In recent years, many people have become distracted from work and listening activities by personal factors (e.g., financial issues, relationship or family problems, schooling, stress because of issues at home) that override their efforts to do a good job each day. When you have personal or other matters on your mind it sometimes becomes difficult to focus on the needs and expectations of the customer. This can frustrate both you and the customer. It is difficult to turn off personal problems, but you should try to resolve them before going to work, even if you must take time off to deal with them. Many companies offer programs to assist employees in dealing with their personal and performance issues. Through **employee assistance programs (EAPs),** many organizations are offering counseling in such areas as finance, mental hygiene (health), substance abuse, marital and family issues, and workplace performance problems. Check with your supervisor to identify such resources in your organization, or ask about these services during the interview process when you apply for a position.

employee assistance program (EAP) Benefit package offered to employees by many organization that provide services to help employees deal with personal problems that might adversely affect their work performance (e.g., legal financial, behavioral, and mental counseling services).

Hearing Loss

Many people suffer from hearing loss caused by physiological (physical) problems or extended exposure to loud noises. Sometimes they are not aware that their hearing is impaired. Often, out of vanity or embarrassment, people take no action to remedy the loss. If you find yourself regularly straining to hear someone, having to turn one ear or the other toward the speaker, or having to ask people to repeat what they said because you

Employees rarely have control over external distractions in the workplace. *What are some strategies to help cope with a noisy work environment?*

external obstacles Factors outside an organization or the sphere of one's influence that can cause challenges in delivering service.

information overload Refers to having too many messages coming together and causing confusion, frustration, or an inability to act.

External Obstacles

You cannot remove all barriers to effective listening, but you should still try to reduce them when dealing with customers. Some typical examples of **external obstacles** include the following.

Information Overload

Each day you are bombarded with information from many sources. You get information in meetings, from the radio and television, from customers, and in a variety of public places. In many instances, you spend as much as 5 to 6 hours a day listening to customers, co-workers, family members, friends, and strangers. Such **information overload** can result in stress, inadequate time to deal with individual situations, and reduced levels of customer service.

Other People Talking

It is not possible for you to give your full attention to two speakers simultaneously. In order to serve customers effectively, deal with only one person at a time. If someone else approaches, smile, acknowledge him or her, and say, "I'll be with you in just a moment" or at least signal that message by holding up your index finger to indicate "1 minute" while you smile.

Ringing Phones

Ringing telephones can be annoying, but you shouldn't stop helping one customer to get into a discussion with or try to serve another customer over the phone. This creates a dilemma, for you cannot ignore customers or others who depend on you to serve their needs over the telephone.

Several options are available in such instances. You might arrange with your supervisor or co-workers to have someone else take the calls. Those people can either provide service or take messages (as we'll explore in Chapter 10), depending on the business your organization conducts. Another option is the use of a voice mail system, answering service, or pager for message collection. Still another possibility would be to ask the person to whom you are speaking face-to-face to excuse you, professionally answer the phone, and either ask the caller to remain on hold or take a number for a callback.

No one solution is best. You can only try to provide the best service possible, depending on your situation. Before such situations develop, it is a good idea to speak with your supervisor or team leader and peers to determine the policy and procedures for handling customers in these instances.

THINK ABOUT A SITUATION IN WHICH YOU WERE TALKING TO A CUSTOMER OR SOMEONE ELSE AND ANOTHER PERSON ARRIVED, INTERRUPTED, AND STARTED ASKING QUESTIONS OR TALKING TO YOU.

What was the reaction of the first person to whom you were talking?

What was your reaction?

How did you handle the situation?

Office and Maintenance Equipment

Noisy printers, computers, photocopying machines, electric staplers, vacuum cleaners, and other devices can also be distractions. When servicing customers, eliminate or minimize the use of these types of items. If others are using noisy equipment, try to position yourself or them as far away from the customer service area as possible.

Speakerphones

These devices allow for hands-free telephone conversations. They are great because you can continue your conversation while searching for something the customer has requested. Unfortunately, many people put callers on the loudspeaker while continuing to do work not related to the caller. This not only is rude but it results in ineffective communication. Because the speakerphone picks up background noise, it is often difficult to hear the caller, especially if you are moving around the room and are not next to the phone. Many people dislike speakerphones. Be aware that improper use of the speakerphone could cause customers to stop calling or to complain. An additional issue with the speakerphone is confidentiality. Since others can hear the caller's conversation, the caller may be reluctant to provide certain information (credit card and social security numbers, medical information, or personal data). Whenever you use a speakerphone, inform the caller if someone else is in the room with you and/or close your office door, if possible.

Physical Barriers

Desks, counters, furniture, or other items separating you from your customer can stifle communication. Depending on your job function, you might be able to eliminate barriers. If possible, do so. These obstacles can distance you physically from your customer or depersonalize your service. If you have an option, be conscious of how you arrange your office or work space. Side-by-side (facing the customer at an angle) seating next to a table is preferable to sitting across from a customer in most situations. That is because having a table between you nonverbally creates an obstacle to effective interaction. An exception to this approach

Inattentive Listening Behavior

TO HELP YOU IMPROVE YOUR LISTENING SKILLS AND OFFER BETTER SERVICE TO YOUR CUSTOMERS, COMPLETE THE FOLLOWING ACTIVITY.

Think of a time when someone was trying to verbally communicate ideas to you and they realized (from your verbal and nonverbal responses) that you were distracted and not really listening to them.

1. What was going on that prevented you from listening effectively?
2. What reaction did your listener have to your distraction or lack of focus?

Compare your answers with other students. Use the collective responses to these questions to improve your listening skills.

would be appropriate if you provide service to customers who might become agitated or violent. Some examples: city or state clerks who deal with people who have been charged with traffic or other violations of the law; public utility employees who deal with people who are complaining about service problems; employees in motor vehicle offices where people may have frustrating problems with drivers' licenses or vehicle registration. In these types of situations, a physical barrier can sometimes be a wise choice.

An Additional Obstacle

In addition to the issues already addressed, customers themselves can negatively affect communication—through their inability to convey a message.

Although it is not specifically a listening issue, if customers are unable to deliver their message effectively, you will be unable to receive and properly analyze their meaning. No amount of dedication and effort on your part will make up for a language barrier, a disability (speech, physical) that limits speech and nonverbal body language, or poor communication skills. In these situations, it is often necessary to seek out others to help (translators, signers) or to use alternative means of communication [gestures, written, symbols, or a text telephone (TTY/TDD)] to discover the customers' meaning and satisfy their needs.

By recognizing these limiting factors, you can improve your chances of communicating more effectively. Use Worksheet 5-4 (see www.mhhe.com/customerservice) to evaluate listening distractions in your environment.

LO 5-5 Strategies for Improved Listening

Concept You can improve your listening skills in several different ways. One important way is to listen more than you talk.

Numerous techniques can be used to become a more effective listener. The following tips can be used as a basis for improvement.

Correcting Common Listening Problems

WORK IT OUT
5.6

HERE ARE SOME COMMON LISTENING PROBLEMS.
Work in a small group with other students to try to think of one or two means for reducing or eliminating these problems in your customer service.

Listening to words, not concepts, ideas, or emotions.

Pretending interest in a customer's problem, question, suggestion, or concern.

Planning your next remarks while the customer is talking.

Being distracted by external factors.

Listening only for what you perceive is the real issue or point.

Reacting emotionally to what the customer is saying.

Stop Talking!

You cannot talk and actively listen at the same time. When the customer starts talking, stop talking and listen carefully. One common mistake that many people make is to ask a question, hesitate, and if no answer is immediately offered, ask a second question or "clarify" their meaning by providing additional information. A habit like this is not only confusing to the listener, but rude. Some people (e.g., people who speak a different language, elderly, or people with certain disabilities) take a bit more time to analyze and respond to messages they receive. Others may be simply trying to formulate just the right answer before responding. If you interrupt with additional information or questions, you may interfere with their thought patterns and cause them to become frustrated or forget what they were going to say. The end result is that the listener may not speak or respond at all because he or she believes that you aren't really listening or interested in the response anyhow, or because he or she is embarrassed or confused. This could then lead to a complaint to your supervisor because of what they believe to be your rude, uncaring, or unprofessional service attitude. To avoid such a scenario, plan what you want to say, ask the question, and then stop speaking. You might ask, "Mr. Swanson, how do you think we might resolve this issue?" Once you have asked the question, stop talking and wait for a response. If a response does not come in a minute or so, or the customer states that he or she is unsure or seems confused by what you said, try asking the question another way (paraphrase), possibly offering some guidance to a response and concluding with an open-end question (one that encourages the listener to give opinions or longer responses). You might say, "Mr. Swanson, I'd really like to help resolve this issue. Perhaps we could try _____ or _____. How do you think that would work?"

Prepare Yourself

Before you can listen effectively to someone, you must be ready to receive what this person has to say. Stop reading, writing, talking to others, thinking

Active Listening Strategies

about other things, working on your computer, answering phones, and dealing with other matters that distract you. For example, if a customer approaches while you're using a calculator to add up a row of figures, smile and say, "I'll be with you in just a moment" or smile and hold up your index finger to indicate "1 minute." As quickly as possible, complete your task, apologize for the delay, and then ask, "How may I assist you?"

Listen Actively

Use the basics of sound communication when a customer is speaking. The following strategies are typically helpful in sending an "I care" message when done naturally and with sincerity:

SMILE!

Do not interrupt to interject your ideas or make comments unless they are designed to clarify a point made by the customer.

Sit or stand up straight and make eye contact with the customer.

Lean forward or turn an ear toward the customer, if appropriate and necessary.

Paraphrase the customer's statements occasionally.

Nod and offer affirmative paralanguage statements ("I see," "Uh-huh," "Really," "Yes") to show that you're following the conversation.

Do not finish a customer's sentence. Let the customer talk.

In addition, focus on complete messages. A complete message consists of the words, nonverbal messages, and emotions of the customer. If a customer says that she's satisfied with a product but is sending nonverbal signals that contradict her statement, you should investigate further. Suppose that the supply of blue bowls being given away as gifts to people who stop by your trade show exhibit is gone. The customer might say, "Oh, that's okay. I guess a green one will do." Her tone and facial expression may, however, indicate disappointment. You could counter with, "I'm sorry we're out of the blue bowls, Mrs. Zagowski. If you'd like one, I can give you a certificate that will allow you to pick one up when you visit our store, or I can take your address and ship one to you when I get back to the store. Would you prefer one of those options?" By being "tuned in" to your customer and taking this extra initiative, you have gone beyond the ordinary and moved into the realm of exceptional customer service. Mrs. Zagowski will probably appreciate your gesture and tell others about the wonderful, customer-focused person she met at the trade show exhibit.

❋ Ethical Dilemma 5.2

Suppose that you work in a college registrar office. You see lots of students and hear lots of stories when they try to change from one class to another or drop a course. One day a student comes into your office and asks to cancel her registration in one class in order to register for another even though the designated time for such a change has passed. Your immediate inclination might be to quote policy since you've "heard this one before." Your response might sound like, "I'm sorry, Ms. Molina, the period for adds or drops has passed," but don't respond so quickly; instead, hear the student (customer) out. She may provide information (verbally or nonverbally) that will change your view. For example, Ms. Molina (crying) might emotionally say, "I've got to get out of that class. I need one more course to graduate, but I can't stay in this class."

If you are proactive in this situation and practicing active listening, you will pick up on the emotions and ask some questions in order to find out her real need or issue. For example, you might say, "Ms. Molina, you seem very upset, is anything wrong?" She might respond, "Yes. I need to graduate this semester and return to my country to help support my family. But I can't stay in Mr. Broward's class. He's . . . he's always leering at me and making lewd remarks. And, in a previous class, he would regularly massage my shoulders and that of other girls during class."

1. Is the student's request to transfer reasonable even though the add/drop period has passed? Explain.

2. Would you allow the student (customer) to transfer to another class? Why or why not?

3. As an employee of the college, do you have any further responsibilities? Explain.

Show a Willingness to Listen

By eliminating distractions, sending positive verbal and nonverbal responses, and actively focusing on what is being said, you can help the customer relax and have a more meaningful dialogue. For example, when dealing with customers, you should make sure that you take some of the positive approaches to listening outlined earlier (turning off noisy equipment, facing the person, making eye contact, and smiling while responding in a positive manner). These small efforts can pay big dividends in the form of higher satisfaction, lower frustration, and a sense of being cared for on the customer's part.

Show Empathy

Put yourself in the customer's place by empathizing, especially when the customer is complaining about what he or she perceives to be poor service or inferior products. This is sometimes referred to as "walking a mile in your customer's shoes." For example, if a customer complains that she was expecting a specific service by a certain date but didn't get it, you might respond as follows: "Mrs. Ellis, I apologize that we were unable to complete _____ on the tenth as promised. We dispatched a truck, but the driver was involved in an accident. Can we make it up to you by _____?

service recovery The process of righting a wrong or correcting something that has gone wrong involving provision of a product or service to a customer. The concept involves not only replacing defective products, but also going the extra step of providing compensation for the customer's inconvenience.

(Offer a gift, suggest an alternative such as hand delivery and so on.) This technique, known as **service recovery,** is a crucial step in delivering quality service and remaining competitive into the twenty-first century. You will learn more about this service recovery in Chapter 7.

Listen for Concepts

Instead of focusing on one or two details, listen to the entire message before analyzing it and responding. For example, instead of trying to respond to one portion of a message, wait for the customer to provide all the details. Then ask any questions necessary to get the information you need to respond appropriately. For example, "Mr. Chi, if I understand you correctly, you'd like us to build a new prototype part to replace the one currently being used in the assembly. You're looking for a total cost for development and manufacture not to exceed $10,000. Is that correct?"

Be Patient

Not everyone communicates in the same manner. Keep in mind that it is your job to serve the customer. Do your best to listen well so that you can get at the customer's meaning or need. Don't rush a customer who seems to be processing information and forming opinions or making a decision. This is especially important after you have presented product information and have asked for a buying decision. Answer questions, provide additional information requested, but don't push. Doing so could frustrate, anger, and ultimately alienate the customer. You could end up with a complaint or lost customer.

Listen Openly

Avoid the biases discussed earlier. Remember that you don't have to like everyone you encounter, but you do have to respect and treat customers fairly and impartially if you want to maintain a positive business relationship. For example, whenever you encounter a person who is rude or is the type of person for whom you have a personal dislike, try to maintain your professionalism. Remember that you represent your organization and that you are paid by your employer to serve the customer (whoever he or she is). If a situation arises that you feel you cannot or prefer not to handle, call in a co-worker or supervisor. However, be careful in taking this action because you will likely reveal a personal preference or bias that could later be held against you when you

Note taking can help focus listening and later aid recall of what was discussed. *What system do you use to take notes while talking on the phone or to follow up on customer issues?*

apply for other positions in your organization or positions in other companies. Try to work through your differences or biases rather than let them hinder your ability to deal with others or your career potential. Your ability to serve each customer fairly and competently is important to your job success.

Send Positive Nonverbal Cues

Be conscious of the nonverbal messages you are sending. Even when you are verbally agreeing or saying yes, you may be unconsciously sending negative nonverbal messages. When sending a message, you should make sure that your verbal cues (words) and nonverbal cues (gestures, facial expressions) are in **congruence**. For example, if you say, "Good morning. How may I help you?" in a gruff tone, with no smile, and while looking away from the customer, that customer is not going to feel welcome or believe that you are sincere in your offer to assist. (Nonverbal cues were covered in detail in Chapter 4.)

congruence In communication, this relates to ensuring that verbal messages sent match or are in agreement with the nonverbal cues used.

Don't Argue

Remember the "Did not," "Did too" quarrels you had with others when you were a child? Such verbal exchanges got heated, voices rose, and tempers escalated, and someone might have started hitting or pushing. Who won? No one. You should avoid similar childish behaviors in dealing with others—especially your customers or potential customers. Don't let these memories or "tapes" in your head get in the way of good service.

When you argue, you become part of the problem and cannot be part of the solution. Learn to phrase responses or questions positively (as discussed in Chapter 3). Even when you go out of your way to properly serve customers, some of them will respond negatively. Some people seem to enjoy conflict. In such situations, maintain your composure (count to 10 silently before responding), listen, and attempt to satisfy their needs. If necessary, refer such customers to your supervisor or a peer for service rather than let the encounter turn confrontational or emotional.

Take Notes, If Necessary

If information is complicated, or if names, dates, numbers, or numerous details are involved in a customer encounter, you may want to take notes for future reference. Notes can help prevent your forgetting or confusing information. Once you have made your notes, verify your understanding of the facts with your customer before proceeding. For example, in an important client or customer meeting, you may want to jot down key issues, points, follow-up actions, or questions. Doing so shows that you are committed to getting it right or taking action.

Ask Questions

Use questions to determine customer needs and to verify and clarify information received. This will ensure that you thoroughly understand the customer's message prior to taking action or responding. For example, when you first encounter a customer, you must discover his or her needs or what is wanted. Through a series of open-end questions (typically used to seek substantial amounts of information and encourage dialogue) and closed-end questions (they often start with words such as *do*, *did*, *are*, and *will*, and elicit one-syllable or single-word responses), you can gain useful information.

LO 5-6 Information-Gathering Techniques

Concept   Use questions to sort out facts from fiction.

Your purpose in listening to your customers is to gather information about their needs or wants on which you can base decisions on how to best satisfy them. Sometimes, you will need to prompt your customers to provide additional or different types of information. To generate and gather information, you can use a variety of questions. Most questions are either open-end or closed-end.

Open-End Questions

This type of questioning follows the time-tested approach of the five Ws and one H used by journalists who ask questions that help determine who, what, when, where, why, and how. Basically, **open-end questions** establish a number of facts. They:

Identify Customer Needs

open-end questions Typically start with words like who, when, what, how, and why and are used to engages others in conversation or to gain input and ideas.

customer needs Motivators or drivers that cause customers to seek out specific types of products or services. These may be marketing-driven by advertising they have seen or may tie directly to Dr. Abraham Maslow's Hierarchy of Needs Theory.

By asking questions, you can help determine **customer needs,** what he or she wants or expects. This is a crucial task because some customers are either unsure of what they need or want or do not adequately express their needs or wants.

Examples

"Ms. Deloach, what type of car are you looking for?"

"Mr. Petell, why is an extended warranty important to you?"

Gather a Lot of Information

Open-end questions are helpful when you're just beginning a customer relationship and aren't sure what the customer has in mind or what's important. By uncovering more details, you can better serve your customer.

Example

"Mr. and Mrs. Milton, to help me better serve you, could you please describe what your ideal house would look like if you could build it?"

Uncover Background Data

When a customer calls to complain about a problem, often he or she has already taken unsuccessful steps to solve it. In such cases, it is important to find out the background information about the customer or situation. By asking open-end questions, you allow customers to tell you as much information as they feel is necessary to answer your question. This is why open-end questions are generally more effective for gathering data than are closed-end questions. If you feel you need more information after your customer responds to an open-end question, you can always ask further questions.

Example

"Mrs. Chan, will you please tell me the history behind this problem, including all of your previous contacts with this office?"

Uncover Objections during a Sale

If you are in sales or cross-selling or upselling products or services (getting a customer to buy a higher quality or different brand of product or extend or enhance existing service agreements) to current customers as a service representative, you will likely encounter **objections.** The reasons for a customer not wanting or needing your product and/or service can be identified through the use of open-end questions.

Such questions can be used to determine whether your customer has questions or objections. Many times, people are not rejecting what you are offering outright; they simply do not see an immediate need for the product or cannot think of appropriate questions to ask. In these cases, you can help them focus their thinking or guide their decision through the use of open-end questions. Be careful to listen to your customer's words and tone when he or she offers objections. If the customer seems adamant, such as, "I really don't want it," don't go any further with your questions. The customer will probably become angry because he or she will feel that you are not listening. A fine line exists between helping and pushing, and if you cross it, you could end up with a confrontation on your hands. Often active listening and experience will help you determine what course of action to take.

objections Reasons given by customers for not wanting to purchase a product or service during an interaction with a salesperson or service provider (e.g., "I don't need one," "I can't afford it," or "I already have one").

Example

"Ms. Williams, from what you told me, all the features of the new RD10 model that we talked about will definitely ease some of your workload, so let me get the paperwork started so you can take it home with you. What do you think?"

Give the Customer an Opportunity to Speak

Although it is important to control the conversation in order to save time and thus allow you to serve more customers, sometimes you may want to give the customer an opportunity to talk. This is crucial if the customer is upset or dissatisfied about something. By allowing a customer to "vent" as you listen actively, you can sometimes reduce the level of tension and help solve the problem. You might also discover other details that will more appropriately allow you to address the situation.

"What suggestions for improving our complaint-handling process should I present to my supervisor?"

"Why is this feature so important to you?"

"How has the printer been malfunctioning, Jim?"

"What is the main use of this product?"

"What are some of the common symptoms that you have been experiencing?"

"When would you most likely need to have us come out each month?"

"Where have you seen our product or similar ones being used?"

"Why do you feel that this product is better than others you've tried?"

"How do you normally use the product?"

"How has the new hearing aid been performing for you?"

"Mr. O'Connell, I can see you're unhappy. What can I do to help solve this problem?"

Closed-End Questions

closed-end questions
Inquiries that typically start with a verb and solicit short one-syllable answers (e.g., yes, no, one word, or a number) and can be used for such purposes as clarifying, verifying information already given, controlling conversation, or affirming something.

Open-end questions are designed to draw out a lot of information. Traditionally, **closed-end questions** elicit short, one-syllable responses and gain little new information. Many closed-end questions can be answered yes or no or with a specific answer, such as a number or a date. Closed-end questions can be used for:

Verifying Information

Closed-end questions are a quick way to check what was already said or agreed on. Using them reinforces that you're listening and also helps prevent you from making mistakes because you misinterpreted or misunderstood information.

Example

"Mr. Christopherson, earlier I believe you said you saw Doctor Naglapadi before about this problem. Is that correct?"

Closing an Order

Once you've discovered needs and presented the benefits and features of your product and service, you need to ask for a buying decision. This brings closure to your discussion. Asking for a decision also signals the customer that it is his or her turn to speak. If the customer offers an objection, you can use the open-end questioning format discussed earlier.

Example

"Mr. Jones, this tie will go nicely with your new suit. May I wrap it for you?"

Gaining Agreement

When there has been ongoing dialogue and closure or commitment is needed, closed-end questions can often bring about that result.

Example

"Veronica, with everything we've accomplished today, I'd really like to be able to conclude this project before we leave. Can we work for one more hour?"

Clarifying Information

Closed-end questions can also help ensure that you have the details correct and thus help prevent future misunderstandings or mistakes. Closed-end questions also help save time and reduce the number of complaints and/or product returns you or someone else will have to deal with.

Example

"Ms. Jovanovich, if I heard you correctly, you said that the problem occurs when you increase power to the engine. Is that as soon as you turn the ignition key or after you've been driving the car for a while?"

Examples of Closed-End Questions

"Do you agree that we should begin right away?" (obtaining agreement).

"Mrs. Leonard, did you say this was your first visit to our restaurant?" (verifying understanding).

"Mr. Morris, did you say you normally travel three or four times a month and have been doing so for the past 10 years?" (verifying facts).

"Is the pain in your tooth constant or just periodic?"

"How many employees do you have, Mr. Carroll?" (obtaining information)

LO 5-7 Additional Question Guidelines

> **Concept** Use questions to further your feedback.

In order to generate meaningful responses from customers, keep the following points in mind.

Avoid Criticism

Be careful not to seem to be critical in the way you ask questions. For example, a question like, "You really aren't going to need two of the same item, are you?" sounds as if you are challenging the customer's decision making. And the bottom line is that what customers choose should not be your concern. Your job is to help them by providing excellent service. Also, as you read in Chapter 4, nonverbal messages delivered via tone or body language can suggest criticism, even if your spoken words do not.

Ask Only Positively Phrased Questions

You can ask for the same information in different ways, some more positive than others. As you interact with your customers, it is crucial to send messages in an open, pleasant manner. This is done by tone of voice and proper word selection. In the examples, you can see how a negative or positive word choice affects meaning.

Examples

"You really don't want that color do you, Mrs. Handly?" (potentially negative or directive).

"We offer a wide selection of colors. Would you consider another color as an alternative, Mrs. Handly?" (positive or suggestive).

Ask Direct Questions

You generally get what you ask for. Therefore, being very specific with your questions can often result in your receiving useful information. Being specific can also save time and effort. This should not be construed to mean that you should be abrupt or curt in your communication with customers or anyone else.

Example

If you want to know what style of furniture the customer prefers, but you know that only three styles are available, don't ask a general open-end question, such as "Mrs. Harris, what style of furniture were you looking for?" Instead, try a more structured closed-end question, such as "Mrs. Harris, we stock Colonial, French provincial, and Victorian styles. Do any of those meet your needs?"

This approach prevents you from having to respond, "I'm sorry, we don't stock that style," when Mrs. Harris answers your open-end question by telling you that she's looking for Art Deco or Contemporary style furniture.

Ask Customers How You Can Better Serve

You will find no better or easier way to determine what customers want and expect than to ask them. They'll appreciate it, and you'll do a better job serving them. Note: If appropriate, a good follow-up question to gain additional information after a customer has responded to a question is "That's interesting, will you please explain to me why you feel that way or believe that's true?"

Small Business Perspective

Listening to the customer makes all the difference in the world when you are the owner or employee of a small business. Because many small business people typically work with established customers for long periods once they establish a good service relationship, they often have the chance to get to know customers on a more personal basis. This affords them the opportunity to learn not only about immediate product and service needs, but often about business goals, likes and dislikes about competitors, and why they choose to do business with the organization. If an organization has a physical presence (bricks and mortar store or shop) as opposed to a primarily technology-based (Internet/E-commerce) one, owners can often gain customer feedback on a regular basis. This is true because many of their customers are from the same local geographic location. This provides opportunity for the owners and employees to encounter customers in more relaxed settings (e.g., golf course, supermarket, restaurant, or repair shop) and talk about things other than business. There is also the potential for inviting customers in for social functions such as holiday parties or to have them participate in focus groups where they answer questions about needs, products, and services. In a globally competitive marketplace, smart small business owners and employees take advantage of some of these strategies. While they may not have a large staff or budget, they can capitalize on these strategies to better position themselves competitively and show customers that they truly do listen to and care about their wants, needs, comments, and suggestions. In effect, they put a personal face on service by doing this.

Impact on Service

Based on personal experience and what you just read, answer the following questions:

1. Have you ever experienced a situation as a customer where you felt an employee of a small business was not listening to you? What did you do as a result?
2. What is the impact on a small business if its employees fail to listen to their customers? Explain.
3. Why might small business employees not listen to their customers?
4. If you were a small business employee, what would you do to enhance your own listening skills?

Summary

No matter what your current level of listening skill is, there is usually room for improvement. Customers expect and should receive your undivided attention in any encounter they have with you. You should continually reevaluate your own listening style, decide which areas need development, and strive for improvement. In addition, you should keep in mind that active listening involves more than just focusing on spoken words. Remember that there are many obstacles that can impede listening. To overcome them, you need to develop the characteristics of an effective listener and strive to minimize negative habits. Through the use of the active listening process and positive questioning, you can better determine and satisfy customer needs.

Review Questions

1. What phases make up the active listening process?
2. How does hearing differ from listening?
3. According to studies, what is the average rate of listening efficiency for most adults in the United States? Why is this significant in a customer service environment?
4. List 14 characteristics of effective listeners.
5. What is an important reason for practicing good listening skills in a customer service environment.
6. Of the characteristics common to good listeners, which do you consider the most important in a customer service organization? Explain.
7. What obstacles to effective listening have you experienced, either as a customer service professional or as a customer?
8. How can you determine when someone is not listening to what you say?
9. What techniques or strategies can be used to improve your listening skills?
10. How is the outcome of customer service encounters improved by using a variety of questions?

Search It Out

Search the Internet for Items on Listening Skills

To find out more about the listening process and how you can improve your listening skills, log on to the Internet and type in "Listening" or any of the other topic headings or subheadings in this chapter. Search for the following items:

Listening activities
Quotations about listening

Books and articles on listening (create a bibliographic list) or interpersonal communication
Research data on listening
Any other topic covered in this chapter (open-end or closed-end questions, handling sales objections)

Bring your findings to class and be prepared to discuss them with your group.

Collaborative Learning Activity

Developing Team Listening Skills

To give you some practical experience in using the techniques described in this chapter, you will now have an opportunity to interact with others in your group. The activity will be done in groups of three or four members. One person will be the listener, one the speaker, and one or two will be observers. Each person will have an opportunity to play the different roles. For example, if there are four people in the group, there will be four rounds of activity. In the first round, one member of the group will be the listener, one will be the speaker, and the other two will be observers. The roles will change in each of the next three rounds so that everyone will have had a turn at each role.

The speaker will spend about five to seven minutes sharing a customer service experience he or she has had in the past few weeks (it can be positive or negative). The experience should have been one that lasted for several minutes so that there will be enough detail to share with the other members of the group. The speaker should describe the type of organization, why he or she was there, how he or she was greeted, the behavior of the customer service provider, how the provider dealt with concerns and questions, and any other important point the speaker can recall. As the speaker talks, the listener should pay attention and use as many of the positive listening skills discussed in this chapter as possible. The observers should watch and take notes on what they see. Specifically, they should look for use of the positive listening skills and any other behaviors exhibited (positive or negative). After each speaker has finished his or her story, the listener, then the speaker, and finally the observers (in that order) should answer the following questions about the listener's behavior:

What was done well from a listening standpoint?
What needed improvement?
What comments or suggestions came to mind?

Face to Face

Handling an Irate Customer at Regal Florists

Background

Regal Florists is a small, third-generation family-owned flower shop in Willow Grove, Pennsylvania. Most customers are local residents, but Regal has a Web site and an FTD delivery arrangement so that it serves customers throughout the United States. Mr. and Mrs. Raymond Boyle have been doing business with Regal for more than 20 years and know the owners well. Quite often they order centerpiece arrangements for holidays and dinner parties, which they host frequently because of Mr. Boyle's position with a public relations firm. They also occasionally send flowers to their six children and four grandchildren living in various parts of the United States and overseas. Regal's owners and employees are usually especially cheerful, helpful, and efficient. That's one of the reasons the Boyles are loyal customers even though Regal's prices have risen about the industry average in recent years.

Your Role

During the past four years you have worked part-time at Regal's, at first delivering arrangements and for the past year creating arrangements and managing the shop. Mr. Boyle stopped by first thing this morning, just as you were opening the store. He was irate, demanding to know what happened with the arrangement delivered yesterday to his assistant for Secretary's Day, and swearing he'd never patronize Regal's again. Apparently, he had phoned in the order last week. The order was taken by a 16-year-old part-time employee who has since resigned. According to Mr. Boyle, he'd ordered a small arrangement with carnations and various other bright spring flowers for his assistant. Instead, his assistant received a dozen red roses along with a card, on the outside of which was a border of little hearts and the statement "Thinking of you." Inside the card was a message intended for his wife: "I don't know what I'd do without you." Unfortunately, Mrs. Boyle had dropped by Mr. Boyle's office and was near the assistant's desk when the flowers arrived, saw the card and flowers, and was quite upset. Rumor has it that Mr. and Mrs. Boyle are having marital problems. You were the only person in the shop when Mr. Boyle came in. Answer these questions.

Critical Thinking Questions

1. Do you think that Mr. Boyle should take Regal's past performance record into consideration? Why or why not?

2. What listening skills addressed in this chapter should you use in this situation? Why?

3. What can you possibly do or say that might resolve this situation positively?

4. Based on information provided, how would you have reacted in this situation if you were Mr. Boyle? Why?

5. If you were Mr. Boyle, what could be done or said to convince you to continue to do business with Regal?

Planning to Serve

Using the content of this chapter, create a personal action plan focused on improving your listening skills when providing service to your customers. Begin by taking an objective assessment of your current listening strengths and areas for improvement. Once you have identified deficit areas, set goals for improvement.

Start your assessment by listing as many strengths and areas for improvement as you are aware of. Share your list with other people who know you well to see if they agree or can add additional items. Keep in mind that you will likely be more critical of yourself than other people will. Additionally, you may be sending nonverbal signals related to listening that you are not aware of. For those reasons, keep an open mind when considering their comments.

Once you have a list, choose two or three items that you think need the most work and can add the most value when you are interacting with others. List these items on a sheet of paper along with specific courses of action you will take for improvement, the name of someone you will enlist to provide feedback on your behavior, and a specific date by which you want to see improvement. Related to the latter, keep in mind that research shows that it takes on average 21 to 30 days to see behavioral change; therefore, set a date that is at least in this range.

Listening		Areas for Improvement	

	Top Three Items	Who Will Help	Date for Change
1.			
2.			
3.			

Quick Preview Answers

1. F	3. T	5. T	7. T	9. F	11. F
2. T	4. F	6. T	8. T	10. T	12. T

Ethical Dilemma Summary

Ethical Dilemma 5.1 Possible Answers

1. What would you say to this customer? Explain.

   There are a couple issues in this scenario. First, there is the fact that she is cursing and screaming, which is not conducive to effective conflict resolution. She also has her children with her and they are being exposed to not only their mother's attitude and demeanor but also whatever you decide to do. This could leave a negative impression on them related to public utility workers in the future. Finally, there is the fact that she is providing potentially untrue information.

   Before you can even begin to deal with the water issue, you should address her use of profanity and her emotion. Try using the Emotion

Reducing Model that you will read about in Chapter 7 (Figure 7.3). Explain in an assertive manner that her tone and language are interfering with your ability to help her and that if she wants to get this issue resolved, she needs to calm down, and treat you in a more civil manner. Should she be unwilling to do so, excuse yourself, and get a supervisor to intervene.

2. What actions would you take to remedy the situation and get her water back on so that she and her children would have access to services?

To deal with this situation, you should keep in mind some of the strategies for effective listening and apply some of the information-gathering techniques described in this chapter. Specifically, be careful of faulty assumptions (e.g., that everything she is telling you is untrue). Spend a bit of time asking open-end questions, such as "Who did you speak with that promised to turn on your water on Friday" and " I see that you were to come in last Wednesday with a money order. When did you make payment on the account?" (This affords her the benefit of the doubt that she did make payment and no one updated your system).

Once you have determined whether payment was or was not made and that your department either did not fail to deliver service as promised, or failed to follow though as promised, proceed as you normally would to collect payment and /or schedule to have services reinstated.

As an added service touch to reinforce your concern for the customer as a person, if you have lollipops or candy available, ask the customer if she would mind if the children have a piece.

Ethical Dilemma 5.2 Possible Answers

1. Were you practicing good service skills in this situation? Explain.

Yes. By making the effort to listen to Ms. Molina's spoken and unspoken messages, you were able to pick up emotion that was driving her feelings or needs. Had you not been watching for nonverbal cues or practicing active listening skills, you might have simply told her that she could not transfer because she had missed established cutoff dates.

2. Is the student's request to transfer reasonable even though they do not meet policy guidelines? Explain.

Yes. In these extenuating circumstances, you should certainly permit a change of classes if you are authorized to do so. If not, you should check with your supervisor to get permission to make the change immediately.

3. Would you allow the student (customer) to transfer to another class? Why or why not?

Obviously, the rules don't apply in this case. If you didn't listen, you'd never know, and there would be a dissatisfied and distraught customer as a result. If you fail to do so, you might be setting up the institution for a harassment lawsuit by forcing Ms. Molina to stay in the class or could create other situations in which Ms. Molina feels compelled to take other actions to remedy the situation (e.g., lawsuit, violence, or going to the media to expose the teacher and the institution).

In a positive customer service environment, there are only a few instances (except where exceptions would violate regulatory or legal guidelines) in which exceptions to organizationally established policies cannot be modified.

4. As an employee of the college, do you have any further responsibilities? Explain.

Absolutely, you have a moral and legal obligation to immediately bring this situation to the attention of your supervisor, who should take prompt action to document and report the behavior to Human Resources or other appropriate authorities at the college. The institution and employees are compelled by state and federal laws to prevent discrimination of any type and to protect students, customers, employees, and vendors from exposure to inappropriate behavior.

Part Three

Building and Maintaining Relationships

Customer Service Interview

John Gregory

Small Business Owner—Guardian Pest Management

1 What are the personal qualities that you believe are essential for anyone working with customers in a service environment?

I believe that sincerity, honesty, and trust are the foremost important qualities needed, while showing true concern, a readiness to listen, and truly helping solve customer issues and concerns are also crucial. Also, promptness in responding to customers' calls is also important.

2 What do you see as the most rewarding part of working with customers? Why?

True relationships are built on trust and quality of service. Customer retention is proof of quality and success. Accomplishing the latter gives me a sense of satisfaction for a job well done. We all need a pat on the back now and again.

3 What do you believe is the most challenging part of working with customers? Why?

A customer's expectations are not always obtainable. Since my industry is agriculture and directly affected by the weather and the availability of materials needed to perform our work, these issues sometimes make it impossible to achieve perfection—but I always try—and customers appreciate the effort.

4 What changes have you seen in the customer service profession since you took your first service provider position?

For one, customer expectations are getting pretty unrealistic. They are often expecting perfection and are less tolerant of basic human mistakes or issues that are uncontrollable. For instance, in my industry acts of God (e.g., hurricanes, heavy rains, and cold/frost) and changes in the law (e.g., water restrictions and the types of chemicals that we can use) impact our work, yet customers still expect guaranteed results. The customer service industry is becoming increasingly more difficult as consumers expect more. Even with all this, I always give my best since this helps create loyalty with our customers.

I am not quite sure why but, it seems that I now see a much higher turnover rate with employees in our industry. I don't often see long-term or career service people. Instead they are quickly trained and then they move on. My answer to Question 3 may help explain this a bit along with monetary issues. Unfortunately, sales have become the main goal for many people in the industry. If companies would only remember that it's cheaper and easier to keep a current customer than to generate a new one!

Another change that I have seen in our industry is in the area of technology. In my business, technology helps our efficiency by doing such things as routing customers who are close together in order to save labor and fuel costs. We can then pass on savings to our customers. Providing quality service for less is high on most customers' list. Technology also reduces billing mistakes, which is good for both us and our customers. Additionally, technology increases communication between companies and customers since e-mail is quicker and more convenient. Ultimately, for my company, "keeping it personal" when using technology seems to be appreciated by our customers. I am always getting big "thank yous" for just returning a phone call promptly.

5 What issues do you see evolving related to dealing with customers in your profession and why do you think these are important?

There are several factors affecting our industry. First are the restrictions on the chemicals we can use. Several have been removed from commercial use, leaving us with fewer materials to do our job as well as we did in the past. Secondly, the weather conditions are always changing. This not only affects the types and quantities of insects that show up, but another issue is the restriction on watering, which affects insect issues and how well our chemical applications work. These obstacles force us to improve our communication with customers. We now have to reeducate them on new methods we now use due to changes. We also need to encourage realistic expectations rather than expect perfection every time.

I've found that if you tell customers what to really expect, they do much more understand. Remember—"Say what you are going to do, then do what you say." You would want no less for yourself!

Customer Service and Behavior

To be successful, you have to be able to relate to people; they have to be satisfied with your personality to be able to do business with you and to build a relationship with mutual trust.

—George Ross

Learning Outcomes

After completing this chapter, you will be able to:

6-1 Explain what behavioral styles are and why you should be concerned with them.

6-2 Identify four key behavioral styles and the roles they play in customer service.

6-3 Develop strategies for communicating effectively with each behavioral style.

6-4 Respond to customer problems effectively while building relationships.

6-5 Use knowledge of behavioral styles to help manage perceptions of others.

Key Terms

behavioral styles	perceptions	rational style
decisive style	primary behavior pattern	seamless service
expressive style	problem solving	stereotype
inquisitive style	process improvement	win-win situation

In the Real World   Government—Orange County Clerk of Courts

LIKE MOST CLERK OF COURTS OFFICES AROUND THE UNITED STATES, THE OFFICE of the Orange County Clerk of Courts in Orlando, Florida, is focused on courtroom support functions and services. Among other things, the office maintains records of civil, juvenile, and criminal court cases, collects fines and funds due as a result of trials, traffic citations, and child support judgments, and oversees cases involving mental health and the probate process in Orange County. Unlike many such operations, Orange County is not typical of the government entities that people often experience. The employees and processes for delivering customer service to citizens are actually focused on effectiveness and efficiency. This is primarily due to the vision of the Clerk of Courts, the Honorable Lydia Gardner, who was elected to office in 2000 and re-elected in 2004 and 2008. Her dedication and approach to service and process improvement is exceptional from any type of business standpoint. Unlike many CEOs and members of senior management in organizations, she really "walks the talk." Not only is she personable and willing to get involved in issues when necessary, but she encourages employees to always strive to be better and look for enhanced ways to accomplish their job. An example of how she has encouraged better service can be found in the area in which citizens come to pay fines and make other payments due. When Ms. Gardner took over as the Clerk of Courts, she started visiting various areas to get to know employees and observe operations. In doing so, she realized that people were standing in a limited number of lines for excessive amounts of time as a few service representatives accepted payments. She immediately directed that the system be modified to enhance efficiency and make a typically negative requirement less stressful or frustrating. Visitors to the area now find a more open environment, with multiple cashier windows and a wait ticket system. When they arrive, they take a numbered ticket from the dispenser and have a seat to wait until their number appears on an electronic screen. They then proceed to an open window and make their transaction. Since implementing this, and many other changes, the office actually gets positive feedback from citizens (customers). Another example can be found in the fact that the organization contracted with the performance improvement firm, Global Performance Strategies, LLC to conduct an assessment of operational functions to help determine which areas had duplicated functions. Following that review, the organization worked with management to develop a process that streamlined and standardized the way employees were trained to perform similar tasks across the organization. This makes it easier for employees transferring from one area to another and doing the same type of work to know how to perform their tasks without a lot of additional training. This means that customers receive the same type of efficiency and quality service no matter what department they visit in the Clerk's office.

Because of the accomplishments in making systems more efficient and customer-centric at the Clerk's office, Ms. Gardner and her staff have received numerous accolades, including the prestigious 2008 Governor's Sterling Award, which is based on the National Malcolm Baldrige Criteria for Performance Excellence. The award evaluates an organization's performance in the following areas and only the premier submissions receive the award.

1. Leadership
2. Strategic Planning
3. Customer Focus
4. Measurement, Analysis, and Knowledge Management
5. Workforce Focus
6. Process Management
7. Results

Much of how employees approach the concept of service and the drive for excellence is articulated in the organization's Value Statement:

Trust and respect are the foundation of our success.

We treat each other with civility, striving to maintain open and honest lines of communication. We apply our policies in a fair and equal manner to all concerned.

We only have one chance to make a good first impression.

We believe in best serving the public by developing a team of committed and knowledgeable professionals who provide quality customer service that meets the need the first time in a prompt, courteous, and competent manner.

Together we make good things happen.

Through teamwork, we seek partnerships with our customers and our community to achieve mutual goals.

We are accountable for our actions.

We commit to demonstrating fiscal responsibility as well as maintaining a high level of accountability to our community, judicial partners, and employees.

Actions speak louder than words.

We believe our actions should parallel our commitment to excellence. It is through our integrity that we gain the confidence and trust of our employees and the public we serve.

Creativity is the window to our future.

We embrace responsible risk taking that will keep us on the leading edge of quality and innovation.

Diversity makes us stronger.

We strive to create a workforce that reflects the community we serve while creating a workplace that respects and includes differences.

Think About It

Visit www.myorangeclerk.com/ and conduct an Internet search for additional information about Lydia Gardner and her organization. Based on what you find and read above, answer the following questions.

1. What is your experience related to customer service from local government organizations with which you have experience? Explain.

2. How does the approach that the Orange County Clerk of Court's Office takes to service differ from others that you have experienced? Explain.

3. How does the behavior of Lydia Gardner, related to customer service, help set the tone for others in the organization to follow? Explain.

4. Would you want to work for this organization as a service representative? Why or why not?

Quick Preview

Before reviewing the chapter content, respond to the following questions by placing a "T" for true or an "F" for false on the rules. If you do not know an answer, put a question mark. Use any questions you miss as a checklist of material to which you will pay particular attention as you read through the chapter. For those you get right, congratulate yourself, but review the sections they address in order to learn additional details about the topic.

_____ **1.** Understanding behavioral styles can aid in establishing and maintaining positive customer relationships.

_____ **2.** You should treat others as individuals, not as members of a category.

_____ **3.** People whose primary behavioral style category is "E" focus their energy on working with people.

_____ **4.** People whose primary behavioral style category is "D" focus their energy on tasks or getting the job done.

_____ **5.** Some behavioral styles are better than others.

_____ **6.** People who exhibit the "D" style often tend to move slowly and speak in a low-key manner.

_____ **7.** People who exhibit the "E" style often tend to be highly animated in using gestures and speaking.

_____ **8.** People who exhibit the "R" style often tend to be very impatient.

_____ **9.** People who exhibit the "I" style often tend to express their emotions easily.

_____ **10.** You should attempt to determine a customer's behavioral style and then tailor your communication accordingly.

_____ **11.** To deliver total customer satisfaction, you need to make your customers feel special.

_____ **12.** When you say no to a customer, it is important to let him or her know what you cannot do and why.

_____ **13.** Service to your customers should be seamless; customers should not have to see or deal with problems or process breakdowns.

_____ **14.** Perceptions are based on education, experiences, events, and interpersonal contacts, as well as a person's intelligence level.

_____ **15.** Once you've made a perception, you should evaluate its accuracy.

Answers to Quick Preview can be found at the end of the chapter.

LO 6-1 What Are Behavioral Styles?

Concept Behavioral styles are actions or reactions exhibited when you and others deal with tasks or people. As a customer service professional, you need to be aware that everyone is not the same.

For thousands of years, people have devised systems in an attempt to better understand why people do what they do and how they accomplish what they do—and to categorize behavioral styles. Many of these systems are still in use today.

Behavioral styles are observable tendencies (actions that you can see or experience) that you and other people exhibit when dealing with tasks or people. As you grow from infancy, your personality forms, based on your experiences and your environment. These form the basis of your behavioral style preference(s).

Have you ever come into contact with someone with whom you simply did not feel comfortable or someone with whom you felt an immediate bond? If so, you were possibly experiencing and reacting to the effect of behavioral style. As a customer service professional, you need to be aware that everyone is different. Not everyone behaves as you do, yet many still demonstrate behaviors that are similar to yours. For this reason, you should strive to provide service in a manner that addresses not only the behaviors that you prefer, but also those that fulfill the needs and desires of others as well.

As a customer service professional, you need to understand human behavioral style characteristics. The more proficient you become at identifying your own behavioral characteristics and those of others, the better you will be at establishing and maintaining positive relationships with customers. Self-knowledge is the starting point. To help in this effort, we will examine some common behavior that you exhibit and that you may observe in customers.

When dealing with your customers, you should recognize that someone else doing something or acting differently from the way you do doesn't mean that the person is wrong. It simply means that they approach situations differently. Relationships are built on accepting the characteristics of others. In customer service, adaptability is crucial, for many people do not always act the way you want them to. As you will read later in this chapter, there are many strategies that can be used to help modify and adapt your behavior so that it does not clash with that of your customers. This does not mean that you must make all the concessions when behaviors do not mesh. It simply means that, although you do not have control over the behavior of others, you do have control over your own behavior. Use this control to deal more effectively with your customers.

LO 6-2 Identifying Behavioral Styles

Concept Each contact in a customer service environment has the potential for contributing to your success. Each person should be valued for his or her strengths and not belittled for what you perceive as shortcomings.

Through an assessment questionnaire you can discover your own behavioral tendencies in a variety of situations. An awareness of your own style

behavioral styles Descriptive term that identifies categories of human behavior identified by behavioral researchers. Many of the models used to group behaviors date back to those identified by Carl Jung.

Customer Service Success Tip

Take the time to obtain one or more of the commercial self-assessment surveys available on the Internet (e.g., DiSC, DISC, or Myers-Briggs Type indicator) in order to learn more about yourself and be better equipped to interact with others in the workplace.

preferences can then lead you to a better understanding of customers, since they also possess style preferences. By understanding these characteristics, you can improve communication, build stronger relationships, reduce conflict and misunderstandings, and offer better service to the customer.

Many self-assessment questionnaires and much of the research related to behavioral styles are based on the work begun by psychiatrist Carl Jung and others in the earlier part of the twentieth century. Jung explored human personality and behavior. He divided behavior into two "attitudes" (introvert and extrovert) and four "functions" (thinking, feeling, sensing, and intuitive). These attitudes and functions can intermingle to form eight psychological types; knowledge of these types is useful in defining and describing human behavioral characteristics.

From Jung's complex research (and that of others) has come many variations, additional studies, and a variety of behavioral style self-assessment questionnaires and models for explaining personal behavior. Examples of these questionnaires are the Myers-Briggs Type Indicator (MBTI) and the Personal Profile System (DiSC). Several organizations allow you to complete free surveys online. You can find these by searching the Internet for the topics and Web sites listed in "Search It Out" at the end of this chapter.

Although everyone typically has a **primary behavior pattern** (the way a person acts or reacts under certain circumstances) to which he/she reverts in stressful situations, people also have other characteristics in common and regularly demonstrate similar behavioral patterns. Identifying your own style preferences helps you relate to behaviors in others.

primary behavior pattern
Refers to a person's preferred style of dealing with others.

To informally identify some of your own behavioral styles preferences, complete Work It Out 6.1. This is not a validated behavioral survey but will give a strong indication of your behavioral preferences in dealing with others.

Note: Keep in mind that this is only a quick indicator. A more thorough assessment, using a formal instrument (questionnaire), will be better at predicting your style preferences. For more information or to obtain written or computer-based surveys and reports, write the author at the address shown in the author information section of this book or do an Internet search as suggested in the Search It Out section of this chapter.

Because of the complexities of human behavior, you should not try to use behavioral characteristics and cues as absolute indicators of the type of person you are dealing with. (This is similar to the situation with nonverbal cues.) You and others have some of the characteristics listed for all four style categories shown in this chapter; you simply have learned through years of experience which behavior you are most comfortable with and when adaptation is helpful or necessary. Generally, most people are adaptable and can shift style categories or exhibit different characteristics depending on the situation. For example, a person who is normally very personable and amiable can revert to more directive behavior, if necessary, to manage an activity or process for which he or she will be held accountable. Similarly, a person who normally exhibits controlling or task-oriented behavior can socialize and react positively in "people" situations.

Describing Your Behavior

AS A QUICK WAY TO DETERMINE YOUR BEHAVIORAL STYLE PREFERENCE, MAKE A COPY OF THIS PAGE AND THEN COMPLETE THE FOLLOWING SURVEY.

Step 1. Read the following list of words and phrases and rate yourself by placing a number (from 1 to 5) next to each item. A 5 means that the word is an accurate description of yourself in most situations, a 3 indicates a balanced agreement about the word's application, and a 1 means that you do not feel that the word describes your behavior well. Before you begin, refer to the sample assessment in Figure 6.1.

Relaxed	Enthusiastic
Logical	Sincere
Decisive	Accurate
Talkative	Pragmatic (practical)
Consistent	Popular
Nonaggressive (avoids conflict)	Patient
Calculating	Detail-oriented
Fun-loving	Objective
Loyal	Optimistic
Quality-focused	TOTAL R = I = D = E =
Competitive	

Step 2. Once you have rated each word or phrase, start with the first word, Relaxed, and put the letter "R" to the right of it. Place an "I" to the right of the second word, a "D" to the right of the third word, and an "E" to the right of the fourth word. Then start over with the fifth word and repeat the "RIDE" pattern until all words have a letter at their right.

Step 3. Next, go through the list and count point values for all words that have an "R" beside them. Put the total at the bottom of the grid next to "R = ." Do the same for the other letters. Once you have finished, one letter will probably have the highest total score. This is your natural style tendency.

For example, if "R" has the highest score, your primary style preference is rational. If "I" has the highest score, you exhibit more inquisitive behavior. "D" indicates decisive, and "E" is an expressive style preference.

If two or more of your scores have the same high totals, you probably generally put forth similar amounts of effort in both these style areas.

Most people have a primary and secondary style (one they revert to frequently).

An important point to remember is that there is no "best" or "worst" style. Each person should be valued for his or her strengths and not belittled because of what you perceive as shortcomings. In a customer environment, each contact has the potential for contributing to your success and that of your organization. By appreciating the behavioral characteristics of

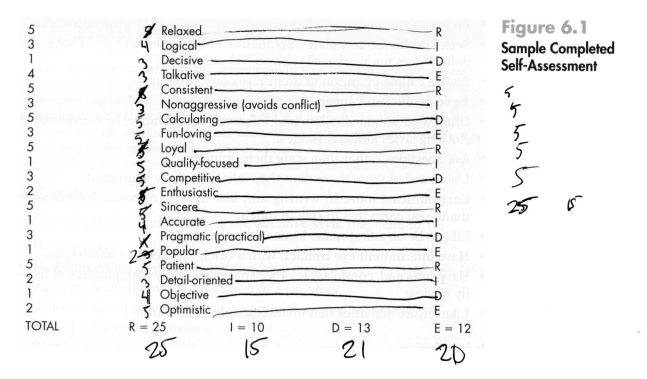

Figure 6.1
**Sample Completed
Self-Assessment**

5	Relaxed			R
3	Logical			I
1	Decisive			D
4	Talkative			E
5	Consistent			R
3	Nonaggressive (avoids conflict)			I
5	Calculating			D
3	Fun-loving			E
5	Loyal			R
1	Quality-focused			I
3	Competitive			D
2	Enthusiastic			E
5	Sincere			R
1	Accurate			I
3	Pragmatic (practical)			D
1	Popular			E
5	Patient			R
2	Detail-oriented			I
1	Objective			D
2	Optimistic			E
TOTAL	R = 25	I = 10	D = 13	E = 12

people with whom you interact, you can avoid bias or prejudice and better serve your customers.

How can a person who demonstrates one of the four styles be described? How might this person act, react, or interact? Some generalizations about behavior are listed in this section. Keep in mind that even though people have a primary style, they demonstrate other style behaviors too. By becoming familiar with these style characteristics, recognizing them in yourself, and observing how others display them, you can begin to learn how to better adapt to various behaviors. When interacting with others, remember to monitor their overall actions and behavior in order to get a better perception of their style preferences rather than react to one or two actions. Also keep in mind that these characteristics are generalities and not absolutes when dealing with others. People can and do adapt and change behavior depending on a variety of circumstances. Also, based on your perceptions, you might misinterpret their actions or behaviors.

R: Rational

People who have a preference for the **rational style** may tend to:

- Be very patient.
- Wait or stand in one place for periods of time without complaining, although they may be internally irritated about a breakdown in the system or lack of organization.
- Exhibit congenial eye contact and facial expressions.

rational style One of four behavioral groups characterized by being quiet, reflective, task-focused, and systematic.

Western culture, and specifically males who have "D," "I," and "R" styles and tend to adopt a formal posture when seated, should be aware of the effect of crossing their legs might have on certain customers. ("E" style people tend to be more relaxed and sprawling in their posture.) As for the head, many countries (e.g., in the Far East, especially Thailand)[2] view it as a sacred part of the body. Patting a child on the head is sometimes considered to invite evil spirits or bad omens. This action might easily be taken by people who have high "E" behavioral tendencies, for they tend to be touchy-feely.

Some books listed in the Bibliography address these kinds of issues. Also, we will explore other culturally related subjects in Chapter 8.

To help send a positive message to customers from other cultures, you can do simple things that might have major effects. For example, if you work in a restaurant and want to show appreciation for the large numbers of customers from another country who patronize the restaurant, you might recommend to your boss that a special dish from that area of the world be added to the menu. This offering could be promoted through flyers or advertisements. Such a strategy shows appreciation of the customers and their culture while encouraging them to eat at your establishment. However, be sure that the special dish is correctly prepared and uses the correct ingredients. Otherwise, you might offend rather than please the customer.

All these strategies, combined with a heightened knowledge of behavioral styles, can better prepare you to serve a wide variety of customers.

Know Your Products and Services

Customers expect that you will be able to identify and describe the products and services offered by your company. Depending on the behavioral style of the customer, the type of questions will vary. For example, an "R" personality may want to know who uses your services and products and ask to see the instructions; an "I" may ask many questions related to options, testing, rebates, and similar detailed technical information; a person with a strong "D" behavioral tendency may want to know the "bottom line" of using your service or product; and an "E" may want to talk about uses, colors, and sizes. If you cannot answer their questions, frustration, complaints, and/or loss of a customer may result.

Service providers need to know the products they are offering so that they can provide the best customer service possible. For example, when a new product line is introduced, orientation classes for employees can be arranged. In the classes, the features, benefits, and operation of the new items can be explained and demonstrated. Taking this approach increases knowledge of products and helps ensure better customer service.

Prepare Yourself

Before you come into contact with customers, take a minute to review your appearance. Ask yourself, "What image do I project?" Think about

Determining Styles

READ THE FOLLOWING DESCRIPTIONS AND THEN DETERMINE WHICH
BEHAVIORAL STYLE YOU ARE DEALING WITH.

Keep in mind that each person can switch behavioral styles, depending on the situation. To help you determine styles, refer to the style tendencies described in previous sections of this chapter.

Situation 1

You are a salesperson at a jewelry counter and observe a professionally dressed female customer waiting in line for several minutes. She is checking her watch frequently, anxiously looking around, and sighing often. When she arrives at the counter, she makes direct eye contact with you and without smiling states, "I want to buy a 16-inch 14-karat gold twisted-link necklace like the one advertised in today's paper. I also want a small gold heart pendant and would like these to cost no more than $125. Can you help me? Oh yes, I almost forgot. Wrap that in birthday paper. This gift is for my daughter's birthday."

Situation 2

You stop by the office of a director of a department that provides data you use to prepare your end-of-month reports. As you look around, you see a photograph of his family. Your co-worker smiles weakly and asks you to have a seat. As you begin to state your purpose by saying, "Thanks for taking the time to see me, Mr. Cohen," he interrupts and says, "Call me Lenny, please."

Situation 3

As a customer service representative for an automobile dealer, you return a phone message from Cynthia McGregor. When the phone is answered, you say, "Good morning, may I speak with Cindy McGregor?" The curt response is, "This is Cynthia McGregor. How may I help you?" During the conversation, Ms. McGregor asks a variety of very specific questions about an automotive recall. Even though it seems obvious that the recall does not apply to her car, she asks very detailed follow-up questions such as why the recall was necessary, who was affected, and what was being done. Throughout the conversation, she is very focused on facts, times, dates, and technical aspects of the recall.

Situation 4

You are a teller in a bank. Mrs. Vittelli, one of the customers, comes into your branch several times a week. You know that she has just become a grandmother because she has brought along photos of her grandson. She has shared them, and all the details of her daughter's pregnancy, in a loud, exuberant manner with several of your coworkers. As she speaks, you have noticed that she has a beautiful smile, and that throughout conversations she is very animated, using gestures and often reaching over to lightly touch others as they speak.

Quick Preview Answers

1. T	4. T	7. T	10. T	13. T
2. T	5. F	8. F	11. T	14. F
3. T	6. F	9. F	12. F	15. T

Ethical Dilemma Summary

Ethical Dilemma 6.1 Possible Answers

High "D" behavior can be frustrating and create challenges in the workplace. If you have observed your supervisor exhibiting the behavior in question on numerous occasions to arrive at your conclusions, and have validated them by talking to some of your co-workers, you may be doing the supervisor and employees a good deed by bringing your perceptions to her attention. This is because most people exhibit behavior of which they are often unaware. Such unintentional displays can create communication and relationship breakdowns if the person is not made aware or does not change them. In a service environment, this can be a real issue.

The key to providing such feedback is to do so at a nonemotional time (e.g., not immediately following an event in which the supervisor does not get input or listen and you are upset about it). Try the following approach:

Pick a time when both of you can calmly and rationally sit down to discuss the issue, perhaps over a cup of coffee in the break room when no one else is present. Doing this might prevent a situation in which the supervisor feels that she has to "stand her ground" because of having to maintain an image of being in control (remember they do have a high "D" type of personality preference). Also, remember the old adage of "The boss may not always be right, but he/she is always the boss."

When sharing your observations, focus on specific examples of her behavior and not on the person. For example, you might say something like, "Susan, I wanted to share my perceptions about how we are allowed to provide suggestions or feedback in the department. I have discussed my feelings with a couple of other people and they mentioned that they have had similar reactions or experiences. A specific example of what I am referring to happened when Matt, Shirley, and I offered a suggestion about … and then the process changed to something totally different without any explanation about why our idea could not be used. It made us feel that our opinion and experience are really irrelevant. " Notice in this example, the word "you" (referring to the supervisor) is avoided. Instead, the focus is on what you and others did, the end action or behavior, and how it made you feel. This potentially reduces the chance that your supervisor will feel attacked or threatened and therefore may seriously consider your feedback, or at least offer an explanation about why she took the action that she did.

Ethical Dilemma 6.2 Possible Answers

Comments about factors that someone cannot change (e.g., culture or physical characteristics) are often a sign of more underlying prejudices against a group or type of people. They can lead to bias and discrimination as well as to provoking emotional confrontations with others.

In the workplace, you sometimes have to walk a fine line between doing what is right and potentially offending your co-workers. In this case, if you have a good rapport with the co-worker, you

Determining Styles

READ THE FOLLOWING DESCRIPTIONS AND THEN DETERMINE WHICH
BEHAVIORAL STYLE YOU ARE DEALING WITH.

Keep in mind that each person can switch behavioral styles, depending on the situation. To help you determine styles, refer to the style tendencies described in previous sections of this chapter.

Situation 1

You are a salesperson at a jewelry counter and observe a professionally dressed female customer waiting in line for several minutes. She is checking her watch frequently, anxiously looking around, and sighing often. When she arrives at the counter, she makes direct eye contact with you and without smiling states, "I want to buy a 16-inch 14-karat gold twisted-link necklace like the one advertised in today's paper. I also want a small gold heart pendant and would like these to cost no more than $125. Can you help me? Oh yes, I almost forgot. Wrap that in birthday paper. This gift is for my daughter's birthday."

Situation 2

You stop by the office of a director of a department that provides data you use to prepare your end-of-month reports. As you look around, you see a photograph of his family. Your co-worker smiles weakly and asks you to have a seat. As you begin to state your purpose by saying, "Thanks for taking the time to see me, Mr. Cohen," he interrupts and says, "Call me Lenny, please."

Situation 3

As a customer service representative for an automobile dealer, you return a phone message from Cynthia McGregor. When the phone is answered, you say, "Good morning, may I speak with Cindy McGregor?" The curt response is, "This is Cynthia McGregor. How may I help you?" During the conversation, Ms. McGregor asks a variety of very specific questions about an automotive recall. Even though it seems obvious that the recall does not apply to her car, she asks very detailed follow-up questions such as why the recall was necessary, who was affected, and what was being done. Throughout the conversation, she is very focused on facts, times, dates, and technical aspects of the recall.

Situation 4

You are a teller in a bank. Mrs. Vittelli, one of the customers, comes into your branch several times a week. You know that she has just become a grandmother because she has brought along photos of her grandson. She has shared them, and all the details of her daughter's pregnancy, in a loud, exuberant manner with several of your coworkers. As she speaks, you have noticed that she has a beautiful smile, and that throughout conversations she is very animated, using gestures and often reaching over to lightly touch others as they speak.

how well your appearance is in tune with that of your typical customer. Evaluate your knowledge of your job and of the products and services offered by your organization. Are you ready and able to describe them to people regardless of their style preference? If not, start getting ready by learning as much as you can and practicing your message delivery by reviewing and implementing some of the strategies related to each style preference discussed earlier in this chapter.

LO 6-5 Dealing with Perceptions

Concept Often there are many different perceptions of an event. Our perceptions are often influenced by many factors such as physical qualities, social roles and behaviors, psychological qualities, and group affiliations.

perceptions How someone views an item, situation, or others.

Everyone has **perceptions** about the people and events he or she encounters (see Figure 6.4). A person's behavioral style as well as background, based on education, experiences, events, and interpersonal contacts, can influence how he or she views the world. In effect, there are sometimes as many different perceptions of an event as there are people involved.

Perceptions and Stereotypes

People's perceptions of events vary greatly, as do their perceptions of each other. As a customer service provider, you should be aware of how you perceive your customers and, in turn, how they perceive you.

How are our perceptions shaped within a customer service framework? In essence, there are five categories that form the basis of many perceptions. We tend to base our perceptions of others and categorize people by thinking about the following:

- *Physical qualities.* What does a person look like? What gender? What body shape? Color of skin? Physical characteristics (hair color or type, facial features, height, or weight)?
- *Social roles.* What is a person's position in society? Job title? Honors received? Involvement in social or volunteer organizations?
- *Social behaviors.* How does this person act, in terms of the behavioral style characteristics? What social skills does he or she exhibit in social and business settings? How well does he or she interact with people (peers, customers, seniors, subordinates, and people of other races, gender, or backgrounds)?
- *Psychological qualities.* How does he or she process information mentally? Is this person confident? Stressed out? Insecure? Curious? Paranoid?
- *Group affiliations.* Does this person belong to a recognizable religious, ethnic, or political group? What kinds of qualities are associated with each group? Does he or she assume leadership roles and demonstrate competence in such roles?

Figure 6.4 Factors Affecting Perceptions

✳ Ethical Dilemma 6.2

You often hear one of your co-workers making improper and derogatory comments about customers from other cultures (e.g., the way they dress, their accent, their values and beliefs, and so on). Often this occurs when other people from outside the organization (e.g., vendors, suppliers, or customers) can hear. Assume that another employee tries to engage you in a conversation in which they are making derogatory comments about people from another culture while there are people from a variety of countries within hearing range.

What would you do about the situation, if anything?

In some cases, you may **stereotype** people and, in doing so, adversely affect delivery of services. For example, your perception of older customers may be that they are all slow, hard of hearing, cranky, and politically conservative. This perception may be based on past experiences or from what you've heard or seen on television. This view might cause you to treat most older people in the same way, rather than treating each person as unique. However, you are basing your behavior on a stereotype, not on reality. Think about it—aren't there many older people who don't have these characteristics? Thus, you need to be very careful that your perceptions are not influenced by stereotypes, because this clearly works against treating each customer as an individual.

Stereotyping people affects our relationships with customers. For this reason, you should consciously guard against stereotyping when you interact with others. If you pigeonhole people right away because of preconceptions, you may negatively affect future interactions. For example, suppose

stereotype Generalization made about an individual or group and not based on reality. Similar people are often lumped together for ease in categorizing them.

Many preconceived ideas about an individual or group can lead to disparate treatment and poor service. *What preconceived ideas might affect how one group of diners is treated versus the other group?*

Discovering Common Characteristics

REFER TO WORK IT OUT 6.1 (DESCRIBING YOUR BEHAVIOR).
Select four to eight friends or co-workers and ask them to rate themselves using Work It Out 6.1. Next, ask each person to answer the following questions:

What do I look for when I shop?

What is my main reason for shopping?

What do I do when I need to buy or replace something?

What is the most important thing to me when I'm looking to replace something?

Once everyone has finished, gather in a group to compare and discuss answers. Focus on the fact that each person and each style is unique but that we all have common characteristics and needs. Discuss how this knowledge of common needs or drives can be used to provide customer service more effectively.

you use your new knowledge about behavioral styles to walk up to a co-worker and say something like, "I figured out what your problem is when dealing with people. You're a 'D.'" Could this create a confrontational situation? Might this person react negatively? What impact might your behavior have on your relationship with your co-worker (and possibly others)? Based on what you have read regarding communication in earlier chapters, several things are wrong with such an approach. First of all, no one is always a "D." Although a person might exhibit this behavior a lot, he or she draws from all four styles, just as you do. Second, exhibiting any particular style is not a "problem." As you have seen in this chapter, "D" behavior can provide some valuable input to any situation. And finally, although a behavioral style may contribute to a person's actions, many other factors come into play (communication ability, timing, location, situation, etc.).

To avoid categorizing people, spend time observing them, listen to them objectively, and respond according to each situation and person. Doing this can lead to better relationships and improved customer service.

Small Business Perspective

Since many small business employees often deliver service face-to-face with customers and have an opportunity to get to know their customers on a more personal basis, knowledge of behavioral styles can come in handy. As noted in the chapter, by recognizing specific traits or behaviors related to the various style preferences, you can adjust your service delivery to better meet the likes of customers if you work for a small company. You might even keep an informal file on each customer that you can reference when a planned meeting is coming. In it, you can note what you believe to be the customer's primary, and any secondary, style preferences. When possible before actually meeting with the customer, refer to the file and mentally think of ways to deal with the customer.

If service interactions are typically over the telephone, you can still use the strategies you read about in this chapter. Simply by listening to tone, timing, and delivery of messages, you can adjust your tone, selection of words, and the approach you take to handling the interaction.

Impact on Service

Based on personal experience and what you just read, answer the following questions:

1. How might behavioral styles play an important role in dealing with fellow employees in a small company? Explain.
2. If you worked for a small business, what strategies for using what you read in this chapter might help strengthen your service to customers? Explain.
3. What specific challenges could you have in dealing with a customer who has a different style preference than your own? Explain.

Summary

Everything a customer experiences from the time he or she makes contact with an organization, in person, on the phone, or through other means, affects that customer's perception of the organization and its employees. To positively influence the customer's opinion, customer service professionals must be constantly alert for opportunities to provide excellent service. Making a little extra effort can often mean the difference between total customer satisfaction and service breakdown.

As you have seen in this chapter, people are varied and have different behavioral styles. Recognizing the differences and dealing with customers on a case-by-case basis is the foundation of solid customer service. By examining individual behavioral tendencies, actions, communication styles, and needs, you can better determine a course of action for each customer. The test of your effectiveness is whether your customers return and what they tell their friends about you and your organization.

Review Questions

1. What are behavioral styles?
2. What are the four behavioral style categories discussed in this chapter?
3. What are some of the characteristics that can help you identify a person who has the following style preferences: R, I, D, E?
4. When communicating with someone who has an "R" preference, what can you do to improve your effectiveness?
5. When communicating with someone who has an "I" preference, what can you do to improve your effectiveness?
6. When communicating with someone who has a "D" preference, what can you do to improve your effectiveness?
7. When communicating with someone who has an "E" preference, what can you do to improve your effectiveness?

8. What are some strategies for eliminating service barriers by using your knowledge of behavioral styles?

9. What are perceptions?

10. How can perceptions affect customer relations?

Search It Out

Search for Behavioral Styles on the Internet

Log onto the Internet and look for information and research data on behavioral styles and other types of personal surveys. Specifically look for the various theories and surveys that describe and categorize behavior. Also try to find information about some of the people who have done research on behavior:

Sigmund Freud
Carl Jung
Alfred Adler
Abraham Maslow

William Moulton Marston
Ivan Pavlov
B. F. Skinner
Behavioral style surveys
Personality surveys
www.myersbriggs.org
www.inscapepublishing.com
www.tickle.com
www.tracomcorp.com
www.personalitypathways.com

Be prepared to present some of your findings at the next scheduled class.

Collaborative Learning Activity

Observing and Analyzing Behavioral Styles

With a partner or team, go to a public place (park, mall, airport, train or bus station, or restaurant) to observe three different people. Using Worksheet 6.1 on the McGraw-Hill Web site www.mhhe.com/customerservice, note the specific behaviors each person exhibits. After you have finished this part of the activity, take a guess at each person's behavioral style preference based on behaviors you saw. Compare notes with your teammates and discuss similarities and differences among findings. Also, discuss how this information can be helpful in your workplace to deliver better customer service.

Face to Face

Working through Technology and People Problems at Child's Play Toy Company

Background

Since opening its newest store in Princeton, New Jersey, Child's Play Toy Company of Minneapolis, Minnesota, has been getting mixed customer reviews. Designed to be state of the art, open, and customer-friendly, the store includes an attended activity area where small children can play while parents shop. In addition, an innovative system makes it possible for local customers to order products from catalogs or from the company's Web site and then go to a drive-up window to pick up their purchases without leaving their cars. Another creative feature involves interactive television monitors in the store—where customers can see a customer service representative at the same time the representative sees them. To reduce staffing costs, the customer service representatives are actually at a Philadelphia, Pennsylvania, location and are remotely connected via satellite and computer to all new stores. This system is used for special ordering, billing questions, and complaint resolution. Customers can also use a computer keyboard to enter data or search for product information online through the company's Web site while in the store.

In recent months, the number of customer complaints has been rising. Many people complain about not getting the product that they ordered over the system, some are uncomfortable using the computer keyboard, while others dislike the impersonal touch and the fact that they have to answer a series of standard questions asked by a "talking head" on the screen, they have encountered system or computer breakdowns, and they cannot get timely service or resolution of problems.

Your Role

As a customer service representative and cashier at the store, you are responsible for operating a cash register in the store at Child's Play when all lines are operational and more than two customers are waiting in each line. You are also responsible for supervising other cashiers on your shift and dealing with customer questions, complaints, or problems. You report directly to the assistant store manager, Meg Giarnelli. Prior to coming to this store, you worked in two other New Jersey store branches during the five preceding years.

This afternoon, Mrs. Sakuro, a regular customer, came to you. She was obviously frustrated and pointed her finger at you as she shouted, "You people are stupid!" She also demanded to speak with the manager and threatened that, "If you people do not want my business, I will go to another store!" Apparently, a doll that Mrs. Sakuro had ordered two weeks ago over the in-store system had not arrived. The doll was to be for her daughter's birthday, which is in two days. Although Mrs. Sakuro has a heavy accent, you understood that she had been directed by a cashier to check with a customer service representative via the monitor to determine the status of the order. When she did this, she was informed that there was a problem with the order. The representative who took the original order apparently wrote down the credit card number incorrectly, and the order was not processed. When Mrs. Sakuro asked the customer service representative why someone hadn't called her, the representative said that the customer service department was in another state and that long-distance calls were not allowed by frontline employees. She was told that the local store where she was picking up is responsible for verifying order status, contacting the customer via telephone, and handling problems. There was no valid explanation given when Ms. Sakuro asked why someone in New Jersey had not just e-mailed her, since they had her e-mail address. Mrs. Sakuro's behavior and attitude are upsetting to you.

Critical Thinking Questions

1. From the behavioral style information in this chapter and other subjects discussed in this book, what do you think is causing the complaints being made?

2. What system changes would you suggest for Child's Play? Why?

3. What can you do at this point to solve the problem?

4. What primary behavioral style is Mrs. Sakuro exhibiting? What specific strategies should you use to address her behavior?

Planning to Serve

In order to ensure that you are prepared to provide premium service to your customers, take some time to think about typical customer situations in which you were personally involved or that you have witnessed. Answer the following questions on the basis of situations recalled.

1. What types of behaviors does the average customer exhibit?

2. Based on what you learned about behavioral styles in general, and your preferred style, what service strategies could you use if you were involved with the behaviors identified in Question 1?

3. In difficult or emotional service situations, what behaviors often manifest themselves?

4. What strategies might help you in dealing with such customer behaviors?

Quick Preview Answers

1. T	4. T	7. T	10. T	13. T
2. T	5. F	8. F	11. T	14. F
3. T	6. F	9. F	12. F	15. T

Ethical Dilemma Summary

Ethical Dilemma 6.1 Possible Answers

High "D" behavior can be frustrating and create challenges in the workplace. If you have observed your supervisor exhibiting the behavior in question on numerous occasions to arrive at your conclusions, and have validated them by talking to some of your co-workers, you may be doing the supervisor and employees a good deed by bringing your perceptions to her attention. This is because most people exhibit behavior of which they are often unaware. Such unintentional displays can create communication and relationship breakdowns if the person is not made aware or does not change them. In a service environment, this can be a real issue.

The key to providing such feedback is to do so at a nonemotional time (e.g., not immediately following an event in which the supervisor does not get input or listen and you are upset about it). Try the following approach:

Pick a time when both of you can calmly and rationally sit down to discuss the issue, perhaps over a cup of coffee in the break room when no one else is present. Doing this might prevent a situation in which the supervisor feels that she has to "stand her ground" because of having to maintain an image of being in control (remember they do have a high "D" type of personality preference). Also, remember the old adage of "The boss may not always be right, but he/she is always the boss."

When sharing your observations, focus on specific examples of her behavior and not on the person. For example, you might say some-thing like, "Susan, I wanted to share my perceptions about how we are allowed to provide suggestions or feedback in the department. I have discussed my feelings with a couple of other people and they mentioned that they have had similar reactions or experiences. A specific example of what I am referring to happened when Matt, Shirley, and I offered a suggestion about ... and then the process changed to something totally different without any explanation about why our idea could not be used. It made us feel that our opinion and experience are really irrelevant. " Notice in this example, the word "you" (referring to the supervisor) is avoided. Instead, the focus is on what you and others did, the end action or behavior, and how it made you feel. This potentially reduces the chance that your supervisor will feel attacked or threatened and therefore may seriously consider your feedback, or at least offer an explanation about why she took the action that she did.

Ethical Dilemma 6.2 Possible Answers

Comments about factors that someone cannot change (e.g., culture or physical characteristics) are often a sign of more underlying prejudices against a group or type of people. They can lead to bias and discrimination as well as to provoking emotional confrontations with others.

In the workplace, you sometimes have to walk a fine line between doing what is right and potentially offending your co-workers. In this case, if you have a good rapport with the co-worker, you might consider approaching the person in a non-threatening, rational manner and using unemotional language (see Chapter 3). If you do not know the person well, perhaps you can get one of his or her friends to take action to correct the situation.

If you do decide to speak to your co-worker, point out that such language is offensive and can actually get him/her into trouble with the customer and the organization. It can also be viewed as discriminatory and can lead to possible legal action against the employee and the organization. This is often best done through a question format (e.g., "When you say things like that about people from other countries, do you really dislike them or are you just trying to be funny?"). Depending on the answer, you may want to try to get the co-worker to see that others might perceive him or her as being prejudiced because of such comments. In some cases, depending on the remarks, attitude of the co-worker, and situation, it may even be appropriate to point out the comments to a supervisor. The bottom line is to try to share your views in a manner that helps the other person see that such actions may not be appropriate and to help that person curtail future such language without damaging your work relationship or creating more serious situations.

Service Breakdowns and Service Recovery

Never underestimate the power of the irate customer.

—Joel Ross

Learning Outcomes

After completing this chapter, you will be able to:

7-1 Define what a service breakdown is.

7-2 Apply knowledge of behavioral styles in difficult customer situations.

7-3 Recognize different types of difficult customers and effectively deal with them.

7-4 Use the emotion-reducing model to help keep difficult situations from escalating.

7-5 Explain why customers defect.

7-6 Develop effective strategies for working with internal customers.

7-7 Identify strategies for preventing customer dissatisfaction and problem solving.

7-8 Explain the six steps of the problem-solving model.

7-9 Implement a front-line service recovery strategy, and spot roadblocks to service recovery.

Key Terms

- angry customers
- customer defection
- customer expectations
- demanding or domineering customers
- difficult customers
- dissatisfied customers
- emotion-reducing model
- indecisive customers
- needs
- Problem-Solving Model
- prohibitions
- rude or inconsiderate customers
- service breakdowns
- service options
- strategies for preventing dissatisfaction
- talkative customers
- underpromise and overdeliver
- wants

In the Real World Food Processing/ Manufacturing—H. J. Heinz Company

HEADQUARTERED IN PITTSBURGH, PENNSYLVANIA, THE COMPANY WAS
founded by Henry John Heinz in Sharpsburg, Pennsylvania, in 1869. It is world-
renowned for the thousands of sauces, soups, seafood, snacks, meals, frozen foods,
and infant and pet food products that it manufactures in plants in six countries. The company is a $10 billion dollar global business that markets products in more than 200 coun-
tries and territories. Over 100 of its products occupy the number 1 or 2 spots in sales in
50 countries. Two of its best known products are ketchup and the Ore-Ida frozen potato
line, which maintain over a 50-percent market share in the United States.

According to the company's Web site, day-to-day business operations
are guided by a Global Code of Conduct, which outlines expected behavior for employees at all levels of the organization. "It is the foundation
of comprehensive and continuous compliance with all corporate policies
and procedures, an open relationship among colleagues that contributes
to good business conduct, and an abiding belief in the integrity of our
employees. These principles and policies make ethics a way of life at
Heinz."[1] In addition to their commitment to ethical compliance, every
employee at Heinz is expected to adhere to an established value code
written as the acronym PREMIER:

- *P*assion—to be passionate about winning and about our brands, products,
  and people, thereby delivering superior value to our shareholders.
- *R*isk tolerance—to create a culture where entrepreneurship and
  prudent risk taking are encouraged and rewarded.
- *E*xcellence—to be the best in quality and in everything we do.
- *M*otivation—to celebrate success, recognizing and rewarding the
  achievements of individuals and teams.
- *I*nnovation—to innovate in everything, from products to processes.
- *E*mpowerment—to empower our talented people to take the initiative and to do
  what is right.
- *R*espect—to act with integrity and respect toward all.[2]

Since its inception, the organization has been driven by high standards of quality and a focus on providing the best products and service to customers. As part of
the organization's commitment to its employees (internal customers), a wide variety of
benefits are available. In addition to traditional healthcare, dental, 401K retirement
plan, insurance, and other employee benefits, Heinz offers such added incentives as
gym membership subsidies and facilities (at some locations), employee store discounts,
tuition reimbursement, flexible work schedules, and travel and adoption assistance.

On the Heinz Web site, visitors can view additional guiding principles and other
tenets related to how the organization conducts business and views its relationship
with customers, employees, partners, the environment, and the world. Heinz has
very specific written guidelines for employees and anyone who wants to do business
with the company. Failure to adhere to these specifications can lead to lost employment and business opportunity. Areas such as diversity, abuse and harassment,
forced labor, working conditions, food and work safety, and much more are covered

in detail in the company's operating principles. These are the types of things that add to an atmosphere of empowerment and gratification that many employees express in written and video tributes to the organization that are posted on the Web site.

Take some time to visit Heinz Company (www.heinz.com) to explore the way it conducts business operations, and its values toward people and the environment, then answer the following questions and discuss your responses with others in class.

Think About It

1. Why do you think some companies like Heinz survive for long periods while their competitors come and go. Explain.
2. What role do you think customer service (internal and external) plays in the Heinz Company success? Explain.
3. What positive aspects about the company help contribute to its worldwide success? Explain.
4. How do you think elements like the Global Code of Conduct and value code affect customer service and impact employee and management relationships? Explain.
5. Would you want to work for a company like Heinz? Why or why not?

Quick Preview

Before reviewing the chapter content, respond to the following questions by placing a "T" for true or an "F" for false on the rules. Use any questions you miss as a checklist of material to which you will pay particular attention as you read through the chapter. For those you get right, congratulate yourself, but review the sections they address in order to learn additional details about the topic.

_____ 1. Service breakdowns often occur because customer needs and wants are not met.

_____ 2. Customer expectations do not affect how service is delivered.

_____ 3. Behavioral style preferences do not affect customer needs or satisfaction levels.

_____ 4. An upset customer is usually annoyed with a specific person rather than the organization or system.

_____ 5. When you cannot comply with the demands of an angry customer, you should try to negotiate an alternative solution.

_____ 6. Competency in communicating can eliminate the need for service recovery.

_____ 7. Demanding customers often act in a domineering manner because they are very self-confident. This is a function of behavioral style.

_____ 8. Service recovery occurs when a provider is able to make restitution, solve a problem, or regain customer trust after service breakdown.

_____ 9. One key strategy for preventing dissatisfaction is to learn to think like a customer.

_____ 10. Adopting a "good neighbor policy" can help in dealings with internal customers.

_____ 11. As part of trying to help solve a customer problem, you should assess its seriousness.

_____ 12. When something does not go as the customer needs or expects, service recovery becomes a vital step in maintaining the relationship.

Answers to Quick Preview can be found at the end of the chapter.

LO 7-1 What Is a Service Breakdown?

Concept Service breakdowns occur whenever any product or service fails to meet the customer's expectations.

Service breakdowns occur daily in all types of organizations. They happen whenever the product or service delivered fails to meet customer expectations (see Figure 7.1). In some cases the product or service delivered may function exactly as it was designed, but if the customer perceived that it should work another way, a breakdown occurs. Additionally, when a product or service fails to meet what the customer **wants** or **needs** or does not live up to advertised promises or standards, dissatisfaction and frustration can result.

service breakdown Situations when customers have expectations of a certain type or level of service that are not met by a service provider.

wants Things that customers typically desire but to not necessarily need.

needs Motivators or drivers that cause customers to seek out specific types of products or services. These may be marketing-driven, based on advertising they have seen, or may tie directly to Abraham Maslow's hierarchy of needs theory.

Figure 7.1 Examples of Service Breakdowns

Here are some examples of service breakdowns:

- A food service professional brings a meal containing an ingredient not expected or wanted by the customer, or one that the customer specified should not be added. For example, a customer orders a hamburger with only lettuce, tomato, and mayonnaise, and specifically tells the server she wants no onion or pickle on the plate. The burger arrives with both onion and pickle and the server states, "I told them not to put that on there, but they preset the condiments for sandwiches before lunch to save time. Can't you just pick it off?"

  A note of caution: If you are in food service, be vigilant in monitoring orders when customers ask that certain ingredients not be used. Check food and drinks before you deliver them to your customer to be sure that the cook staff or bartender did not forget the special request. Also, do not simply remove a food item if it was placed on a plate inadvertently. Some people have severe allergies to certain foods that could cause serious illness and even death—and a huge liability for you and your organization.

- On Friday morning, you realize that the pain medication you are taking following surgery is about to run out and there are no refills left on the prescription. You call your doctor's office at 9:00 A.M. and are put through to an automated nurse's hotline, which tells you the office will return calls by the end of the day or the next business day. At 4:00 P.M. you check with the pharmacy and find the prescription has not been called in from the doctor, so you call back to the doctor's office only to find that the office closes at 3:30 on Fridays. You now have no pain medication for the weekend.

- A hotel room is not available when the customer arrives. (In some cases a stated check-in time may exist and the customer may be early. Make every effort to accommodate the customer if this happens.)

- According to the customer, room service food was cold when delivered (e.g., not at the degree of warmth desired or expected).

- An optometrist provides glasses or contact lenses that do not adequately correct a patient's vision because a technician misread the prescription.

- A volunteer at a silent auction for charity misplaces an item won by a donor.

- A co-worker expects your assistance in providing information needed for a monthly report, but you failed to get it to her on time or as agreed.

- A manufacturer does not receive a parts delivery as you promised, and an assembly line has to be shut down.

- A garment you needed for a meeting is returned from the laundry with broken buttons and cannot be worn.

In any of the situations described, customers may have not received what they were promised or expected, or at least they perceived that they did not. When such incidents occur, there is a breakdown and they often lead to emotional or difficult situations. In many instances service providers are uncomfortable and unprepared to deal with such events.

Handling Service Breakdowns

PAIR UP WITH ONE OR TWO OTHER STUDENTS AND DISCUSS POSSIBLE WAYS TO PREVENT THE SERVICE BREAKDOWNS LISTED IN FIGURE 7.1 AND SOLUTIONS IF THEY DO OCCUR.

customer expectations
The perceptions that customers have when they contact an organization or service provider about the kind, level, and quality of products and services they should receive.

In addition, **customer expectations** can affect how service is delivered and perceived. Today's customers are more discerning and better educated, have access to more up-to-date and accurate information, and are often more demanding than in the past. They have certain expectations about your products and services, and the way that you will provide them. Figure 7.2 shows some common expectations customers might have of a service organization. Failure to fulfill some or all of these expectations can lead to dissatisfaction and in some cases confrontation and/or loss of business. Keep in mind that they also have many more options offered by your competitors.

Figure 7.2
Typical Customer Expectations

Customers come to you expecting that certain things will occur in regard to the products and services they obtain. Customers typically expect the following:

Expectations Related to People

Friendly, knowledgeable service providers
Respect (they want to be treated as if they are intelligent)
Empathy (they want their feelings and emotions to be recognized)
Courtesy (they want to be recognized as "the customer" and as someone who is important to you and your organization)
Equitable treatment (they do not want to feel that one individual or group gets preferential benefits or treatment over another)

Expectations Related to Products and Services

Easily accessible and available products and services (no lengthy delays)
Reasonable and competitive pricing
Products and services that adequately address needs
Quality (appropriate value for money and time invested)
Ease of use
Safe (warranty available and product free of defects that might cause physical injury)
State-of-the-art products and service delivery
Easy-to-understand instructions (and follow-up assistance availability)
Ease of return or exchange (flexible policies that provide alternatives depending on the situation)
Appropriate and expedient problem resolution

Ethical Dilemma 7.1

You are an employee of a local retail organization that typically closes at 6:00 P.M. At 5:52 P.M., your supervisor tosses you the keys to the front door and tells you to lock up for the evening because he wants to get out early so that he can pick up his wife. They have tickets for a play and are going out to dinner to celebrate their anniversary.

As you lock the door and start to return to your cash register to begin your end-of-day activities, you hear a frantic knock on the front door. An obviously distraught customer is yelling that she needs to by a gift for her son's birthday and is pointing to the clock on the wall next to your register that indicates 5:56 P.M. There is a sign on the door that lists the closing time as 6:00 P.M.

1. What would you do in this situation?

2. How do you think the customer will view this matter?

3. Are there possible repercussions from a service standpoint? If so, what are they?

LO 7-2 The Role of Behavioral Style

Concept Behavioral preferences have a major effect on the interactions of people. The more you know about style tendencies, the better you will understand your customers.

As you read in Chapter 6, behavioral style preferences play a major part in how people interact. Styles also affect the types of things people want and value. For example, those with high expressive behavioral tendencies will probably buy more colorful and people-oriented items than will those who have high decisive tendencies.

The more you know about style preferences, the easier it becomes to deal with people in a variety of situations and to help match their needs with the products and services you and your organization can provide. The suggested strategies found in Chapter 6 can assist you in dealing with customers who exhibit a specific behavioral style preference and are upset, irrational, or confrontational. Keep in mind that everyone possesses all four behavioral styles discussed in Chapter 6 and can display various types of behavior from time to time. Therefore, carefully observe your customer's behavior and use the information you learned about each style as an indicator of the type of person with whom you are dealing. Do not use such information as the definitive answer for resolving the situation. Human beings are complex and react to stimuli in various ways—so adapt your approach as necessary. In addition, learn to deal with your emotions so that you can prevent or resolve heated emotional situations.

Customer Service Success Tip

Be prepared and conscientious and think like a customer in order to identify and satisfy customer needs and expectations.

Service Breakdown Examples

WHAT EXAMPLES OF SERVICE BREAKDOWN HAVE YOU EXPERIENCED OR CAN YOU RECALL FROM SOMEONE ELSE'S STORY?
List and then discuss them with classmates. After discussing your lists, brainstorm ways that the organization did or could have recovered.

LO 7-3 Difficult Customers

Concept Successful service will ultimately be delivered through effective communication skills, positive attitude, patience, and a willingness to help the customer.

difficult customers
People who challenge a service provider's ability to deliver service and who require special skills and patience.

You may think of **difficult customer** contacts as those in which you have to deal with negative, angry, demanding, or aggressive people. These are just a few of the types of potentially difficult interactions. From time to time, you will also be called upon to help customers who can be described in one or more of the following ways:

Dissatisfied with your service or products.

Indecisive or lacking knowledge about your product, service, or policies.

Rude or inconsiderate of others.

Talkative.

Internal customers with special requests.

Speak a primary language other than yours (discussed in Chapter 8).

Elderly and need extra assistance (discussed in Chapter 8).

Have some type of a disability (discussed in Chapter 8).

Each of the above categories can be difficult to handle, depending on your knowledge, experience, and abilities. A key to successfully serving all types of customers is to treat each person as an individual. If you stereotype people, you will likely damage the customer-provider relationship. Avoid labeling people according to their behavior. Do not mentally categorize people (put them into groups) according to the way they speak or act or look—and then treat everyone in a "group" the same way.

Ultimately, you will deliver successful service through your effective communication skills, positive attitude, patience, knowledge, service experience, and willingness to help the customer. Your ability to focus on the situation or problem and not on the person will be a very important factor in your success. Making the distinction between the person and the problem is especially important when you are faced with difficult situations in the service environment. Although you may not understand or approve of a person's behavior, he or she is still your customer. Try to make the interaction a positive one, and if necessary ask for assistance from a co-worker or refer the problem to an appropriate level in your operational chain of command.

Many difficult situations you will deal with as a service provider will be caused by your customer's needs, wants, and expectations. You will read about service challenges in this chapter, along with their causes and some strategies for effectively dealing with them.

Demanding or Domineering Customers

Customers can be **demanding or domineering** for a number of reasons. Many times, domineering behavior is part of a personality style or simply behavior that they have learned, as discussed in Chapter 6. In other instances, it could be a reaction to past customer service encounters. A demanding customer may feel a need to be or stay in control, especially if he or she has felt out of control in the past. Often, such people are insecure. Some strategies for effectively handling demanding customers are discussed in the following sections:

Handling difficult customers will be one of your biggest challenges so be prepared. *How would you deal with an unhappy customer?*

demanding or domineering customers Customers who have definite ideas about what they want and are unwilling to compromise or accept alternatives.

- *Be professional.* Don't raise your voice or retaliate verbally. Children engage in name-calling, which often escalates into shoving matches. Unfortunately, some adults "regress" to childish behavior. Your customer may revert to negative behavior learned in the past. Both you and the customer lose when this happens.

- *Respect the customer.* Showing respect does not mean that you must accommodate your customer's every wish. It means that you should make positive eye contact (but not glare), remain calm, use the customer's name, apologize when appropriate and/or necessary, and let the customer know that he or she is important to you and your organization. Work positively toward a resolution of the problem. If accommodations are appropriate and possible, consider making them. If they are not, perhaps you might explain why something cannot be done. Most adults can be reasoned with if you take the time to talk to them on a professional and equal level.

- *Be firm and fair and focus on the customer's needs.* As you read in Chapter 3, assertive behavior is an appropriate response to a domineering or demanding person; aggression is not. Also, remember the importance of treating each customer as an individual. If you are dealing with a customer who is being unreasonable, contact your supervisor, then try to get them to accompany you to a more private location where the three of you can discuss the issue in an unemotional manner out of sight of other customers, if possible.

Handling the Demanding Customer

SURVEY CUSTOMER SERVICE PROFESSIONALS IN VARIOUS PROFESSIONS TO SEE HOW THEY HANDLE DEMANDING OR DOMINEERING CUSTOMERS.
Make a list for future reference and role-play a variety of scenarios involving demanding customers with a peer.

✳ Customer Service Success Tip

Put yourself in a customer's situation when he or she is demanding and trying to control you. Ask yourself, "Is there something that I have said or done that might have escalated or added to this situation?" If the answer is "yes," apologize, listen and move toward resolution. If you do not believe that you are at fault, engage the customer with nonthreatening but firm language and explain that your goal is to help the customer, but that you need that person to calmly explain the issue so that you can figure out what needs to be done. If all else fails, you may eventually have to call in a supervisor or other employee to handle the customer's issue.

- *Tell the customer what you can do.* Don't focus on negatives or what can't be done when dealing with your customers. Stick with what is possible and what you are willing to do. Be flexible and willing to listen to requests. If something suggested is possible and will help solve the problem, compliment the person on his or her idea (e.g., "Mr. Hollister, that's a good suggestion, and one that I think will work"), and then try to make it happen. Doing this will show that you are receptive to new ideas, are truly working to meet the customer's needs and expectations, and value the customer's opinion. Also, remember that if you can psychologically partner with a customer, he or she is less likely to attack. You do need to make sure that your willingness to assist and comply is not seen as giving in or backing down. If it is, the customer may make additional demands or return in the future with similar demands. To avoid this, you could add to the earlier statement by saying something like, "Mr. Hollister, that's a good suggestion, and although we cannot do this in every instance, I think that your suggestion is one that will work at this time." This puts the customer on alert that although he or she may get his or her way this time, it will not necessarily happen in the future. Another strategy is to make a counteroffer in an effort to find a win-win solution in which the customer and your organization gets partial satisfaction and needs fulfillment.

By being thoroughly familiar with your organization's policies and procedures and your limits of authority, you will be prepared to negotiate with demanding customers. If they want something you cannot provide, you might offer an alternative that will satisfy them. Remember that your goal is complete customer satisfaction, but not at the expense of excessive loss to your organization.

Indecisive Customers

You will encounter people who cannot or will not make a decision. They sometimes spend long periods of time vacillating. They might even leave and come back later to continue their decision-making effort. Sometimes, they will bring along a friend on the second visit. In some cases, **indecisive customers** truly do not know what they want or need, as when they are looking for a gift for a special occasion. Sometimes such customers are afraid that they will choose incorrectly or need reassurance that the

indecisive customers
People who have difficulty making a decision or making a selection when given choices of products or services.

Indecisive people can be frustrating as you try to serve their needs. *What steps would you take to help a customer make a decision?*

product has the features they really need or will use later. In these situations, use all your product or service knowledge and communication skills. Otherwise, indecisive customers will occupy large amounts of your time and detract from your ability to do your job effectively or to assist other customers.

Be aware, however, that some people really are just looking as they check out sales, kill time between appointments, or relax, or they may be lonely and want to be around others. Strategies for dealing with an indecisive person are:

- *Be patient.* Keep in mind that, although indecisive people can be frustrating (especially if you have a high "D" behavioral style preference), they are still customers.

- *Ask open-ended questions.* Just as you would do with a customer who is dissatisfied, try to get as much background information as possible. The more data you can gather, the better you can evaluate the situation, determine needs, and assist in the solution of any problems.

- *Listen actively.* Focus on verbal and nonverbal messages for clues to determine emotions, concerns, and interests.

- *Suggest other options.* Offer alternatives that will help in decision making and reduce the customer's anxiety. Suggesting a warranty or exchange option may make the customer more secure in the decision-making process.

- *Guide decision making.* By assertively, not aggressively, offering suggestions or ideas and providing product and/or service information, you can help customers make a decision. Note that you are helping them, not making the decision for them. If you push your preferences on them, they may be dissatisfied later or have buyer's remorse, where they regret their decision and return the item. Then you, or someone else, will have to potentially deal with an unhappy customer.

Dissatisfied and Angry Customers

Occasionally, you will encounter **dissatisfied customers** or angry ones. Possibly they have been improperly served by you or one of your peers, or by a competitor in the past. Even if you were not personally involved in their previous experience, you represent the organization or you may be considered "just like that last service employee." Unfair as this may be, you have to try to make these customers happy. To do so, try the following strategies:

- *Listen.*
- *Remain positive and flexible.*
- *Smile, give your name, and offer assistance.*
- *Be compassionate and empathize without making excuses.*
- *Ask open-ended questions and verify information.*
- *Take appropriate action.*

Remember: if you get defensive, you become part of the problem and not part of the solution. Keep in mind what you read about the power of positive wording in Chapter 3. Figure 7.3 shows some examples of negative wording and some possible alternatives.

Dealing with angry people requires a certain amount of caution. For you to effectively serve an **angry customer,** you must move beyond the emotions to discover the reason for his or her anger. *Note*: Before dealing with customers, check with your supervisor to find out what your policies are

dissatisfied customer
Someone who either does not (or perceives that he or she does not) receive promised products or services.

angry customers
Customers who become emotional because either their needs are not met or they are dissatisfied with the services or products purchased from an organization.

Figure 7.3
Positive Wording

When faced with a customer encounter that isn't going well, remain positive in language. This will help you avoid escalating the situation.

Negative Words or Phrases	Positive Alternatives
Problem	Situation, issue, concern, challenge
No	What I (or) we can do is . . .
Cannot	What I (or) we can do is . . .
It's not my job (or my fault)	Although I do not normally handle that, I'm happy to assist you.
You'll have to (or you must . . .)	Would you mind . . . ? Would you please . . . ?
Our policy says . . .	While I'm unable to . . . What I can do is . . .

Dealing with Angry Customers

WORK IT OUT
7.4

WORK WITH A PARTNER.
Discuss situations in which you had to deal with an angry person. Think about what made the person angry and what seemed to reduce tension. Make a list of these factors and be prepared to share your list with the class. Use the results of this discussion to develop strategies to help calm angry people in the future.

and what level of authority you have in making decisions. This relates to empowerment discussed earlier in the book. By having this information before a customer encounter, you will have the tools and knowledge necessary to handle your customers effectively and professionally. Here are some possible tactics:

- *Be positive.* Tell the customer what you can do rather than what you cannot do.
- *Acknowledge the customer's feelings or anger.* By taking this approach, you've acknowledged the customer's feelings, demonstrated a willingness to assist, and asked the customer to participate in solving the problem. For example, "Mr. Philips, I can see that you are obviously upset by _____ and I want to help find a solution to this issue, however, I need your assistance to do that. Can you please explain what _____?"
- *Reassure.* Indicate that you understand why he or she is angry and that you will work to solve the problems. For example, "Ms. O'Hara, based on what you have explained, I can see why you are not satisfied with this product. I am going to immediately see what we can do to repair or replace the unit."
- *Remain objective.* Remember, angry customers are usually angry at the organization, product, or service that you represent, not at you.
- *Listen actively; determine the cause.* Whether the customer is "right" or "wrong" makes no difference in situations like these. Actively listening and trying to discover the problem will assure the customer that you are trying to take care of it for him or her.
- *Reduce frustrations.* Don't say or do anything that will create further tension. Do your best to handle the situation with this customer before serving another.

Before you can deal with a customer's business needs, you must first address the customer's emotional issues and try to calm him or her. *What would you do to calm such customer?*

Responding to Rudeness

WORKING WITH A PARTNER, DEVELOP A LIST OF RUDE COMMENTS THAT A CUSTOMER MIGHT MAKE TO YOU.

For example, the comment might be, "If you're not too busy, I'd like some assistance." Also list the responses you might give; for example, "If you could please wait, I'll be happy to assist you as soon as I finish, sir (or madam). I want to be able to give you my full attention and don't want to be distracted."

Customer Service Success Tip

Strive to do the unexpected and provide quality service to create a memorable customer experience— **underpromise and overdeliver** and do whatever you can (within your authority) to rectify a situation in which a customer is dissatisfied with your product or service in order to ensure customer satisfaction.

underpromise and overdeliver
A service strategy in which service providers strive for excellent customer service and satisfaction by doing more than they say they will do for the customer or exceeding customer expectations.

rude or inconsiderate customers People who seem to take pleasure in being obstinate and contrary when dealing with service providers and who seem to have their own agenda without concern for the feelings of others.

- *Negotiate a solution and conduct a follow-up.* Elicit ideas or negotiate an alternative with the customer. Follow up as soon as you can. Don't assume that the organization's system will work as designed.

Rude or Inconsiderate Customers

Some people seem to go out of their way to be offensive or to get attention. Although they seem confident and self-assured outwardly, they are often insecure and defensive. Some behaviors they might exhibit are raising the voice, demanding to speak to a supervisor, using profanity, cutting in front of someone else in a line, being verbally abrupt (snapping back at you) even though you're trying to assist, calling you by your last name, which they see on your name tag (e.g., "Listen, Smith"), ignoring what you say, or otherwise going out of the way to be offensive or in control. Try the following strategies for dealing with **rude or inconsiderate customers**:

- *Remain professional.* Just because the customer is exhibiting inappropriate behavior does not justify your reacting in kind. Remain calm, assertive, and in control of the situation. For example, if you are waiting on a customer and a rude person barges in or cuts off your conversation, pause, make direct eye contact, smile, and firmly say, "I'll be with you as soon as I finish with this customer, sir (or madam)." If he or she insists, repeat your comment and let the person know that the faster you serve the current customer, the faster you can get to the person waiting. Also, maintaining decorum may help win over the person or at least keep him or her in check.

- *Don't resort to retaliation.* Retaliation will only infuriate this type of customer, especially if you have embarrassed him or her in the presence of others. Remember that such people are still customers, and if they or someone else perceives your actions as inappropriate, you could lose more than just the battle at hand.

Talkative Customers

Some people phone or approach you and then spend excessive amounts of time discussing irrelevant matters such as personal experiences, family, friends, schooling, accomplishments, other customer service situations,

Building Your Skills

WORK IT OUT 7.6

GO ON A FIELD TRIP TO A VARIETY OF BUSINESSES OR STORES (POSSIBLY A MALL). As you visit these establishments, play the role of a customer and engage customer service professionals in lengthy conversation. Take note of the techniques they use to regain control of the conversation. Chances are, most, especially the more experienced, will allow you to talk and will respond to you rather than risk being rude. Remember the effective techniques described and jot them down.

and the weather. The following tips might help when dealing with **talkative customers**:

talkative customers
Customers exhibiting extroverted behavior who are very people-oriented.

- *Remain warm and cordial, but focused.* Recognize that this person's personality style is probably mainly expressive and that his or her natural inclination is to connect with others. You can smile, acknowledge comments, and carry on a brief conversation as you are serving this customer. For example, if the person comments that your last name is spelled exactly like his or her great aunt's and then asks where your family is from, you could respond with "That's interesting. My family is from . . . but I don't believe we have any relatives outside that area." You have responded but possibly cut off the next question. Anything less would probably be viewed as rude by the customer. Anything more could invite additional discussion. Your next statement should then be business-related (e.g., "Is there anything else I can assist you with today?").
- *Ask specific open-ended questions.* These types of questions can assist in determining needs and addressing customer concerns.
- *Use closed-end questions to control.* Once you have determined the customer's needs, switch to closed-end (discussed in Chapter 3) questions to better control the situation and limit the opportunity for the customer to continue talking.
- *Manage the conversation.* Keep in mind that if you spend a lot of time with one customer, other customers may be neglected. You can manage a customer encounter through questioning and through statements that let the customer know your objective is to serve customers. You might say, "I know you said you have a lot of shopping to do, so I won't keep you any longer. Thanks for coming in. Please let me know if I can assist in the future." Imply that you are ending the interaction to benefit the customer.

LO 7-4 Handling Emotions with the Emotion-Reducing Model

Concept Using the emotion-reducing model helps to calm the customer so that you can then solve the problem.

It is important to remember when dealing with people who are behaving emotionally (e.g., irritated, angry, upset, crying, or raising their voice) that they are typically upset with the structure, process, organization, or other factors over which you and/or they have no control. They are usually not upset with you (unless you have provoked them by exhibiting poor customer service skills or attitude). Remain rational and do not react to them emotionally.

Before you can get your customer to calm down, listen, and address the situation, you must first deal with her or his emotional state. Once you do this, you can proceed to use problem-solving strategies (discussed later in this chapter) to assist in solving the problem. Until you reduce the customer's emotional level, he or she will probably not listen to you or be receptive to what you are saying or your attempts to assist. In some cases, she or he may even become irritated because you seem uncaring.

To help calm the customer down, you must send customer-focused verbal and nonverbal messages. You need to demonstrate patience and use all the positive communication skills you read about in Chapters 3 to 5. Most important among those skills are the ability and the willingness to listen calmly to what the customer has to say without interrupting or interjecting your views. This lesson is taught to many law enforcement officers to help them deal with crisis situations such as domestic disturbances in order to help prevent situations from emotionally escalating. If your customer perceives that you are not attuned to his or her emotional needs or thinks that you are not working in his or her best interest, you become part of the problem, rather than part of the solution.

Keep in mind that a customer generally wants to be respected and acknowledged as an individual and as being important. As you interact with the customer, you can soften the situation and reduce emotion by providing customer-focused responses. Simple customer-focused messages can put you on a friendly (human) level while at the same time helping to calm the emotion.

The key to helping resolve any service breakdowns is to frame your problem resolution with customer-focused messages through use of the emotion-reducing model (Figure 7.4). Here's how the **emotion-reducing model** works: Assume a customer has a problem. As the customer approaches (or when you answer the telephone), greet him or her with "Good morning (or afternoon)," a smile, and open body language and gesturing (1. customer-focused message). Then, as the customer explains the issue

emotion-reducing model Process for reducing customer emotion in situations when frustration or anger exists.

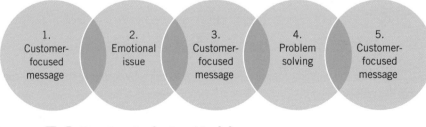

Figure 7.4 Emotion-Reducing Model

(emotional issue), you can offer statements such as, "I see," "I appreciate your concern (or frustration, or anger)," or "I understand how that can feel" (2. customer-focused). Such statements can help you connect psychologically with the customer. Continue to use positive reinforcement and communication throughout your interaction. Once the problem has been defined and resolved (3. problem solving), take one more opportunity at the end of your interaction to send a customer-focused message by smiling and thanking the customer for allowing you to assist. Also, one last apology may be appropriate for inconvenience, frustration, mistreatment, and so on (4. customer-focused).

LO 7-5 Reasons for Customer Defection

Concept Failing to meet the customer's needs, handling problems inefficiently, treating the customer unfairly, and using inadequate systems are reasons for the customer to leave you and go elsewhere.

Following a service breakdown, there is often a possibility that you may never see the customer again. This is potentially disastrous to your organization, because it costs five to six times as much to win a new customer as it costs to retain a current one. And, as we saw earlier in this chapter, a dissatisfied customer is also likely to tell other people about the bad experience. Thus, you and others in your organization must be especially careful to identify reasons for **customer defection** (Figure 7.5) and remedy potential and actual problems before they negatively affect customers.

customer defection
Customers often take their business to competitors when they feel that their needs or wants are not met or if they encounter breakdown in customer service or poor quality products.

Figure 7.5 Reasons for Customer Defection

Poor service and complacency. If customers perceive that you and/or your organization do not sincerely care about them or about solving their problems, they may go elsewhere. If a concern is important enough for the customer to verbalize (formally or informally) or to write down, it is important enough for you to take seriously. You should immediately address the problem by listening, gathering information, and taking appropriate action. Customer comments might be casual, for example, "You know, I sure wish you folks stocked a wider variety of rose bush colors. I love shopping here, but your selection is so limited." In this instance, you might write down the customer's name, phone number, and address and then follow up with your manager or buyers about it. Also, practice your questioning skills by asking, "What color did you have in mind?" or "What is your favorite color?" If the customer has a specific request, you could pass that along. You or someone else should try to obtain the item and then contact the customer to discuss your efforts and findings. Sometimes the obvious solutions are the ones that are overlooked, so be perceptive when dealing with customers and look for little clues such as these. It could mean the difference in continued business and word-of-mouth advertising by your customer.

Inappropriate complaint resolution. The key thing to remember about complaint resolution is that it is the customer's perception of the situation, not yours, that counts. If customers believe that they were not treated fairly, honestly, in a timely manner, and in an appropriate fashion, or if they are still dissatisfied, your efforts failed. Remember that only a small percentage of your customers complain. Second attempts at resolution by customers are almost unheard of.

Unmet needs. Customers have very specific needs to which you must attend. When these needs are not addressed or are unsatisfactorily met, the customer is likely to seek an alternative source of fulfillment.

So often, service providers make the mistake of trying to project their personal needs onto others. Their feeling is that "I like it, so everybody should like it." However, as you will read in Chapter 8, today's diverse world requires you to be more knowledgeable and accepting of the ideas, values, beliefs, and needs of others. Failure to be sensitive to diversity may set you, your organization, and your customers on a collision course. Remember what you have read about trust and how quickly it can be destroyed in relationships.

LO 7-6 Working with Internal Customers (Co-workers)

Concept Relationships with your internal customers are important. You should meet your commitments and build a professional reputation.

As we discussed in earlier chapters, you have to deal with internal as well as external customers. Although your interactions with internal customers may not be difficult, they can often be more sensitive than your dealings with outsiders. This is because if someone within your organization becomes irritated or dissatisfied with you, they don't necessarily go away. Instead, they might tell co-workers or your supervisor about the encounter, which can damage your reputation. They might also withdraw, which means that you might lose access to knowledge, information, or support that you need from them in the future.

After all, you see peers and co-workers regularly, and because of your job, office politics, and protocol, your interactions with them are ongoing. Therefore, extend all the same courtesies to internal customers that you do to external ones—in some cases, more so.

The importance of effective internal customer service cannot be underestimated. That is because your relationships with individuals and departments within your organization have far-reaching effects on the organization. Sound internal customer service practices can help to boost employee communication and morale while helping to enhance processes and procedures, reduce costs, increase productivity, and replace interdepartmental competition with interdepartmental cooperation. Through such internal cooperation, external customer service is enhanced. Some suggestions that might help you enhance your interactions with internal customers are given below.

Stay Connected

Since relationships within the organization are so important, go out of your way to make contact with internal customers periodically. You can do this by dropping by their work area to say hello, sending an e-mail, or leaving a voice mail message. If you know of a special occasion (e.g., birthday, anniversary, or the birth or adoption of a child, consider sending a card or an e-card to congratulate them. This helps strengthen the relationship and can keep the door to communication open so that if service does break down someday, you will have a better chance of hearing about it and solving the problem amiably. You might describe your co-workers as your "normal" internal customers, but do not forget the importance of your relationships with other employees, such as the cleaning crew (they service your office and work area), security force (they protect you, your organization, and your vehicle), support staff (who provide services like purchasing, payroll, travel, mail, and print services, and logistical assistance), and the information technology people (they maintain computer equipment). All these groups and many others within the organization add value and can be a big help to you at some point. Go out of your way to build and maintain strong interpersonal relationships with others in the workplace, especially if you have a behavioral style to which personal interactions are not second nature or as comfortable. A little extra effort to say good morning or do something nice for others can pay big dividends in the future. For example, if you have good rapport with co-workers and are someday downsized, you still have a support network or people who may know other people in the industry where you might find another job.

Meet All Commitments

Too often, service providers forget the importance of internal customers. Because of familiarity, they sometimes become lax and tend to not give the attention to internal customers that they would give to external customers. This can be a big mistake. For example, if you depend on someone else to obtain or send products or services to external customers, that relationship is as crucial as the ones you have with external customers. Don't forget that if you depend on internal suppliers for materials, products, or information, these people can negatively affect your ability to serve external customers by delaying or withholding the items you need. Such actions might be unintentional or intentional, depending on your relationship. Either way, your external customers suffer and your reputation and that of the organization are on the line.

To prevent, or at least reduce, the possibility of such breakdowns, honor all commitments you make to internal customers. If you promise to do something, do your best to deliver, and in the agreed-upon time. If you can't do something, say so when your internal customer asks. If something comes up that prevents you from fulfilling your commitment, let the customer know of the change in a timely manner.

Remember, it is better to exceed customer expectations than not meet them. If you beat a deadline, they will probably be pleasantly surprised and appreciative.

Ethical Dilemma 7.2

A co-worker promised to help you complete a project where you were to compile information and mail it to customers on Tuesday even though it was not her job. You have helped her in similar situations in the past. It is now Thursday and the co-worker still has not come to your aid and you are now behind schedule.

1. How would you handle this situation? Why?
2. Would you report the situation to your supervisor? Why or why not?
3. What effect might her behavior have on your relationship? Why?

Don't Sit on Your Emotions

Some people hold on to anger, frustration, and other negative emotions rather than get their feelings out into the open and dealing with them. Not only is this potentially damaging to health, for it might cause stress-related illnesses, but it can also destroy working relationships. Whenever something goes wrong or you are troubled by something, go to the person and, using the feedback skills you learned in Chapter 3, talk about the situation. Failure to do so can result in disgruntled internal customers, damage to the customer-supplier relationship, and damage to your reputation. Don't forget that you will continue to rely on your customer in the future, so you cannot afford a relationship problem.

Build a Professional Reputation

Through your words and actions, go out of your way to let your customer and your supervisor know that you have a positive, can-do, customer-focused attitude. Let them know that you will do whatever it takes to create an environment in which internal and external customers are important. Also, regularly demonstrate your commitment to proactive service. This means gathering information, products, and other tools before coming into contact with a customer so that you are prepared to deal with a variety of situations and people. It also means doing the unexpected for customers and providing service that makes them excited about doing business with you and your organization.

Adopt a Good-Neighbor Policy

Take a proactive approach to building internal relationships so that you can head off negative situations. If your internal customers are in your department, act in a manner that preserves sound working relationships. You can accomplish this in part by avoiding the following negative work habits:

- *Avoid gatherings of friends and loud conversation in your work space.* This can be especially annoying if the office setup consists of cubicles, as sound travels easily. Respect your co-workers' right to work in

Customer Service Tip

Be proactive in dealings with individuals and departments in your organization. This can go a long way to building and strengthening relationships and support. Instead of waiting for someone to ask for information, anticipate needs and provide it to them before they need it. Think of information, data, statistics, or pertinent information that would benefit others in the organization, as you read articles or attend training programs and share it with them. Most people will appreciate your interest and initiative and will likely reciprocate.

a professional environment. If you must hold meetings or gatherings, go to the cafeteria, conference room, or break room or some other place away from the work area.

- *Maintain good grooming and hygiene habits.* Demonstrate professionalism in your dress and grooming. Avoid excessive amounts of colognes and perfumes. This is important because some people have severe allergies to such products and if you are creating an environment where they cannot work, their performance and health suffer.

- *Don't overdo call forwarding.* Sometimes you must be away from your work space. Company policy may require that you forward your calls. Do not overdo forwarding your calls. Your co-workers may be inconvenienced and resentful if you do.

- *Avoid unloading personal problems.* Everyone has personal problems now and then. Do not bring personal problems to the workplace and burden coworkers with them. If you have personal problems and need assistance, go to your supervisor or team leader or human resources department and ask for some suggestions. Many organizations have professionally trained counselors available through their Employee Assistance Programs. If you get a reputation for often having personal problems—and bringing them to the workplace—your career could suffer.

- *Avoid office politics and gossip.* Your purpose in the workplace is to serve the customer and do your job. If you have extra time to spread gossip and network often with others, you should approach your supervisor or team leader about job opportunities in which you can learn new skills or take on additional responsibilities. This can increase your effectiveness and marketability in the workplace and enhance your value to the organization. The latter can be important in a bad economy where downsizing staff to save costs is an option used by many organizations.

- *Pitch in to help.* If you have spare time and your co-workers need assistance with a project, volunteer to help out. They may do the same at some point in the future when you are feeling overwhelmed with a project or assignment.

- *Be truthful.* One of the fastest ways for you to suffer a damaged relationship, or lose the trust and confidence of your co-workers and customers, is to be caught in a lie. Regard your word as your bond.

LO 7-7 Strategies for Preventing Dissatisfaction and Problem Solving

Concept Focusing on the customers' needs and seeking ways to satisfy their needs quickly while exceeding customer expectations are ways to prevent dissatisfaction.

The best way to deal with a service breakdown is to prevent it from occurring. Here are some specific **strategies for preventing dissatisfaction.**

strategies for preventing dissatisfaction Techniques used to prevent a breakdown in needs fulfillment when you are dealing with customers.

Think Like the Customer

Learn to use the interactive communication techniques described in this book. Once you've mastered them, set out to discover what customers want by observing nonverbal behavior, asking specific questions, and listening to their comments and responses. Learn to listen for their unspoken as well as verbalized needs, concerns, and questions. Think about how you would like to be served under the conditions you are dealing with and act accordingly.

Pamper the Customer

You do not have to give into a customer's every whim and request, but you should certainly attempt to provide the products and services promised, provide the best quality of service that you can deliver, and address their concerns professionally.

Make customers feel special and important. Treat them as if they are the center of your attention and that you are there for no other purpose than to serve them. Do the unexpected, and take any extra effort necessary to meet and exceed their needs. Even if you can't satisfy all their wishes, if you are positive, enthusiastic, and show initiative, customers can walk away feeling good about the encounter.

Respect the Customer

Before you begin focusing on customers' problems, take time to listen and show that you support them and their viewpoint. By using a people-centered approach to problem analysis and problem solving, you can win the customer over. With both of you working together, you can define the problem and jointly reach an acceptable solution. See Figure 7.6 for some strategies to focus on the customer's concerns.

Exceed Expectations

Go the extra mile by giving your customers exemplary service. Strive to get the highest rating possible on the relationship-rating point scale (see Chapter 10). To do so, work hard to understand what the customer wants and expects. Observe customers, monitor trends, and talk to customers. Constantly look for ways to go beyond the expected or what the competition provides. Provide it faster, better, and more efficiently than others, and exceed customer expectations. Do things for your customer that set your service attitude apart from that of other providers. Some things cost little or nothing and return your "investment" many times over through goodwill and positive word-of-mouth publicity. To raise your rating and please your customers, try some of these simple strategies:

> *Auto repair technician*: "After I rotated and balanced your tires, I checked and filled all your fluids, and also inspected all your hoses free of charge."

Focusing on the Customer

THINK ABOUT THE TECHNIQUES DESCRIBED IN THIS CHAPTER FOR FOCUSING ON THE CUSTOMER.

Make a list of additional strategies that you can you think of and then work with others to see what they came up with. Discuss how to implement the strategies in the workplace.

Clothing salesperson: "While you try on that outfit, I'll go pick out a couple of other blouses that would suit you perfectly."

Bank customer service representative: "While you are waiting for a loan officer, can I get you a cup of coffee?"

Hotel operator: "Along with your wake-up call, I'll have some complimentary coffee or tea brought up. Which would you prefer?"

Restaurant host: "The wait for a table is approximately 30 minutes. Can I get you a complimentary glass of wine or soft drink from the bar?"

When a customer takes the time to share a concern, complaint, or question, take the following actions:

React to remarks or actions. Let customers know that you heard what they said or received their written message. If the information is given in person, remember to use the verbal, nonverbal, and listening skills discussed earlier in this book. Smile and acknowledge their presence and comments. If you can't deal with them at that moment because you are serving another customer, let them know when you will be available. If customer comments are in writing, respond quickly. If a phone number is available, try calling to speed up the response and then follow up in writing.

Empathize. Let customers know that you are concerned, that you do appreciate their views, feelings, or concerns, and that you'll do your best to serve them. Really try to "feel their pain" and act as if you were resolving a personal issue of your own. Chances are you will then put more effort into it and appear more sincere.

Take action. Once you've gathered enough information to determine an appropriate response, get agreement from your customer and then act. The faster you act, the more important the customer will feel.

Reassure or reaffirm. Take measures to let customers know that you and the organization have their best interests at heart. Stress their value to you and your commitment to resolving their complaints. Part of this is providing your name and phone number, and telling them what actions you will take; for example, "Mrs. Lupe, I appreciate your concern about not receiving the package on time. My name is Bob Lucas, my number is 407-555-6134, and I will research the problem. Once I've discovered what happened, I'll call you back. If it looks as though it will take more than a day, I'll call you by 4 P.M. tomorrow to update you. Is that acceptable?"

Follow up. Once a customer transaction is completed, make sure that any necessary follow-up actions are begun. For example, if appropriate, make an additional phone call to customers to be sure that they received their orders, that they are satisfied with your actions, or simply to reassure them and provide an opportunity for questions. If you promised to take some action, do so and coordinate with others who need to be involved.

Figure 7.6
Customer Focus Strategies

Problem-Solving Model
The process used by a service provider to assist customers in determining and selecting appropriate solutions to their issues, concerns, or needs.

Travel agent: "Since this is your honeymoon cruise, I've arranged for a complimentary bottle of champagne to be delivered to your room along with a book of discount coupons for onboard services."

Call center representative: "Because you were on hold so long to place your order, I'm taking 10 percent off your order."

Dentist: "For referring your friend to us, I've told my receptionist to take $25 off your next cleaning fee."

Plumber: "While I was fixing your toilet stopper, I noticed that the lift arm was almost rusted through, so I changed it too, at no charge."

LO 7-8 The Problem-Solving Process

Concept Helping customers find a solution to a problem through use of the six-step Problem-Solving Model to strengthen customer provider relationships.

To solve a problem, you need to first identify the problem and determine if the problem is one that should be solved. For instance, some customers will complain about things that are legitimately not your responsibility (e.g., a customer bought a drill and used it for over 30 days, then wanted to return it for a replacement because he left it outside on a construction site during a rain shower and now it will not work). Once you decide to solve the problem, follow the six proven steps to problem solving. Figure 7.7 shows a concise six-step **Problem-Solving Model.**

Before you begin to solve a customer's problem, consider the fact that he or she may not really want you to "solve the problem." In some cases, a person simply wants to vent frustration or be heard. This is where the empathetic listening you have read about will come in handy. In many cases, your customer will often have a solution in mind when he or she calls or comes in. Your role may be to simply listen and offer to facilitate the implementation of the suggested solution. In some situations, you may have to "plant a seed" by asking an open-ended question that suggests a solution. If the customer picks up on your "seed" and nourishes it, you end up with an outcome for which he or she feels ownership. For example, assume that a customer wants a product that you do not have in stock. Instead of saying, "I'm sorry, that item is out of stock," you could ask a

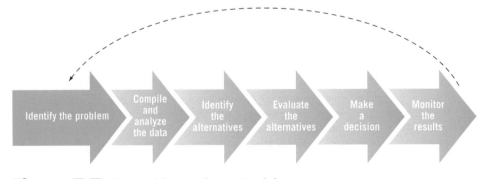

Figure 7.7 **The Problem-Solving Model**

question such as "How do you think _____ would work as an alternative?" You have now subtly made a suggestion without saying, "You could use _____ instead. It does the same thing."

If you jointly solve a problem, the customer often feels ownership for the solution—that he or she has made the decision. This customer is likely to be a satisfied customer. The following six steps describe some key actions involved in this process.

1. Identify the Problem

Before you can decide on a course of action, you must first know the nature and scope of the issue you are facing. Often, the customer may not know how to explain his or her problem well, especially if he or she speaks another language primarily or has a communication-related disability. In such cases, it is up to you to do a little detective work and ask questions or review available information. In some cases, you might have to seek the assistance of someone else (a co-worker or nearby customer) to act as a translator. In the case of persons with a disability, perhaps they can write down their message.

Begin your journey into problem solving by apologizing for any inconvenience you or your organization has caused. The customer likely wants someone to be responsible. A simple, "I'm sorry you were inconvenienced, how may I assist you?" coupled with some of the other techniques listed in this book can go a long way to mending the relationship. Take responsibility for the problem or concern, even if you didn't actually cause it. Remember that you represent the organization to the customer. Since you are representing the company, you are "chosen" to be responsible. Don't point fingers at other employees, policies, procedures, or other factors. It is also important to let the customer know that you are sincerely remorseful (on behalf of the organization) and that you will do whatever possible to quickly and effectively resolve the issue.

To learn as much about the issue as you can, start by speaking directly to the customer, when possible. Collect any documentation or other background information available.

For example if the problem were a malfunctioning television, ask questions of your customers similar to the following:

When and where did you buy the unit?

When did you first notice the issue?

What model is it?

What, exactly, is wrong?

Does it have an antenna attached?

Is there a remote control?

Have you checked to see that the power cord is firmly attached?

Have you tried using a different electrical outlet?

Have you checked to make sure that the power strip is turned on?

it is probably best to approach the co-worker in a friendly and nonthreatening manner, using some strategies you read about in Chapters 3 and 4. Ask why she failed to assist as she agreed and listen to her response rationally. Depending on what she tells you, let her know that you are disappointed that she failed to either help or come to you before now to explain that she could not do so. Also, let her know how you feel about her failure to come forward. The last is important because people often do not realize the effect their behavior has on others and how it might impact relationships.

2. Would you report the situation to your supervisor? Why or why not?

Since this was not a task assigned to both of you, it is probably best not to go to your supervisor or to point fingers and blame your co-worker for your missing the deadline. After all, it is your job and not hers.

3. What effect might her behavior have on your relationship? Why?

Because relationships are built on trust, your co-worker's behavior could certainly negatively affect your relationship in the future, depending on her reason for failing to assist you. Even if she has a good reason, the fact that she did not at least let you know of the obstacle could influence how you feel toward her and your ability to trust and work with her effectively in the future.

Customer Service in a Diverse World

chapter 8

Diversity is the one true thing we all have in common. Celebrate it every day.
—Anonymous

Learning Outcomes

After completing this chapter, you will be able to:

8-1 Recognize that diversity is not a bad thing.

8-2 Describe some of the characteristics that make people unique.

8-3 Embrace the need to treat customers as individuals.

8-4 Determine actions for dealing with various types of people.

8-5 Identify a variety of factors that make people diverse and that help to better serve them.

8-6 Communicate effectively with a diverse customer population.

Key Terms

- Americans with Disabilities Act of 1990
- attitudes
- baby boomer
- beliefs
- blogs
- Chicano culture
- collective cultures
- concept of time
- conflict resolution style
- cultural diversity
- customers with disabilities
- diversity
- expectations of privacy
- face
- foreign-born people
- form of address
- gender roles
- hearing disabilities
- Hispanic culture
- inclusive
- individualistic cultures
- interpersonal relationship
- Latino culture
- mobility or motion impairments
- modesty
- monochronic
- ownership of property
- Platinum Rule
- podcasts
- polychronic
- respect for elders
- Telecommunications Relay Service (TRS)
- Telecommunications Device for the Deaf (TDD)
- values
- vision disabilities
- wiki
- younger customers

In the Real World Online Retail—Netflix, Inc.

NETFLIX, INC. HAS REVOLUTIONIZED THE WAY PEOPLE RENT MOVIES BY BRINGING the content directly to the consumer. They do this by providing more movies and television episodes over the Internet and through the mail than any other company. This approach better meets the needs of a fast-paced, in-a-hurry, got-to-have-it-now society where customers demand what they want immediately, coupled with more control and value for their money. Because of their innovative approach to product and service delivery, they have in effect shut out traditional home entertainment companies like Blockbuster, which filed for Chapter 11 bankruptcy in September 2010 and restructured in an attempt to compete and survive. In Blockbuster's case, management did not recognize changing trends and needs in the industry and society fast enough and failed to modify its business model to address the needs of a technology-literate and driven customer base.

Founded in Scotts Valley, California, in 1997, Netflix had over 14 million members early in 2010 and over 4,000 employees at its headquarters and in shipping centers; the company continually exceeds earnings expectations on Wall Street. On a typical business day, the company ships over 2 million DVDs of 56,000 unique titles. With the addition of compatibility to Nintendo Wii, Xbox 360, PlayStation 3, IPad, and numerous other home entertainment systems, the organization is positioned to continue its stellar growth as each new technology-savvy generation comes forward.

Like any highly visible organization, Netflix has had its share of complaints and lawsuits filed by customers and groups that were not pleased with operating policies and procedures. Even so, the organization continues to receive high praises from various sources for its level of service. Among its many service accolades and awards, Netflix has been recognized for 10 out of 11 years since 2005 by ForeSee Results as the number one retail Web site for customer satisfaction. It also received:

Fast Company magazine 2005 Customers First Award.

Retail Innovator of the Year award by the National Retail Federation.

Number one online retailer by Nielsen Online in 2007.

Number one company for customer satisfaction in 2010 by the American Customer Satisfaction Index.

Think About It

Based on this organization's profile, what you can locate on the Internet and what you know about the company, answer the following questions. Be prepared to discuss your responses.

1. What do you feel are the strengths of the company from a customer perspective? Explain.
2. How do you feel that Netflix has done in dealing with more established competition from a service perspective? Explain.

3. What diversity factors in society do you feel have allowed Netflix to gain and maintain popularity and growth? Explain the relationship of these factors to Netflix's growth.
4. What do you think are Netflix's future growth opportunities related to customer service? Explain.
5. Are you a customer of Netflix? Why or why not?
6. Would you want to work for Netflix? Why or why not?

Quick Preview

Before reviewing the chapter content, respond to the following questions by placing a "T" for true or an "F" for false on the rules. Use any questions you miss as a checklist of material to which you will pay particular attention as you read through the chapter. For those you get right, congratulate yourself, but review the sections they address in order to learn additional details about the topic.

_____ **1.** Diversity is an important aspect of everyone's life that can present many positive opportunities or negative challenges depending on your knowledge of other people and groups.

_____ **2.** Many people only associate the term diversity with the word cultural, which describes the differences between groups of people from various countries and with differing beliefs.

_____ **3.** The diverse nature of your customer population requires you to be aware of the various ways people from different cultures interact in the business setting.

_____ **4.** Values are the "rules" that people use to evaluate situations, make decisions, interact with others, and deal with conflict.

_____ **5.** In some cultures, direct eye contact is often discouraged, for it suggests disrespect or overfamiliarity.

_____ **6.** Today, all cultures use less formality in the business environment and do not stress the importance of using titles and family names as often as they did in the past.

_____ **7.** When encountering someone who speaks a language other than yours, you should avoid jokes, words, or acronyms that are tied to sports, historical events, or specific aspects of your own culture.

_____ **8.** In serving customers from some cultures, it is important to avoid the use of the word "no" because this word may cause the customer to become embarrassed or experience a "loss of face."

_____ **9.** According to the U.S. Census Bureau, over 54 billion Americans have some level of disability.

_____ **10.** When a customer has a disability, the disability should be deemphasized by thinking of the person first and the disability second.

_____ **11.** When dealing with an elderly customer, you should always be respectful.

_____ **12.** Younger customers are as valuable as those in any other group and should be served professionally.

Answers to Quick Preview can be found at the end of the chapter.

LO 8-1 The Impact of Diversity

Concept Diversity is an important aspect of everyone's life. Encounters with others give us an opportunity to expand our knowledge of others.

As the world grows smaller economically and otherwise (e.g., in world trade, international travel, outsourcing and offshoring of jobs, international partnerships between organizations and technologically transmitted information exchange), the likelihood that you will have contact on the job with people from other cultures, or who are different from you in other ways, increases significantly. This likelihood also carries over into your personal life. **Diversity** is encountered everywhere (over the telephone and Internet and in supermarkets, religious organizations, public transportation) and so is an important aspect of everyone's life. Although it presents challenges in making us think of differences and similarities, it also enriches our lives—each encounter we have with another person gives us an opportunity to expand our knowledge of others and build relationships, while growing personally.

LO 8-2 Defining Diversity

Concept Diversity is not a simple matter; it is not difficult to deal with if you are fair to people and keep an open mind.

The word *diversity* encompasses a broad range of differences. Many people only associate the term diversity with **cultural diversity,** which has to do with the differences between groups of people, depending on their country of origin and their beliefs. They fail to recognize that diversity is not just cultural. Certainly, diversity occurs within each cultural group; however, many other characteristics are involved. For example, within a group of Japanese people are subgroups such as males, females, children, the elderly, athletes, thin people, gay or lesbian people, Buddhists, Christians, married and single people, to mention just a few of the possible diverse characteristics, beliefs, and values.

Diversity is not a simple matter, yet it is not difficult to deal with. Start your journey to better understanding of diversity by being fair to people and keeping an open mind when interacting with them. In fact, when you look more closely at, and think about, diversity it provides wonderful opportunities because people from varying groups and geographic locations bring with them special knowledge, experience, and value. This is because even though people may have differences or potentially look different, they also have many traits in common. Their similarities form a solid basis for successful interpersonal relationships if you are knowledgeable and think of people as individuals; you can then capitalize on their uniqueness. If you cannot think of the person instead of the group, you may stereotype people—lump them together and treat them all the same. This is a recipe for interpersonal disaster, service breakdown and organizational failure.

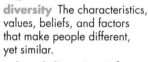

diversity The characteristics, values, beliefs, and factors that make people different, yet similar.

cultural diversity Refers to the differences and similarities attributed to various groups of people within a culture.

Platinum Rule Term coined by speaker and author Tony Alessandra related to going beyond the step of treating customers the way you want to be treated, to the next level of treating them the way they would like to be treated.

Customer Service Success Tip

To better ensure service success, find out what customers want and treat them as they want to be treated. This concept has been termed the **Platinum Rule.**[1]

A key point to remember is that the concept of treating others as you would like to be treated (a value common in many religions—e.g., The Golden Rule) can lead to service breakdowns. This is because your customers are unique and may not value what you do or want to be treated as you do.

Encountering Diversity

TAKE A FEW MINUTES TO THINK ABOUT DIVERSITY AND WHAT IT
MEANS TO YOU.
Write your own definition of diversity.

During the past week, in what situations have you encountered someone from a
different culture, group, or background in the workplace or at school (someone whose
values or beliefs differed from yours or who looked or dressed differently from you or
your group)? Make a list of the diverse people that you met (e.g., where they were
from, why they were different from you, and how they were similar to you) and the
situations encountered.

Once you have created your responses, form a group with two to three other
students, share your responses, and discuss the implications of providing quality
service to customers who are different from you.

The basic customer service techniques related to communication found
in this book can be applied to many situations in which you encounter
customers from various groups. Coupled with specific strategies for adapting to special customer needs, these techniques provide the tools you need
to provide excellent customer service.

Some factors that make people different are innate and they are born
with them, such as height, weight, hair color, gender, skin color, physical
and mental condition, and sibling birth order. All these factors contribute
to our uniqueness and help or inhibit us throughout our lives, depending
on the perceptions we and others have. Other factors that make us unique
are learned or gained through our environment and our life experiences.
Examples of these factors include religion, **values, beliefs,** economic level,
lifestyle choices, profession, marital status, education, and political affiliation. These factors are often used to assign people to categories. Caution
must be used when considering any of these characteristics, since group-
ing people can lead to stereotyping and possible discrimination.

The bottom line is that all of these factors affect each customer encounter. Your awareness of differences and of your own preferences is crucial in
determining the success you will have in each instance.

values Long-term appraisals
of the worth of an idea, person, place, thing, or practice
held by individuals, groups, or
cultures. They affect attitudes
and behavior.

beliefs Perceptions or
assumptions that individuals or
cultures maintain. These perceptions are based on past
experiences, memories, and
interpretations and influence
how people act and interact
with certain individuals or
groups.

LO 8-3 Customer Awareness

Concept Applying your own cultural practices and beliefs to a situation involving someone from another culture can result in frustration, anger, poor service, and lost business.

Aren't all customers alike? Emphatically, no! No two people are alike, no
two generations are alike, and no two cultures are alike. In addition, as we
discussed in Chapter 7, each customer has needs based on his or her own
perceptions and situation.

In our highly mobile, technologically connected world, it is not unusual to
encounter a wide variety of people with differing backgrounds, experiences,

religions, modes of dress, values, and beliefs within the course of a single day. All these factors affect customer needs and create situations in which you must be alert to the verbal and nonverbal messages that indicate those needs. Moreover, the diverse nature of your customer population requires you to be aware of the various ways people from different cultures or groups interact in the business setting. Applying your own cultural practices and beliefs to a situation involving someone from another culture can result in frustration, anger, poor service, and lost business.

LO 8-4 The Impact of Cultural Values

Concept Values often dictate which behaviors and practices are acceptable or unacceptable. These values may or may not have a direct bearing on serving the customer.

Although many cultures have similar values and beliefs, specific cultural values are often taught to members of particular groups starting at a very young age. This does not mean that a particular group's values and beliefs are better or worse than those of any other culture; they are simply important to that particular group. These values often dictate which behaviors and practices are acceptable or unacceptable. They may or may not have a direct bearing on serving the customer, but they can have a very powerful influence on what the customer wants, needs, thinks is important, and is willing to seek or accept. Values can also influence your perceptions and actions toward others. Being conscious of differences can lead to a better understanding of customers and potentially reduce conflict or misunderstandings in dealing with them.

The mobility of modern-day society may put you in regular contact with customers from a variety of cultures. The more informed you are about similarities and differences, the greater the likelihood that you will provide quality service. *How should you provide customer service to someone of another culture?*

Many service providers take values for granted. This is a mistake. Values are the "rules" that people use to evaluate issues or situations, make decisions, interact with others, and deal with conflict. As a whole, a person's value system often guides thinking and helps him or her determine right from wrong or good from bad. From a customer service perspective, values often strongly drive customer needs and influence the buying decision. Values also differ from one culture to another, depending on its views on ethics, morals, religion, and many other factors. For example, if customers perceive clothing as either too sexy or too conservative, they may not purchase the items, depending on what need they are trying to meet. Or they may not buy a house because it's in the perceived "wrong" neighborhood.

Values are based on the deeply held beliefs of a culture or subculture. These beliefs might be founded in religion, politics, or group mores. They drive thinking and actions and are so powerful that they have served as the basis for arguments, conflicts, and wars for hundreds of years.

To be effective in dealing with others, service providers should not ignore the power of values and beliefs, nor should they think that their value system is better than that of someone else's. The key to service success is to be open-minded and accept that someone else has a different belief system that determines his or her needs. With this in mind you, as a service provider, should strive to use all the positive communication and needs identification you have read about thus far in order to satisfy the customer.

Cultural values can be openly expressed or subtly demonstrated through behavior. They can affect your interactions with your customers in a variety of ways. In the next few pages, consider the connection of values with behavior, and how you can adjust your customer service to ensure a satisfactory experience for diverse customers. Keep in mind that the degree to which customers have been acculturated to prominent cultural standards will determine how they act.

Your goal is to provide excellent service to the customer. In order to achieve success in accomplishing this goal, you must be sensitive to, tolerant of, and empathetic toward customers. You do not need to adopt the beliefs of others, but you should adapt to them to the extent that you provide the best service possible to all of your customers. As mentioned earlier, apply the Platinum Rule of service when dealing with customers.

Modesty

Modesty is exhibited in many ways. In some cultures (e.g., Muslim and Quaker) conservative dress by women is one manifestation of modesty. For example, in some cultures women demonstrate modesty and a dedication to traditional beliefs by wearing a veil or head dress. Such practices are tied to religious and cultural beliefs that originated hundreds of years ago. In other cultures, nonverbal communication cues send messages. For example, direct eye contact is viewed as an effective communication approach in the many Western cultures, and lack of eye contact could suggest dishonesty or lack of confidence to a Westerner. In some cultures (India, Iran, Iraq, and Japan), direct eye contact is often discouraged, in particular between men and women or between people who are of different social or business status, for it is considered disrespectful or rude. Often a sense of modesty is instilled into people at an early age (more so in females). Modesty may be demonstrated by covering the mouth or part of the face with an open hand when laughing or speaking, or through avoiding direct eye contact in certain situations.

Another way that you might offend someone's modesty is through your environment. For example, if you have a waiting room that has magazines which show advertisements with scantily clad models or a television or radio station broadcasting for customers that contains sexual situations (e.g., soap operas) or racy talk show hosts, you may want to rethink the situation.

modesty Refers to the way that cultures view propriety of dress and conduct.

surnames: one from their father (listed first) and one from their mother (e.g., Jose Ricardo Gutierrez (father's surname) Martinez (mother's surname). Usually, when addressing the person, use a title only with the father's surname (e.g., Mr. or Mrs. Gutierrez).

Impact on Service

A customer's preference for a particular name or form of address can have an impact upon your ability to effectively deal with him or her. If you start a conversation with someone and immediately alienate the person by incorrectly using his or her name, you may not be able to recover. Moreover, informality or improper use of family names could send a message of lack of knowledge or concern for the customer as an individual or as being important to you.

Respect for Elders

In most cultures, some level of respect is paid to older people. Often this **respect for elders** is focused more on males (when older men are viewed as revered, as among Chinese). This arises from a belief that with age come knowledge, experience, wisdom, authority, and often, higher status. Thus, respect for or deference to elders is normal. Also, in many cultures age brings with it unique privileges and rights (such as the right to rule or to be the leader). For example, this is true in many Native American cultures.[2]

respect for elders A value held by people from many cultures.

interpersonal relationship Focuses on the need for service providers to build strong bonds with customers.

Impact on Service

You must be careful to pay appropriate respect when speaking to older customers (of both sexes). Further, you should be sensitive to the fact that if the customer demands to speak to a senior person or to the manager or owner, he or she may simply be exhibiting a customary expectation for his or her culture or generation. If you can assist without creating conflict in such situations, do so; if not, honor the request when possible.

Importance of Relationships

In many Asian, Latin American, and Middle Eastern cultures, the building of a strong **interpersonal relationship** is extremely important before business is conducted. For example, in Indonesia, Egypt, El Salvador, Myanmar (Burma), Korea, China, and Japan it is not unusual to have a number of meetings with people in an organization before coming to an agreement. Lunch, dinner, and office meetings often occur for weeks before an agreement is reached. Also, unless you reach the right level of management in the organization for these meetings, all your efforts may be wasted. Figure 8.1 shows a partial listing of some of the world's more relationship-focused countries where building relationships before conducting business is often crucial.

Bangladesh	Indonesia	Myanmar	Saudi Arabia
Brazil	Iran	Pakistan	Singapore
China	Iraq	Philippines	South Korea
Columbia	Japan	Poland	Thailand
Egypt	Kuwait	Qatar	Turkey
Greece	Malaysia	Romania	Vietnam
India	Mexico	Russia	

Figure 8.1

Relationship-Focused Countries (Partial Listing)

Impact on Service

Failure to establish support or an environment of trust could lead to a breakdown in service and/or lost customers. This does not mean that you should hesitate to assume a quicker familiarity with customers from such cultures. This could also alienate them. Instead, when you will be having ongoing contact or doing repeat business, follow the customers' lead. Get to know them and share information about your organization and yourself that can lead to mutual respect and trust. You may find that you also have to take time at the beginning of each encounter with your established customers to reestablish the relationship. This may involve spending time in conversations related to nonbusiness topics (e.g., their health, sports, hobbies, pets, or other topics in which the customer is interested). Just remember to familiarize yourself with cultural manners and etiquette for the customer's country before meeting in order to avoid cultural taboos. For example, it is inappropriate for a male to ask a male counterpart from many Middle Eastern countries about his wife or daughter.

Relationship building may also involve presenting gifts to persuade various people in the organization that you are a friend and have their interests at heart. Only then can you proceed to determine needs and provide service. People from many countries view this as an appropriate form of etiquette, while others may label such gratuities as bribes. Whatever your belief, if the practice is a cultural norm, you may do well to follow it when dealing with customers from other regions of the world.

Gender Roles

Culturally and individually, people view the role of men and women differently. Although **gender roles** are continually evolving throughout the world, decision making and authority are often clearly established as male prerogatives within many cultures, subcultures, or families. For example, in many Middle Eastern, Asian, South American, and European countries, women have often not gained the respect or credibility in the business environment that they have achieved in many parts of North

gender roles Behaviors attributed to or assigned by societal norms.

262   Part Three   Building and Maintaining Relationships

America. In some countries it is not unusual for women to be expected to take a "seen and not heard" role or to remain out of business transactions. In Korea and other Pacific Rim countries, it is rare for women to participate in many business operations. Men often still have higher social status than females. You do not have to agree with these practices, but you will need to take them into consideration when facing them in some customer encounters. When serving customers from different countries, you would do well to remember that people leave a country, but they take their cultural norms and values with them. Failure to consider alternative ways of dealing with people in certain instances might cause you to react negatively to a situation and nonverbally communicate your bias.

Impact on Service

If you are a female dealing with a male whose cultural background is like one of those just described, he may reject your assistance and ask for a male service provider. If you are a male dealing with a male and female from such a culture, do not be surprised if your conversation involves only the male. Attempts to draw a woman into such a transaction or make direct eye contact and smile may embarrass, offend, or even anger customers and/or their family members who are present. Generally, people who have lived or worked in Western cultures for longer periods will acculturate and not take offense to more direct behaviors that are meant to convey friendliness and to engage customers (e.g., smiling, engaging in small talk about families, or compliments on dress).

Attitude toward Conflict

Conflict is possible when two people come together in a customer environment, but it does not have to happen. By recognizing your biases and preferences, and being familiar with other cultures, you can reduce the potential for disagreement. Certainly, there will be times when a customer initiates conflict. In such instances all you can do is to use the positive communication techniques described throughout this book.

Many times, **attitudes** toward conflict are rooted in the individual's culture or subculture and based on behavioral style preference (discussed in Chapter 6). Some cultures are **individualistic cultures** (emphasis is placed on individuals' goals, as in Western countries), and some are **collective cultures** (individuals are viewed as part of a group, as in Japan or in Native American cultures). Members of individualistic cultures are likely to take a direct approach to conflict, whereas people whose culture is collective may address conflict indirectly, using an informal mediator in an effort to prevent loss of face or embarrassment for those involved. Even within subcultures of a society, there are often differing styles of communication and dealing with conflict. Of course, regardless of culture or group, people choose different forms of **conflict resolution styles** on the basis of personality style preferences.

attitudes Emotional responses to people, ideas, and objects. They are based on values, differ between individuals and cultures, and affect the way people deal with various issues and situations.

individualistic cultures Groups in which members value themselves as individuals who are separate from their group and responsible for their own destiny.

collective cultures Members of a group sharing common interests and values. They see themselves as an interdependent unit and conform and cooperate for the good of the group.

conflict resolutions style The manner in which a person handles conflict. People typically use one of five approaches to resolving conflict— avoidance, compromise, competition, accommodation, or collaboration.

Impact on Service

Depending on the individuals you encounter and their cultural background, you and your customers may deal differently with conflict. If you use the wrong strategy, emotions could escalate and customer dissatisfaction could follow. The key is to listen and remain calm, especially if the customer becomes agitated.

The Concept of Time

In relation to time, people and societies are often referred to as being either **monochronic** or **polychronic.** People from monochronic societies tend to do one thing at a time, take time commitments seriously, are often focused on short-term projects or relationships, and adhere closely to plans. On the other hand, polychronic people are used to distractions, juggle multiple things (e.g., conversations) without feeling stressed, consider time as a guide and flexible commodity, work toward long-term deadlines, and base promptness on relationships.

People from the United States are typically very time-conscious (monochronic). You often hear such phrases as "time is money," "faster than a New York minute," and "time is of the essence," which stress their impatience and need to maximize time usage. Similarly, in Germany, punctuality is almost a religion, and being late is viewed as very unprofessional and rude. In most business settings in the United States, anyone over 5 minutes late for a meeting is often chastised. In many colleges and universities, etiquette dictates that students wait no longer than 15 to 20 minutes when an instructor (depending on whether he or she is a full or associate professor) is late for a class. North Americans tend to expect people from other cultures to be as time-conscious as they are; however, this is not always the case. For example, it is not unusual for people from Arab countries (polychronic) to be a half hour or more late for an appointment or for a person from Hispanic and some Asian cultures to be an hour late. It is also not unusual for people from such cultures to fail to show up for an appointment at all. A phrase used by some Asian Indians sums up the concept and justifies the lateness: "Indian standard time." Such tardiness is not viewed as disrespect for the time of others or rudeness; it is simply indicative of a cultural value or way of life. Figure 8.2 lists countries according to their **concept of time.**

monochronic
Refers to the perception of time as being a central focus with deadlines being a crucial element of societal norms.

polychronic Refers to the perception of time as a fluid commodity that does not interfere with relationships and elements of happiness.

concept of time Term used to describe how certain societies view time as either polychromic of monochronic.

Impact on Service

In Western and other monochronic cultures you are expected to be punctual. This is a crucial factor in delivering effective service. Although others may not have the same beliefs and may be late for meetings, you must observe time rules in order to project an appropriate image and to satisfy the needs of your customers and organization.

Figure 8.2
Monochronic and Polychronic Countries

Most cultures can be described as either monochronic or polychronic. Some are both in that people exhibit one focus in the workplace and another with relationships. In some countries, a monochronic approach is prevalent in major urban areas, whereas a polychronic view is taken elsewhere. The following is a sampling of countries and their perspective on time.

Monochronic	Polychronic		Both
Australia	Africa	Latvia	Brazil
England	Bahrain	Lebanon	France
Canada	Bangladesh	Mexico	Japan
Czech Republic	Cambodia	Myanmar	Spain
Germany	China	Native American tribes	
Hungary	Croatia	Pakistan	
New Zealand	Ethiopia	Philippines	
Norway	Estonia	Portugal	
The Netherlands	Greece	Romania	
Poland	India	Russia	
Slovakia	Indonesia	Saudi Arabia	
Sweden	Ireland	Serbia	
Switzerland	Italy	South Korea	
United States	Java	Thailand	
	Jordan	Turkey	
	Kuwait	Ukraine	
	Laos	Vietnam	

Ownership of Property

ownership of property
Refers to how people of a given culture view property.

In many cultures (e.g., Buddhist, certain African tribes, and the Chickasaw Indian Nation) **ownership of property,** or accumulation of worldly goods or wealth, is frowned upon. In the case of the Chickasaw Indians and other native tribes in North America, such things as the earth, nature, natural resources, possessions, and individual skills are shared among the tribal group. They are not to be owned or kept from others, for the Creator gave them.[3] Many devout Buddhists believe that giving away personal belongings to others can help them reach a higher spiritual state. Thus the amassing of material things is not at all important to them and is often frowned upon.

Customer Service Success Tip

By being aware of the time values that you and your customers have and proceeding accordingly; you can reduce your own stress level when dealing with customers or clients from other cultures.

Impact on Service

People have differing levels of needs. Ask customers what their needs are and listen to their responses. Don't persist in upgrading a customer's request to a higher level or more expensive product if he or she declines your suggestion. You may offend and lose a customer. Of course, if you are in sales, you must make a judgment on whether an objection is one that you should attempt to overcome or whether it is culturally based and means no.

✳ Ethical Dilemma 8.2

Assume that you work for an organization that has a zero tolerance policy related to discrimination based on characteristics such as race, color, national origin, and other protected categories. While working one day, you overhear one co-worker talking to another about a customer from a Middle Eastern country who just walked out of the store. The customer had been dressed in his native garb (e.g., a flowing floor-length garment called a *Jellabiya* with a turban). Apparently the customer did not speak English well and had difficulty getting his point across to your co-worker. You heard the co-worker remark to his peer, "It really makes me mad that these rag heads come over here, don't learn our language and then expect us to go out of the way to provide them with what they want. If I had my way, I'd put them all back on a camel and send them packing back to whatever hole they crawled out of." He continued, "That guy might have gotten what he wanted, but I'll have the last laugh. I told him that I would make sure his credit card gets credited for an overcharge as soon as the system comes back on line, but that is never going to happen." The workers both laughed as they walked away.

You are well aware of the organization's nondiscrimination policy and have respect for anyone who comes to this country and makes an effort to assimilate into the culture. This is because your parents and grandparents all immigrated from Eastern Europe and you are first-generation North American.

1. Have you ever witnessed similar situations in the workplace? Explain.
2. From a service perspective, is this situation a problem? Explain.
3. What would you do or say about the incident that you just witnessed? Explain.
4. If you fail to act in this situation, what are possible repercussions? What about if you do act?

LO 8-5 Providing Quality Service to Diverse Customer Groups

Concept As a service provider, you should become proficient in working with customers with language differences and disabilities; you also need to work with young and elderly customers.

Given the potential diversity of your customer base, it may be impossible to establish a service strategy for each group. However, you should think of what you might do to address the needs of some of the larger categories of customers with whom you will probably come into contact. The next few sections provide some strategies for dealing effectively with people from four diverse groups: customers with language differences, those with disabilities, elderly customers, and young customers.

Customers with Language Differences

One major obstacle for service providers in the United States is that many adults believe that just over half (52 percent) of the world's population

foreign-born people
Refers to people not born in a given country.

speaks English. According to findings from the National Foreign Language Center in Washington, DC, cited by Harris Interactive,[4] the number is closer to 20 percent.

Bureau of Labor Statistics figures estimate that over 34 24.1 million (15.6%) of the U.S. workforce are **foreign-born people**.[5] These figures are representative of the number of people who live in the United States but were not born in the country. The key to effectively serving all customers, and particularly people from different cultures, is flexibility. Since you are likely to encounter customers from virtually any country in the world when you work in today's business environment, you need to be prepared. You need to have a way to use alternative methods or strategies for providing service. For example, you might identify people in your organization who speak languages other than English so that you can call upon them, if necessary. Some larger organizations provide an on-call list of translators who can assist at point of sale locations. There is a posted listing in different languages next to the cash register that says something like, "Point to the text that you can read." This allows a service provider to see what language the person speaks and dial a phone code that connects to an appropriate translator. Another strategy for dealing with people from other countries is to do research on the Internet and at the library to learn about different cultures or countries. To help accomplish this, you might subscribe to publications that focus on cultural issues and a variety of countries, such as *National Geographic*.[6] If a customer speaks a little English, or has a heavy accent, try the strategies described in the following sections.

Let Your Customer Guide the Conversation

When possible, let your customer take the lead in guiding the service interaction. Some customers may want to spend time getting to know you, others may take a rigid or formal approach and get right down to business by taking the lead, and still others may choose to have someone else act as a mediator or an intermediary. Learn to recognize the cues and follow along when you can.

Be Flexible

Communicating with people from other cultures who do not speak your language fluently can be frustrating and complicated. Even if you do not understand their culture or language, using the positive listening, nonverbal, and verbal techniques you read about in Chapters 3 through 6 can help. If you are having difficulties, try some of the specific ideas included in this section of the book. Part of being flexible is recognizing that your views are not the way of the world. Making the mistake of believing that everyone has the same experiences and sees things the way you do can lead to communication and relationship breakdown. It is probably wise to assume that people from other cultures with whom you come into contact do not have the same knowledge and experience that you have. You can then proceed to share information with each other openly and freely. Listen for points of agreement or commonality.

Listen Patiently

You may be frustrated, but so is the other person. Focus on what he or she is saying and try to understand the meaning of the message and the needs being communicated by your customer.

Speak Clearly and Slowly

Depending on what survey results you view, most adults in the United States speak at a rate of about 125 to 150 words a minute. Other cultures have different rates of speech. The key to successful customer service is to speak at a rate slow enough that allows your customers to understand you without being insulting.

Speak at a Normal Volume and Tone

Yelling or changing tone does nothing to enhance understanding. A customer who is unable to speak your language is not necessarily deaf. You may naturally raise your voice if a customer cannot speak your language, but if you do the customer may become offended or think that you are hard of hearing and raise his or her voice also. This is not an effective way to communicate or provide effective customer service.

Use Open-End Questions

Open-end questions encourage customers to share information. On the other hand, closed-end questions do not allow you to accurately gauge a customer's viewpoint or understanding. Either because of embarrassment or to avoid saying no, some customers from other cultures may not admit that they do not agree, have an answer, or want to do something if you used a closed-end question. This reluctance can lead to misunderstandings and possibly resentment if you do not recognize a customer's nonverbal signals.

Pause Frequently

Pausing allows your customer to translate what you have said into her or his language, comprehend, and then respond in your language or ask questions.

Use Standard English

Avoid technical terms, contractions (e.g., *don't, can't*), slang (e.g., *like, you know, whoopee, rubberneck*), or broken language (e.g., sentences that fail to follow standard rules of grammar or syntax). Some people, when encountering non-native-language speaking customers, revert to an insulting singsong, almost childish, form of communication (e.g., in English, this might sound like, "You wantee me to takee this back?"). This does nothing to aid communication, for it is offensive and any language that the customer does understands gets lost in translation. Remember, some people understand your language though they may not be able to speak it well. Also, some people do not speak your language because they are self-conscious about their ability or choose not to out of fear of being embarrassed or losing esteem from you or others who hear them. Many cultures value and use silence as an important aspect to communication, something that some people of Western cultures find difficult to understand. Many Westerners often believe that silence means that a person does not understand or has nothing to add.

A scene in the first *Rush Hour* movie, with Chris Tucker and Jackie Chan, is a perfect example of how some people make assumptions about people from other cultures and end up communicating ineffectively. Tucker (playing a Los Angeles police officer) is sent to the airport to pick up a Chinese police officer (Chan). Tucker immediately makes assumptions about Chan's ability to communicate in English:

Tucker [upon meeting Chan]: "Please tell me you speak English."

Chan [gives no response; just looks at a Chinese airline pilot standing next to him]

Tucker [raises his voice]: "I'm Detective Carter. You speaka any English?"

Chan [again looks at others and says nothing]

Tucker [in a loud, exaggerated voice and gesturing toward his mouth]: "Do you understand the words coming out of my mouth?"

Chan [smiles and says nothing]

Later in the movie, as the two are riding in Tucker's car, Chan finally speaks in English.

Tucker: "All of a sudden, you're speaking English now."

Chan: "A little."

Tucker: "You lied to me."

Chan: "I didn't say I didn't speak English. You assumed I didn't. Not being able to speak is not the same as not speaking."

Use Globally Understood References

To reduce the risk of misunderstandings by people who speak your language as a second language, stick with basic verbiage. Avoid jokes, words, or acronyms that are uniquely tied to sports, historical events, or your culture. For example, people from the United States should avoid these types of statements:

- "I'll need your John Hancock on this form" (referring to John Hancock signing the Declaration of Independence).
- "If plan A fails, we'll drop back and punt" (referring to North American football).
- "We scored a base hit with that proposal yesterday" (referring to baseball).

These phrases might be understood by someone acculturated to North American society but will likely make no sense to many others.

Be Conscious of Nonverbal Cues

Continually monitor nonverbal reactions as you converse with a customer. If you sense confusion or lack of comprehension, stop and try to reestablish a bond. Also, be aware of the cues you send and make sure that they are in line with your verbal message.

Paraphrase the Customer's Message

After focusing on what you think is the customer's message, you may convey your understanding to the customer in your own words. When you think that you don't understand, either paraphrase the part of the customer's message up to the point at which you did understand or ask clarifying questions. For example, "Mr. Rasheed, I understand your complaint, but I'm not sure I understand what you expect us to do. How can I help make this better for you?"

Try Writing Your Message

Some people who speak another primary language understand written English words better than they speak them. If a customer seems to be having trouble understanding what you are saying, try printing your message (legibly) to see if he or she can understand your meaning. You might even try using recognizable symbols, if appropriate (e.g., a stop sign when you are giving directions or a picture of an object if you are describing something).

Try a Different Language

If you speak a second language, try using it. Your non–native-language-speaking customers may understand, since many countries require students to learn multiple languages in school. At the very least, they will appreciate your efforts to communicate with them.

Avoid Humor and Sarcasm

Humor and sarcasm are common to many Westerners but do not work well with customers whose first language is not English. They could lead to customer confusion and embarrassment. Differing cultural values and beliefs result in alternative points of view about what is socially acceptable. Also, jokes and other types of humor are typically based on incidents or people connected to a specific culture. They do not "travel well" and may not be understood by someone not of that culture.

Look for Positive Options

Many North Americans are often very direct. Many tend to use an abrupt no in response to a request they cannot fulfill. This behavior is viewed as rude, arrogant, and closed-minded in many cultures. Some countries do not even have a literal word in their language for no (e.g., Burmese). In many cases (e.g., parts of Asia) the response *no* in a conversation may cause a person embarrassment or loss of **face** (the esteem of others). Many people try to avoid such embarrassment at all costs. In some instances, people from certain parts of Asia may even say yes to your proposal and then not follow through on your suggestion rather than tell you no. Such behavior is acceptable in some cultures.

If you are dealing with customers who might react to your saying no in these ways—and you must decline—smile, apologize, and then try something like, "I am not sure we can do this" or "That will be difficult to do." Then, offer an alternative.

Use Questions Carefully

As mentioned earlier, phrase questions simply and avoid the use of closed-end questions that require a yes or no. Watch your customer's nonverbal responses so that you will be able to gauge his or her reactions to your questions.

In some cultures, people believe that questioning someone is intrusive, and they therefore avoid it. This is especially true if the questions are personal (e.g., "How is your family?").

Use a Step-by-Step Approach

When explaining something, outline exactly what you will do or what will be expected of the customer. Write this information down for the customer's future reference in order to prevent misunderstandings. If the customer cannot read it, and does not want to admit this out of embarrassment, he or she now has something to take to someone else for translation.

Keep Your Message Brief

Avoid lengthy explanations or details that might frustrate or confuse your customer. Use simple one-syllable words and short sentences. But also avoid being too brisk. Make sure you allow time for interpretation of, translation of, and response to your message.

Check Frequently for Understanding

In addition to using short words and sentences, pause often to verify the customer's understanding of your message before continuing. Avoid questions such as "Do you understand?" Not only can this be answered with a "yes" or "no" as you read in an earlier chapter, but it can also offend someone who speaks and understands English reasonably well. The nonverbal message is that the person may not be smart enough to get your meaning. Instead, try tie-in questions such as "How do you think you will use this?" or others that will give you an indication of whether the customer understands the information you have provided. These types of questions help

face Refers to the important concept of esteem in many Asian cultures. In such cultures one tries not to cause embarrassment or otherwise create a situation in which someone looks bad in the eyes of others.

Customer Service Success Tip

Do not point out the mistake if a customer makes an error or is wrong about something (e.g., improperly fills out a form or uses an incorrect word when speaking). Instead, take responsibility for correcting the error or clearing up the misunderstanding (e.g., "I am sorry that these forms are so confusing. I have trouble with them too." or "I apologize that I did not clearly explain what you needed to do to get a refund."). This strategy allows you to assume responsibility and helps them avoid embarrassment (save face) and sends a nonjudgmental message that you are there to assist them.

you and the customer visualize how the information will be put to use. They also give you a chance to find out if the person has misunderstood what you explained.

Keep Smiling

Smiling is a universal language; speak it fluently (when appropriate).

Customers with Disabilities

The U.S. Census Bureau reported in 2008 that of the 291.1 million people in the population, 54.4 million (18.7 percent) had some level of disability and 35 million (12 percent) had a severe disability.[7] These numbers are projected to continue to grow as the population ages.

From a customer service perspective, it is certain that you will encounter someone in the workplace who has a disability that may require your assistance in serving him or her. Some service professionals are uncomfortable working with **customers with disabilities** because they have had little prior exposure to people who have special needs, they are uninformed about various disabilities, or they have unfounded fear or anxiety in relating to them. Even though you may be unfamiliar with how people with disabilities adapt to life experiences, you should strive to provide excellent service to them. In most cases, customers who have disabilities do not want to be treated differently; they want to be treated equally.

In addition to all the factors you have read about previously, to be effective in dealing with customers in the United States, you must be aware of the **Americans with Disabilities Act of 1990** (ADA), ADA Amendments Act of 2008 and other legislation passed by Congress to protect individuals and groups. Similar legislation now exists in many other countries as well, so if you work in such an area, you should familiarize yourself with the laws. You should also understand the court interpretations of these laws that require businesses to provide certain services to customers with disabilities and to make certain premises accessible to them. The laws also often prohibit any form of discrimination or harassment related to a disability.

Since the passage of the ADA, much has been published about the rights of and accommodations for people with disabilities. Figure 8.3 provides general strategies for working with customers and others with disabilities and complying with the ADA. In addition, the following sections discuss specific approaches you can take to work well with people with certain disabilities.

Customers with Hearing Disabilities

Hearing loss is common as people age or because of a medical condition and can be a real challenge in service environments. For example, about 17 percent (36 million people) of adults in the United States have some form of hearing loss.[8] Remember that customers who have **hearing disabilities** may have special needs, but they also have certain abilities. Do

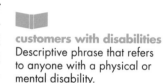

customers with disabilities Descriptive phrase that refers to anyone with a physical or mental disability.

Americans with Disabilities Act of 1990 A United States federal act signed into law in July of 1990 guaranteeing people with disabilities equal access to workplace and public opportunities.

hearing disabilities Conditions in which the ability to hear is diminished below established auditory standards.

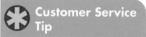

Customer Service Tip

Do not assume that just because someone has an obvious disability that he or she requires or wants your assistance. Offer assistance, if appropriate, and follow your customer's lead in offering assistance. Unsolicited assistance can be offensive and might even be dangerous if it is unexpected and causes the person to lose his or her balance.

Figure 8.3
General Strategies for Servicing Customers with Disabilities

In addition to the suggestions offered in this chapter for serving customers with specific disabilities, here are some general guidelines for success:

Be prepared and informed. You can find a lot of literature and information about disabilities. Do some reading to learn about the capabilities and needs of customers with disabilities.

Be careful not to patronize. Refrain from talking "down" to customers with disabilities. Just because they have a physical or mental disability does not mean that they should be valued less as a customer or person.

Treat them equally, not differently. Just as you would other customers, work to discover their needs and then set about satisfying them.

Refer to the person, not the disability. Instead of referring to the *blind man,* refer to the *man wearing the red shirt* or *man who is standing by the . . . ,* or better yet, *the man who needs . . . .*

Offer assistance, but do not rush to help without asking. Just as you would ask someone without a disability whether you might assist them, hold a door or carry a package, do the same for a person with a disability.

Be respectful. The amount of respect you show to all customers should be at a consistently high level. This includes tone of voice (showing patience), gestures, eye contact, and all the other communication techniques you have learned about.

not assume that people who are hearing impaired are helpless. In interactions with such customers, you can do a variety of things to provide effective service:

- Face your customer directly when speaking
- Speak louder (assuming they only have partial hearing loss).
- Provide written information and instructions where appropriate and possible.
- Use pictures, objects, diagrams, or other such items to communicate more clearly, if appropriate.
- To get the person's attention, use nonverbal cues such as gesturing.
- Use facial expressions and gestures to emphasize key words or express thoughts.
- Enunciate your words and speak slowly so that the customer can see your mouth form words.
- Use short sentences and words.
- Check for understanding frequently by using open-end questions to which the customer must provide descriptive answers.
- Communicate in a well-lighted room when possible.
- Watch backlighting (light coming from behind you that can cast a shadow on your face), which may reduce the ability to see your mouth.
- Reduce background noise, if possible.

If you serve customers over the telephone or Internet, you may find yourself interacting with a **Telecommunications Relay Service (TRS),** also called Relay Service, Relay Operator, and IP-Relay. Through such

Telecommunications Relay Service (TRS) Through such services, specially trained operators act as intermediaries between people who are deaf, hard-of-hearing, speech disabled, or deaf and blind and standard telephone users.

services, specially trained operators act as intermediaries between people who are deaf, hard-of-hearing, speech disabled, or deaf and blind and standard telephone users. This is accomplished when a disabled customer uses a keyboard or assistive device to contact the operator service. Those people then add the intended service provider onto the call and translate messages verbally back and forth between the customer and provider. The customer types comments and the operator then relays them to the service provider. When the provider responds, the operator responds back to the customer in writing. As you can imagine, this is a time-consuming process. If you are contacted by such an operator, be patient and speak slowly so your message gets translated properly.

Originally, relay services were designed to be connected through a **Telecommunications Device for the Deaf (TDD), or Telephone Typewriter (TTY),** or other assistive telephone device. In recent years, assistive services have expanded to include many connected devices, such as personal and laptop computers, cell phones, and personal digital assistants (PDA).

Like many other aspects of life involving technology these days, there are people who try to abuse "the system." There are many scam artists (e.g., Nigerian-based con artists) who attempt to use the TRS systems to steal from unsuspecting organizations, especially small businesses. This can create a potential trust issue between you and legitimate customers with disabilities who contact you via an assistance system. Provide quality service whenever you are contacted by a relay operator; however, always beware. To protect your organization, make sure that you receive payment in advance via a credit card or a money order or check (ensure the check clears your bank) before shipping products.

Customers with Vision Disabilities

As with hearing loss, many people experience vision loss because of medical conditions or as a result of the aging process. According to the National Center for Health Statistics, 21.2 million people in the United States reported having difficulty seeing or being unable to see.[9] This means that you are likely to encounter someone with a vision impairment. Like people who have hearing impairments, customers with **vision disabilities** may need special assistance, but are not helpless. Depending on your organization's product and service focus, you can do things to assist visually impaired customers. Be aware that, depending on the type of impairment, a person may have limited vision that can be used to advantage when serving them. Here are some strategies to use:

- Talk to a visually impaired person the same way you would talk to anyone else.
- You do not have to raise your voice; the person is visually impaired, not hard of hearing.
- Do not feel embarrassed or change your vocabulary. It is okay to say things like "Do you see my point?" or "Do you get the picture?"

Telecommunications Device for the Deaf (TDD) or Telephone Typewriter (TTY) A typewriter-type device used by people with hearing disabilities for typing messages back and forth via telephone lines.

vision disabilities Condition resulting from lost visual acuity or disability.

- Speak directly to the customer.
- Speak to the person as he or she enters the room or approach the person so that he or she knows where you are. Also, introduce others who are present, or at least inform the customer of their presence.
- If appropriate, ask how much sight he or she has and how you can best assist.
- Give very specific information and directions (e.g., "A chair is approximately 10 feet ahead on your left").
- If you are seating the person, face him or her away from bright lights that might interfere with any limited vision he or she may have.
- When walking with someone who is blind, offer your arm. Do not take the person's arm without permission; this could startle him or her. Let the person take your elbow and walk slightly behind you.
- When helping a blind person to a chair, guide his or her hand to the back of the chair. Also, inform the person if a chair has arms to prevent him or her from overturning the chair by leaning or sitting on an arm.
- Leave doors either completely closed or open. Partially open doors pose a danger to visually impaired people.

Customers with Mobility or Motion Impairments

In the United States in 2008, about 19.2 million people or 6.9 percent of the civilian noninstitutionalized population 5 years and older had an ambulatory difficulty.[10] The term "mobility impairment" typically refers to disabilities that impact someone's ability to move without assistance, manipulate objects, and interact with the physical world. Mobility impaired users include the users who are confined to bed, use a wheelchair or other assistive device to navigate, or have permanently incapacitated or reduced hand movements. Customers who have **mobility or motion impairments** often use specially designed equipment and have had extensive training in how to best use assistive devices to compensate for the loss of the use of some part of their body. You can best assist them by offering to help and then following their lead or instructions. Do not make the assumption that they need your assistance and then set about giving it. You can cause injury if you upset their balance or routine. Here are some strategies for better serving these customers:

- Prior to a situation in which you may have to accommodate someone who uses a walker, wheelchair, crutches, or other device, do an environmental survey of your workplace. Note areas where space is inadequate to permit mobility (a minimum of 36 inches is needed for a standard wheelchair) or where hazards exist. If you can correct the situation, do so. For example, move or bring in a different table or chair or rearrange furniture for better access. Otherwise, make suggestions for improvements to the proper people in your organization. Remind them that the ADA and state regulations require an organization to accommodate customers with such disabilities.

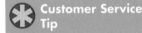

Customer Service Tip

Do not pet, feed, or otherwise distract a guide dog without the owner's permission. A guide dog is specially trained to perform specific functions. If you interfere, the dog might become confused and the owner could possibly be injured as a result.

mobility or motion impairments Physical limitations that some people have, requiring accommodation or special consideration to allow access to products or services.

- Do not assume that someone who has such an impairment cannot perform certain tasks. As mentioned earlier, people who have disabilities are often given extensive training. They have learned how to overcome obstacles and perform various tasks in different ways.
- Make sure that you place information or materials at a level that makes it possible for the person to see without undue strain (e.g., eye level for someone in a wheelchair so that he or she does not have to look up).
- Do not push or lean on someone's wheelchair without his or her permission.

Customer Service Tip

Stand or sit so that you can make direct eye contact with a person in a wheelchair without forcing the person to look up at an uncomfortable angle for extended periods. This reduces discomfort and neck strain on their part.

Elderly Customers

Being elderly does not make a person or a customer less valuable. In fact, many older customers are in excellent physical and mental shape, are still employed, and have more time to be active now than when they were younger. Studies show that senior citizens have more disposable income now than at any other time in history. And, as the **baby boomer** population (people born between 1946 and 1964) ages, there are more senior citizens than ever (35.9 million in 2003).[11] Moreover, as the population ages, there will be a greater need for services—and service providers—to care for people and allow them to enjoy a good quality of life. Figure 8.4 shows the U.S. population aged 65 and older between 2000 and 2050. Consider the following strategies when you are interacting with an elderly customer.

baby boomer A term applied to anyone born between 1946 and 1964. People in this age group are called "boomers."

Be Respectful

As you would with any customer, be respectful. Even if the customer seems a bit arrogant, disoriented, or disrespectful, don't lose your professionalism. Recognize that sometimes these behaviors are a response to perceptions based on your cues. When this happens, quickly evaluate your behavior and make adjustments, if necessary. If an older customer seems abrupt in his or her response, think about whether you might have

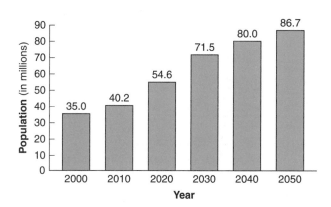

Figure 8.4 **Population Aged 65 and Older: 2000 to 2050 (in Millions)**

Note: The reference population is the resident population.

Sources: 2000, U.S. Census Bureau, 2001, Table PCT 12; 2010 to 2050. U.S. Census Bureau, 2004.

Identifying Resources

CHECK WITH LOCAL ADVOCACY GROUPS OR ON THE INTERNET FOR INFORMATION ON THE TYPES OF ACCOMMODATIONS YOU MIGHT MAKE FOR PEOPLE WITH VARIOUS DISABILITIES AND HOW BEST TO INTERACT WITH PEOPLE WHO HAVE SPECIFIC DISABILITIES (E.G., SIGHT, MOBILITY, HEARING IMPAIRMENT). Collect and read literature on the subject. Share the information with other students and/or co-workers (if you currently work in a customer service environment).
What to look for:

> Definitions of various disabilities.
>
> Strategies for better communication.
>
> Accommodations necessary to allow customer access to products and services.
>
> Resources available (e.g., tools, equipment, training, or organizations).
>
> Bibliographic information on disabilities (e.g., books or articles).

nonverbally signaled impatience because of your perception that he or she was slow in acting or responding.

**Customer Service
Success Tip**

Use the following strategies to help enhance communication with all customers:

- Face the person.
- Talk slowly and enunciate words clearly.
- Keep your hands away from your mouth.
- Talk without food or chewing gum in your mouth.
- Observe the customer's nonverbal cues.
- Reword statements or ask questions again, if necessary.
- Be positive, patient, and practice the good listening skills covered in Chapter 5.
- Stand near good lighting, and keep background noise to a minimum, when possible.
- If an interpreter is with the customer, talk to the customer and not the interpreter. The interpreter will know what to do..

Be Patient

Allow older customers the time to look around, respond, react, or ask questions. Value their decisions. Also, keep in mind that as some people age, their ability to process information lessens and their attention span becomes shorter. Do not assume that this is true of all older customers, but be patient when it does occur.

Answer Questions

Providing information to customers is crucial in order to help them make reasonable decisions. Even though you may have just explained something, listen to the customer's questions, respond, and restate. If it appears that the customer has misunderstood, try repeating the information, possibly using slightly different words.

Try Not to Sound Patronizing

If you appear to talk down to older customers, problems could arise and you could lose a customer. Customers who are elderly should not be treated as if they are senile! A condescending attitude will often cause any customer, elderly or otherwise, to take his or her business elsewhere.

Remain Professional

Addressing senior citizens accompanied by their children or grandchildren with "Good morning, Grandma" because one of their family members used that language is inappropriate, disrespectful, and rude.

Guard against Biases

Be careful not to let biases about older people interfere with good service. Don't ignore or offend older customers by making statements such as "Hang on, old timer. I'll be with you in a minute." Such a statement might be in jest, but is nonetheless potentially offensive to the person, and to others who might hear it. Similarly, do not use such age-based comments when referring to an older co-worker or external customer since these might be overheard by others and may cause people to form opinions about your level of professionalism or your beliefs regarding older people as a result. Either could cause problems in the workplace and ultimately impact service potential.

Younger Customers

You have heard the various terms describing the "younger generation"—Generation Y, Nexters, MTV generation, Millennial Generation, or cyber kids. Whatever the term, this group follows Generation X (born 1964–1977) and is now entering the workplace in great numbers as employees and consumers. Financially, the group accounts for billions of dollars in business revenue for products such as clothes, music, videos, electronic entertainment equipment, and entertainment consumption. Generation Y is a spending force to be reckoned with, and marketers are going after them with a vengeance. If you don't believe this, pick up a magazine and look at the faces of the models, look at the products being sold, and watch the shows being added to television lineups each year. All of this affects the way you will provide service to this generation of customers. Depending on your own age, your attitude toward them will vary. If you are of Gen Y, you may make the mistake of being overly familiar with your age group in delivering service. If you are a baby boomer or older, you may feel paternalistic or maternalistic or might believe some of the stereotypical rhetoric about this group (e.g., low moral values, fragmented in focus, overprotected by legislation and programs). Although some of these descriptions may be accurate for some members of the group, it is dangerous to pigeonhole any group or individual, as you have read. This is especially true when providing service, since service is based on satisfying personal needs and wants.

Younger customers can often have a completely different set of needs. *What are some effective strategies for handling customers of a younger generation?*

Serving a Variety of Customers

PAIR UP WITH A PEER AND USE THE FOLLOWING SCENARIOS AS THE BASIS OF ROLE-PLAYS TO GIVE YOU PRACTICE AND FEEDBACK IN DEALING WITH VARIOUS CATEGORIES OF CUSTOMERS.

Before beginning, discuss how you might deal with each customer in a real-life situation. After the role-plays, both persons should answer the following questions and discuss any ideas for improvement.

Questions

1. How well do you feel that service was provided?

2. Were any negative or unclear messages, verbal or nonverbal, communicated? If yes, discuss.

2. What open-end questions were used to discover customer needs? What others could have been used?

4. How can identified areas for improvement be incorporated into a real customer service encounter?

Scenario 1. You are a shuttle driver for the airport and just received a call from your dispatcher to proceed to 8172 Dealy Lane to pick up Cassandra Fenton. You were told that Ms. Fenton is blind and will need assistance getting her bags from the house to the bus. Upon arrival, you find Ms. Fenton waiting on her front porch with her bags.

Scenario 2. Mrs. Zagowski is 62 years old and is in the library where you are working at the circulation desk. As you observe her, you notice that she seems a bit frustrated and confused. You saw her browse through several aisles of books, then talk briefly with the reference librarian, and finally go to the computer containing the publication listings and their locations. You are going to try to assist her. Upon meeting her, you realize that she has a hearing deficit and has difficulty hearing what you are saying.

Scenario 3. You are the owner of a small hobby shop that specializes in coins, stamps, comics, and sports memorabilia. Tommy Chin, whom you recognize as a regular "browser," has come in while you are particularly busy. After looking through numerous racks of comic books and trading cards, he is now focused on autographed baseballs in a display case. You believe that he cannot afford them, although he is asking about prices and for other information.

younger customers
Subjective tern referring to anyone younger than the service provider. Sometimes used to describe members of Generation X (born to baby boomers) or later.

Remember when you were young and felt that adults didn't understand or care about your wants or needs? Well, your **younger customers** probably feel the same way and will remember how you treat them. Their memories could prompt them to take their business elsewhere if their experience with you is negative. If you are older, you may be tempted to talk down to them or be flippant. Don't give in to the temptation. Keep in mind that they are customers. If they feel unwelcome, they will take their business and money elsewhere, and they will tell their friends of the poor treatment they received. Just as with older customers, avoid demeaning language and condescending forms of address (*kid, sonny, sweetie, sugar, or young woman/man*).

Additional points to remember when dealing with younger customers is that they may not have the product knowledge and sophistication in communicating that older customers might have. You can decrease confusion and increase communication effectiveness by using words that are appropriate for their age group and by taking the time to explain and/or demonstrate technical points. Keep it simple without being patronizing if you are older than your customers.

LO 8-6 Communicating with Diverse Customers

Concept Many considerations need to be taken into account when you are delivering service to a diverse customer base. Appropriate language usage is a meaningful tool that you should master for good customer service.

Given all this diversity, you must be wondering how to provide service that is acceptable to all of these customer groups. As you've seen, there are many considerations in delivering service to a diverse customer base. Therefore, consider the following basic guidelines for communicating; these tips are appropriate for dealing with all types of customers.

Be Careful with Your Remarks and Jokes

Comments that focus on any aspect of diversity (religion, sexual preference, weight, hair color, age) can be offensive and should not be made. Also, humor does not cross cultural boundaries well. Each culture has a different interpretation of what is humorous and socially acceptable.

Make Sure That Your Language Is "Inclusive"

When speaking, address or refer to the people from various groups that are present. If you are addressing a group of two men and one woman, using the term *guys* or *fellows* excludes the woman and thus is not **inclusive.**

Respect Personal Preferences When Addressing People

As you read earlier, don't assume familiarity when addressing others. (Don't call someone by her or his first name unless she or he gives permission.) Don't use *Ms.* if a female customer prefers another form of address. Also, avoid derogatory or demeaning terms such as *honey, sugar,* and *sweetheart* or other overly familiar language.

Use General Terms

Instead of singling a customer out or focusing on exceptions in a group, describe people in general terms. That is, instead of referring to someone as a *female supervisor, black salesperson,* or *disabled administrative assistant*, say *supervisor, salesperson,* or *administrative assistant.*

Customer Service Success Tip

Learn as much technology as you can if you plan to effectively provide service to members of Generations X and Y, since they are very technically savvy. Technology examples include smart phones, iPods, iPads, computer hardware and software, Internet options and services, and service delivery technology such as **wiki**, **blogs** (Web logs), and **podcasts.**

wiki A form of server software that allows nontechnical personnel to create and edit Web site pages using any Web browser and without complex programming knowledge.

blogs Online journals (Web logs) or diaries that allow people to add contents. Many organizational Web sites use them to post "what's new" sections and to receive feedback (good and bad) from customers and Web site visitors.

podcasts A word that is a derivative of Apple® Computer's iPod® media player and the term broadcasting. Through podcasts, Web sites can offer direct download or streaming of their content (i.e., music or video files) to customers or Web site users.

inclusive The concept of ensuring that people of all races, genders, and religious and ethnic backgrounds, as well as a multitude of other diverse factors, are included in communications and activities in the workplace.

Recognize the Impact of Words

Keep in mind that certain words have a negative connotation and could insult or offend. Even if you do not intend to offend, the customer's perception is the deciding factor of your actions. For example, using the terms *handicapped* or *crippled, boy, girl, homo, retard,* or *idiot* may conjure up a negative image to some groups or individuals and label you as unprofessional, biased, and inconsiderate. Using such terminology can also reflect negatively upon you and your organization and should never be used.

Use Care with Nonverbal Cues

The nonverbal cues that you are familiar with may carry different meanings in other cultures. Be careful when you use symbols or gestures if you are not certain how your customer will receive them. Figure 8.5 lists some cues that are common in Western cultures but have negative meanings in other cultures.

Small Business Perspective

In order for small businesses to compete effectively with larger ones, they must utilize all resources available to them. That means that they must openly embrace a diverse workforce and learn more about people from various cultures, races, generations, genders, religions, and other diverse factors. They must also be aware of the laws regarding fair and equitable treatment of others. By recognizing the needs and preferences of different groups and individuals, employers can better prepare their employees, products, and services to address what customers want.

Part of the initiative to prepare to better deal with diversity involves providing training and job aids that can support employees as they serve customers. Programs such as effective multicultural communication, cultural sensitivity, diversity awareness, behavioral styles, and others that provide insights into how people behave, what they value and believe, special needs, and cultural background information are valuable in educating employees about others.

By doing research on the products and services desired and typically used by various groups of customers, small businesses and their employees can become a valuable resource for those seeking specific products and services. This can lead to them being recognized as a prime source or organization that specializes in particular products or in the delivery of culturally and group-specific products and help themselves stand out from the competitive crowd.

Impact on Service

Based on personal experience and what you just read, answer the following questions:

1. What specific customer needs might employees of a small business have to meet? Explain.

The following are symbols and gestures that are commonly used in the United States but have different—and negative or offensive—meanings in other parts of the world:

Figure 8.5
Nonverbal Cue Meanings

American Gesture or Symbol	Meaning in Other Cultures	Country
Beckoning by curling and uncurling index finger*†	Used for calling animals or ladies of the evening	Hong Kong, Australia, Indonesia, Yugoslavia, Malaysia
V for victory sign (with palm facing you)*†	Rude gesture	England
Sole of foot pointed toward a person*‡	You are lowly (the sole is lowest part of the body and contacts the ground).	Thailand, Saudi Arabia, Singapore, Egypt
"Halt" gesture with palm and extended fingers thrust toward someone*†‡	Rude epithet	Greece
Thumb up (fingers curled) indicating *okay, good going,* or *everything is fine**‡	The number 5 Rude gesture	Japan, Nigeria, Australia
Thumb and forefinger forming an O, meaning okay*‡	Zero or worthless Money Rude gesture	France Japan Brazil, Malta, Greece, Tunisia, Turkey, Italy, Paraguay, Russia
Waving good-bye with fingers extended, palm down, and moving the fingers up and down toward yourself*‡	Come here	Parts of Europe, Myanmar, Colombia, Peru
Patting the head of a child	Insult, inviting evil spirits	Parts of the Far East
Using red ink for documents	Death; offensive	Parts of Korea, Mexico, and China
Passing things with left hand (especially food)	Socially unacceptable	India, Pakistan

*R. Axtell, *Gestures: The Do's and Taboos of Body Language Around the World*, John Wiley and Sons, New York, 1991.

†A. Wolfgang, *Everybody's Guide to People Watching*, International Press, Yarmouth, Mass., 1995.

‡D. Morris, *Bodytalk, The Meaning of Human Gestures*, Crown Trade Paperback, New York, 1994.

2. How does the changing demographic environment impact the ability of small businesses to compete for customers? Explain.

3. If you worked for a small business, what do you think you would need to know in order to deliver appropriate service to a diverse customer base? Explain.

Summary

Opportunities to deal with a diverse customer base will increase as the global economy expands. With continuing immigrations, an aging world population, shifts in cultural values, and increased ease of mobility, the only thing certain is that the next customer you speak with will be different from you. Remember, however, that he or she will also be similar to you in many ways and that both of you will have a basis for discussion.

The success you have in the area of dealing with others is totally dependent on your preparation and attitude toward providing quality service. Learn as much as you can about various groups of people in order to effectively evaluate situations, determine needs, and serve all customers on an equal basis.

Review Questions

1. What are some innate qualities or characteristics that make people unique?
2. What external or societal factors affect the way members of a group are seen or perceived?
3. What are values?
4. Do beliefs differ from values? Explain.
5. Why would some people be reluctant to make eye contact with you?
6. When dealing with customers with a disability, how can you best help them?
7. How can recognition of the cultural value of "importance of family" be helpful in customer service?
8. What are some considerations for improving communication in a diverse environment?
9. How can you effectively communicate with someone who has difficulty with the English language?
10. What are some techniques for effectively providing service to older customers?

Search It Out

Search the Internet for Diversity Information

Log on to the Internet to locate information and articles related to topics covered in this chapter. Be prepared to share what you found at your next scheduled class or session. The following are some key words you might use in your search:

Any country name (e.g., Australia, Canada, Sri Lanka)
Baby boomers
Beliefs
Any religion (e.g., Muslim, Hindu, Buddhist, Christian)
Cultural diversity
Cultural values
Disabilities

Disability advocacy
Diversity
Elderly
Generation X
Generation Y
Intercultural communication
Intercultural dynamics
IP-Relay
Jellabiya
Population projections
Relay Operator
Relay Service
Telecommunications Device for the Deaf (TDD)
Telecommunications Relay Service (TRS)
Telephone Typewriter (TTY)
Turban

Collaborative Learning Activity

Awareness of Diversity

To help raise your awareness of diversity in the customer service environment, try the following activities:

1. Pair up with someone to role-play scenarios in which you are a service provider and have customers from the following groups:

   An elderly person who has a hearing loss and wants directions on how to use some equipment (you choose the equipment and provide instruction).

   Someone who speaks English as a second language (with a heavy accent) and needs to fill out a credit card application or some other form.

   Someone with a sight impairment who wants to "see" several blouses or shirts or needs directions to another part of your store.

   A 10-year-old who wants a new computer and has questions about various types, components, and how they work.

2. Interview a variety of people: from different cultures, from various age groups, with disabilities, male or female (opposite of your sex), or gay or lesbian. Find out whether they have preferences in the type of customer service they receive or in the kind of language used to refer to their group. Also, ask about ways you can better communicate with and understand them and people from their group.

3. Suggest to your supervisor, team leader, or work group peers that employees meet as a group to discuss situations in which all of you have encountered people from different cultures or groups. Exchange ideas on how to better serve such people in the future. Report the results of your efforts to your class members at the next scheduled meeting.

4. Working in teams assigned by your instructor, set up an appointment to visit a local advocacy group for the disabled or aging, or contact a national group (e.g., the National Society to Prevent Blindness, assisted-living facilities, World Federation of the Deaf, National Information Center on Deafness, National Eye Institute, National Institute on Aging). Focus on gathering information that will help you understand various disabilities and develop strategies for effectively communicating with and serving people who have disabilities. Write a brief summary of your experience and report back to your peers.

Face to Face

Dealing with Difficult People on the Phone at MedMobile

Background

MedMobile is a medical supply business located in Los Angeles employing 62 full-time and 11 part-time workers. The company specializes in equipment designed to improve patient mobility (walkers, motorized carts, wheelchairs, mechanized beds, and chairs). Average yearly sales are in the area of $1.5 million.

The primary client base for the company is insurance companies that pay for rehabilitation after worker accidents or injuries. Medical professionals who conduct the patient medical case file reviews and recommend treatment programs are in regular contact with the account representatives for MedMobile.

Your Role

As an account representative with MedMobile, you have been with the company for about 18 months. Your main job is to help clients determine and obtain the correct equipment needed to assist their patients. To do this, you spend hours on the phone daily and often know clients by voice. In the past month you have become extremely frustrated, almost to the point of anger. A new claims adjuster works for one of your primary account companies, TrueCare Insurance

Company. His name is Abeyola Pepukayi, and he has been with TrueCare 8 weeks. He has been an adjuster for a little over a year.

You just got off the phone after a lengthy conversation with Abeyola and you are agitated. For over half an hour you tried unsuccessfully to explain why you felt the equipment being ordered by Abeyola was not the best for the patient's injury, as he described it to you.

Because this isn't the first time such an encounter has taken place, you are now in your supervisor's office venting. While discussing the situation with your boss, you note the following about Abeyola:

He doesn't listen. No matter what you say, he asks totally irrelevant questions about other equipment.

He usually has no idea what you're talking about.

He is rude and interrupts, often making statements such as "One moment, please. That makes no sense."

You have spent hours discussing equipment design and function because he doesn't know anything about it.

He spends endless amounts of time getting offtrack and trying to discuss other issues or topics.

After your conversation, your boss called a friend at True Care to see what he knew of the situation. The friend, David Helmstedter, supervises Abeyola. Apparently, Abeyola has been venting to David about you. From what David has been told:

You are rude and abrupt and aren't very friendly. Abeyola has tried to establish a relationship, but you have ignored his efforts.

Abeyola is trying hard to learn the terminology and equipment but you are unwilling to help.

You speak rapidly, using a lot of technical language that you don't explain.

Critical Thinking Questions

1. What seems to be happening here? Does Abeyola have any legitimate complaints? If so, what are they?

2. What steps or process can you use to clarify understanding?

3. What cultural differences might be involved in this scenario?

Planning to Serve

Identifying Your Biases

We sometimes have biases that interfere with our interactions with others. Typically, these biases are learned behavior (something we have personally experienced or have been taught by others). By thinking of your biases and bringing them to a conscious level, you can better control or eliminate them in dealing with your customers and others.

Think about the qualities of other people or groups that you do not like or prefer to avoid. List them, along with the basis (why you believe them to be true) for each.

Share your list with other students and discuss their potential impact on service.

Quick Preview Answers

1. T	3. T	5. T	7. T	9. T	11. T
2. T	4. T	6. F	8. T	10. T	12. T

Ethical Dilemma Summary

Ethical Dilemma 8.1 Possible Answers

1. What action should you take, if any?

   As an employee of any type of organization (retail or otherwise) you should take ownership of your environment. After all, your employer pays you to be professional and alert on the job. In this situation, the customer seems to be acting in an unusual and possibly suspicious manner. Certainly, security is a concern for anyone these days. You would be correct and prudent to monitor the man's actions and to notify your supervisor, a coworker, and/or security of the situation just in case the person is up to some unlawful or otherwise inappropriate activity. Because of potential risk, you should not confront such a person yourself, and certainly not alone without others watching the situation.

2. If you decide to take some action, why would you do so?

   Any action you take would likely be precautionary to prevent loss (financial or physical) to your organization yourself and others. Also, in the event that the person is really up to illegal activity, you would likely be doing it out of concern for safety (yours and others).

3. What are possible repercussions if you either act or decide not to act?

   If you fail to act and the person is engaged in some unlawful or mischievous activity, you, others, and the organization could sustain loss, damage, and possible injury. If you do act, and the man is not doing anything more than "killing time," the person's perception could be that you are targeting him and potentially could become upset or even claim some sort of discrimination. You could also lose his business and that of anyone to whom he relates his experience.

Ethical Dilemma 8.2 Possible Answers

1. Have you ever witnessed similar situations in the workplace? Explain.

   Spend some time discussing your experience(s) with other students along with the results of such behavior.

2. From a service perspective, is this situation a problem? Explain.

   Even though the customer may not have heard the remarks in this situation, this is unacceptable behavior. You (and possibly others, including customers may have overheard the remarks). As a service provider, employees represent not only themselves, but also the organization. People form opinions based on what they see workers do and say. This type of incident can lead to lost business, negative word of mouth publicity, and claims of defamation and discrimination. Not only is there potential for financial loss, but also damage to the reputation of the service providers involved, other workers, and the organization.

3. What would you do or say about the incident that you just witnessed? Explain.

   At the very least, you should intervene to point out that the language is disrespectful, derogatory, discriminatory, and can cause problems for the two employees, others at the organization, and the organization itself. Depending on the reaction you get when approaching the others, you may need to escalate this matter to your supervisor for appropriate action.

Customer Service via Technology

In the world of Internet Customer Service, it's important to remember that a competitor is only one mouse click away.

—Doug Warner

Learning Outcomes

After completing this chapter, you will be able to:

9-1 Recognize the extent to which customer service is facilitated by the effective use of technology.

9-2 Use technology to enhance service delivery capabilities.

9-3 Communicate effectively via e-mail, the Internet, and fax.

9-4 Deliver quality service through effective telephone techniques.

Key Terms

automated attendants
automatic call
   distribution (ACD)
   system
automatic number
   identification (ANI)
   system
blind transfer
computer telephony
   integration (CTI)
electronic mail (e-mail)
emoticons (emotional
   icons)

facsimile (fax) machine
fax on demand
fee-based 900 numbers
help desk
interactive voice
   response (IVR) system
Internet callback
Internet telephony
iPod
media blending
offshoring
online information
   fulfillment system

outsourcing
predictive dialing system
screen pop-ups
spamming or spam
telecommuting
Telephone Typewriter
   system (TTY)
voice response unit
   (VRU)

In the Real World Technology—Google

ACCORDING TO GOOGLE'S CORPORATE WEB SITE, "FOUNDERS LARRY PAGE and Sergey Brin named the search engine they built 'Google,' a play on the word 'googol,' the mathematical term for a 1 followed by 100 zeros. The name reflects the immense volume of information that exists, and the scope of Google's mission: to organize the world's information and make it universally accessible and useful." One strategy that the company launched in May of 2010 is called "Google Editions." This technology platform allows users to buy e-books directly from the company, or other retailers, and load them onto multiple electronic devices. In effect, this allows books to be read on any Internet-enabled device. Obviously, their goal is to compete with companies such as Amazon.com and Apple, Inc., which manufacture and sell electronic reading devices.

Like many companies, Google began with "seed" money from investors and venture capital firms. They focused on search services and advertising to generate operating capital and expand their offerings. The result has been a steady word-of-mouth customer satisfaction rating that slowly spread the word about their powerful search engine. Since its inception in 1998 in Mountain View, California, Google has continued to grow in stature and visibility by establishing or acquiring more than 150 other Google domains. The organization employs thousands of employees at its corporate headquarters (named Googleplex), and around the world. Virtually any type of information, maps, images, and much more can be found in multiple languages from around the world via the Google search engine. As one of the largest and most well-known search engines on the Internet, Google continues to research and develop new products and services (e.g., Google Chrome, Google Books, Android, Google Earth, Google Apps, Google AdWords and Google AdSense). A recent partnership between Google Earth and Disney involves a new Internet product (Walt Disney World Resort in 3D) that allows users to tour a virtual re-creation of Epcot and the rest of Disney World in Florida. Users can click for more information to assist them in their travel planning.

Management at Google values intelligence, creativity, and the multicultural nature of its workforce and strives to make the work environment creative and employee-friendly. For example, some of the typical workplace amenities in different Google office environments around the world include:

- Bicycles or scooters for efficient travel between meetings, dogs, lava lamps, massage chairs, large inflatable balls.
- Weekly all-hands meetings are held at corporate headquarters where employees can pose questions directly to founders Larry Page and Sergey Brin.
- "Googlers" sharing cubes, yurts, and huddle rooms—and very few solo offices.
- Laptops everywhere—standard issue for mobile coding, e-mail on the go, and notetaking.
- Foosball, pool tables, volleyball courts, assorted video games, pianos, ping pong tables, and gyms that offer yoga and dance classes.

- Grassroots employee groups for all interests (e.g., meditation, film, wine tasting, and salsa dancing).
- Healthy lunches and dinners for all staff at a variety of cafés.
- Break rooms packed with a variety of snacks and drinks to keep Googlers going.

According to an American Customer Satisfaction Index report in the second quarter of 2009, Google has lead other portals and search engines in customer satisfaction for seven of the past eight years. With a score of 86 on a scale of 100 points, Google has lead Yahoo! and Bing in service success. When you consider that Google does 74 percent of all search business on the Internet, while Yahoo! handles 17 percent and Microsoft's new entrant Bing.com is third with 7 percent, this index indicates a solid lead for the organization.[1]

For more information about this organization, visit www.google.com. Look at their historical and other information about the organization on their Web site.

Think About It

Based on this organization's profile, answer the following questions and be prepared to discuss your responses.

1. From your personal experiences, what you just read about the company, and what you found on the Google Web site, what do you feel are the strengths of the company from an external customer perspective? Explain.

2. How do you view Google's internal customer environment and its impact on employees? Explain.

3. What factors in society do you feel have allowed Google to attain such phenomenal popularity and growth, and have such an impact on the Internet environment, in a relatively short time period? Explain the relationship of these factors to Google's growth.

4. What do you think are Google's future opportunities for growth related to customer service? Explain.

5. As an Internet user, are you a fan of Google and what it has accomplished? Why or why not?

6. Take a look at the management Operating Committee at www.google.com/intl/en/corporate/execs.html and offer thoughts on how the makeup of that team might impact internal and external service levels at Google.

Quick Preview

Before reviewing the chapter content, respond to the following questions by placing a "T" for true or an "F" for false on the rules. Use any questions you miss as a checklist of material to which you will pay particular attention as you read through the chapter. For those you get right, congratulate yourself, but review the sections they address in order to learn additional details about the topic.

_____ **1.** According to the Cellular Telecommunications Industry Association, over 276 million people in the United States subscribe to a wireless telephone service.

_____ **2.** E-commerce is a term that means that the commerce of the United States is in excellent condition.

_____ **3.** A customer service representative might also have one of the following job titles: associate, sales representative, consumer affairs counselor, consultant, technical service representative, operator, account executive, attendant, or engineer.

_____ **4.** The acronym TTY is used by call center staff members to indicate that something is to be done today.

_____ **5.** Many organizations think of technology as a way to reduce staff and save money.

_____ **6.** One way to improve your image over the telephone is to continually evaluate your speech.

_____ **7.** Jargon, slang, and colloquialisms can distort message meaning.

_____ **8.** Adjusting your rate of speech to mirror a customer's rate can aid comprehension.

_____ **9.** Quoting policy is one way to ensure that customers understand why you can't give them what they want.

_____ **10.** To ensure that accurate communication has taken place, you should summarize key points at the end of a telephone conversation.

_____ **11.** Blind transfers are effective if you don't take too much time explaining who is calling.

_____ **12.** Chewing food and gum, drinking, or talking to others while on the telephone can be distracting and should be avoided.

_____ **13.** Using voice mail to answer calls is an effective way to avoid interruptions while you are speaking to a customer.

_____ **14.** Planning calls and the information you will leave on a voice mail is an effective way to avoid service breakdown.

_____ **15.** Because of the cost of technology, small businesses cannot effectively benefit from its use as a customer service tool.

Answers to Quick Preview can be found at the end of the chapter.

LO 9-1 The Role of Technology in Customer Service

Concept Customer service is a 24/7 responsibility, and technology can assist in making it effective.

To say that technology has permeated almost every aspect of life in most developed countries would be an understatement. With the number of Internet users continuing to climb throughout the world, it is no wonder that online sales of products and services continue to rise. Of the estimated $906 billion dollars in retail sales in the second quarter 2009, 3.6 percent $32.4 billion was from e-commerce sales.[2] According to Internet World Stats (www.internetworldstats.com/stats.htm) there were an estimated 1,802,330,457 Internet users worldwide as of December 31, 2009. Further, the site indicates that 259,561,000 people, or 76.2 percent of the population

fax-on-demand Technology that allows information, such as a form, stored in a computer to be requested electronically via a telephone and transmitted to a customer.

Internet callback Technology that allows someone browsing the Internet to key a prompt on a Web site and have a service representative call a phone number provided.

Internet telephony Technology that allows people to talk to one another via the Internet as if they were on a regular telephone.

interactive voice response (IVR) system Technology that allows customers to call an organization 24 hours a day, 7 days a week to get information from recorded messages or a computer by keying a series of numbers on the telephone keypad in response to questions or prompts.

voice response unit (VRU) System that allows customers to call 24 hours a day, 7 days a week by keying a series of numbers on the telephone keypad in order to get information or answers to questions.

media blending Technology that allows a service provider to communicate with a customer via telephone while at the same time displaying information to the customer over the computer.

online information fulfillment system Technology that allows a customer to access an organization's Web site and click on desired information without having to interact with a service provider.

computer equipped with a modem. Information can be sent anywhere in the world in minutes, or a customer can make a call, key in a code number, and have information delivered to his or her fax machine or computer without ever speaking to a person (**fax-on-demand** system).

Internet Callback

An **Internet callback** system allows someone browsing the Internet to click on words or phrases (e.g., *Call me*), enter his or her phone number, and continue browsing. This triggers a predictive dialing system (discussed later in this chapter) and assigns an agent to handle the call when it rings at the customer's end.

Internet Telephony

Internet telephony allows users to have voice communications over the Internet. Although widely discussed in the industry, call center Internet telephony is in its infancy, lacks standards, and is not currently embraced by consumers. Power outages, quality issues with transmissions, and other technical glitches have prevented this medium from becoming widely used by most organizations.

Interactive Voice Response (IVR) or Voice Response Unit (VRU)

An **interactive voice response (IVR) system** or a **voice response unit (VRU)** allows customers to call in 24 hours a day, 7 days a week, even when customer service representatives are not available. By keying in a series of numbers on the phone, customers can get information or answers to questions. Such systems perform a text-to-speech conversion to present database information audibly to a caller. They also ensure consistency of information. Banks and credit card companies use such systems to allow customers to access account information.

Media Blending

Media blending allows agents to communicate with a customer over a telephone line at the same time information is displayed over the Internet to the customer. As with Internet telephony, this technology has not yet been taken to its full potential.

Online Information Fulfillment System

An **online information fulfillment system** allows customers to go to the World Wide Web, access an organization's Web site, and click on desired information. This is one of the fastest-growing customer service technologies. Every competitive business will eventually use this system so that customers can get information and place orders.

Predictive Dialing System

A **predictive dialing system** automatically places outgoing calls and delivers incoming calls to the next available agent. This system is often used in outbound (telemarketing/call center) operations. Because of numerous abuses, the government is continually restricting its use.

Screen Pop-Ups

Screen pop-ups are used in conjunction with ANI and IVR systems to identify callers. As a call is received and dispatched to an agent, the system provides information about the caller that "pops" onto the agent's screen before he or she answers the telephone (e.g., order information, membership data, service history, contact history).

Speech Recognition

Speech recognition programs allow a system to recognize keywords or phrases from a caller. These systems can be for routing callers to a representative and for retrieving information from a database. This technology is incorporated into a customer contact center's voice response system. It is typically used by individuals to dictate data directly into a computer, which then converts the spoken words into text. There is a variety of potential applications for voice-recognition systems for all contact centers. Some organizations are recording customers' voices (passwords and phrases) as a means of identification so that customers can gain access to their accounts without allowing unauthorized persons to break into them and steal personal information. With other applications, agents speak into a computer, instead of typing data, and people who have disabilities can obtain data from their accounts by speaking into the computer.

Telephone Typewriter System (TTY)

Partly because of the passage of the 1990 Americans with Disabilities Act in the United States, and similar laws in other countries, which required that telecommunication services be available to people with disabilities, organizations now have the technology to assist customers who have hearing and speech impairments. By using a **Telephone Typewriter system (TTY)**—a typewriter-type device for sending messages back and forth over telephone lines—a person who has a hearing or speech impairment can contact someone who is using a standard telephone. The sender and the receiver type their messages using the TTY. To do this, the sender or receiver can go through an operator-assisted relay service provided by local and long-distance telephone companies to reach companies and individuals who do not have TTY receiving technology, or the user can get in touch directly with companies that have TTYs. The service is free of charge. Operators can help first-time hearing-disabled users understand the rules in using TTY. Also, local speech and hearing centers can often provide training on the use of TTY in a call center environment.

predictive dialing system
Technology that automatically places outgoing calls and delivers incoming calls to the next available service representative in a call center.

screen pop-ups Small screen images that are programmed to appear on someone's computer monitor when a Web site is accessed.

Telephone Typewriter system (TTY) A typewriter-like device used by people with hearing disabilities for typing messages back and forth via telephone lines. It is also known as Telecommunications Device for the Deaf (TDD).

The federal government has a similar service (Federal Information Relay Service, or FIRS) for individuals who wish to conduct business with any branch of the federal government nationwide.

Video

For customers and customer contact centers equipped with video camera–computer hookups, this evolving technology allows customers and agents to interact via the computer. Like the interactive video kiosks discussed earlier in this book, this technology allows customers and agents to see one another during their interactions. Because of privacy concerns or preference, some software allows customers to block their image, yet they still see the agent to whom they are speaking.

Some organizations are exploring other types of technology to serve customers better, including biometric technology. See Figure 9.4 for some examples of how biometric technology is being used.

Advantages and Disadvantages of Technology

Like anything else related to customer service, technology offers advantages and disadvantages. The following sections briefly review some of the issues resulting from the use of technology.

Organizational Issues

Distinct advantages accrue to organizations that use technology. Through the use of computers, software, and various telecommunication devices, a

Figure 9.4
Technology in Action

In addition to telephonic and call center–based technology used to serve customers better, there are other types being explored by various organizations. One example is a Biometric Entry System. Many larger organizations are using fingerprint or thumbprint and retinal eye verification to prohibit unauthorized entry into restricted areas and from preventing access to a customer's personal data or property without permission. For example, Walt Disney World in Orlando requires guests who purchase an annual pass to their parks in Florida to provide a fingerprint at time of purchase. Subsequently, when using their pass at the security/entrance gate at one of the parks, they must place their finger onto the security pad three times to verify they are the authorized user. This prevents fraudulent users from getting into the park and costing the company money, since Disney often provides specials at different times (e.g., discounted passes to military family members or Florida resident discounts). It also protects a guest who loses a pass from having an unauthorized person use it. In the latter instance, customers can rest assured that if they buy a pass in January and subsequently misplace or lose it, they will be able to replace it and prevent some unauthorized person from using their visits.

Financial institutions and retail organizations are using evolving biometric technology to reduce customer wait times by speeding up the customer authentication process for sensitive transaction (e.g., check cashing) and to help deter identity thieves and fraudsters. Additionally, security agencies in over 100 countries are using biometric passports (called e-passports) to decrease the likelihood of counterfeit documentation and strengthen border security.

company can extend its presence without physically establishing a business site and without adding staff. Simply by setting up a Web site, organizations can become known and develop a worldwide customer base while helping to equalize the playing field with larger competitors. This is because, on the Internet, visitors do not know how many employees or buildings and how much money an organization has when they view a Web site. Information and services can be provided on demand to customers. Often, many customers can be served simultaneously through the telephone, fax, and so on.

The challenge for organizations is to have well-maintained, state-of-the-art equipment and qualified, competent people to operate it. In a low-unemployment period, this can be a challenge and can possibly result in disgruntled customers who have to wait on hold for service until an agent is available to help them.

Staying on top of competition with technology is an expensive venture. New and upgraded software and hardware appear almost every day. If a company is using systems that are six months old, these systems are on their way to becoming obsolete. Also, new technology typically brings with it a need to train or retrain staff. The end result is that employees have to be taken away from their jobs for training.

Customer Service Success Tip

Take the time to read equipment manuals and clarify operational issues and questions before customers contact you. Technology can aid service efficiency and reduce your stress levels if you learn to master and use it effectively.

Employee Issues

Technology brings many benefits to employees. The greatest benefit is that it frees them from mundane tasks such as taking information and mailing out forms, information, or other materials. These tasks can be done by using fax-on-demand, IVR, or online fulfillment systems. Technology also allows employees to serve more people in a shorter period of time—and to do it better.

The downside for employees is that many organizations see technology as a way to reduce staff costs and overhead related to employees, and they therefore eliminate positions. Moreover, as mentioned before, new technology requires new training and skills. Some people have difficulty using technology and are not able to master it. This in turn can lead to reassignment or dismissal. To avoid such negative outcomes, you and your peers should continually work to stay abreast of technology trends by checking the Internet or taking refresher courses through your organization's training department or local community resources.

Another problem created is an increase in stress levels of both employee and customer. This arises from the increased pace of business and daily life, from the need for employees to keep up to date with technology, and so on. Stress accounts for some of the high turnover rate in call center staff and for customer defection. But it doesn't necessarily have to be that way. For more information on dealing with stress and time more effectively in a service environment, visit www.mhhe.com/customerservice.

Customer Issues

In the age of technology, people contacting your organization typically expect immediate responses or assistance. They do not care about problems with your system. They likely expect that issues related to services, phone systems, and other equipment are anticipated and an alternative is available—and that you have a backup plan in place to handle them when something fails. If that is not the case and you make excuses for why you cannot deliver service (e.g., "I'm sorry, my system just went down. Can you call back later?"), chances are that you may never again hear from the person. If you do, it is often in a form of complaint to your supervisor.

It is not the customers' fault, nor their responsibility to call you back. There should either be a process for circumventing technical problems and you should take the initiative to get the information they need and get back to them as soon as possible (e.g., "My apologies Mr. Hernandez, my computer system just went offline. Rather than keep you waiting, please tell me exactly what information you need. As soon as the system comes back online, I will research the issue and get back to you with an answer. Is that acceptable?" If the customer agrees, say something like, "Please give me a phone number and an e-mail address where I can reach you."). If customers tell you they need an answer right away, ask them to hold while you check with someone else to try and get an answer. Certainly, these steps will not work in every situation or satisfy every customer; however, you should make a positive good faith effort to assist them right away.

From a customer standpoint, technology can be a blessing. From the comfort and convenience of a home, office, car, or anywhere a customer may have a telephone or laptop computer, he or she can access products and services. More people than ever have access to the Internet and computers. Technologies allow a customer to get information, order products, have questions about billing or other matters answered, and access virtually anything she or he wants on the World Wide Web.

However, this convenience comes with a cost to customers, just as it does for organizations. To have the latest gadgets is costly in terms of time and money. For example, when a customer calls an 800 or 888 support number, or must pay for a call to a support center, it is not unusual for the customer to wait on hold for the next available agent. Also, technology does not always work as it is designed to. For example, a Web site might not provide clear instructions about how to enter an account number or how to get a password. Even if a customer follows the instructions exactly, he or she might repeatedly get a frustrating error message instructing him or her to reenter the data. At some point, the customer will simply give up and go to another Web site. Another example would be to get caught in "voice mail jail." In this situation the customer follows the instructions, pressing the appropriate phone keys to get to a representative, only to find that the representative has forwarded his or her calls to another voice mailbox. Eventually the instructions either lead the customer back to the first message or the customer is disconnected.

Another major consumer issue related to telephone usage is that many organizations conduct direct marketing (telemarketing) and/or collections

Customer Service Success Tip

Make sure that you have a "backup plan" to use in case technology fails (e.g., the electricity fails and the cash register will not work or the computer system goes down). Discuss this with your supervisor before something goes wrong.

activities via the telephone. Unfortunately, many unscrupulous telemarketers pressure-call recipients, illegally take advantage of them, and/or violate personal privacy. As a result many states and the federal government have passed laws dictating how business via the telephone can be done. If you are involved in this type of outbound calling, it is crucial that you and your organization adhere to laws prohibiting when you may call someone and how business can be conducted. Consumers can now apply to be on a national do-not-call list. Many states have similar lists. Organizations and representatives who continue to call phone numbers that appear on this list, if they have not been given permission to do so by the consumer and/or have no preexisting business relationship, can face stiff financial and legal penalties.

Additional Issues

Just as with any system, there are people who will take advantage of it. Technology, especially the Internet, has spawned a new era of fraud and manipulation. This is a major concern for consumers and can create many challenges for you and your peers when you work in a call center. Some of the biggest problems you must deal with are customers' fear of fraud, violation of privacy, and concerns that their personal and financial information might be compromised, leading to future issues with their credit.

Informed customers go to great lengths to protect credit card, merchant account, and social security numbers, addresses, and personal data (e.g., arrest records, medical history, and family data). Many news stories have warned of criminal activity associated with technology. The result is that customers, especially those who are technically naive, have a level of distrust and paranoia related to giving information via the Internet and over the phone to unsolicited callers. This is why many Web sites involved in e-commerce offer the option of calling an 800 number instead of entering credit card and other personal information into an Internet order form. If you, as a customer service provider, encounter a lot of this type of reluctance, notify your supervisor. Some systemic issues may be adding to your customers' fears. You have a personal responsibility and a vested interest to improve processes and procedures in the organization. Helping identify these issues and dealing with them can make life easier for you and your customers while helping the organization improve the quality of service delivered and potentially increasing revenue streams. The latter can lead to more available cash for new equipment, facilities, salaries, and benefits.

One thing to remember is that a customer's reluctance to provide you with information is not necessarily a reflection on you or your service-providing peers; it is based more on a distrust in the system. Figure 9.5 lists some strategies you can use to help reduce customer fears related to communicating via technology.

Figure 9.5
Reducing Customer Fears about Technology

Avoiding customer concerns is often as simple as communicating effectively. Try some of the following approaches to help reassure your customers about the security of technology.

- Emphasize the organization's policy on security and service. If customers voice concerns about providing a credit card number over the phone or on the Internet, you might respond with "This is not a problem. You can either fax or mail the information to us."
- Stress participation in consumer watchdog or community organizations (e.g., Better Business Bureau or Chamber of Commerce), if your organization participates.
- Direct customers to areas on your Web site that show your digital certificate or security level (e.g., a Secure Socket Layer [SSL] logo from a third-party certifying source like VeriSign or Thawte) that indicate the encryption of information entered into the order system and transferred electronically.
- Point out any Web site page that shows the organization's history and shows how long you have been in business (assuming there has been a period of time since establishment). The longevity of a company can subconsciously allay fears and convince people that you have been around for awhile and not likely to go out of business tomorrow.
- Ask for only pertinent information.
- Answer questions quickly and openly (e.g., if a customer asks why you need certain information, respond in terms of customer service, such as "We need that information to ensure that we credit the right account.").
- Avoid asking for personal and financial account information when possible.
- Offer other options for data submission, if they are available.
- When using the telephone, smile and sound approachable in order to establish rapport (customers can "hear" a smile over the telephone).
- Listen carefully for voice tones that indicate hesitancy or uncertainty and respond appropriately (e.g., "You sound a bit hesitant about giving that information, Mr. Hopkins. Let me assure you that nothing will be processed until we have actually shipped your order.").
- Communicate in short, clear, and concise terms and sentences. Also, avoid technical or "legal" language that might confuse or frustrate the customer.
- Explain how personal information will be used or stored.

LO 9-3 Technology Strategies

There are numerous ways to incorporate technology into an organization's marketing, sales, and customer service initiatives. By creating opportunities to maintain regular contact with customers, you can help build a stronger relationship, reassure them, and show continuing support. All this leads to more customer loyalty and potentially higher levels of revenue generation from existing customers and those they refer. The following are some strategies that many organizations use to maintain a high touch relationship with current and potential customers.

Social Networking (e.g., LinkedIn and Facebook)

As you read earlier, people are using social networking Web sites to connect with one another, while businesses are starting to approach such Web sites from a sales generation and customer contact perspective. Organizations are beginning to recognize that such sites provide access to a wealth of customer data and opportunities to showcase themselves and their services and products. These sites provide a convenient, free, and widely accepted vehicle for sharing ideas and information with current and potential customers. For example, Web sites such as LinkedIn and Facebook, which allow users to create a free profile then connect with limitless numbers of people around the world, are perfect sources for gathering personal contact information. In effect, people who set up such accounts are putting their name and contact information in a public forum from which savvy organizations can "mine" the data. In the past, companies had to pay a lot of money for such information. Now, it is there for the choosing and many organizations have employees whose job it is to search and retrieve such data, and then pass it along to marketing and sales staff or others in the organization. Such information can be used to e-mail or push information to potential customers via cell phones and other technology.

Tied closely to social networking sites is the practice of publishing articles and other materials on self-help and professional Web sites that others can download and share with others. For example, the author of this book regularly posts articles that he has written on customer service and workplace topics on Web sites such as www.selfgrowth.com and www.ezinearticles.com. He also creates a personal profile about himself on those sites for potential readers (customers) to review. His articles are often picked up and used in corporate newsletters and magazines around the world as a result of this approach. Additionally, by placing a short sentence and Web site links about his company at the end of each article, he is in effect able to get free publicity and brand recognition for himself and organization. This in turn can lead potential clients and customers to his Web sites and result in future business opportunities. Thus, marketing and customer service initiatives are closely aligned.

Another growing trend for marrying common technology to customer service and marketing is the placement of video segments on YouTube. According to www.mashable.com (a site that tracks social media), YouTube serves 100 billion videos per day and around 20 million unique visitors a month. The site has a 29 percent share of the U.S. multimedia entertainment market accounting for 60 percent of all online videos watched. With this clout, organizations realize the full potential for getting their message in front of customers free each month. Many organizations have developed commercials, infomercials, and instructional videos that they have posted on the site. While many add value through step-by-step instructions and useful information for viewers, they often have promotional information (e.g., banners with corporate names and Web sites posted in the background).

MP3 and other audio files

With so many people using iPods and other MP3 player devices to listen to songs and other aural information, this tool is being tapped by a number of organizations to provide instructional materials, self-help presentations tied to their products and other materials that are of interest to a variety of people. They often allow people to download materials free from organizational Web site, subscribe through services online, or purchase the materials through Amazon, Walmart, and similar organizations. In effect, these organizations are providing useful information that have a secondary potential of spreading the word about their products and services.

Push Technology/Text Messages

Sending targeted text messages out to cell phone users is an example of how information is "pushed" out to customers without waiting for them to request it. For example, new and updated product information, customer satisfaction surveys, Web links, special sales offers, discounts, and other information that might benefit current and potential customers are automatically forwarded by the organization's server. Such information might be targeted at all existing customers in a database. Because of the potential cost involved to customers from their cell phone providers, smart companies are being cautious about how they use this form of communication. Someone who is going to be charged a fee for an unsolicited message is not likely to be a satisfied customer and the organization's efforts at cementing the relationship might actually backfire. The result could be negative word-of-mouth publicity or a complaint. SPAM email messages that you receive in your inbox daily is also an example of push technology in use.

Many organizations are also starting to use this vehicle to update and communicate with employees (internal customers) when they travel or work from virtual offices. They can quickly share information, images, data, changes, ideas and other crucial business-related information that allows workers to remain informed and have the latest information to better serve their customers and clients.

Tied to this push concept, many people use micro-blogging technology, such as Twitter, to send out short messages to large numbers of people and to allow people to "follow" them. In doing so, a service provider can quickly announce sales, updates to products and services, recalls, "thank you" messages, or whatever they like through the technology.

E-newsletters

Periodic electronic publications are a great way for organizations and business people to offer a value-added service to current and potential customers, suppliers, employees, and other interested parties. By producing a free e-newsletter that is e-mailed and/or posted on a Web site for customers to download, an organization can share ideas and product, service, and company information, along with useful tips, ideas, and information. The key is to make sure that anything e-mailed is to people who want to receive it. Anything that is unsolicited could be viewed as spam and result in repercussions from Web site hosting companies and government agencies. Such broadcast e-mail deliveries should always contain an "opt out" option that is clearly visible to recipients and that allows them to notify senders not to continue sending the files. An example of an e-newsletter for trainers, educators, and presenters can be found at www.globalperformancestrategies.com/ under the Monthly Newsletter section of the home page.

E-books/White Papers

Similar to the concept of e-newsletters, many organizations have subject matter experts whom they employ to create electronic books and research or white papers on topics of interest to customers. These books are then typically offered free through their Web site, e-mail or text messages, and social networking sites or in stores. Often, to get the publications, customers and other visitors must sign up for an e-newsletter, buy a product, or register their contact information on a Web site. This information then becomes a way of contacting people and pushing information to them later.

Webinars

Many organizations provide new product and usage demonstrations through scheduled training programs or webinars in which customers can register, obtain a password and call-in phone number, then join others in a technology-based learning event. They might log onto a designated Web site to view a slide show, call the designated number, and log into a telephone conference call where an organizational employee discusses a specific topic (e.g., product or service). Handouts might also be provided by emailing them to attendees in advance.

Satellite Technology

Depending on the industry in which you work, you may find yourself serving customers remotely through the use of satellite-based technology. For example, General Motors uses a system called OnStar to assist drivers of its vehicles. The system allows service representatives in service centers to remotely communicate with drivers in cases of accident, to remotely unlock a vehicle when someone locks the keys inside, or to provide data electronically (e.g., turn-by-turn directions through a partnership with Google). The company can also provide a detailed electronic diagnostic report of vehicle function to a customer's e-mail inbox monthly. In addition, drivers can use the system to make hands-free voice-activated telephone calls or to contact the service center with questions. The system can also use Global Positioning System (GPS) technology to pinpoint a car's location in cases of theft or automobile accident. All of this adds to customer peace of mind and provides an instant connection with a service representative in time of need.

Telecommuting

telecommuting A trend seen in many congested metropolitan areas and government offices. To reduce traffic and pollution and to save resources (e.g., rent, telephone, and technology systems), many organizations allow employees to set up home offices and from there electronically communicate and forward information to their corporate offices.

Many organizations have discovered that they can save money, adapt to employee lifestyle needs (e.g., single parents, people with disabilities, and parental caregivers), and provide service from remote locations through the use of technology through a process known as **telecommuting.** By allowing workers to work full- or part-time from home, organizations can eliminate the need for large facilities, telephone lines, support staff, and many other costly factors involved when there is a central building to which employees report for work.

When employees work from their own homes, they are often more satisfied, less stressed, and just as productive as when they come to an established office. Scheduling flexibility saves money (e.g., lunch at a restaurant or cafeteria, gas, vehicle maintenance, and business clothing), commuting time, wear and tear on their vehicles, and allows them to take care of personal tasks more easily (e.g., care for small children, parents, or someone with a disability, or be home when their school-aged children come home). All of this can lead to greater employee loyalty and job satisfaction.

By using dedicated telephone, facsimile, or cell phone lines, computers, and other customer service technology, employees can provide online and phone support to customers from home without their clients ever knowing that the employee is wearing a pair of shorts and t-shirt while sitting in a small home office.

Sometimes, an organization might have a remote office where employees report a couple days a week to take care of administrative reports, meet with customers or clients face to face, or attend staff meetings and training. In other instances, supervisors may do all their coaching, mentoring, and communication via technology with employees. This is all driven by the culture and purpose of the organization and the type of jobs that are involved.

LO 9-4 Technology Etiquette and Strategies

Concept Using technology ethically and with correct etiquette is important.

As with any other interaction with people, you should be aware of some basic dos and don'ts related to using technology to interact with and serve your customers. Failure to observe some commonsense rules can cause loss of a customer.

E-mail

The e-mail system was designed as an inexpensive, quick way of communicating via the World Wide Web. E-mail was not originally intended to replace formal written correspondence, although many organizations now use it to send things like attached correspondence and receipts and to notify customers of order status, to gather additional information needed to serve a customer, and for other business-related issues. No matter what the function, e-mail has its own set of guidelines for effective usage to ensure

LOL	Laugh out loud or lots of luck	ROTFL	Rolling on the floor laughing
BCNU	Be seeing you	TTFN	Ta ta for now
FYI	For your information	TTYL	Talk to you later
IMHO	In my humble opinion	BTW	By the way
FWIW	For what it's worth	ASAP	As soon as possible

Figure 9.6
Common Abbreviations

that you do not offend or otherwise create problems when dealing with customers via e-mail. Here are some e-mail tips to remember, as well as some etiquette for effective usage.

- *Use abbreviations and initials.* Since e-mail is an informal means of communicating, using acronyms and other short forms or abbreviations (e.g., USA versus United States of America) works fine in some cases. Just be sure that your receiver knows what the letters stand for; otherwise miscommunication could occur. Figure 9.6 lists some common abbreviations employed by e-mail users who typically know and e-mail one another frequently (e.g., internal customers, friends, and family members). When communicating with external customers, you may want to use abbreviations sparingly or avoid them altogether in order to prevent confusion, communication breakdown, and the perception that you are unprofessional.

- *Proofread and spell-check before sending a message.* Checking your message before sending an e-mail may help prevent damage to your professional image. This is especially true when writing customers, because you are representing your organization. Poor grammar, syntax, spelling, and usage can paint a poor picture of your abilities and professionalism and can leave a bad impression about your organization and its employees.

- *Think before writing.* This is especially important if you are answering an e-mail when you are upset or emotional. Take time to cool off before responding to a negative message (an insulting or provocative e-mail message is called a flame) or when you are angry. Remember that once you send an e-mail, you cannot take back your words. Your relationship with your receiver is at stake and the recipient can easily share your message with others (think about all the e-mailed messages you get regularly that have been forwarded to many other people and whose names appear in the text section of the e-mail). The latter is why you should never forward jokes, articles, or other materials that could be viewed as discriminatory or racist, or could cast a negative light on you and your organization. It is also why most companies do not allow personal use of their e-mail systems.

- *Use short, concise sentences.* The average person will not read lengthy messages sent by e-mail. Scrolling up and down pages of text is time-consuming and frustrating. Therefore, put your question or key idea in the first sentence or paragraph. Keep your sentences short and use new paragraphs often, for easier reading. A good rule of thumb is that if the entire message does not fit on a single viewing screen, consider whether another means of communication is more appropriate. An option would be to use the attachment feature so that lengthy documents can be printed out.

- *Use both upper- and lowercase letters.* With e-mail, writing a sentence or message in all-capital letters is like shouting at a person and could offend or cause relationship problems. In addition, reading a message written in all-capital letters is difficult and is likely to annoy your customer, whether or not he or she perceives it as "shouting."

- *Be careful with punctuation.* As with all-capital letters, you should use caution with punctuation marks, especially exclamation points, which can cause offense because, like all-capital letters, they indicate strong emotion.

- *Use e-mail only for informal correspondence.* Although it is becoming more acceptable to send business correspondence (e.g., contracts, resumes, and other information) via e-mail, it is probably better to use a more formal format in most instances (see the additional information at www.mhhe.com/customerservice). For example, it would be inappropriate to send a cancellation notice via e-mail. The receiver might think that the matter is not significant enough to warrant your organization's buying a stamp to mail a letter. However, this caution does not mean that you should not attach letters or other documents to an e-mail. Just consider the effect on the recipient. Another important thing to remember about e-mail is that it is sometimes unreliable. Many people do not check their e-mail regularly, especially if they use free e-mail accounts offered by yahoo.com, gmail.com, google.com, and other companies. Computer systems also fail and individuals often change service providers without notifying you. If your message is critical and delivery is time-sensitive, choose another method (e.g., a telephone call or express mail). If nothing else, call as a follow-up to ensure that the e-mail was received. Do not assume the addressee got your message.

In some cases, e-mail that is not delivered is not returned to the sender, so you may not know why the recipient did not respond. If your computer system allows, you can also request a return receipt notification showing the time and date that a message was opened. The

A recipient cannot always decipher your intended tone when reading an e-mail. What are some things to keep in mind when composing professional e-mails to avoid unnecessary conflict and/or frustration?

downside of that is that your receivers can cancel the return notification on their end and you will still not know if the message ever arrived.

- *Use organization e-mail for business only.* Many companies have policies prohibiting sending personal e-mail via their system. Some companies have started to actively monitor outgoing messages and many now can use unauthorized use of the e-mail as grounds for dismissal. Avoid violating your company's policy on this. Remember, too, that while you are sending personal messages, you are wasting productive time and your customers may be waiting.

  Unless you have security software that will decode and mask the information, hackers or others who do not have a right or need to know such information can gain access to it. A good rule of thumb is to never send anything by e-mail that you would not want to see in tomorrow's newspaper.

- *Use blind courtesy copies sparingly.* Most e-mail systems allow you to send a copy to someone without the original addressee knowing it (a blind courtesy copy, or bcc). If the recipient becomes aware of the bcc, your actions might be viewed as suspicious, and your motives brought into question. A customer might view your actions as an attempt to hide something from him or her. Thus, a relationship breakdown could occur if the original recipient discovers the existence of the bcc or if the recipient of the bcc misuses the information.

- *Copy only necessary people.* Nowadays, most people are overloaded with work and do not have the time to read every e-mail. If someone does not need to see a message, do not send that person a copy with the "reply to all" function available in e-mail programs. When you do the latter, anyone listed as a recipient or copied will get the return e-mail.

- *Get permission to send advertisements or promotional materials.* As mentioned earlier, people have little time or patience to read lengthy e-mail messages, especially from someone trying to promote or sell them something. This is viewed the same way you probably think of unsolicited junk mail or telemarketing calls at home. Companies should routinely have an "opt-out" check box available when they are soliciting e-mail information from their customers. If your company does not have this option, it might be well for management to consider such an option as a service to their customers and potential customers.

- *Be cautious in using emoticons.* **Emoticons (emotional icons)** are the faces created through the use of computer keyboard characters. Many people believe that their use in business correspondence is inappropriate and too informal. Also, since humor is a matter of personal point of view, these symbols might be misinterpreted and confusing. This is especially true when you are corresponding with someone from a different culture. Figure 9.7 shows examples of emoticons.

- *Fill in your address line last.* This is a safety mechanism to ensure that you take the time to read and think about your message before you

Customer Service Success Tip

Never send financial, proprietary, or confidential information (e.g., credit card numbers, medical information, social security numbers, or personal or employment history information) via e-mail since it is an unsecured method of communicating.

emoticons (emotional icons) Humorous characters that send visual messages such as smiling or frowning. They are created with various strokes of the computer keyboard characters and symbols.

Figure 9.7
Some Emoticons

:-)	Happy	:-}	Embarrassment or sarcasm
:-(	Sad	:-D	Big grin or laugh
;-)	Flirting or wink	<:-)	Stupid question (dunce cap)
O /\	Defiant or determined	O:-)	Angel or saint
:-O	Yelling or surprise	>:-)	Devil
:-x	Lips are sealed	:~/	Really confused

send the e-mail. The message cannot be transmitted until you address it. You will have one last chance to think about the effect of the message on the recipient.

Facsimile

As with any other form of communication, there are certain dos and don'ts to abide by when you use a fax machine to transmit messages. Failing to adhere to these simple guidelines can cause frustration, anger, and a breakdown in the relationships between you and your customers or others to whom you send messages.

- *Be considerate of your receiver.* If you plan to send a multipage document to your customer, telephone in advance to make sure that it is OK and a good time to send it. This is especially true if you will be using a business number during the workday or if there is only one line for the telephone and fax machine. It is frustrating and irritating to customers when their fax is tied up because large documents are being transmitted. If you must send a large document, try to do so before or after working hours (e.g., before 9 A.M. or after 5 P.M.). Also, keep in mind geographic time differences. Following these tips can also help maintain good relationships with co-workers who may depend on the fax machine to conduct business with their customers.

- *Limit graphics.* Graphic images that are not needed to clarify written text waste the receiver's printer cartridge ink, tie up the machine unduly, and can irritate your receiver. Therefore, delete any unnecessary graphics (or solid colored areas) including your corporate logo on a cover sheet if it is heavily colored and requires a lot of ink to print. (If appropriate, create a special outline image of your logo for your fax cover sheets.)

- *Limit correspondence recipients.* As with e-mail and memorandums, limit the recipients of your messages. If they do not have a need to know, do not send them messages. Check your broadcast mailing list (a list of people who will receive all messages, often programmed into a computer) to ensure that it is limited to people who "have a need to know." This is also important from the standpoint of confidentiality. If the information you are sending is proprietary or sensitive in any way, think about who will receive it. Do not forget that unless the document is going directly to someone's computer fax modem, it may be lying in a stack of other incoming messages and accessible by people other than your intended recipient.

LO 9-5 The Telephone in Customer Service

Concept The telephone is the second most important link in customer service.

Not all service via technology, and specifically the telephone, is delivered from a customer contact center. Although many small- and medium-size organizations may have dedicated customer service professionals to staff their telephones, others do not. In the latter cases, the responsibility for answering the telephone and providing service falls on anyone who is available and hears the telephone ring (e.g., administrative assistant, salesperson, driver, nurse, partner, owner, or CEO).

Modern businesses rely heavily on the use of telephones to conduct day-to-day operations and communicate with internal as well as external customers. Effective use of the telephone saves employee time and effort. Employees no longer have to take time to physically travel to another location to interact with customers and vendors. By simply dialing a telephone number or typing in a text message on a cell phone, you are almost instantaneously transported anywhere in the world. And with the use of the fax and computer modem, documents and information can also be sent in minutes to someone thousands of miles away—even during nonbusiness hours. Figure 9.8 lists some advantages of telephone customer service.

With these tools, more businesses are setting up inbound (e.g., order taking, customer service, information sources) and outbound (e.g., telemarketing sales, customer service, customer surveys) telephone

Customer Service Success Tip

When a customer calls or contacts your organization, you should personally accept responsibility and do whatever you can to help ensure that he or she gets the finest level of service available. Remember that, in order to provide quality customer service, everyone in the organization has to take ownership for customer satisfaction. The first person interacting with a current or potential customer sends a powerful message about the organization and may be the only person with whom that customer ever deals. The way that person is treated will often determine the memory of the organization and whether he or she becomes a supporter or spreads the word about the poor service received.

Even though there are some disadvantages to telephone communication (e.g., lack of face-to-face contact with the customer), there are many advantages. Some of the advantages are discussed in the following sections.

- *Convenience.* Sales, information exchange, money collection, customer satisfaction surveys, and complaint handling are only a few of the many tasks that can be effectively handled by using the telephone and related equipment. If a quick answer is needed, the telephone can provide it without the need to travel and meet with someone face to face or to endure the delays caused by the mail.

- *Ease of communication.* Although some countries have more advanced telephone systems and capabilities than others, you can call someone in nearly any country in the world. And, with advances in cellular phone technology, even mobile phones have international communication capability.

- *Economy.* Face-to-face visits or sales calls are expensive and can be reduced or eliminated by making contacts over the telephone as opposed to traveling to a customer's location. With competitive rates offered by many telephone companies since the deregulation of the telecommunication industry years ago, companies and customers have many options for calling plans. For example, customers can purchase a calling card and use it from any telephone. All of this makes accessing customer services a simple and relatively inexpensive task, especially when combined with the other technology discussed in this chapter.

- *Efficiency.* You and your customer can interact without being delayed by writing and responding. Telephone usage is so simple that it is taught to kindergarten and grade school children.

Figure 9.8

Advantages of Telephone Customer Service

staffs. Through these groups of trained specialists, companies can expand their customer contact and be more likely to accomplish total customer satisfaction.

Communication Skills for Success

In Chapters 3 through 5, you read about the skills you need in face-to-face customer service. The same skills apply to providing effective customer service over the telephone, especially the use of vocal quality and listening skills. Your customer cannot communicate with or understand you if she or he doesn't accurately receive your message. To reduce the chances of message failure, think about the communication techniques discussed below.

- *Speak clearly*. By pronouncing words clearly and correctly, you increase the chances that your customer will accurately receive your intended message. Failure to use good diction could decrease a customer's comprehension of your message and be interpreted as a sign that you are lazy, unprofessional, or lack intelligence and/or education. If you are unsure how to improve your diction, review Chapter 3.

- *Limit jargon, slang, and colloquialisms*. Technical jargon (terms related to technology, an industry, a specific organization, or a job), slang (informal words used to make a message more colorful; e.g., *whoopee, blooper, bummer*), and colloquialisms (regional phrases or words such as, "fair to middling," "as slow as molasses," "if the good Lord's willing and the creek don't rise," or "faster than a New York minute") can distort your message and detract from your ability to communicate effectively. This is especially true when your recipient speaks English as a second language (see Chapter 8 for more information on this topic). By using words or phrases unfamiliar to the customer, you draw the customer's attention away from listening to your message. This is because, when people encounter a word or phrase that is unfamiliar, they tend to stop and reflect on that word or phrase. When this occurs, the next part of the message is missed while the mind tries to focus on and decipher the unfamiliar element it encountered. You must then repeat the missed portion or end up with a miscommunication.

- *Adjust your volume*. As your conversation progresses, it may become apparent that you need to speak more loudly or more softly to your customer. Obvious cues are statements from the customer, such as, "You don't have to yell" or "Could you speak up?" Or if your customer is speaking really loudly, he or she may have a hearing impairment. To find out if this is the case, you could say, "I'm sorry, Mrs. Reynolds, are you able to hear me clearly? I'm having trouble with loud volume on my end."

- *Speak at a rate that allows comprehension*. Depending on the person to whom you are speaking, you may find yourself having to adjust your rate of speech (covered in Chapter 3) by either speeding up or slowing down. A good rule of thumb is to mirror or match the other person's rate of speech to some extent, since he or she is probably comfortable with it. Otherwise you risk boring the customer by speaking too slowly, or confusing the customer by speaking too rapidly. Be careful not to be too obvious or unnatural when doing this; otherwise, some customers may think that you're making fun of them.

- *Use voice inflection*. By using inflection and avoiding a tendency to speak in a monotone, you can help communicate your message in an interesting manner that will hold your customer's attention. The result might be saved time, since your message may be received correctly the first time and you will not have to repeat it.

- *Use correct grammar*. Just as important as enunciation, good grammar helps project a positive, competent image. When you fail to use good grammar in your communication, you may be perceived as lazy or uneducated. Keep in mind that your customer forms an image of you and the company you represent simply by listening to you and the way you speak. (Grammar is covered in more detail at www.mhhe.com/customerservice).

- *Pause occasionally*. This simple yet dramatic technique can sometimes affect the course of a conversation. By pausing after you make a statement or ask a question, you give yourself time to breathe and think. You also give your customer an opportunity to reflect on what you have said or to ask questions. This practice can greatly aid in reducing tension when you are speaking with an upset customer or one who does not speak your language fluently.

- *Smile as you speak*. By smiling, you project an upbeat, warm, and sincere attitude through the phone. This can often cheer the customer, diffuse irritation, and help build rapport. A technique some telephone professionals use to remind themselves to smile when placing or answering a call is to put a small mirror or a picture of a "smiling face" in front of them or next to their telephone. This reminds them to smile as they talk.

- *Project a positive image and attitude*. All the tips related to using your voice that were presented in earlier chapters contribute to how people envision you. Customers generally do not want to hear what you cannot do for them or about the bad day you're having. They want a timely, affirmative answer to their questions or solution of their problems. Giving anything less is likely to discourage or annoy them and result in a service breakdown.

- *Wait to speak*. Many people tend to interrupt a customer to add information or ask a question. As you read in Chapter 5, this is not only rude but

Customer Service Success Tip

Avoid distractions while you are on the phone in order to help prevent breakdowns in communication. It is difficult to listen effectively when you are reading something, writing notes to yourself, using a cash register, typing, polishing your fingernails, and so on.

Never underestimate the importance of smiling when you speak to customers. They can hear it in your voice!

can cause a breakdown in communication and possibly anger the customer. If you ask a question or if the customer is speaking, allow him or her to respond or to finish speaking before interjecting your thoughts or comments.

- *Listen actively*. Just as with face-to-face communication, effective listening is a crucial telephone skill for the customer service provider. The need to focus is even more important when you are speaking on the phone, since you do not have nonverbal cues or visual contact to help in message delivery or interpretation. Information on active listening was covered in Chapter 5.

Tips for Creating a Positive Telephone Image

People quickly form an opinion of you and your organization. The message they receive often determines how they interact with you during the conversation and in your future relationship. Keep in mind that when you answer your organization's telephone, or call someone else as part of your job, you represent yourself and the organization. Since many telephone calls are short, you have limited opportunity to make a positive impression.

❋ Ethical Dilemma 9.1

Before discussing the following dilemma with other students, research the National Do-Not-Call Registry on the Internet.

You have heard that there are federal laws that prohibit call centers from contacting people with whom they have no prior business relationship or who are a National Do-Not-Call Registry. Your organization has recently started a phone campaign to identify potential customers and is using a number of phone lists obtained from various other companies. When you remind your supervisor about the nonsolicitation law, she tells you not to worry about it, and instructs you that if someone complains or states they are on a do not call list when you call, to just hang up.

1. Are there any potential legal problems with this policy? If so what might they be?

2. Are there any ethical issues here? Explain.

3. What should you do in this situation?

When you feel good about yourself, you normally project a naturally confident and pleasant image. On days when things aren't going so well for you, your self-image may tend to suffer. Here are some suggestions to help serve your customers effectively and leave them thinking well of you and your organization.

- *Continually evaluate yourself*. You are your own best critic. From time to time, think about your conversation—what went well, what could have been improved. If possible, occasionally tape-record your conversations and evaluate your voice qualities and message delivery. Have someone else listen to the tape and provide objective feedback.

To help in your self-assessment, you may want to make copies of Worksheet 9.1 (see www.mhhe.com/customerservice) and evaluate all your calls for a specific period of time (for example, a couple of hours or a day).

- *Use proper body posture*. The following can negatively affect the sound and quality of your voice:

  Slouching in your chair.

  Sitting with your feet on a desk with your arms behind your head as you rock back and forth in your chair.

  Looking down, with your chin on your chest, to read or search through drawers.

  Resting the telephone handset between your cheek and shoulder as you do other work (e.g., type data into a computer, look for something, write, or doodle).

  Strive to sit or stand upright and speak clearly into the mouthpiece whether you are using a headset or handheld receiver. If you are using a handheld receiver, make sure that the earpiece is placed firmly against your ear and the mouthpiece is directly in front of your mouth.

- *Be prepared*. Answer a ringing phone promptly and use a standard greeting as outlined later in this chapter.

- *Speak naturally*. Whether you are calling someone or providing information to a caller, speak in a conversational voice. Don't use a "canned" or mechanical presentation, and don't read from a prepared script, unless you are required to do so by your company. If you must read from a script, *practice, practice, practice*. Before you connect with a customer, become very comfortable with your presentation so that you can deliver it in a fluid, warm, and sincere manner. Nothing sends a more negative message than a service provider who mispronounces a customer's name, stumbles through opening comments, and seems disorganized.

- *Be time-conscious*. Customers appreciate prompt, courteous service. Be aware that time is money—yours, your organization's, and the customer's. Have your thoughts organized when you call a customer. It is a good idea to have a list of questions or key points ready before calling (see Worksheet 9.2 at www.mhhe.com/customerservice as an example). If a customer calls you and you don't have an answer or information readily available, offer to do some research and call back instead of putting the customer on hold. Respect your customer's time. Chances are that customers will prefer to hold if they will be waiting only a short time, but give them the option. In addition to helping better organize your calls, a written call-planning sheet will provide a good record of the call.

- *Be proactive with service*. If you must say no to a customer, do so in a positive manner without quoting policy. Tell the customer what you can do. For example, if your policy prohibits refunds on one-of-a-kind or closeout items, you might make an offer such as this (depending on your level of authority or empowerment):

"Mr. Targowski, I see that the computer you ordered from our Web site was a closeout item. I understand that you have decided that you need more RAM. Although I cannot give refunds on a closeout item, I can give you a voucher good at any of our retail locations for a $50 discount on a memory chip upgrade or free installation, whichever you prefer."

- Doing more than the customer expects after a breakdown (this is called *service recovery* and is discussed in Chapter 7) is important, especially if you or your company made an error. When you or your company is not responsible for the error, but you want to maintain a positive customer-provider relationship, going out of your way to help make it better is just good business practice.

- *Conclude calls professionally*. Ending a call on an upbeat note, using the caller's name, and summarizing key actions to be taken by both parties are all recommended practices. For example, you might say, "All right, Ms. Herrick, let me confirm what we've discussed. I'll get _____ by the 23rd, and call you to confirm _____. You'll take care of _____. Is that correct?" Once agreement has been reached, thank the customer for calling, ask what other questions he or she has or what else you can assist with, and then let the customer hang up first. By following this type of format, you can reduce misunderstandings and elicit any last-minute questions or comments the customer might have. If you fail to bring the conversation to a formal close and hang up abruptly, the customer may feel you are in a hurry to finish servicing him or her (regardless of the fact that you have just spent 15 minutes talking with him or her!). Think of this final step as wrapping a gift: it looks fine, but adding a nice ribbon and bow makes it look even better. The thank-you and polite sign off are your ribbon and bow.

Effective Telephone Usage

One basic strategy for successfully providing effective customer service over the telephone is to thoroughly understand all phone features and use them effectively. This may seem to be a logical and simple concept, but think about times when you called a company and someone attempted to transfer you, or put you on hold, or did not communicate clearly. If the transfer was successful, you were lucky (Figure 9.9 gives tips for effectively using the hold and transfer features). If not, you probably couldn't understand what happened, got disconnected, were connected to the wrong party, or heard the original person come back on the telephone to apologize and say something like, "The call didn't go through. Let me try again." Sound familiar? If so, use the following strategies to ensure that you do not deliver similar poor service.

- *Eliminate distractions*. Do not eat food, chew gum, drink, talk to others, read (unless for the purpose of providing the customer with information),

Be sure you understand how the telephone transfer (sometimes called the link) and hold functions work. Nothing is more frustrating or irritating for callers than to be shuffled from one person to the next or to be placed on what seems to be an endless hold. Here are some suggestions that can help to increase your effectiveness in these areas:

Always request permission before transferring a caller. This shows respect for the caller and psychologically gives the caller a feeling of control over the conversation. You can also offer options (you can ask the caller to allow a transfer or let you take a message). This is especially helpful when the customer is already irritated or has a problem. Before transferring the call, explain why you need to do so. You might say, "The person who handles billing questions is Shashandra Philips at extension 4739. May I transfer you, or would you rather I take a message and pass it along to her?" This saves you and the caller time and effort, and you have provided professional, courteous service. If the caller says, "Yes, please transfer me," follow by saying something like, "I'd be happy to connect you. Again, if you are accidentally disconnected, I'll be calling Shashandra Philips at extension 4739."

Once you have successfully reached the intended person, announce the call by saying, "Shashandra, this is (your name), from (your department). I have (customer's name) on the phone. She has a (question, problem). Are you the right person to handle that?" If Shashandra answers yes, connect the caller and announce, "(Customer's name), I have Shashandra Philips on the line. She will be happy to assist you. Thanks for calling (or some similar positive disconnect phrase)." You can then hang up, knowing that you did your part in delivering quality customer service.

   If the call taker is not available or is not the appropriate person, reconnect with the customer and explain the situation. Then offer to take a message rather than trying to transfer to different people while keeping the customer on hold. You would make an exception if the call taker informed you of the appropriate person to whom you should transfer, or if the customer insisted on staying on the line while you tried to transfer to the right person.

You should avoid making a blind transfer. This practice is ineffective, rude, and not customer-focused. A **blind transfer** happens when a service provider asks a caller, "May I transfer you to Cathy in Billing?" or may even say, without permission, "Let me transfer you to Tom in Shipping." Once the intended transfer party answers, the person transferring the call hangs up. Always announce your caller by waiting for the phone to be picked up and saying, "This is (your name) in (your department). I have (customer's name) on the line. Can you take the call?" Failure to do this could result in a confrontation between the two people. If the calling customer is already upset, you have just set up a situation that could lead to a lost customer and/or angry coworker.

If you place someone on hold, it is a good idea to go back on the line every 20 to 30 seconds to let the person know that you have not forgotten the call. This action becomes more important if the phone system you are using does not offer information or music that the customer hears during the holding time.

One final word about holds. Once you return to the phone to take the call, thank the caller for waiting.

Figure 9.9
Transfer Calls and Use the Hold Function Properly

blind transfer The practice of transferring an incoming caller to another telephone number.

or handle other office tasks (filing, stapling, stamping, sealing envelopes, etc.) while on the phone. Your voice quality will alert the customer to the fact that you are otherwise occupied.

- *Answer promptly*. A lot is communicated by the way a phone call is handled. One tip for success is to always answer by the third or fourth ring. This sends a nonverbal message to your customers of your availability to serve them. It also reduces the irritating ringing that you, co-workers, or customers have to hear.

- *Use titles with names*. It has been said that there is nothing sweeter than hearing one's own name. However, until you are told otherwise, use a person's title (e.g., Mr., Mrs., Ms., or Dr.) and last name. Do not assume that it is alright to use first names. Some people regard the use of their first name as insolent or rude. This may especially be true of older customers and people from other cultures where respect and use of titles are valued. When you are speaking with customers, it is also a good idea to use their name frequently (don't overdo it, though, or you'll sound mechanical). Repeat the name directly after the greeting (e.g., "Yes, Dr. Carmine, how may I help you?"), during the conversation (e.g., "One idea I have, Mr. Perrier, is to . . ."), and at the end of the call (e.g., "Thanks for calling, Mrs. Needham. I'll get that information right out to you. Is there anything else I can do to assist you today?").

- *Ask questions*. You read about the use of questions earlier in the book. Use them on the telephone to get information or clarify points made by the customer. Ask open-end questions; then listen to the response carefully. To clarify or verify information, use closed-end questions.

- *Use speakerphones with caution*. Speakerphones make sense for people who have certain disabilities and in some environments (where you need free hands or are doing something else while you are on hold or are waiting for a phone to be answered). From a customer service standpoint, they can send a cold or impersonal message, and their use should be minimal. Many callers do not like them and even think that speakerphone users are rude. Also, depending on the equipment used and how far you are from the telephone, the message received by your customer could be distorted, or it might seem as though you are in an echo chamber. Before using a speakerphone, ask yourself whether there is a valid reason for not using a headset or handheld phone.

  When you are using a speakerphone, make sure that your conversation will not be overheard if you are discussing personal, proprietary, or confidential information. Also, if someone is listening in on the customer's conversation, make sure that you inform the customer of that fact and explain who the listener is and why he or she is listening. As you read earlier, some people are very protective of their privacy and their feelings should be respected.

- *Use call waiting*. A useful feature offered by many phone systems is call waiting. While you are on the phone, a signal (usually a beep) indicates that there is an incoming call. When you hear the signal, you have a

---

✳ Customer Service Success Tip

Use equipment properly. Ensure that the earpiece and mouthpiece rest squarely against your ear and in front of your mouth, respectively when speaking to customers. This allows you to accurately hear what is said and accurately and clearly transmit your words to the customer. Your success or failure in receiving and delivering messages often hinges on simply holding the receiver or wearing a headset properly. This allows you to accurately hear what is said and accurately and clearly transmit your words to the customer.

couple of options: excuse yourself from your current call, by getting permission to place the person on hold, or ignore the second caller. If you have a voice mail system, the system makes the choice for you by transferring incoming calls to your message system. Both options have advantages and disadvantages.

By taking the second call, you may irritate your current caller, who might hang up. This results in lost business. On the other hand, by not taking the second call, you might miss an important message and/or irritate that caller.

By ignoring the signal, you might offend the second caller. Research indicates that many customers forget to or decide against placing later calls to busy numbers, especially if they have already made several attempts. Customers may feel that you're too busy to properly serve them.

So, how do you handle the dilemma? Make a judgment about how the customer to whom you are speaking might react and then act accordingly. In some instances, company policies tell you what to do, so you don't have to decide.

Voice Mail and Answering Machines or Services

Although voice mail is hailed by many people as a time-saver and vehicle for delivering messages when an intended recipient is unavailable, many other people have difficulty dealing with this technology (including answering machines) or simply refuse to interact with a machine. Let's take a look at some ways to use voice mail.

* *Managing incoming calls*. To effectively use voice mail, you must first understand how your system works. Check the manuals delivered with your system or speak with your supervisor and/or the technical expert responsible for its maintenance.

  A key to using voice mail effectively is to keep your outgoing message current, indicating your availability, the type of information the caller should leave, and when the caller can expect a return call. If your system allows the caller the option of accessing an operator or another person, you should indicate this early in your outgoing message to save the caller from having to listen to unnecessary information. Figure 9.10 provides

---

* "Hello. This is (your name) of (company and department).
* I'm unavailable to take your call at the moment, but if you leave your name, number, and a brief message, I'll call you as soon as possible.
* Thanks for calling."

If you know when you will be returning calls (e.g., at the end of the workday), tell the caller so. If your voice mail system offers callers the option to press a number to speak with someone else, let them know this right after you tell them whose voice mail they have reached. This avoids requiring them to listen to a lengthy message before they can select an option.

Figure 9.10
Sample Outgoing Message

Evaluating Voice Mail

TO HELP INCREASE YOUR AWARENESS OF THE EFFECT OF VOICE MAIL MESSAGES, MAKE NOTE OF THE FOLLOWING QUESTIONS DURING THE COMING WEEK.

As you call people or organizations, consider the outgoing messages that they leave on their voice mail or answering machines and evaluate them, using the following questions.

1. Was the call answered by the fourth ring?

2. Did the announcement contain the following:

Greeting (hello, good morning, or good afternoon)

Organization's name

Departmental name

A statement of when the person will return

An early announcement of an option to press a number for assistance

Instructions for leaving a message

When calls will be returned

a sample outgoing message. Also, Work It Out 9.1 can be used to evaluate the voice mail messages of others when you call them. Another key to effective voice mail usage is to retrieve your calls and return them as soon as possible. Usually 24 hours, or by the next working day, is a good guideline for returning calls. Doing so sends a positive customer service message.

- *Placing calls to voice mail.* Many normally articulate people cannot speak coherently when they encounter an answering machine or voice mail. One technique for success is to plan your call before picking up the phone. Have a 30-second or less "sales" presentation in mind that you can deliver whether you get a person or machine. For example, if you get a person, try, "This is (your first and last name) from (company) calling (or returning a call) for Wilhelm Tackes. Is he available?" Also, have available a written list of the key points you want to discuss so you don't forget them as you talk.

    If you get a machine, try "This is (first and last name) from (company) calling (returning a call) for Inez Montoya. My number is _____. I will be available from _____ to _____." If you are calling to get or give information, you may want to add, "The reason I am calling is to _____." This allows the return caller to leave information on your voice mail or with someone else and thus avoid the game of telephone tag.

- *Avoiding telephone tag.* You have probably played telephone tag. The game starts when the intended call receiver is not available and a message is left. The game continues when the call is returned, the original caller is not available, a return message is left, and so on.

  Telephone tag is frustrating and a waste of valuable time. It results in a loss of efficiency, money, and in some cases, customers. To avoid telephone tag, plan your calls and make your messages effective by giving your name, company name, phone number, time and date of your call, and a succinct message, and by indicating when you can be reached. If appropriate, emphasize that it is all right to leave the information you have requested on your voice mail or with someone else. Also, you may suggest that your message recipient tell you a time when you can call or meet with him or her face to face. By doing this, you end the game and get what you need. Use Worksheet 9.3 (see www.mhhe.com/customerservice) to help plan your calls effectively.

Taking Messages Professionally

If you have ever received an incomplete or undecipherable telephone message, you can appreciate the need for practice in this area. At a minimum, when you take a message you should get the following information from the caller:

Name (correctly spelled—ask caller for spelling)

Company name

Phone number (with area code and country code, if appropriate)

Brief message

When call should be returned

Time and date of the call and your name (in case a question about the message arises)

If you are answering someone's phone while he or she is away, let the caller know right away. This can be done by using a statement such as, "Hello, (person's name) line. This is (your name). How may I assist you?" In addition, be cautious of statements you make regarding the intended recipient's availability. Sometimes, well-meant comments can send a negative message to customers. See Figure 9.11 for typical problem messages and better alternatives.

General Advice for Communicating by Telephone

Don't communicate personal information (someone is at the doctor's, on sick leave, etc.), belittle yourself (e.g., "I don't know," "I'm only . . .") or the company (e.g., "Nobody knows"), or use weak or negative language (e.g., "I think," "I can't"). Instead, simply state "Malik is unavailable. May I take a message?" or if appropriate, "I'd be happy to assist you."

Figure 9.11
Communicating Messages

Message	Possible Interpretation	Alternative
"I'm not sure where he is" or "He's out roaming around the building somewhere."	"Don't they have any control or structure at this company?"	"He's not available. May I take a message?"
"I'm sorry. She is *still* at lunch."	(Depending on the time of the call.) "Must be nice to have two-hour lunch breaks!"	Same as above or "I'm sorry, She is at lunch or is unavailable. May I assist you or take a message?"
"We *should* have that problem taken care of soon."	"Don't you know for sure?"	"I apologize for the inconvenience. We'll attempt to resolve this by _____."
"He isn't available right now. He's taking care of a crisis."	"Is there a problem there?"	"He isn't available right now. May I assist you or take a message?"
"She's not in today. I'm not sure when she'll be back."	Same as above.	"She's not in today. May I assist you or take a message?"
"He left early today."	"Obviously, you people are not very customer-focused or he would be there during normal business hours to assist me."	"He is out of the office. May I assist you or take a message?"
"I don't know where she is. I was just walking by and heard the phone ringing."	"Nice that you're so conscientious. Too bad others are not."	"She isn't available right now, but I'd be happy to take a message."
"I'll give him the message and try to get him to call you back."	"So there's a 50-50 chance I'll be served."	"I'll give him the message when he returns and ask him to call you back."
"Hang on a second while I find something to take a message with."	"Doesn't sound as if people at this company are very prepared to serve customers."	"Would you mind holding while I get a pen and paper?"

After you have taken the message, thank the caller before hanging up and then deliver the message to the intended receiver in a timely manner. If you discover that the receiver will not be available within a 24-hour period, you may want to call the customer and convey this information. If you do so, again offer to assist or suggest some other alternative, if one is available.

Small Business Perspective

Small businesses can benefit from technology in ways similar to larger organizations. Even though many may not have the human resources and finances to have their own call centers and internal support staff members, they have options for applying technology to their day-to-day operations. The Internet has provided a tremendous resource that allows even single-person or small family-run, home-based businesses to look like a much larger organization. By setting up a professional looking Web site, arranging to accept credit cards and/or PayPal as cash transaction systems, they can now participate in e-commerce activities. To get an idea of how this might appear online, visit Web site www.presentationre-sources.net. This family-run e-commerce business has operated since the mid-1990s with over 1,000 items offered online and thousands of custom-ers all over the world. Internally, tracking of revenue and expenses is han-dled on an off-the-shelf accounting software package. When there is a need for specialized services, such as printing, shipping and freight, legal, or graphic design, the owner simply contracts professionals who special-ize in those areas.

By setting up contracting arrangements with third-party organizations, small businesses can look like a major player in the business world. For example, Creative Presentation Resources, Inc. offers many large and elec-tronic items that would require a lot of warehouse space and tie up large amounts of revenue if they were stocked internally. Instead, special orders are handled through established business accounts with major manufac-turers and distributors who drop ship the items ordered by customers around the world through when they are ordered via the Web site, tele-phone or fax. When an order arrives, it is processed, and a purchase order is faxed to a supplier, who in turn ships the item and invoices the author's company. That company in turn invoices or collects payment from the cus-tomer placing the order. There are many small businesses using this pro-cess all over the world. According to Joanne Pratt in a report for the U.S. Small Business Administration, "Leading edge entrepreneurs are demon-strating that the Internet offers unparalleled opportunities for small busi-ness by developing imaginative ways to conduct e-business." That report pointed out that:

- Sixty-five percent of small, niche firms make a profit or cover the costs of their Web sites.
- Less than 10 percent of small businesses' online commerce is business-to-business.
- The smallest firms (fewer than 10 employees) benefit the most from be-ing online.[6]

The key to a successful e-commerce for a small business is to plan be-fore getting involved. There are many elements that must be considered (e.g., Web site design, maintenance and support, merchandise types and sources, marketing, distribution, payment processing, and staffing). To be successful, small businesses need a high-quality computer system with quality printer, fax machine, telephone, answering machine, and copier. A toll-free number is also valuable and sends a subliminal message that the company is larger and more professional.

Impact on Service

Based on personal experience and what you just read, list three to five small businesses with which you had business dealings within the past month, then answer the following questions about them:

1. What are some of the types of technology that you have witnessed these businesses using to serve their customers?
2. How successful were their employees in using the technology provided to them to service customers? Explain and give examples.
3. In what ways has technology hindered one or more of these companies from delivering effective customer service? Explain.
4. How could these companies improve service with new, different or upgraded technology?

Summary

Delivering customer service via technology can be an effective and efficient approach to use to achieve total customer satisfaction. However, you must continually upgrade your personal technology knowledge and skills, practice their application, and consciously evaluate the approach and techniques you use to provide service.

In the quality-oriented cultures now developing in the United States and in many other countries, service will make the difference between survival and failure for individuals and organizations. You are the front line, and you are often the first and only contact a customer will have with your company. Strive to use technology to its fullest potential, but do not forget that you and your peers ultimately determine whether expectations are met in the eyes of your customer.

Whether a company is large or small, technology can help make them successful when properly utilized. Smart and successful managers stay current of trends in society and act quickly to implement strategies that incorporate technology to address evolving customer needs.

Review Questions

1. In what ways can technology play a role in the delivery of effective customer service? Explain.
2. What are some advantages of using technology for service delivery?
3. What are some disadvantages of using technology for service delivery?
4. What are some of the communication skills for success?
5. How can you project a more positive image over the telephone?
6. What information should you always get when taking telephone messages?
7. When transferring calls, what should you avoid and why?
8. When you leave a message on voice mail, what information should you give?
9. What is telephone tag, and how can it be avoided or reduced?
10. How are small businesses benefitting from today's technology?

Search It Out

Search the Internet for Customer Service Technology

1. Visit www.youtube.com and search the phrase "customer service." Identify and download one example of a positive and a negative customer service experience that you can share with the class.

2. Log onto the Internet and search for sites that deal with customer service and the technology used to deliver quality customer service. Also, look for the Web sites and organizations that focus on the technology and people involved in the delivery of customer service. Be prepared to share what you find with the class.

3. Log onto the Internet and search for additional information about one of the technologies addressed in section LO 9-2 of this chapter. Report your findings to your classmates.

4. Log onto the Internet to search for books and other publications that focus on customer service and technology. Develop a bibliographic listing of at least seven to ten publications, make copies of the list, and share it with your classmates.

Collaborative Learning Activity

Practice Customer Service with Your Team Members

Get together in teams of three members each. One person will take the role of a customer service provider, one will be a customer, and one will be the observer. Use the following scenarios to practice the skills you have learned in this chapter. Incorporate other communication skills covered in previous chapters as you deal with your "customer." Use three of the four scenarios so that each person in a group has a chance to play each of the three roles. Depending on the scenario, you might use copies of Worksheet 9.2 (see www.mhhe.com/customerservice) to plan your call.

Scenario 1

You are a customer service representative in a customer contact center that provides service to customers who have purchased small appliances from your company. A customer is calling to complain that she purchased a waffle iron from one of your outlet stores two weeks ago and it no longer works. She is upset because her in-laws and family are arriving in two days for an extended visit and they love her "special" waffles.

Scenario 2

You are a customer care specialist for a company that provides answers to travel-related questions for a national membership warehouse retail store. A customer calls to find out about the types of travel-related discounts for which he qualifies through his membership.

Scenario 3

You are a telemarketing sales representative for a company that sells water filtration systems. You are calling current customers who purchased a filtration system seven to 10 years ago to inform them of your new Oasis line of filters, which is better than any other system on the market. You can offer them:

A 30-day money-back guarantee.

Billing by all major credit cards or invoice.

A one-year limited warranty on the system that replaces all defective parts but does not cover labor.

If they find a less expensive offer for the same product, a refund for the difference and an additional 50 percent of the difference.

Scenario 4

This scenario has two parts. In Part 1, you are a mechanic in an automotive repair shop. You answer a phone call from an irate customer calling to complain about what he perceives is an inflated billing charge for a recent air-conditioner repair. He is asking for your manager, who is at lunch and won't be back for 45 minutes. You take the incoming call, using the message-taking format covered in this chapter. In Part 2, you are the manager. You have just returned from lunch and find a message from the irate customer described in Part 1 and must call the customer. Use Worksheet 9.3 (see www.mhhe.com/customerservice) to plan your return call based on the message you received.

Face to Face

Telephone Techniques at Staff-Temps

Background

Staff-Temps International is a temporary employment agency based in Chicago, Illinois. It has six full-time and three part-time employment counselors. The office is part of a national chain owned by Yamaguchi Enterprises Ltd., headquartered in Tokyo. The chain annually places over 100,000 temporary employees in a variety of businesses and offices.

Most of Staff-Temps' contacts are made by telephone; therefore, greater emphasis is placed on selecting and training employees who have a good phone presence. Each employee is required to meet certain standards of quality in dealing with customers on the telephone. To ensure that these standards are applied uniformly, an outside quality control company (Morrison and Lewis) is used to make "phantom calls" to staff members. In these calls, Morrison and Lewis staff pretends to be potential clients seeking information. Employee-customer calls are also randomly taped. Through the calls and tapes, levels of customer service are measured.

Your Role

Your name is Chris Walker. As an employment counselor with Staff-Temps, you are aware of the customer service standards, which include the following:

Answer a ringing telephone within three rings. Smile as you speak.

Use a standard salutation (good morning, afternoon, or evening).

Give your name and the name of your department and company.

Offer to assist the customer ("How may I assist you?").

On the way back to the office after lunch, you were involved in a minor automobile accident. Even though it was not your fault, you are concerned that your insurance may be canceled since you had another accident and got a speeding ticket earlier this year. Because of the accident, you were an hour late in returning from lunch. Upon your arrival, the receptionist handed you six messages from vendors and customers. Two of the messages were from Aretha Washington, human resources director for an electronics manufacturing firm that has been a good client for over two years. The two of you had spoken earlier in the day.

As you walked into your office, the telephone started to ring. By the time you took your coat off and got to your desk, the phone had rung five or six times.

When you answered, you heard Aretha's voice on the line. Her tone told you that she was upset. This was the conversation:

You: "Staff-Temps. Chris speaking."

Aretha: "Chris, what's going on? You told me when I called first thing this morning that you would find out why my temp didn't show up today and would call me back. I've left messages all day and haven't heard a thing! We've got a major deadline to meet for a very important client, and I can't get the work done. My boss has been in here every half hour checking on this. What is going on?"

You: Aretha, I'm sorry. I just got in from lunch and haven't been able to get back to you."

Aretha: "Just got back from lunch! It's after 2:30! It must be nice to have the luxury of a long lunch break. I didn't even get to eat lunch today!"

You: "Listen, Aretha, I couldn't help . . ." Obviously anxious and raising your voice.

Aretha: "Don't you 'listen' me! I'm the customer, and if you can't handle my needs, I know someone else who can. If I don't hear from you within the next half hour, I don't ever want to hear from you again! Goodbye!"

[Slamming receiver down.]

Critical Thinking Questions

1. How well was this customer call handled? Explain.

2. What should you have done differently?

3. Do you believe that Aretha was justified in how she treated you? Explain.

4. How do personal problems or priorities sometimes affect customer service?

Planning to Serve

To get a better idea of how well your own organization uses technology to serve customers, use the following checklist to ensure that you and the organization are delivering the best possible service to customers, using technology effectively, and sending a positive image to others.

Call your own organizational (office) telephone number, or choose any large company or government agency from the phone book, to determine:

- How many times the telephone rings before being routed to another person or voice mail. (Four rings should be the maximum unless your organization has another standard.)
- If the "O" (operator) option is chosen, does the call go to a live person at another number? In other words, do you have service coverage when you are away from your telephone?

If you choose the voice mail option, is your outgoing message:

- Upbeat and friendly?
- Concise?
- In compliance with organizational guidelines for voice messages? If no standards exist, does your message comply with the suggested message format in this chapter?

E-mail yourself to determine:

- If the message is delivered properly to your mailbox.
- If your "out of office" message is sent automatically (assuming that you have this option on your system and have activated it). For example, a response might be generated that tells correspondents that "I'll be out of the office from (date) until (date) but I will be checking my e-mail during that period and will respond as soon as possible."

Examine your fax cover sheets (if used) to ensure that excessive information and graphics (e.g., bulky logos or icons) have been removed and that your name and phone number are provided.

Quick Preview Answers

1. T	4. F	7. T		10. T	13. T
2. F	5. T	8. T		11. F	14. T
3. T	6. T	9. F		12. T	15. F

Ethical Dilemma Summary

Ethical Dilemma 9.1 Possible Answers

1. Are there any potential legal problems with this policy? If so, what are they?

   The National Do-Not-Call Registry is managed by the Federal Trade Commission (the consumer protection agency in the United States) and applies to any plan, program, or campaign selling goods or services through interstate phone calls.

This includes telemarketers who solicit consumers, often on behalf of third-party sellers. It also includes sellers who provide, offer to provide, or arrange to provide goods or services to consumers in exchange for payment.

The National Do-Not-Call Registry does not limit calls by political organizations, charities, or telephone surveyors.

Under the law, a telemarketer or seller may call a consumer with whom it has an established business relationship for up to 18 months after the consumer's last purchase, delivery, or payment—even if the consumer's number is on the National Do-Not-Call Registry. In addition, a company may call a consumer for up to three months after the consumer makes an inquiry or submits an application to the company. And if a consumer has given a company written permission, the company may call even if the consumer's number is on the National Do-Not-Call Registry.

If a consumer asks a company not to call, the company may not call, even if there is an established business relationship. Indeed, a company may not call a consumer—regardless of whether the consumer's number is on the registry—if the consumer has asked to be put on the company's own do-not-call list.

Since 2005, telemarketers and sellers have been required to search the registry at least once every 31 days and drop from their call lists the phone numbers of consumers who have registered. A consumer who receives a telemarketing call despite being on the registry will be able to file a complaint with the FTC, either online or by calling a toll-free number. Violators could be fined up to $16,000 per incident.

2. Are there any ethical issues here? Explain.

   Yes, if you know that the supervisor is asking you to violate a federal law; you have to decide whether to participate in the illegal activity or to take some type of action.

3. What should you do in this situation?

   Ethically, you have to decide whether you want to escalate your concerns about calling people illegally to your supervisor's boss, report the company to the FTC, and/or resign from the company.

Encouraging Customer Loyalty

You don't earn loyalty in a day. You earn loyalty day-by-day.

—Jeffrey Gitomer

Learning Outcomes

After completing this chapter, you will be able to:

10-1 Establish and maintain trust with customers.

10-2 Explain customer relationship management and explain its importance to quality service.

10-3 Develop the service provider characteristics that will enhance customer loyalty.

10-4 Describe the provider's responsibility for establishing and maintaining positive customer relationships.

10-5 Identify strategies that can be used to make customers feel like they are number one.

10-6 Discuss strategies that can enhance customer satisfaction.

10-7 Define quality service.

Key Terms

channel partner
churn
code of ethics
contact points
contingency plans
cost of dissatisfied
  customers
customer loyalty
customer relationship
  management (CRM)

customer relationships
customer retention
customer satisfaction
ethical behavior
moment of truth
Planning Process Model
relationship-rating
  points
relationship-rating point
  scale

Technical Assistance
  Research Program
  (TARP) Worldwide
total quality
  management (TQM)
  and continuous quality
  improvement (CQI)
touch point
trust

In the Real World   Small Business—Stoner, Inc.

IN 2003 STONER, INC. BECAME THE SMALLEST COMPANY TO EVER WIN THE prestigious Malcolm Baldrige National Quality Award. The company is a small, family-owned business located in Lancaster County, the heart of Pennsylvania Amish country. Paul Stoner, an orphan, chemist, and entrepreneur, started the company to make inks at the end of World War II. In 1986, the company was purchased by Paul Stoner's grandson, Rob Ecklin, who had a vision of repositioning the organization for expansion. He guided the company's growth to a point where it now has over 300 specialized cleaners, lubricants, coatings, and car care products. As a result of Ecklin's vision, Stoner is now the largest supplier in the United States of aerosol and bulk release agents for plastics and other molded materials. Since the early 1990s, Stoner has increased sales 400 percent and has won three times as many customers as it has lost. While Ecklin is still the sole owner, he empowered a six-member senior leadership team to manage the business in 1990. These hands-on leaders facilitate strategic planning, develop team processes, and mentor team members daily in order to implement the company's strategy.

Part of what has lead to Stoner's success is its approach to doing business, which is highlighted in the company's core values—*exceed customer expectations,* foster and develop a *motivated team,* be *safety/health/environment* responsible, *innovate* new and better solutions, and *continuously improve.* All Stoner employees, known as team members, understand that continuous improvement is the key to sustaining competitive success and are focused on finding and implementing ways to add value for customers.

Creating stakeholder value at Stoner begins with the customer. Product managers meet with more than 100 customers per year and sales team members speak by phone with more than 1,000 customers each week to help define the company's direction based on what their customers want or need. Results from a national industry survey show that Stoner's attention to its customers pays off. The company ranks first in satisfaction on four of the five factors most important to its customers: quality, delivery, service, and value. It is in the top quartile for the fifth factor, price. Manufacturing productivity has increased 150 percent since 1991, and weekly average output of aerosol can products has increased 33 percent from 1998 to 2003. Stoner's 39 percent return on assets exceeds the industry average by 29 percent and its best competitor by 14 percent.

Think About It

Now that you have read the background on Stoner Inc., spend a bit of time researching the organziation on the Internet at www.nist.gov/public_affairs/baldrige2003/ Stoner_3.3.04.pdf and http://stonersolutions.com/.

1. As an organization, do you believe that Stoner is truly customer focused? Explain why or why not.
2. Based on what you know about Stoners, what roles do you believe that its mission and values play in its organizational strategy of helping customers? Explain.

3. Why do you think some small businesses succeed and become award winning and others do not? Explain.

4. From a customer perspective, did you find Stoner's Web site customer-friendly or not? Explain?

5. How do Stoner's products tie into the theme of time management?

Quick Preview

Before reviewing the chapter content, respond to the following questions by placing a "T" for true or an "F" for false on the rules. Use any questions you miss as a checklist of material to which you will pay particular attention as you read through the chapter. For those you get right, congratulate yourself, but review the sections they address in order to learn additional details about the topic.

_____ **1.** Customer satisfaction and loyalty are the result of effective product and service delivery, resolution of problems, and elimination of dissatisfaction.

_____ **2.** The number of customers with major problems who continue to do business with an organization if their complaint is resolved is about 9 percent.

_____ **3.** One way to take responsibility for customer relationships is to personalize your approach when dealing with customers.

_____ **4.** Customers usually decide to purchase or repurchase from a supplier on the basis of the quality and performance of the products and services.

_____ **5.** Many customers return to organizations because of relationships established with employees even though comparable products and services are available elsewhere.

_____ **6.** As customers develop long-term relationships with an organization, they tend to become more tolerant of poor service.

_____ **7.** Projecting an enthusiastic "I'm happy to serve you attitude" is one way to have a positive effect on customer relationships.

_____ **8.** Customers usually exhibit six common needs that must be addressed by service providers in order to ensure customer loyalty.

_____ **9.** Using a customer's name is a good way to personalize your relationship with a customer.

_____ **10.** Trust is not a major concern for most customers.

_____ **11.** Handling complaints quickly and effectively is a good strategy for aiding customer retention.

_____ **12.** An important step often overlooked in dealing with customers is follow-up.

Answers to Quick Preview can be found at the end of the chapter.

LO 10-1 The Role of Trust

Concept Trust is the most important criterion for a relationship. Trust depends on many factors. Communicating effectively, keeping your word, caring, and trusting your customers are some of these factors.

Customer loyalty is an *emotional* rather than a *rational* thing. Tied to commitment, loyalty is typically based on customer interest in maintaining a relationship with your organization. Often, customer interest is created and maintained through one or more positive experiences that lead to a relationship.

Relationships are built on **trust!** The most important thing to remember about trust is that, without it, you have no relationship. This applies to all human situations, not just the customer service environment. In the business world, trust typically results in positive word-of-mouth advertising. This mode of endorsement can be powerful and contribute to organization or product success. According to research published in a white paper for Harris Interactive, "Beyond permissive email, supplier and brand Web sites, and the like, customer trust is consistently highest for word-of-mouth. . . . While the aggregate value of print and electronic advertising as a decision-making influence has remained about the same since 1977, word-of-mouth advertising has doubled in leveraging power to the point where it is the dominant communication device in our society . . . more than 90 percent of customers identify word-of-mouth as the best, most reliable and relevant source of ideas and information about products and services."[1] Further, "In a time when mom and pop shops have shuttered their doors and have been replaced by nationwide chains, consumers still have the most powerful tool for ensuring that they receive the best possible customer service: their mouths. A recent online survey of more than 8,000 consumer-packaged-goods consumers, conducted by TARP Worldwide, found that more than 60 percent of consumers who hear of a first-hand positive or negative experience will change their buying habits."[2]

For customers to continue doing business with you, they must trust you and your organization. Trust has to be earned, and it does not happen overnight. Only through continued positive efforts on the part of everyone in your organization can you demonstrate to customers that you are worthy of their trust and thereby positively affect customer retention. Through actions and deeds, you must deliver quality products, services, and information that satisfy the needs of your customers. Every **touch point** with a customer is an opportunity for you and your organization to influence customer loyalty. Even when you win trust and achieve customer satisfaction, the customer relationship is very fragile. It is easy to destroy trust quickly: an inappropriate tone, a missed appointment, failure to follow through on a promise, a lie, or a misleading statement to a customer are just some of the ways you can sabotage this relationship. The good news for North American businesses is that as the economic recession started to show signs of slowing down and reversing, customer satisfaction levels for a

customer loyalty Term used to describe the tendency of customers to return to a product or organization regularly because of the service and satisfaction they receive.

trust Key element in cementing interpersonal relationships.

touch point Any instance in which a service provider or organization (e.g., face to face, in writing, through technology) comes in contact with a customer; it is an opportunity to influence customer loyalty and enhance the customer relationship.

number of industries have reached higher points than they have in several years on the University of Michigan American Customer Service Index (ACSI) scale of 100 possible points[3]:

Automobiles and light vehicles	84
Electronics (TV, VCR, DVD)	83
Internet portals and search engines	83
Manufacturing and durable goods	81.6
Major appliances	81
Personal computers	75

In a poll[4] by Harris Interactive, five dimensions of trust were identified that help explain why customers trust one organization over others. These types of trust can be used by organizations to create systems and staffing strategies that foster trust. The dimensions are:

- Personal experience.
- Organizational knowledge (of the company).
- Deference (trust of companies in general).
- Reference (what one learns about a company from others).
- Glitz (advertising, packaging, and high pricing).

To gain and maintain trust, you and the organization must actively work toward incorporating the values and beliefs you read about in other chapters into daily actions. Failure to do so can send a message that you are not trustworthy or that you act according to a double standard of saying one thing but doing another. You must exhibit trustworthiness in words and actions, for although it takes a long time to gain trust, it can be lost in seconds. Once trust is gone, if you do not act quickly to correct the situation, you may never regain total customer confidence. An example of how customer trust can erode was found in a 2007 Harris Interactive poll related to ongoing recalls in the pet and food product markets. The poll found that "consumers are concerned about the incidence of recalls among manufacturers and suppliers of food and pet food products. More than four in five (86 percent) mentioned at least some concern with three in ten (29 percent) indicating that these recalls are a serious concern for them."[5] These continued recalls, and those of many consumer products in the past (e.g., toys, tire, car, and

Displaying caring and respect for customers is essential. What are some ways you can go "above and beyond" when providing customer service?

dishwasher manufacturers that produce products that cause death, injury, and product loss to users), are causing a lot of uneasiness and distrust of many manufacturers.

There are numerous things that you can do to personally help build trust with your customers. Some potential trust building success strategies include:

Communicate Effectively and Convincingly

Customer Service Success Tip

Always act in the best interest of your customers. Listen to them, ask questions, anticipate their needs, deliver what you promise, and exhibit high levels of professionalism in every thing that you do whether your customers are present or not.

If you cannot articulate or clearly explain (verbally and in writing) information in a manner that customers can comprehend and act upon, they will not believe in you. You must provide more than facts and figures; you must send a message of sincerity, knowledge, and honesty.

As you communicate, project your feelings and emotions by being positive and enthusiastic. Let customers know that you are human and approachable. Also, communicate frequently and keep customers informed. This is especially important when they are awaiting a product or service that has been delayed. If you fail to update them regularly, they may become frustrated and could cancel their order, complain, take their business elsewhere, and tell others about their disappointing experience.

Display Caring and Concern

Emphasize to your customers that you have their best interests at heart. Work to demonstrate that you are willing to assist in satisfying their needs. Asking questions that uncover their needs and then taking positive action to satisfy them can do this. It can also be accomplished through passionate efforts to solve problems. Remember that their problem is your problem. Too often, service providers send a message that customers are not really that important. This can happen when service providers adopt a "next" mentality and treat customers as if they were numbers, not people. For example, think about the difference wording can make. Which of the following sends a more caring message to a group of customers standing in line as they wait for service?

1. A provider calls out "Next."
2. A provider looks over to the next person in line, smiles, and motions the person over with a waving hand gesture while saying, "May I help the next person in line?"

If you chose No. 2, you are on your way to providing caring service.

Be Fair

Make sure that you treat all customers (internal and external) with respect and consistency. For example, if you give special discounts to established or return customers while other customers are present, do so discreetly. Failure to exercise discretion in these cases could cause other customers to be offended because they perceive "preferential treatment" and they might take their business elsewhere. People like to feel that they are special. If a customer believes that another customer is getting something that they are not, you could have problems. Such perceptions might even lead to legal action if customers perceive that your actions are discriminatory.

Admit Errors or Lack of Knowledge

You are human and are expected to make mistakes. The key is to recover from errors by apologizing, accepting responsibility, and then quickly and appropriately solving the problem or getting the necessary information. One of the biggest mistakes a service provider can make is to deny accountability in dealing with a customer. When you or your organization, or the products or services it sells, cause customer inconvenience or dissatisfaction, take responsibility and work toward an acceptable resolution with the customer. To do otherwise is courting disaster. In some cases, even if a customer incorrectly perceives that you contributed to his or her dissatisfaction, it may be wise to take responsibility.

✳ Ethical Dilemma 10.1

You work as a pharmacy technician at a major drugstore chain and you have hopes of one day being selected for the company's management training program after graduating from college.

A patient calls to complain that the medication she was given causes headaches when she takes it and the symptoms for which it was prescribed are not going away. You instruct her to stop by the pharmacy at her convenience and to bring the prescription with her. Once the pharmacist sees the pills, and compares it to her doctor's prescription, he realizes that the patient was given the wrong medication. The pharmacist instructs you to tell the patient that he will call the doctor to get a new prescription, but actually just refills the original prescription and gives it to her.

1. What would you say or do to the pharmacist? Explain.
2. Should you notify anyone else about the incident? Explain.
3. What do you do or say to the patient? Explain.
4. What are the ethical issues here and how would you deal with them?

A story about the power of such action has been circulated for years. It involves the highly successful department store Nordstrom. As the story goes, a disgruntled customer brought a used car tire into a Nordstrom's store and complained that it was defective. After some discussion, the manager looked at the customer's receipt and cheerfully accepted the tire and refunded the customer's money. This may not seem too unusual, except that Nordstrom does not sell automobile tires! So, why would the manager take such an extreme action? Think about the word-of-mouth publicity (how many people in your class now know this story from just reading it?) and the customer loyalty that likely resulted from it. Whether the event actually took place or someone made it up is irrelevant. The point is that taking unusual actions to solve ordinary customer problems can pay dividends long into the future.

In another classic example of taking responsibility for a problem, in 1982 an unknown person or group contaminated bottles of Extra-Strength Tylenol with cyanide. Seven people used the product and died. Upon finding out about the situation, the parent company (Johnson and Johnson) immediately called a press conference to announce the total recall of the product from store shelves (approximately 264,000 bottles). Johnson & Johnson started a major media campaign to reassure the public that its other products were safe. The company also helped lead the way in developing tamper-resistant packaging. The cost—millions. The result—walk into any store that sells over-the-counter drug products and look for Extra-Strength Tylenol. Tylenol is right there with all its competitors and is a strong seller. How did Johnson & Johnson pull this off? The actions of the company in taking responsibility for a situation that was not of its making communicated strong values and concern for public safety, and the public remained loyal as a result.

Other companies have not fared so well in the face of adversity. For example, think about the Exxon oil tanker Valdez, which spilled more than 200,000 gallons of crude oil along the Alaska coastline in 1989. The fishing and associated industries in the region were devastated and many people and animals suffered in various ways as a result. This disaster caused major environmental as well as financial losses in the millions of dollars. This does not include the almost $3 billion Exxon has spent cleaning up the environmental damage and paying legal settlements. Similarly, when the oil platform in the Gulf of Mexico exploded in 2010, killing several workers and pumping millions of gallons of oil and gas into the water, outrage was swift and people were unforgiving of British Petroleum (BP), which owned the platform. In both cases, the companies were slow to react and did not initially take responsibility. As a result, both organizations are still the object of litigation and jokes. From a trust standpoint, people harbor resentment over the incidents, and, in protest, many people will still not patronize Exxon and BP gas stations.

In light of the costs associated with procuring new customers, a customer loss study of over 500 sales, marketing, and corporate buying executives found that "A massive 62 percent of buyers surveyed who recently dismissed a key supplier reported choosing another supplier that offered basically the same product or service. This finding indicates that the lost account's needs have not changed and can still be filled by the dismissed supplier. Importantly, buyers also report their dismissed suppliers do not even attempt to win them back. Only 25 percent reported the dismissed supplier offered an apology and only 14 percent of buyers said dismissed suppliers adopted a keep-in-touch strategy with them."[6]

In an era of strong competition worldwide, the policy identified in the study above makes little fiscal sense and does nothing to stimulate and maintain customer loyalty.

Trust Your Customers

Most customers are not out to cheat or "rip you (or your organization) off." They do want the best value and service for their money and expect you to provide it. Make a good-faith effort to accomplish this and deal effectively with customers by communicating openly, listening objectively to their questions and concerns, providing service to the best of your ability, showing compassion for their needs, and demonstrating that you are their advocate when things go wrong (if appropriate).

One of the most common mistakes service providers make in dealing with customers who have a complaint or problem is to verbally acknowledge and agree, but nonverbally send a message of skepticism. For example, suppose a customer comes in to complain about a defective product she purchased. As she is describing the symptoms of the problem, you use some of the paralanguage discussed in earlier chapters (e.g., "Uh huh," "I see," "Hmmm"); however, the inflection you use or your tone of voice communicates questioning or doubt (e.g., "I seeee?" or "Hmmm?"). How do you think the customer might feel or perceive you at that point?

> ✳ **Customer Service Success Tip**
>
> If you seek trust; communicate it through your words and nonverbal cues.

Keep Your Word

Customers have many choices in selecting a service or product provider. If they feel you cannot be depended upon to take action, they simply leave, often without complaint or comment. When you tell customers you will do something, do it. Do not promise what you cannot deliver; many people take your word as your bond. Break the bond, and you risk destroying the relationship. If feasible after providing service, contact your customer to make sure that he or she was satisfied and that your service met expectations. This follow-up can be an informal call, a more formal questionnaire, or a friendly e-mail or text message (assuming they authorized you to send such correspondence). Always strive to underpromise and overdeliver. An example of this concept in action would be for you to suppose that a customer drops off film to be processed at your store on Tuesday. The store guarantees that the photos will be ready on Saturday. If possible, develop the film before Saturday, and call to tell the customer it is ready. When he or she comes to pick it up, give a coupon for a discount on the next roll of film. Such actions help secure customer loyalty.

Provide Peace of Mind

Be positive and assertive. Assure customers through your words and actions that you are confident, have their best interests at heart, and are in control of the situation. Let them know that their calls or messages, questions, and needs will be addressed professionally and in a timely manner. Reassure them that what they purchase is the best quality, has a solid warranty, will be backed by the organization, and will address their needs while providing many benefits. Also, assure them that their requests and information will be processed rapidly and promises will be met.

Problem Solving

WORKING IN TEAMS OF THREE OR FOUR MEMBERS, DECIDE ON A COURSE OF ACTION TO RESOLVE THE PROBLEM POSED IN THE FOLLOWING SCENARIO.

You have been a cashier at Gifts Galore for a little over two months. A customer comes into your gift shop and wants to return a lamp that she says she purchased from your store as a gift for a wedding. Apparently, she discovered later that the intended recipient already had a lamp exactly like the one she bought. She tells you that she remembers the salesperson, Brittney, because her daughter's name is spelled the same way. You know that Brittney used to work at the gift shop, but quit about the time you started. The customer has no receipt, and you do not recognize the product as one that your store sells. You are empowered to make exchanges and give refunds up to a product value of $50. The customer says the lamp was $49.95 before tax. Store policy says that the customer must have a receipt if a refund is to be made. What questions would you ask to clarify the situation? How would you handle the problem?

All of these things can lead them to the belief that they made the right decision in selecting you and your organization and that you will take care of their needs.

Be Responsible for Your Customer Relationships

Taking a concerned, one-on-one approach to working with customers helps satisfy immediate needs while building a basis for long-lasting relationships. Customers tend to enjoy dealing more with people whom they believe are caring and have their best interests at heart. Interacting with someone they like is a pleasant experience and is likely to encourage trust and an enhanced relationship.

Personalize Your Approach

Think of the theme song for the syndicated television show *Cheers*. The idea of the theme song was that *Cheers* was a great place to go because "everyone knows your name." For the most part, people are a social species and need to be around others to grow and flourish. Helping your customers feel accepted can create a bond that will keep them coming back.

To create a social bond with customers, you will need to take time to get to know your regular customers and serve them individually. Recognizing them and using their names while interacting goes a long way toward creating that bond. For new customers, immediately start using the positive interpersonal communication skills you have learned. Treating customers as individuals and not as a number or one in a series is a very important step in building rapport and loyalty.

Keep an Open Mind

To develop and maintain an open mind, make it a habit to assess your attitude about your job, customers, products, and services before making contact with your customers. Make sure that you are positive, objective, prepared, and focused. Don't let negative attitudes block good service. Many service providers, even the more seasoned ones, go through slumps during which they feel down about themselves, their job, supervisors, organizations, customers, and so on. This is normal. Customer service is a stressful job, and external and internal factors (e.g., circadian rhythm, workload, and personal problems) influence one's perceptions of people and the world in general; however, guard against pessimism.

   If you are facing personal problems that seem overwhelming, contact your supervisor, human resources, or personnel department, or any other appropriate resource [e.g., Employee Assistance Program (EAP) representative] to help you sort out your problems. Failure to do so could lead to poor customer service or a less-than-professional image.

Individualize Service

Each customer is unique and has his or her own desires and needs. For that reason, every situation you handle will be slightly different. As you read in Chapter 8, you should view each person as an individual and not deal with customers on the basis of preconceived ideas or the demographic group of which they are part. By addressing a customer as an individual, listening so that you can discover his or her personal needs and problems, and then working to satisfy the needs or solve the problems, you potentially create a loyal customer. A simple way of accomplishing individualized service is to ask what else the customer would like. For example, in the case of a restaurant server who uses such a question, a customer might respond, "Do you have any (item)?" If the item is available, the server could cheerfully reply, "We certainly do. I'll get it for you right away." If the item is not available, the server might reply, "I'm sorry we do not have (item). However, we do have (alternative item). Would that be acceptable?"

> **✳ Customer Service Success Tip**
>
> Remember to remain positive when dealing with customers and tell them what you can do, not what you cannot do.

Show Respect

Even if you don't agree with a customer, respect his or her point of view or need and provide the best possible service. In return, the customer will probably respect and appreciate you and your efforts. A variation of an old adage may help put this concept into perspective: *The customer may not always be right, but he or she is still the customer.*

   If you lose sight of the fact that it is the customer who supports the organization, pays your salary, provides for your benefits, and gives you a job, you may want to examine why you are working in your current position. By acknowledging the value of your customers and affording them

Showing Respect

TAKE A FEW MINUTES TO THINK OF OTHER WAYS THAT YOU CAN SHOW RESPECT FOR A VARIETY OF CUSTOMERS (E.G., OLDER, YOUNGER, PEOPLE WITH DISABILITIES, OR OF VARIOUS CULTURAL BACKGROUNDS).
Discuss how these can positively influence service.

the respect and service they deserve, you can greatly improve your chances of having a satisfied customer. Some easy ways to show respect to customers include:

- When addressing the customer, use his or her last name and title. (If you are on the telephone, write down the customer's name along with other pertinent information so that you do not forget.)
- Stop talking when the customer begins to speak.
- Take time to address the customer's questions or concerns.
- Return calls or e-mail messages within reasonable amounts of time.
- Show up on time for scheduled meetings.
- Do what you promised to do, and do it right the first time, within the agreed-upon time frame.

Elicit Customer Input

Some people actually encourage rewarding customers who complain. Complaints provide feedback that can enable service providers and organizations to rapidly shift resources to fix things that are not working well in an effort to satisfy the customer. By taking the time to ask for customer input and actually listening to what they have to say, then acting appropriately upon their comments, you can solidify a bond and further enhance their level of trust in you. If you think about it, this makes sense. You cannot fix what you do not know is broken.

Many times, service providers do not take the time to ask for feedback because they are afraid that it may not be good. In other instances, they simply do not think of asking or care to do so. To increase your own effectiveness and that of your organization, actively and regularly seek input from your customers. No one knows better than the customer what he or she likes or needs. Take the time to ask the customer, and then listen and act upon what you are told. By asking customers questions, you give them an opportunity to express interest, concerns, emotion, and even complaints. There are many ways of gathering this information (e.g., customer satisfaction cards, written surveys, and service follow-up telephone calls; see Figure 10.1). The key is to somehow ask the customer "How well did we do in meeting your needs?" or "What do you think?" If this is not a normal procedure in your place of business, you should consider bringing it up at a staff meeting. It will take extra effort on the part of the customer service employees, but the effort will be well-rewarded in the good will it will elicit from your customer base.

Figure 10.1
Customer Information-Gathering Techniques

There are many ways to gather information about customer satisfaction levels. Some of the more common include:

- *Customer comment cards* are simple 5- × 7-inch (approximately) card stock questionnaires that quickly gather customer reactions to their service experiences. These cards are commonly found on restaurant tables and at point-of-sale locations (e.g., cash registers). They typically consist of four or five closed-end questions that can be answered with yes/no or short answers and have a space for general comments.

- *Toll-free numbers* are often used to obtain customer opinions after a service encounter. Customers are provided a toll-free number on their sales receipt and encouraged to call within 24 hours. As a reward, they are often given discount coupons, bonus frequent guest/user points, or other small incentives.

- *Verbal comments* can be elicited from customers and logged in by service providers. By asking customers for feedback on their experiences and paying heed to them, immediate service adjustments can be made.

- *Follow-up telephone surveys* can be done by employees or consultants using a written list of questions. The key is to be brief, not impose on customers, and ask questions that will gather pertinent information (e.g., open-end questions).

- *Service contact surveys* that are mailed or e-mailed (with permission) to people who have contacted an organization for information, to make a purchase, or use a service can gather more in-depth information.

- *Automated surveys* that can be sent to targeted customers and taken through a link to a Web site following transactions or events in order to get their opinion. The Internet offers a variety of Web sites that provide survey services. Some are even free (e.g., www.surveymonkey.com).

- *Exit interviews* conducted by greeters, hosts, or hostesses as customers leave a facility. These are typically one or two quick questions (e.g., "How did you enjoy your stay?," "Were you able to find everything you needed?," or "What can we do to make your next visit more pleasurable?"). The key is to log in responses for future reference.

- *Shopper/customer surveys* that can yield a wealth of information. These are typically longer and more detailed than a comment card. They can be given to a customer as he or she leaves or can be sent to customers later (get names and addresses from checks written). Offer discount coupons or other incentives for returned surveys and provide self-addressed, stamped envelopes.

- *Focus groups* of six to eight internal or external customers can be formed to do in-depth, face-to-face or online (chat) surveys. Often organizations conducting these provide snacks and gifts (e.g., $50) for each participant. Ask open-end questions related to the organization and products and services provided. Often, trained marketing or other facilitators are used to conduct such sessions. They also analyze responses and provide reports to management along with recommendations for improvement.

- *Sales and service records* can provide a wealth of information. They can reflect whether customers are returning and what products and services are being used most, and can show patterns of purchases.

LO 10-2 The Importance of Customer Relationship Management (CRM)

customer relationships
The practice of building and maintaining ongoing friendships with customers in an effort to make them feel comfortable with an organization and its service providers and to enhance customer loyalty.

customer relationship management (CRM)
Concept of identifying customer needs: understanding and influencing customer behavior through ongoing communication strategies in an effort to acquire, retain, and satisfy the customer.

Concept Long-term relationships are the ones that sustain organizations.

Why bother building relationships with customers? The answer would seem obvious—so that you can stay in business. However, when you examine the question further, you may find that there are more reasons than you think. This is where the customer relationship management (CRM) concept comes in. There are actually a number of components in the CRM process:

- Operational (involving sales and service representatives).
- Collaborative (involving interaction with customers through such means as e-mail).
- Web pages and automated voice response, or AVR, systems.
- Analytical (involving analyzing customer data for efforts like marketing and financial forecasting).

Through CRM, organizations and employees get to better know their customers and project needs that can be satisfied through appropriate products and services.

At one point in history, business owners knew their customers personally. They knew their customers' families, what their religious affiliation was, and what was happening in their lives. That was then, and this is now. Our current society is more mobile; people live in large metropolitan areas where relationships are distant, and families live miles apart from one another in many instances. Large multinational organizations provide the products and services once provided by the neighborhood store. All this does not mean, however, that the customer-provider relationship can no longer exist.

Additionally, with B2B (business-to-business), customers are often companies. This makes managing **customer relationships** more difficult because of the number of contacts you might have in an organization and the varying requirements or needs each might have. Also, much of business-to-business service is delivered through technology. Many service organizations use **customer relationship management (CRM)** software to better keep track of customer needs, access multiple sources of customer information (e.g., credit reports, past contacts, and voice and e-mail messages), and to record service provided. CRM is a crucial element of customer loyalty.

Relationships are a crucial part of customer service. By working to build trust and getting to know customer needs, service providers increase their effectiveness. What techniques do you use to build rapport and trust with customers?

Typically, many service providers look at customer interactions from a short-term perspective. They figure that a customer calls or comes in (or they go to the customer), they provide service, and then the customer (or the service provider) goes away. This is a shortsighted viewpoint in that it does not consider the long-term implications. This is not the way to gain and sustain customer loyalty.

A more customer-focused approach is to view customers from a relationship standpoint. That does not mean that you have to become intimate friends with all your customers; it simply means that you should strive to employ as many of the positive relationship-building skills that you have learned as possible. By treating both internal and external customers in a manner that leads them to believe that you care for them and have their best interests at heart, you can start to generate reciprocal feelings. Using the interpersonal communication skills you have learned throughout this book is a great way to begin doing this. People usually gravitate toward organizations and people with whom they have developed rapport, respect, and trust, and who treat them as if they are valued as a person. Relationships are developed and enhanced through one-on-one human interaction. This does not mean that people who provide service via technology cannot develop relationships. Those relationships develop on a different level, using the nonverbal skills addressed in Chapters 4, 6, 8, and 9.

Remember that long-term customer relationships (**customer retention**) are the ones that sustain organizations. Seeking out new or replacement customers through advertising and other means is a very costly proposition. This is because in addition to having to find new customers, you and your organization have to educate and win them over. You have to prove yourself to newly acquired customers. More than likely, new customers are also going to be more apprehensive, skeptical, and critical than customers who have previous experience with your organization. For these reasons, it is imperative that you and every other member of your organization work to develop loyalty on the part of those customers with whom you have an existing relationship.

customer retention The ongoing effort by an organization to meet customer needs and desires in an effort to build long-term relationships and keep them for life.

Many organizations and industries seem to forget the value of fostering solid customer relationships. They often treat existing customers poorly or not as well as newly acquired ones. Examples of this can be found in:

High maintenance and transaction fees charged by financial institutions.

High fees charged by hotels for local calls.

Exorbitant fees charged by airlines for ticket changes and baggage.

Inability for existing cell phone customers locked into contracts to get the same deals as new customers.

Cancellation fees by doctors' and dentists' offices regardless of the reason.

Restocking fees charged by many online retailers for returned items.

Charging for air and water for vehicles at a gas station.

One way that organizations try to cement relationships and encourage customer retention is through loyalty or rewards programs. In many cases this strategy seems to be working. Maritz Loyalty Marketing in a study of 2,178 shoppers who had made purchases in the past six months found that "In an increasingly fragmented retail landscape, customer loyalty programs are an important tool to help retailers maximize their 'share of wallet' among consumers . . . . [R]ewards program members are more likely to have spent a greater amount of money in the past six months across the 11 retail categories examined in the study, including home improvement, electronics, grocery and book stores."[7]

Benefits of Customer Relationship Management

According to a J.D. Powers and Associates North American Hotel Guest Satisfaction Index Study, "The highest-performing hotel brands differentiate themselves by meeting customer expectations consistently, whether it's a guest's first stay with the brand or their fiftieth. . . . By setting and maintaining high brand standards, hotels build a reputation for reliability, which breeds customer loyalty."[8]

When organizations attain a high degree of brand recognition and a reputation for providing quality products and services at a competitive price, while going above and beyond their customers' expectations, they are typically rewarded with customer loyalty and repeat and referral business.

Other direct benefits include:

- Less need to obtain new customers through marketing, since current customers are aware of offerings and take advantage of them.
- Reduced marketing costs, since direct mail, follow-up, and other customer recruitment activities are reduced.
- Increased return on investment (ROI), since marketing can target specific customer needs.
- Enhanced customer loyalty due to pricing and product service offerings that meet current customer needs.
- Elevated profitability due to increased sales, customer referrals, and longer customer retention during life cycle.
- Targeted marketing based on statistics on which customers buy more and on high-ticket item sales.

By providing excellent customer service and dealing with dissatisfaction as soon it is identified, you can help ensure that customers remain loyal and keep coming back. Figure 10.2 shows an equation that conveys the loyalty concept.

Figure 10.2
Loyalty Equation

Effective product/service delivery
+ Proactive relationship building
+ Elimination of dissatisfiers
+ Resolution of problems
+ Follow-up
= Customer satisfaction and loyalty

Traditionally, customers will remain loyal to a product, service, or organization that they believe meets their needs. Even when there is an actual or perceived breakdown in quality, many customers will return to an organization that they believe sincerely attempts to solve a problem or make restitution for an error. According to the **Technical Assistance Research Program (TARP) Worldwide,** many organizations have found that, when complaints were acted upon and resolved quickly, most customers returned to the organization (see Figure 10.3).

The bottom line is that you and other employees must realize that customer service is everyone's business and that relationships are the basis of that business.

Cost of Dissatisfied Customers

Many research studies have been conducted to try to determine the **cost of dissatisfied customers.** Too often, service providers look at the loss of a sale when a customer is dissatisfied as a single event. However, as you saw in the last section, one dissatisfied customer can cost your organization a lot.

To get an idea of what one negative customer experience can cost your organization over a 10-year period, consider the following example:

Ms. Ling comes in to return a product that she paid $22 for over a month ago. She explains that the product did not fit her needs and that she had been meaning to return it since the date she purchased it, but kept forgetting. She also explains that she comes in at least once a week to make purchases. Your company has a three-day return policy, your manager is out to lunch and you do not have the authority to override the policy. Ms. Ling is in a hurry and is upset by your inability to resolve the issue. She leaves after saying, "You just lost a good customer!"

Technical Assistance Research Program (TARP) Worldwide An Arlington, Virginia, based firm specializing in customer service research studies for call centers and many other industries.

cost of dissatisfied customers Phrase that refers to any formula used to calculate the cost of acquiring a new customer or replacing a current one as a result of having a dissatisfied customer leave an organization.

Figure 10.3
The Importance of Customer Loyalty

For almost three decades, the research firm TARP has conducted various studies to determine the effects of customer service. The research has revealed the following:

- It will cost an organization at least five times more to acquire a new customer than it will to keep an existing one.
- On average, 50 percent of consumers will complain about a problem to a frontline person. In business-to-business environments, this figure jumps to 75 percent.
- For small-ticket items, 96 percent of consumers do not complain or they complain to the retailer from whom they bought an item. For large-ticket items, 50 percent complain to front-line employees, and 5 to 10 percent escalate the problem to local managers or corporate headquarters.
- At least 50 percent of your customers who experience problems will not complain or contact your organization for help; they will simply go elsewhere.
- Customers who are dissatisfied will tell as many as 16 friends about a negative experience with your organization.
- The average business loses 10 to 15 percent of its customers per year because of bad service.

Source: Technical Assistance Research Program (TARP), 1300 Wilson Boulevard, Suite 950, Arlington, Virginia 22209.

Personal Customer Relationship Experiences

THINK ABOUT A SERVICE PROVIDER WITH WHOM YOU DEAL FREQUENTLY AND WITH WHOM YOU HAVE ESTABLISHED A BETTER-THAN-AVERAGE CUSTOMER-PROVIDER RELATIONSHIP. PERHAPS YOU HAVE BEEN DEALING WITH THE ORGANIZATION FOR A LONG PERIOD OF TIME OR VISIT FREQUENTLY.

Reflect on the relationship and make a list of positive customer service behaviors exhibited by this person. Then review the list and make it a personal goal to replicate as many of these behaviors as possible when dealing with your own customers.

Let's assume that Ms. Ling spends at least $22 a week in your store and calculate the potential loss to your organization.

$22 × 52 (number of weeks in a year) = $1,144

10 (number of years as a customer) × $1,144 = $11,440

16 (number of people statistically told of her negative experience) × $11,440 = $183,040

These numbers are the bad news. The good news is that you and every other employee in your organization can reduce a large percentage of customer defections by providing quality service.

LO 10-3 The Role of Channel Partner Relationships on Customer Loyalty

Concept Relationship with channel partners is a key component for managing customer loyalty.

channel partner Relationship of two organizations in which they are able to build a larger and stronger competitive presence in the marketplace.

A key component of managing customer loyalty is for organizations to effectively manage its **channel partner** relationships. Such partners can help gain access to new business opportunities at lower costs, without having to merge or acquire more assets and employees. This means that retail and service pricing can be kept down. This provides a more competitive posture for your organization and potentially attracts and holds customers based on reduced pricing and enhanced product and service availability. Through such relationships organizations are able to build a larger and stronger competitive presence in the marketplace, which can help enhance customer trust and loyalty. Harris Interactive reports that "The role that channels and business partners now play in securing end customers' trust, commitment and loyalty cannot be overstated. Given the ever-increasing dependence on Web-based communications and commerce and the breaking down of geographical constraints, it's no surprise that these relationships have become integral to today's extended enterprises, and a fundamental component of successful, customer-focused businesses."[9]

Three Types of Channel Partners

There are three types of typical channel partners with which your organization might have a relationship:

1. **Transactional or indirect.** This type of organization provides a distribution outlet or link for your company's products and services. The challenge is that they maintain no specific loyalty and when the opportunity arises to obtain a newer product or service line, or one that is less expensive, they may move to other suppliers or vendors. Examples of transactional partners are online Web sites (e.g., Amazon.com, Overstock.com, or presentationresources.net), retail stores, or service providers (e.g., plumber, laundry, pest control, masseuse/masseur, and car repair).

2. **Tactical.** This category of partners include organizations that are intricately meshed with your company's internal operations. Examples of such arrangements include mobile phone service providers that use retail outlets (e.g., Best Buy or mall kiosks).

3. **Strategic.** The third type of channel partnership involves signing agreements through which one organization creates long-term alliance with one another to brand, develop, or produce each other's products or services. As example of this is the code sharing that takes place between airlines where two different airlines can sell seats on a single plane under their own individual flight numbers.

LO 10-4 Provider Characteristics Affecting Customer Loyalty

Concept Personal characteristics of a service provider may affect customer loyalty, positively or negatively.

Many of your personal characteristics affect your relationships with customers. In customer service, some circumstances are beyond your control; however, your personal characteristics are not. Some of the most common qualities of service providers that affect customers are described in the next sections.

Responsiveness

Customers typically like to feel that they are the most important person in the world when they come in contact with an organization (see Figure 10.4). This is a human need. If customers feel that they are not appreciated or not welcome by you or another service provider, they will likely take their business elsewhere. However, they will often first complain to management and will tell anyone who will listen about the poor quality of service they received.

A simple way to demonstrate responsiveness is to attend to customer needs promptly. If you get an e-mail or voice mail message, respond to it immediately, if possible. If that is not possible, try to respond within

Training is usually provided by most organizations to increase employee knowledge and effectiveness with customers. What training do you think would be useful to you in a new position in customer service?

Perceptiveness

Recognizing the need to pay close attention to verbal and nonverbal cues, cultural factors, and the feelings or concerns of others is important. If necessary, you may want to review these topics in Chapters 3, 4, and 8. By staying focused on customers and the signals they send, you can often recognize hesitancy, interest in a product or adamant rejection, irritation, anxiety, and a multitude of other unspoken messages. Once you have identified customers' signals, you can react appropriately and address their needs.

One way you can address customer needs is to anticipate them, depending on where you work. Suppose that a customer makes a comment like "Man, is it hot outside. My lips are parched." You might offer a cold drink or direct the customer to a cafeteria or soft drink machine. You might offer a blanket to a family member staying with someone in the emergency room in the middle of the night when it is very cold. Or you might offer a chair to someone who is accompanying a customer while he or she shops and tries on clothing. Such small gestures show that you are astute in noticing their needs and nonverbal cues. Remember, sometimes the little things mean a lot. Moreover, in all of these examples, by taking care of the customer's basic needs, you might encourage him or her to shop longer.

Planning Ability

Planning is a crucial skill to possess when operating in today's fast-paced, changing customer service environment, especially in technology-based environments. To prepare for all types of customer situations, you and your organization must have a strategy. This often involves assessing various factors related to your organization, industry, products, services, policies and procedures, resources, and customer base. Remember that a systemic breakdown on your part or that of your organization is not the responsibility or problem of your customers. In fact, most do not care about your issues; they just want fast, efficient, quality service. If you and your organization fail to provide it, they may take their business elsewhere. By being proactive and thinking about such factors, you will be able to provide better service to your customers.

Also, you should consider alternative strategies for dealing with unusual situations (**contingency plans**). Such alternatives are helpful when things do not go as originally planned (e.g., a computer database fails, service is not delivered as promised, or products that were ordered from another organization for a customer do not arrive as promised).

Figure 10.6 shows the **Planning Process Model,** the basic steps of which are:

Set a goal. In a customer service situation, the obvious goal is to prevent problems from occurring. You also want to successfully address customers' needs, have them leave the service experience satisfied, spread positive word-of-mouth advertising, and return in the future.

Examine and evaluate the situation. In this phase of planning, you should look at all possible factors that could affect a customer interaction (e.g., the environment, policies, procedures, your skills and authority level, management support, and the customer). With these factors in mind, work with your peers and supervisor or team leader to establish criteria for selecting acceptable actions. For example, it might be acceptable to use voice

contingency plans Backup systems or procedures that are implemented when regular ones break down or fail to function as intended.

Planning Process Model Five-step process for creating contingency or backup plans to better serve customers when problems arise or things do not go as expected.

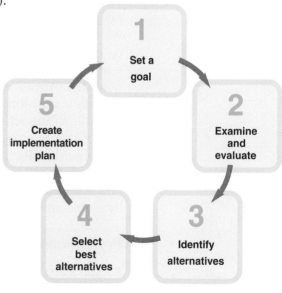

Figure 10.6 Planning Process Model

mail if you are dealing with a customer; however, it is not proper to forward incoming messages to voice mail so that you can meet with a peer on a non-work-related issue.

Identify alternatives. Meet with peers and supervisors or team leaders to develop a list of alternatives for dealing with various customer situations. Consider the advantages and disadvantages of each option.

Select the best alternative. After reviewing all the options, select the one (or more) that best addresses the targeted goal of providing quality service to customers. Do not forget to measure this choice against the criteria you established earlier.

Create an implementation plan. Working with peers and supervisors or team leaders, decide which resources (human and otherwise) will be needed to deliver effective service. Also, develop a system for evaluating success. For example, a customer wants two items, but you have only one in stock. You apologize for not being able to fulfill the customer's needs. Is this "success"? Or, would you be successful if, in addition to the apology, you called other stores, located another item, and had it delivered to the customer's house at no cost?

Problem-Solving Ability

If a customer has a problem, you have a problem. Remembering this simple concept can go a long way in reminding you of your purpose for being a service provider. Your primary job function is to address the needs of your customer. To do this when a customer is dissatisfied or has a concern, you should take responsibility for the problem instead of trying to place blame and defer the issue to someone else. What or who created the problem (e.g., the weather, you, the customer, or the manufacturer) doesn't matter. Your goal is to identify and implement appropriate solutions to the extent that you are authorized to do so. Otherwise, you should seek assistance from the appropriate person according to your organization's policy. To accomplish sound problem solving, you will need a process for gathering and analyzing information. As with the planning process discussed earlier, you should take some specific steps in finding a solution to a customer problem. These steps are described in the following sections. The Problem-Solving Model discussed in Chapter 7 can also be applied when you are trying to encourage and maintain customer loyalty.

Problem resolution is not difficult if it is approached systematically. If you have done the planning described earlier and know what options are available and what authority you have, it becomes much easier.

Professionalism

As you have read in previous chapters, projecting a positive personal image, through manner of dress, knowledge, appearance of your work area, and your mental attitude, is a crucial element in communicating an

Exemplary (4) Service that
category. Examples: An auto
transmission. A beauty salon
patron on her birthday. A res
coupon for a discount on a fu
twice to be cooked properly.
after his 12-hour shift ends to
she needs anything.

Above Average (3) Servi
pleasantly surprise the custo
regular customer at a bar ge
a bank gives a customer a fi
customer's son, who just rec
barber.

Average (2) Service at this
customer drops off laundry ar
requested, on hangers, and ir
"Paper or plastic?" and then
accountant finishes a client's
processes a new dental patie
information in a pleasant mar

Below Average (1) Servic
disappoints customers. Examp
paper after a customer calls t
and departs without apologiz
15 minutes or longer beyond
seen, no one apologizes. A c
on service because the custor
resolved.

Unsatisfactory (0) Service
breakdown in the customer-pr
neutered by a veterinarian wh
advertises "immediate emerge
repairperson to fix a leaking
room is being saturated and c
cuts a large section from a tre
brand-new car. A doctor oper

Establish Rapport

Customers react to and d
ceive as likable, helpful, a
tinue to be helpful, smile,
attend to the customer's n
generate small talk about
goes wrong, people who fe
higher ratings on the **relat**
not feel this connection.

"I care" image to customers and potential customers. By paying close attention to such factors, you better position yourself to establish and maintain a strong customer relationship. This is especially true where attitude is concerned. Attitude can mean success or failure when dealing with customers and can be communicated through the various verbal and nonverbal cues you have read about in other chapters.

LO 10-5 Making the Customer Number One

Concept   Make a good first impression by establishing rapport; then identify and satisfy your customers' needs. Follow up to obtain repeat business.

The days of a customer adopting one product or company for life are long gone. With easy access and global competitiveness, customers are often swayed by advertising and a chance at a "better deal." Quality levels and features between competing brands and organizations are often comparable. The thing that separates competitors is their level of service. It is not unusual for customers to switch back and forth between products or organizations simply because of pricing. This is sometimes referred to as service **churn.** According to research by Harris Interactive, ". . . the majority of companies lose between 10% to 40% of their customers every year. Other calculations show that the average company loses half of its customer base over a 5-year period."[10]

churn The process of a customer switching between products or companies, often simply to get a better price, rebate, or warranty.

Customer loyalty is won by providing extra service for the customer. Organizations must assess individual needs and determine how to meet those needs better than the competition does. In this case, customers who have mobility impairments or limitations will keep coming back to this establishment because they have provided transportation for those with disabilities. How can you provide extra service for customers with special needs?

Per

REFL
EXTE
E-MA
Imme
pape
you,
have

Note
expe
Reco
with
obje

Strategies for Making Customers Number One

ON A SHEET OF PAPER, LIST EACH OF THE INITIATIVES FOR MAKING CUSTOMERS NO. 1 THAT YOU JUST READ ABOUT.

Then, develop an action plan for addressing each of them in your customer contacts. Be specific about exactly what you will do or say to address each strategy. Use the following initiatives and specify your actions and the expected customer response.

Make positive initial contact.

Establish rapport.

Identify and satisfy customer needs quickly.

Exceed expectations.

Follow up.

Encourage customers to return.

moment of truth A phrase popularized by Scandinavian Airlines System President Jan Carlzon in his popular 1987 book of the same name. It is defined as any instance when a customer comes into contact with any element or representative of an organization.

contact points Instances in which a customer connects with a service provider or some other aspect of an organization.

relationship-rating points Values mentally assigned by customers to a service provider and his or her organization. They are based on a number of factors starting with initial impressions and subsequently by the quality and level of service provided.

M
ing
cus
cus
whi

E
hav
serv
in v
tior
deli
disc
enc
ord
len

Mc

Fir
you
ver
itiv
ave
tior
rel
cus
in
Fig
wit

Identify and Satisfy Customer Needs Quickly

Use the questioning, listening, observing, and feedback skills outlined in this book to focus on issues of concern to the customer. By effectively gathering information, you can then move to the next phase of customer service.

Exceed Expectations

As you can see on the relationship-rating point scale, customers typically expect that, if they pay a certain price for a product or service, they will receive a specific quality and quantity in return. This is not an unusual expectation. The average customer looks for value. As you read in Chapter 9, with the Internet and global competition, many products and services are only a mouse click away. If you and your organization fail to deliver as promised or expected, customers may simply go away. In earlier chapters, you also saw that today's customers tend to be better-educated consumers who recognize that if they cannot fulfill their needs in one place, they can easily access the same or similar products and services on the Internet or by visiting a competitor. Therefore, you need to exceed a customer's expectations. Many terms are used to describe the concept of exceeding expectations—knock-their-socks-off service, positive memorable customer experiences, E-plus service, customer delight, dazzling service, fabled service, and five diamond or five star service. All these phrases have in common the concept mentioned before of going above and beyond customer expectations—*under*promise and *over*deliver. By going out of your way not only to satisfy customers but also to "wow" them by doing, saying, or offering the unexpected related to high-quality service delivery, you can exceed expectations. The result could be the reward of continuing patronage by the customer.

An example of unexpected service or going the extra mile follows. A customer bought flooring tiles from a home product warehouse and took

"I care" image to customers and potential customers. By paying close attention to such factors, you better position yourself to establish and maintain a strong customer relationship. This is especially true where attitude is concerned. Attitude can mean success or failure when dealing with customers and can be communicated through the various verbal and nonverbal cues you have read about in other chapters.

LO 10-5 Making the Customer Number One

Concept Make a good first impression by establishing rapport; then identify and satisfy your customers' needs. Follow up to obtain repeat business.

The days of a customer adopting one product or company for life are long gone. With easy access and global competitiveness, customers are often swayed by advertising and a chance at a "better deal." Quality levels and features between competing brands and organizations are often comparable. The thing that separates competitors is their level of service. It is not unusual for customers to switch back and forth between products or organizations simply because of pricing. This is sometimes referred to as service **churn.** According to research by Harris Interactive, ". . . the majority of companies lose between 10% to 40% of their customers every year. Other calculations show that the average company loses half of its customer base over a 5-year period."[10]

churn The process of a customer switching between products or companies, often simply to get a better price, rebate, or warranty.

Customer loyalty is won by providing extra service for the customer. Organizations must assess individual needs and determine how to meet those needs better than the competition does. In this case, customers who have mobility impairments or limitations will keep coming back to this establishment because they have provided transportation for those with disabilities. How can you provide extra service for customers with special needs?

Personal Customer Experiences

REFLECT ON A RECENT INTERACTION YOU HAD WITH AN INTERNAL OR EXTERNAL CUSTOMER AS A PROVIDER (OVER THE TELEPHONE, IN PERSON, VIA E-MAIL, OR THROUGH ANY OTHER MEANS).

Immediately after that interaction, if someone had handed the customer a piece of paper and asked him or her to write down impressions of the treatment received from you, what would he or she likely have said? Why do you believe the customer would have said this?

Note: If you do not deal with customers, think of a situation that you recently experienced as a customer and answer the questions based on your experience. Record your perspective of what your customer's comments would have been, along with anything you could have done differently to improve the situation. Be as objective as you can.

moment of truth A phrase popularized by Scandinavian Airlines System President Jan Carlzon in his popular 1987 book of the same name. It is defined as any instance when a customer comes into contact with any element or representative of an organization.

contact points Instances in which a customer connects with a service provider or some other aspect of an organization.

relationship-rating points Values mentally assigned by customers to a service provider and his or her organization. They are based on a number of factors starting with initial impressions and subsequently by the quality and level of service provided.

Most people like to feel that they are important and valued. By recognizing and acting on that fact, you can go a long way toward providing solid customer service, reducing churn, and building a strong relationship with customers. By being an "I care" person, you can generate much goodwill while meeting customer needs.

Every time you encounter a customer in person or over the phone, you have an opportunity to provide excellent service. Some companies call a service encounter the **moment of truth** or refer to them as **contact points,** in which the customer comes into contact with some facet of the organization. At this point you and other service providers have an opportunity to deliver "knock your socks off" service, as Kristin Anderson and Ron Zemke discussed in several of their books on customer service. Each customer encounter moves through the following stages, although sometimes the order varies. At each step, you have another opportunity to provide excellent customer service.

Make Positive Initial Contact

First impressions are crucial and often lasting. To ensure that you put your best effort forward, remember the basics of positive verbal and nonverbal communication—giving a professional salutation, projecting a positive attitude, and sincerely offering to assist. This is crucial because the average customer will come into an initial contact with certain expectations. If the expectations are not met, you and your organization can lose **relationship-rating points** that can ultimately cost the organization a customer. Such points are like the ones on performance appraisals used in many organizations to evaluate and rate employee performance (see Figure 10.7). Use this scale frequently to evaluate your rating as you deal with various customers.

Figure 10.7
Relationship-Rating Point Scale

Exemplary (4) Service that is out of the ordinary and unexpected falls into this category. Examples: An auto repair shop details a customer's car after replacing a transmission. A beauty salon owner provides a free Swedish massage to a regular patron on her birthday. A restaurant server provides a complimentary meal and a coupon for a discount on a future visit to a customer who had to send her steak back twice to be cooked properly. A nurse visits one of his patients in the intensive care unit after his 12-hour shift ends to ensure that everything is okay and to ask the spouse if she needs anything.

Above Average (3) Service in this category goes beyond the normal and may pleasantly surprise the customer, but does not dazzle the customer. Example: A regular customer at a bar gets a free second drink from the bartender. A clerk at a bank gives a customer a free wall calendar at the end of the transaction. A customer's son, who just received his first haircut, is given a lollipop by the barber.

Average (2) Service at this level is what is expected by a customer. Examples: A customer drops off laundry and when it is picked up, his shirts are starched as requested, on hangers, and in a plastic garment bag. A grocery store bagger asks, "Paper or plastic?" and then proceeds to comply with the customer's request. An accountant finishes a client's tax return on time, as promised. A receptionist properly processes a new dental patient and gathers pertinent health and insurance information in a pleasant manner.

Below Average (1) Service provided at this level is not as expected and disappoints customers. Examples: A newspaper deliverer brings a replacement paper after a customer calls to complain, leaves it on the doorstep, rings the bell, and departs without apologizing. A patient waits in a doctor's waiting room 15 minutes or longer beyond her scheduled appointment, and when she is finally seen, no one apologizes. A call center representative gives a customer a $15 credit on service because the customer had to call back three times to have a problem resolved.

Unsatisfactory (0) Service at this level is unacceptable and typically leads to a breakdown in the customer-provider relationship. Examples: A customer's cat is neutered by a veterinarian when taken in for a flea dip. A plumbing company that advertises "immediate emergency service" takes over four hours to send a repairperson to fix a leaking pipe in a wall; meanwhile, all carpeting in the living room is being saturated and one wall is crumbling. A contracted tree-trimming worker cuts a large section from a tree that crashes through the garage roof and onto a brand-new car. A doctor operates on the wrong leg of a patient.

Establish Rapport

Customers react to and deal effectively with employees whom they perceive as likable, helpful, and effective. Throughout your interaction, continue to be helpful, smile, listen, use the customer's name frequently, and attend to the customer's needs or concerns. Also, look for opportunities to generate small talk about non-business-related matters. When something goes wrong, people who feel a kinship with service providers typically give higher ratings on the **relationship-rating point scale** than people who do not feel this connection.

relationship-rating point scale The mental rating system that customers apply to service and service providers. Ratings range from exemplary to unsatisfactory, with average being assigned when service occurs as expected.

Strategies for Making Customers Number One

ON A SHEET OF PAPER, LIST EACH OF THE INITIATIVES FOR MAKING CUSTOMERS NO. 1 THAT YOU JUST READ ABOUT.

Then, develop an action plan for addressing each of them in your customer contacts. Be specific about exactly what you will do or say to address each strategy. Use the following initiatives and specify your actions and the expected customer response.

Make positive initial contact.

Establish rapport.

Identify and satisfy customer needs quickly.

Exceed expectations.

Follow up.

Encourage customers to return.

Identify and Satisfy Customer Needs Quickly

Use the questioning, listening, observing, and feedback skills outlined in this book to focus on issues of concern to the customer. By effectively gathering information, you can then move to the next phase of customer service.

Exceed Expectations

As you can see on the relationship-rating point scale, customers typically expect that, if they pay a certain price for a product or service, they will receive a specific quality and quantity in return. This is not an unusual expectation. The average customer looks for value. As you read in Chapter 9, with the Internet and global competition, many products and services are only a mouse click away. If you and your organization fail to deliver as promised or expected, customers may simply go away. In earlier chapters, you also saw that today's customers tend to be better-educated consumers who recognize that if they cannot fulfill their needs in one place, they can easily access the same or similar products and services on the Internet or by visiting a competitor. Therefore, you need to exceed a customer's expectations. Many terms are used to describe the concept of exceeding expectations—knock-their-socks-off service, positive memorable customer experiences, E-plus service, customer delight, dazzling service, fabled service, and five diamond or five star service. All these phrases have in common the concept mentioned before of going above and beyond customer expectations—*under*promise and *over*deliver. By going out of your way not only to satisfy customers but also to "wow" them by doing, saying, or offering the unexpected related to high-quality service delivery, you can exceed expectations. The result could be the reward of continuing patronage by the customer.

An example of unexpected service or going the extra mile follows. A customer bought flooring tiles from a home product warehouse and took

them home. Upon opening the box, he discovered that several tiles were broken. After the customer called the store, an employee delivered the replacement tiles and assisted the customer in laying them.

Follow Up

Service professionals regrettably often overlook this important element of the service process, although it can be one of the most crucial in establishing long-term relationships. Follow-through is a major factor in obtaining repeat business. After you have satisfied a customer's needs, follow up with the customer on his or her next visit or via mail, e-mail, or telephone to ensure that he or she was satisfied. For external customers, this follow-up can be coupled with a small thank-you card, coupons for discounts on future purchases, small presents, or any other incentive to reward their patronage. You can follow up with internal customers by using voice mail or e-mail messages, leaving Post-it® notes on their desks, inviting them for coffee in the cafeteria, or any other of a number of ways. The prime objective is to let them know that you have not forgotten them and appreciate their business and support.

Customer Service Success Tip

Smile, remind the customer you are available to help in the future, give an opportunity for last-minute questions, and invite the customer to return. Just as with your initial impression, you need to close on a high note.

LO 10-6 Enhancing Customer Satisfaction As a Strategy for Retaining Customers

Concept Do the unexpected; deal with one customer at a time; handle complaints efficiently. These are just some of the things you can do to enhance customer satisfaction.

Building good relationships in order to increase **customer satisfaction** is valuable—because it can lead to repeat business—the key to keeping a business productive and profitable.

Satisfaction is a big factor for many customers in remaining loyal. In your own organization, your efforts could be a deciding factor in customer ratings for the quality of service rendered.

Keeping customers can be difficult in a competitive, global marketplace because so many companies have joined in the race for customers. By providing a personal, professional strategy, you can help ensure that customers return. Some tips that can help provide quality service to customers are given in the following sections.

Pay Attention

As you listen, focus all your attention on the customer so that you can identify and address his or her needs. If you are serving in person, use positive nonverbal cues (e.g., face the customer, smile, use open gestures, make eye contact, stop doing other things, and focus attention on the customer) and language. Ask open-end questions to determine the customer's needs. Also, use the active listening techniques discussed in Chapter 5 to ensure that you get all the information you need to properly address the customer's needs or concerns.

Deal with One Customer at a Time

You cannot effectively handle two people (on the phone or in person) simultaneously. When more than one call or customer comes in at the same time, seek assistance or ask one customer to either wait or if you might get back to him or her at a later time). Then, give personalized attention to the other customer.

Know Your Customers

This is crucial with long-term customers, but it is also important with everyone. You may see or talk to hundreds of customers a week; however, each customer has only one or two contacts with you. Although you might not recall the name of everyone you speak with during a day, your customers will likely remember what was said or agreed upon previously, and expect you to do the same. For that reason, use notes or your computer to keep a record of conversations with customers. You can review or refer to these notes in subsequent encounters. This avoids having customers repeat themselves, and they will feel "special" because you remembered them. Many professionals use database management programs or contact software (e.g., ACT or Maximizer) or customer contact management systems to log and catalog contacts and customers, as well as to keep detailed notes on each contact with a customer. Consider such programs to be your electronic "cheat sheet" to help you remember important details about all your customers, clients, or patients (e.g., spouse names, favorite colors, birthdays, sizes, last purchase, prior conversations, and other valuable information).

Give Customers Special Treatment

As you read earlier, you should try to take the time for a little small talk once in a while. This will help you learn about your customers and what's important to them (potential needs). Occasionally, paying them compliments also helps (e.g., "That's an attractive tie," or "That perfume is very pleasing").

Service Each Customer at Least Adequately

Take the necessary time to handle your customer's questions, complaints, or needs. If you have a number of customers on the phone or in person, service one at a time and either ask to get back to the others or get help from a co-worker, if possible. You might also suggest alternative information resources to customers, such as fax-on-demand or your Web site, online information system, or interactive voice response. This may satisfy them and help reduce the calls or visits from customers, because they can now get the information they need from alternative sources.

Do the Unexpected

Do not just provide service; provide exceptional service. Provide additional information, offer suggestions that will aid the customer, send articles that

may be of interest, follow up transactions with calls or letters to make sure that needs were met, or send cards for special occasions and to thank customers. These are the little things that mean a lot and can mean the difference between a rating of Average or Exemplary on the relationship-rating point scale.

Give 'Em the Extra Pickle!

An example of doing the unexpected came when Bob Farrell, founder of Farrell's Ice Cream Parlor restaurants, reportedly responded to a customer complaint a number of years ago. Farrell received a letter from a regular customer of many years. The customer had been ordering hamburgers with an extra pickle since he started patronizing Farrell's. At some point, the man went to Farrell's and ordered a hamburger but was told by a new server that the extra pickle would cost an additional 25 cents. When the man protested, the server conferred with her manager and happily reported that the extra pickle would cost only 5 cents. At that point the man left and wrote Farrell, who wrote back enclosing a free coupon, apologizing, and inviting the customer back.

The lesson to be learned here is that when you have a loyal customer whom you might lose because of enforcement of a trivial policy, you should be flexible. When policies inhibit good service and negatively affect customer relationships, they should be pointed out to management and examined for possible modification or elimination.

Customer Service Success Tip

Treat all customers as if they are crucial to the organization—they are! Do whatever is possible and reasonable to maintain a strong customer-provider relationship and keep the customer returning and recommending that others should do likewise. Whether someone is a new or existing customer should make no difference.

Handle Complaints Effectively

Treat complaints as opportunities to redeem missed service expectations, and handle them effectively. Acknowledge any error on your part, and do everything possible to resolve the problem quickly and to the customer's satisfaction. Thank the customer for bringing his or her concerns to your attention.

Sell Benefits, Not Features

An effective approach to increasing sales is used by most salespeople. They focus on benefits and not features of a product or service. A feature differs from a benefit in that it is a descriptive aspect of a product or service (e.g., has a shorter turn radius, has 27 options, comes in five different colors, has a remote control, and uses less energy than competing models).

Show each customer how your product, service, or information addresses his or her needs. What benefit will result? Stress that although other organizations may offer similar products and services, yours fit their needs best (if they do), and how. If your product or service doesn't fit their needs, admit it, and offer any available alternatives (such as referral to a competitor). Your customers will appreciate your honesty, and even if you can't help them, they will probably return in the future because you are trusted.

Know Your Competition

Stay abreast of what other, similar organizations are offering in order to counter comments about them. This does not mean that you should criticize or belittle your competitors or their products and services. Such behavior is unprofessional, unethical, and will likely cause the customer to lose respect for you. And, when respect goes; trust goes.

Staying aware of the competition has the additional benefit of helping you be sure that you can describe and offer the products, services, and features of your organization that are comparable to those being offered by others.

The Marriott hotel chain recognized a need to compete with cheaper reservation rates being offered on the Internet. Marriott announced its "Look No Further Best Rate Guarantee" that matched reservation rates for the same hotel, room type, and reservation dates at all its hotels (excluding Ritz-Carlton) no matter where the customer found them. The chain states as part of its guarantee, "If the lower rate you found qualifies, we will adjust your room rate to reflect that rate, and give you an additional 25% off the lower rate."[11] The hotel chain did this to remain competitive and fill rooms.

LO 10-7 Strive for Quality

Concept A customer's perception of quality service is often one of the prime reasons for his or her return.

A final strategy for helping to increase customer loyalty relates to the quality of service you and your organization provide. So much is written these days about quality—how to measure it and its significance—that there is a temptation to think of it as a fad. In the areas of customer service and customer retention, thinking this way could be disastrous. A customer's perception of quality service is often one of the prime reasons for his or her return.

Terms such as **total quality management (TQM)** and **continuous quality improvement (CQI)** are often used in many industries and by manufacturers to label the goal of improvement. Basically, quality service involves efforts and activities that are done well and that meet or exceed customer needs and expectations. In an effort to achieve quality service, many organizations go to great lengths to test and measure the level of service provided to customers.

On a personal level, you can strive for quality service by working to achieve an Exemplary rating on the relationship-rating point scale. Your organization's ability to deliver quality service depends on you and the others who provide front-line service to customers. If you do not adopt a professional attitude and continually strive to improve your knowledge, skills, and efforts in dealing with customers, failure and customer dissatisfaction can result.

total quality management (TQM) and continuous quality improvement (CQI) A systematic approach to identifying and quantifying best practices in an organization and/or industry in order to make improvements in effectiveness and efficiency.

Small Business Perspective

Like most organizations at the end of the first decade of the twenty-first century, the small business sector has been hit hard financially. The Small Business Administration reported in a 2009 report that "More than half of the 763,000 jobs lost in the first two quarters of 2008 were lost in small firms . . . ."[12] In addition, small businesses have to face competition and strive to maintain customer loyalty on three fronts. First they have to effectively compete with local small business competitors. Second, they have to stave off competition from large chain stores and organizations that maintain a local presence and have large advertising budgets. Finally, they must compete with similar organizations worldwide on the Internet.

Building and maintaining customer loyalty is no easy task for small business owners who typically have limited financial and human resources. Not only must they be concerned with the day-to-day business operations, but they must also continually monitor competitive practices and trends in society that might impact their bottom line. Without the buying clout of larger organizations, they often struggle to maintain a profitable business model while looking for ways to continue to maintain or grow their business. Rising product and distribution costs, fees from banks and credit card processing companies, insurance, state and local taxes, employee expenses and myriad other expenses work to eat away profit margins. These are major reasons why entrepreneurs and small business owners need to focus so heavily on customer loyalty. Those who take a reactive "next" approach to dealing with customers, where they wait for someone to click on their Web site or to walk through the door are doomed to failure. Successful business people continually look for new and innovative approaches to serving their customers. This includes using an integrated approach to doing business (e.g., face-to-face, telephone, computers, and other available technology). Customers expect that anyone who provides products and services will be competitive and prepared to match the service and delivery systems of others in their industry. Those organizations who cannot meet these standards are typically the ones that close their doors.

The cost of getting new customers versus maintaining current ones has traditionally been higher. According to TARP Worldwide, "the real ratio of cost to win a new customer vs. retaining a current customer varies from 2 to 1 to 20 to 1 (this depends on the size and value of the customer to the company/industry); and that it costs five times as much to win a new customer as to keep a current customer. This formed the basis for establishing many of the customer service 800 numbers in the early 1980s."[13]

A prudent business strategy for any size business is to keep the customers you have and try to bring in new ones with low or no-cost initiatives (e.g., referral programs, incentives, discount coupons, brand recognition, and positive word-of-mouth publicity). Typically, some of the factors that can help sustain a loyal customer population for retail organizations include:

- Service representatives who are knowledgeable, helpful, have excellent communication skills, and care about their job and customers.
- Service and assistance that is readily available and easily accessible 24/7/365 and in a variety of formats (e.g., telephone, fax, Internet, face to face).
- Unique products that differentiate you from competitors.
- Creating a one-stop shopping experience where customers can obtain multiple types of products and services at one location.

- High-quality products that require lower levels of maintenance and follow-up service.
- A flexible, "no-hassle" return or exchange policy.

Service organizations should also be concerned about customer loyalty. Some factors that can assist in customer satisfaction and retention include:

- Staff who are experienced, knowledgeable, trustworthy, reliable, and possess a "can-do" attitude.
- The ability to create a true partnership with clients where the success of the customer is a prime consideration as opposed to just fulfilling the requirements of a contract or project.
- The ability to see beyond the obvious and come up with customized, unique strategies and interventions to address client needs.
- Flexibility in dealing with clients who are experiencing a changing environment or situation.

Impact on Service

Based on personal experience and what you just read, answer the following questions:

1. How well do small business do in delivering quality service and retaining customers?
2. What factors have you seen small businesses faced with in the past couple of years?
3. What technology have you witnessed small business owners using to gain and retain customers?
4. Are there issues faced by small businesses that do not impact larger companies as much related to customer service and retention? Explain.

Summary

Build enduring, strong customer relationships based on the principles of trust, responsibility, loyalty, and satisfying customer needs. These are all crucial elements of success in an increasingly competitive business world. Retaining current customers is less expensive and more effective than finding and developing new ones. The key is to provide courteous, professional service that addresses customer needs. Although many factors potentially affect your ability to deliver quality service, you can apply specific methods and strategies to keep your customers coming back.

Too often, service providers lose sight of the fact that they are the organization and that their actions determine the outcome of any customer-provider encounter. By employing the strategies outlined in this chapter, and those you read about previously, you can do much to ensure customer satisfaction and organizational success.

Review Questions

1. How can you build customer trust?

2. What are some key reasons why customers remain loyal to a product, a service, or an organization?

3. What are some of the provider characteristics that affect customer loyalty?

4. What are the steps in the planning process model? Describe.

5. What are six common customer needs?

6. What are ways for service providers to take responsibility for customer relations?

7. What are some techniques for making the customer feel that he or she is No. 1?

Search It Out

Search the Web for Information on Loyalty

Log on to the Internet to search for additional information related to customer loyalty. Select one of the following projects:

1. Go to the Web sites of organizations that deal with customers and service. Identify research data, articles, bibliographies, and other reference sources (e.g., videotapes) related to customer loyalty and create a bibliography similar to the one at the end of this book. Here are a few sites to get you started:

   www.ICSA.com
   www.SOCAP.com
   www.CSR.com

   www.Amazon.com
   www.Barnes&Noble.com
   www.Borders.com

2. Go to various search engines to locate information and articles on *customer loyalty*. To find information, enter terms related to concepts covered in this chapter or locate Web sites dealing with such issues. Here are a few to get you started:

   Customer loyalty
   Customer satisfaction
   Customer retention
   Customer Service Review magazine
   Total quality management in customer service
   Cost of customer service

Collaborative Learning Activity

Building Loyalty

Here are three options for activities that you and others can use to reinforce the concepts of building loyalty that you read about in this chapter.

1. Working with a partner, think of times when you have both been frustrated or dissatisfied with service received from a provider. Make a list of characteristics the service provider(s) exhibited that had a negative impact on you. Once you have a list, discuss the items on the list, and then honestly say

whether either (or both) of you exhibit any of these negative behaviors when dealing with others. For the ones you answered yes, jointly develop a list of strategies to improve each behavior.

2. Take a field trip around your town. Walk through and/or past as many establishments as possible. Look for examples of actions that organizations are doing to encourage and discourage customer loyalty. List the examples on a sheet of paper and be prepared to discuss them in groups assigned by

your instructor when you return to class. Some examples of encouragement might be free samples of a product being distributed at a food court, discount coupons, acceptance of competitor coupons, or free refills on drinks. Negative examples might be signs that say "Restrooms for customers only" or "No change given," and policies that allow discounts only on certain days and no refunds on purchases (exchanges only).

3. Do a survey of at least 20 people of different age groups and cultural and ethnic backgrounds. Ask the following questions related to customer retention and loyalty, then report your findings in class:

- What is the most important thing that a service provider can do to get you to return to a store, organization, or Web site?

- When shopping for a product or service, what referral source do you value most when making a buying decision (e.g., Web site, consumer article or media channel, newspaper, family member or friend)?

- If you are trying to decide where to purchase a product or service and the only two differentiators are slightly higher cost and a better approach to service, which would you choose?

- If you have a choice of choosing to buy an identical product locally or on the Internet, which source are you more likely to select?

Face to Face

Assessing the Need for Reorganization at Get Away

Background

After over 9 years in business, the Get Away travel agency in Des Moines, Iowa, is feeling the pinch of competition. During the past 14 months, the owners, Marsha Henry and Consuela (Connie) Gomez, have seen business profits dwindle by 18 percent. Employee attrition was also over 50 percent in the past 6 months. Neither Marsha nor Connie can figure out what has happened. Although travel reservationists have had to deal with airline fee caps, customers making more reservations on the Internet, and the fact that many industry travel providers are cutting back, competing agencies don't seem to be suffering as much as Get Away. The problem is especially worrisome because Marsha and Connie recently took out a second mortgage on their office building so that they could put more money into promotion and customer acquisition efforts. The more efforts they make at gaining exposure, the more customers they lose, it seems. Recently, they lost a major corporate client that accounted for over $100,000 in business a year. Out of desperation, they have decided to hire you, a seasoned travel agency manager, to try to stop their descent and turn the operation around.

Your Role

As the new manager at Get Away, you have been given the authority to do whatever is necessary to salvage the agency. By agreement with Marsha and Connie, they are delaying the announcement of your hiring to other agency employees. Your objective is to objectively assess the operation by acting as a customer.

Your first contact with the agency came on Thursday morning, when you placed a phone call to the office at 9:00 A.M., posing as a customer. The phone rang 12 times and was curtly answered with "Hello. Please hold (click)." After nearly five minutes, an agent, Sue, came on the line and stated, "Sorry for the wait, we're swamped. Can I get your name and number and call you right back?" Two-and-a-half hours later, you got a call from Tom. He said that Sue had gone home for the day because she was sick, and he was doing her callbacks. Sue would follow up when she came in the next day. You had asked a friend to make a similar call yesterday (Wednesday), and she had similar results.

On Thursday afternoon, you stopped by the office at 1:55 P.M. Of four agents who should have been there, only Claudia was present. Apparently Tom and Sue were still at lunch. Two customers were waiting as you arrived. Aisha greeted you with a small smile and asked you to "Take a number and have a seat." You looked around the office and saw desks piled high with materials, an overflowing trash can, and an empty coffeepot in the waiting area bearing the sign "Please have a cup on us." In talking to your fellow "customers," you learned that one had been there for over 45 minutes. Both were irritated at having to wait, and eventually, one left. You left after 30 minutes and passed Tom and Sue, who came in laughing. You thought you detected an odor of alcohol on Tom. Neither acknowledged you. From the office, you proceeded to a meeting with Marsha and Connie.

Critical Thinking Questions

1. What impressions of the travel agency did you have as a result of your initial phone call?
2. How did your office visit affect you?
3. What will you tell Marsha and Connie about employee professionalism?
4. What customer needs are being overlooked in this scenario?
5. In what ways can this situation be improved?

Planning to Serve

To help enhance customer retention and foster customer loyalty efforts of any organization, think about the following questions:

1. What are some strategies that can be used to show customers that their business is valued?
2. What obstacles exist to customer loyalty and how might they be removed?
3. What are some of the things that positively impact customer loyalty in many organizations?
4. What are some things that differentiate organizations and that can be accentuated to build customer retention and loyalty?
5. When a customer becomes dissatisfied, what can be done to appease and retain that customer's business?
6. What is the most difficult aspect of customer retention in your mind? Explain.

Quick Preview Answers

| 1. T | 3. T | 5. T | 7. T | 9. T | 11. T |
| 2. F | 4. T | 6. F | 8. T | 10. F | 12. T |

Ethical Dilemma Summary

Ethical Dilemma 10.1 Possible Answers

1. What are the ethical issues here and how would you deal with them? Explain.

This is certainly a very awkward, sensitive, and serious issue with which to deal. If you fail to share your concerns and feelings about the way the situation is being handled with the pharmacist, it will possibly be repeated, and potentially have serious medical repercussions or worse. The pharmacist is not only acting unprofessionally, unethically, and potentially illegally, he is also potentially putting himself and the organization in a litigious situation and endangering the lives of patients. Granted, this may have been a legitimate mistake on the part of the pharmacist; however, that does not make it any less serious.

On the other hand, if you refuse to do as the pharmacist tells you; your job and future opportunities might be in jeopardy. This could be a reality; however, remember that federal law protects whistleblowers from retaliation. Also, you have an option of going to the store manager to discuss the issue. The bottom line is that this is a very serious medical issue.

2. What would you say or do to the pharmacist?

Because of the serious nature of this incident, you should not become part in a potentially litigious and health-threatening situation. Tell the pharmacist that you do not feel comfortable not telling the patient the truth and ask him to handle it himself.

3. What do you do or say to the patient? Explain.

In the immediate instance, you should probably defer discussion of the matter and explain that the pharmacist or someone else will be right with the customer.

4. What else would you do in this situation?

Because of the serious nature of this event, you should definitely report it to the store manager and depending on the reaction that you get; you may want to consider whether this organization is really somewhere that you want to continue working. If the situation is not properly resolved with the disciplining and/or removal of the pharmacist, there are going to be major legal and other problems in the future. If it is not handled at a local level, you can always contact the regional store manager and if necessary corporate headquarters. If all else fails, each state has governmental agencies that license and oversee pharmacies and pharmacists. You can report the incident to them for investigation.

5. How do such instances potentially affect customer loyalty?

There have been many media reports of similar incidents in recent years and as a result consumers are very skeptical and leery about going to pharmacies. Typically, when these cases arise, there is an exodus from pharmacies to their competitors. The old adage of "buyer beware" is certainly the watchword for many patients these days. Also, there are many watchdog groups monitoring such cases.

Ethical Dilemma 10.2 Possible Answers

1. Should you say anything to anyone in the office? Explain.

In a situation where you are the "new kid on the block," it is likely that your inclination is to keep your mouth shut, especially since you do not yet have a strong rapport with co-workers. In such situations, most people would not feel comfortable approaching anyone to share their views. However, if you fail to say something to the agents or your supervisor, there is a chance that federal Environmental Protection Agency (EPA) guidelines are going to be violated and children are going to be put in potential physical danger. This is based on research that shows young children assimilate almost 50 percent of any lead that they might ingest (e.g., from eating paint chips they find on the floor). This can lead to mental and physical medical conditions.

You could try approaching the agents casually (in the break room) and sharing some interesting "research" that you read (go on line in advance to read about the EPA rulings) about the effect of lead-based paint in buildings. Ask them how agents normally handle situations where they know about such paint in properties that are listed. This can put the agents on notice without accusing them and might even result in your finding that they were not aware of the EPA guidelines.

Another alternative would be to approach your supervisor and let him or her know that you have heard of a property the agency has listed that might violate EPA guidelines for lead-based paint and ask what types of disclosures agents have to warn potential buyers about. Again, you could do this in a nonaccusatory fashion.

If neither of these approaches have any direct corrective impact, you have a number of additional options. Some of these include:

- Confronting the agents about the conversation that you overheard and let ask them to inform the potential buyer.
- Telling your supervisor of the conversation and asking him or her to speak to the agents.
- Telling the potential buyer of the situation.
- Reporting the incident to the EPA if a sale is made and no legal disclosure was done.
- Quitting your job and saying nothing.

2. Should you say anything to the potential buyer? Explain.

   Before approaching a customer, you should always try to resolve the issue internally within the organization at the lowest possible level.

3. If you do not say anything, is there potential legal liability? Explain.

   If a sale is made and legal disclosure is not made as required by law, the organization and agents could be held legally and potentially civilly liable.

4. If you do say something to either the agents, your boss, or the potential buyer, what are the potential repercussions for you?

   There are a number of potential results if you speak up:

   - You might be thanked for bringing the issue to the attention of the agents, boss, or buyer.
   - You might also be ostracized by your peers for intervening.
   - You might be fired by your boss, if he or she is aware of the practice and wants to keep the illegal activity under wraps.

Reader's Customer Service Survey

Name _____

Title _____

Organization/School _____

Address (where you want booklet mailed) _____

_____

City/State/Zip _____

Phone (   ) _____

Customer feedback is crucial for delivering effective service and addressing specific needs. For us to make necessary additions, deletions, or corrections to this book we need your help. Please take a few minutes to provide feedback in the following areas and return this questionnaire to the address noted. In exchange for your thoughts and time, we'll send you a free booklet, "Communicating One-to-One," on effective interpersonal communication techniques. (Photocopy the questionnaire if you prefer). All the information above is needed to receive the free booklet.

Thank you.

1. Describe yourself in terms of customer contact experience:

    ___ Entry level (up to 1 year) ___ Midlevel (2–5 years) ___ Senior (5+years)

2. Are you currently working in a customer contact position in a business or organization?

    Yes _____ No _____

3. In what industry do you currently work or intend to once you graduate?

    1 _____ 2 _____ 3 _____ 4 _____ 5 _____ 6 _____ 7 _____
    Strongly   Neutral   Strongly
    agree   disagree

4. The information provided in this book was clearly written and easy to read.

    1 _____ 2 _____ 3 _____ 4 _____ 5 _____ 6 _____ 7 _____
    Strongly   Neutral   Strongly
    agree   disagree

5. The techniques outlined in this book are realistic and useful.

    1 _____ 2 _____ 3 _____ 4 _____ 5 _____ 6 _____ 7 _____
    Strongly   Neutral   Strongly
    agree   disagree

6. The design of this book was logical, efficient, effective, and easy to follow.

    1 _____ 2 _____ 3 _____ 4 _____ 5 _____ 6 _____ 7 _____
    Strongly   Neutral   Strongly
    agree   disagree

7. The level of information was well targeted to entry to midlevel customer contact personnel.

1 _____ 2 _____ 3 _____ 4 _____ 5 _____ 6 _____ 7 _____
Strongly   Neutral   Strongly
agree   disagree

8. The text included real-world examples and scenarios that helped make chapter content more relevant to the workplace.

1 _____ 2 _____ 3 _____ 4 _____ 5 _____ 6 _____ 7 _____
Strongly   Neutral   Strongly
agree   disagree

9. I can apply information or ideas learned directly to my current or future job.

1 _____ 2 _____ 3 _____ 4 _____ 5 _____ 6 _____ 7 _____
Strongly   Neutral   Strongly
agree   disagree

10. I plan to use this book as a reference in the future.

1 _____ 2 _____ 3 _____ 4 _____ 5 _____ 6 _____ 7 _____
Strongly   Neutral   Strongly
agree   disagree

11. This book met my overall needs and expectations.

1 _____ 2 _____ 3 _____ 4 _____ 5 _____ 6 _____ 7 _____
Strongly   Neutral   Strongly
agree   disagree

12. I will recommend this book to others.

1 _____ 2 _____ 3 _____ 4 _____ 5 _____ 6 _____ 7 _____
Strongly   Neutral   Strongly
agree   disagree

13. What chapter was most valuable to you? Why? _____
_____

14. In your mind, what is the most critical issue facing customer service professionals today? Why? _____
_____

15. If you rated any question below a 5 above, please explain why you did so. _____
_____

16. What other topics related to customer service are of interest to you? Why?
_____

17. What supplemental Web site content created for this book did you use and what did you think of them?
_____

Send form to: Bob Lucas, President
Creative Presentation Resources Inc.
P.O. Box 180487
Casselberry, Florida 32718-0487

Phone: (800)308-0399/(407)695-5535

Fax: (407)695-7447

E-mail: blucas@presentationresources.net

Glossary

A

acknowledgment   A communication technique for use with customers who have a complaint or are upset. It involves recognizing the customer's level of emotion before moving on to help resolve the issue.

Americans with Disabilities Act of 1990   A United States federal act signed into law in July of 1990 guaranteeing people with disabilities equal access to workplace and public opportunities.

angry customers   Customers who become emotional because either their needs are not met or they are dissatisfied with the services or products purchased from an organization.

appearance and grooming   Nonverbal characteristics exhibited by service providers that can send a variety of messages that range from being a professional to having a negative attitude.

articulation, enunciation, or pronunciation   Refers to the manner or clarity in which verbal messages are delivered.

assertiveness   Involves projecting a presence that is assured, confident, and capable without seeming to be aggressive or arrogant.

assigning meaning   The phase of the listening process in which the brain attempts to match a received sound or message with other information stored in the brain in order to recognize or extract meaning from it.

attending   The phase of the listening process in which a listener focuses attention on a specific sound or message being received from the environment.

attitudes   Emotional responses to people, ideas, and objects. They are based on values, differ between individuals and cultures, and affect the way people deal with various issues and situations.

automated attendants   Provide callers with a menu of options from which they can select by pressing a key on their telephone keypad.

automatic call distribution (ACD) system   Telecommunications system used by many companies in their call centers and customer care facilities to capture incoming calls and route them to available service providers.

automatic number identification (ANI) system   A form of caller identification system similar to home telephone caller ID systems. ANI allows incoming customers to be identified on a computer screen with background information so that they can be routed to an appropriate service representative for assistance.

B

baby boomer   A term applied to anyone born between 1946 and 1964. People in this age group are called "boomers."

behavioral styles   Descriptive term that identifies categories of human behavior identified by behavioral researchers. Many of the models used to group behaviors date back to those identified by Carl Jung.

beliefs   Perceptions or assumptions that individuals or cultures maintain. These perceptions are based on past experiences, memories, and interpretations and influence how people act and interact with certain individuals or groups.

biases   Beliefs or opinions that a person has about an individual or group. Often based on unreasonable distortions or prejudice.

blind transfer   The practice of transferring an incoming caller to another telephone number and hanging up once someone answers without announcing who is calling.

blogs or Web logs   Online journals or diaries that allow people to add content. Many organizational websites use them to post "what's new" sections and to receive feedback (good and bad) from customers and Web site visitors.

body language   Nonverbal communication cues that send powerful messages through gestures, vocal qualities, manner of dress, grooming, and many other cues.

burnout   A category of stress that encompasses personal exhaustion, lack of enthusiasm, reduced productivity, and apathy toward the job and customers.

business-to-business (B2B)   Refers to a business-to-business customer service.

C

channel   Term used to describe the method through which people communicate messages. Examples are face to face, telephone, e-mail, written correspondence, and facsimile.

channel partner   Relationship of two organizations in which they are able to build a larger and stronger competitive presence in the marketplace.

Chicano culture   Refers primarily to people with a heritage based in Mexico.

churn   The process of a customer switching between products or companies, often simply to get a better price, rebate, or warranty.

circadian rhythm   The physiological 24-hour cycle associated with the earth's rotation that affects metabolic and sleep patterns in humans as day displaces night.

closed-end questions   Inquiries that typically start with a verb and solicit short one-syllable answers (e.g., yes, no, one word, or a number) and can be used for such purposes as clarifying, verifying information already given, controlling conversation, or affirming something.

clusters of nonverbal behavior   Groupings of nonverbal behaviors that indicate a possible negative intent (e.g., crossed arms, closed body posturing, frowning, or turning away) while other behaviors (smiling, open gestures with arms and hands, and friendly touching) indicate positive message intent.

code of ethics   A set of standards, often developed by employees, which guide the conduct of all employees.

Cold War   A period of military, economic, and political tension and competition between the United States and the former Soviet Union that lasted from the 1940s through the 1990s.

collective cultures   Members of a group sharing common interests and values. They see themselves as an interdependent unit and conform and cooperate for the good of the group.

comprehending   The phase of the listening process in which the brain attempts to match a received sound or message with other information stored in the brain in order to recognize or extract meaning from it.

computer telephony integration (CTI)   A system that integrates a representative's computer and phone to facilitate the automatic retrieval of customer records and other information needed to satisfy a customer's needs and requests.

concept of time   Term used to describe how certain societies view time as either polychronic or monochronic.

conflict   Involves incompatible or opposing views and can result when a customer's needs, desires, or demands do not match service provider or organizational policies, procedures, and abilities.

conflict resolution style   The manner in which a person handles conflict. People typically use one of five approaches to resolving conflict—avoidance, compromise, competition, accommodation, or collaboration.

congruence   In communication, this relates to ensuring that verbal messages sent match or are in agreement with the nonverbal cues used.

contact points   Instances in which a customer connects with a service provider or some other aspect of an organization.

contingency plans   Backup systems or procedures that are implemented when regular ones break down or fail to function as intended.

cost of dissatisfied customers   Phrase that refers to any formula used to calculate the cost of acquiring a new customer or replacing a current one as a result of having a dissatisfied customer leave an organization.

cottage industries   Term adopted in the early days of customer service when many people started small businesses in their homes or cottages and bartered products or services with neighbors.

crisis manager   A person who waits until the last minute to address an issue or take an action. The result is that others are then inconvenienced and have to shift their priorities to help resolve the issue.

cultural diversity   Refers to the differences and similarities attributed to various groups of people within a culture.

customer-centric   A term used to describe service providers and organizations that put their customers first and spend time, effort, and money identifying and focusing on the needs of current and potential customers. Efforts are focused on building long-term relationships and customer loyalty rather than simply selling a product or service and moving on to the next customer.

customer contact center   A central point within an organization from which all customer service contacts are managed via various forms of technology.

customer defection   Customers often take their business to competitors when they feel that their needs or wants are not met or if they encounter breakdown in customer service or poor quality products.

customer expectations   The perceptions that customers have when they contact an organization or service provider about the kind, level, and quality of products and services they should receive.

customer-focused organization   A company that spends energy and effort on satisfying internal and external customers by first identifying customer needs, then establishing policies, procedures, and management and reward systems to support excellence in service delivery.

customer-friendly systems   Refers to the processes in an organization that make service seamless to customers by ensuring that things work properly and the customer is satisfied.

customer loyalty   Term used to describe the tendency of customers to return to a product or organization regularly because of the service and satisfaction they receive.

customer needs   Motivators or drivers that cause customers to seek out specific types of products or services. These may be marketing-driven by advertising they have seen or may tie directly to Dr. Abraham Maslow's Hierarchy of Needs Theory.

customer relationship management (CRM)   Concept of identifying customer needs: understanding and influencing customer behavior through ongoing communication strategies in an effort to acquire, retain, and satisfy the customer. The ultimate goal is customer loyalty.

customer relationships   The practice of building and maintaining ongoing friendships with customers in an effort to make them feel comfortable with an organization and its service providers and to enhance customer loyalty.

customer retention   The ongoing effort by an organization to meet customer needs and desires in an effort to build long-term relationships and keep them for life.

customer satisfaction   The feeling of a person whose needs have been met by an organization.

customer service   The ability of knowledgeable, capable, and enthusiastic employees to deliver products and services to their internal and external customers in a manner that satisfies identified and unidentified needs and ultimately results in positive word-of-mouth publicity and return business.

customer service environment   An environment made up of and influenced by various elements of an organization. Examples are delivery systems, human resources, service, products, and organizational culture.

customers with disabilities   Descriptive phrase that refers to anyone with a physical or mental disability.

D

decisive style   One of four behavior style groupings characterized by a direct, no-nonsense approach to people and situations.

decoding   The stage in the interpersonal communication process in which messages received are analyzed by a receiver in an effort to determine the sender's intent.

deliverables   Products or services provided by an organization.

delivery system   The method(s) used by an organization to provide services and products to its customers.

demanding or domineering customers   Customers who have definite ideas about what they want and are unwilling to compromise or accept alternatives.

deregulation   Occurs when governments remove legislative or regulatory guidelines that inhibit and control an industry (e.g., transportation, natural gas, and telecommunications).

difficult customers   People who challenge a service provider's ability to deliver service and who require special skills and patience.

dissatisfied customers   Someone who either does not (or perceives that he or she does not) receive promised products or services.

distress   Pain or worry brought on by either internal or external physical or mental strain.

diversity   The characteristics, values, beliefs, and factors that make people different, yet similar.

downsizing   Term applied to the situation in which employees are terminated or empty positions are left unfilled once someone leaves an organization.

E

e-commerce   An entire spectrum of companies that market products and services on the Internet and through other technology, and the process of accessing them by consumers.

electronic mail (e-mail)   System used to transmit messages around the Internet.

e-mail management   System of providing organizational guidelines for effective use of e-mail systems.

emoticons (emotional icons)   Humorous characters that send visual messages such as smiling or frowning. They are created with various strokes of the computer keyboard characters and symbols.

emotional messages of color   Research-based use of color to send nonverbal messages through advertisements and other elements of the organization.

emotion-reducing model   Process for reducing customer emotion in situations when frustration or anger exists.

employee assistance program (EAP)   Benefit package offered to employees by many organizations that provide services to help employees deal with personal problems that might adversely affect their work performance (e.g., legal, financial, behavioral, and mental counseling services).

employee expectations   Perceptions about positive and negative aspects of the workplace.

employee roles   Task assignments that service providers assume.

empowerment   The word used to describe the giving of decision-making and problem-resolution authority to lower-level employees in an organization. This precludes having to get permission from higher levels in order to take an action or serve a customer.

encoding   The stage in the interpersonal communication process in which the sender decides what message will be sent and how it will be transmitted along with considerations about the receiver.

environmental cues   Any aspect of the workplace with which a customer comes into contact. Such things as the general appearance of an area, clutter, unsightly or offensive items, or general disorganization contribute to the perception of an environment.

environmental factors affecting stress   Refers to the workplace, organizational, and societal elements that impact a service provider's mental and physical state.

ethical behavior   Expected performance that sends a message of being trustworthy and honest, and having the intent to provide quality service.

etiquette and manners   Includes the acceptable rules, manners, and ceremonies for an organization, profession, or society.

eustress   A term coined by psychologist Dr. Hans Seyle to describe positive stress that people sometimes experience when they set goals or objectives and exhilaration that are essential for personal expansion and growth.

expectations of privacy   The belief that personal information provided to an organization will be safeguarded against inappropriate or unauthorized use or dissemination.

expressive style   One of four behavior groups characterized as being people-oriented, fun-loving, upbeat, and extroverted.

external customers   Those people outside the organization who purchase or lease products and services. This group includes vendors, suppliers, and people on the telephone, and others not from the organization.

external obstacles   Factors outside an organization or the sphere of one's influence that can cause challenges in delivering service.

F

face   Refers to the important concept of esteem in many Asian cultures. In such cultures one tries not to cause embarrassment or otherwise create a situation in which someone looks bad in the eyes of others.

facsimile (fax) machine   Equipment that converts printed words and graphics into electronic signals and allows them to be transmitted across telephone lines then reassembled into a facsimile of the words and graphics on the receiving end.

faulty assumptions   Service provider projections made about underlying customer message meanings based on past experiences.

fax on demand   Technology that allows information, such as a form, stored in a computer to be requested electronically via a telephone and transmitted to a customer.

fee-based 900 number   A premium telephone number provided by organizations and individuals that, when called, can provide information and services that are billed back to the caller's local telephone bill.

feedback   The stage of the interpersonal communication process in which a receiver responds to a sender's message.

feel, felt, found technique   A process for expressing empathy and concern for someone and for helping them understand that you can relate to their situation.

fight or flight syndrome   A term used by scientists to describe the body's reaction to stressors in which the heart starts pumping the chemical adrenaline into the blood stream and the lungs start taking in more oxygen. This provides the fuel needed to deal with the situation. (See also stressors.)

filters   Psychological barriers in the form or personal experiences, lessons learned, societal beliefs, and values through which people process and compare information received to determine its significance.

foreign-born people   Refers to people not born in a given country.

form of address   Title used to address people. Examples are Mister, Miss, and Doctor.

G

gender communication   Term used to refer to communication between genders.

gender roles   Behaviors attributed to or assigned by societal norms.

globalization   The term applied to an ongoing trend of information, knowledge, and resource sharing around the world. As a result of a more mobile society and easier access to transportation and technology, more people are traveling and accessing products and services from international sources than ever before.

global terms   Potentially inflammatory words or phrases used in conversation. They tend to inappropriately generalize behavior or group people or incidents together (e.g., always, never, everyone, everything, all the time).

H

hearing   A passive physiological process of gathering sound waves and transmitting them to the brain for analysis. It is the first phase of the listening process.

hearing disabilities   Conditions in which the ability to hear is diminished below established auditory standards.

help desk   Term used to describe a service provider trained and assigned to assist customers with questions, problems, or suggestions.

Hierarchy of Needs Theory   Developed by Dr. Abraham Maslow. In studies, Maslow identified five levels of needs that humans possess—physiological (basic), safety, social, esteem, and self-actualization.

Hispanic culture   Refers to people who were born in Mexico, Puerto Rico, Cuba, or Central or South America.

human resources   Refers to the employees of an organization.

hygiene   The healthy maintenance of the body through such practices as regular bathing, washing of hair, brushing of teeth, cleaning of fingernails, and using commercial products to eliminate or mask odors.

I

"I" or "we" messages   Messages that are potentially less offensive than the word "you," which is like nonverbal finger pointing when emotions are high.

impact of culture   Refers to the outcome of people from various countries or backgrounds coming into contact with one another and potentially experiencing misunderstandings or relationship breakdowns.

inclusive   The concept of ensuring that people of all races, genders, and religious and ethnic backgrounds, as well as a multitude of other diverse factors, are included in communications and activities in the workplace.

indecisive customers   People who have difficulty making a decision or making a selection when given choices of products or services.

individualistic cultures   Groups in which members value themselves as individuals who are separate from their group and are responsible for their own destiny.

inflection   The change in tone of the voice as one speaks. This quality is also called pitch and adds vocal variety and punctuation to verbal messages.

information overload   Refers to having too many messages coming together and causing confusion, frustration, or an inability to act.

inquisitive style   One of four behavioral groups, characterized by being introverted, task-focused, and detail-oriented.

interactive voice response (IVR) system   Technology that allows customers to call an organization 24 hours a day, 7 days a week to get information from recorded messages or a computer by keying a series of numbers on the telephone keypad in response to questions or prompts.

interferences   Noises that can interfere with messages being effectively communicated between two people.

internal customers   People within the organization who either require support and service or provide information, products, and services to service providers. Such customers include peers, co-workers, bosses, subordinates, and people from other areas of the organization.

Internet callback   Technology that allows someone browsing the Internet to key a prompt on a Web site and have a service representative call a phone number provided.

Internet telephony   Technology that allows people to talk to one another via the Internet as if they were on a regular telephone.

interpersonal relationship   Focuses on the need for service providers to build strong bonds with customers.

interpersonal skills   The skills used by people to relate to and communicate effectively with others. Examples are verbal and nonverbal communication skills and the ability to build trust, empathy, and compassion.

iPod   A brand of portable media player that has been manufactured and marketed by Apple® computer since 2001. It can play digital audio files and videos and can also function as an external data storage unit.

J

job factors affecting stress   Refers to the elements of a job that frustrate or pressure someone.

job stress   Term coined to describe the impact of the internal and external elements of the workplace that cause service providers to feel mentally and physically pressured or to become ill.

L

lag time   The term applied to the difference in the rate at which the human brain can receive and process information and at which most adults speak.

Latino culture   Refers to people of Hispanic descent.

learning organizations   A term used by Peter Senge in his book *The Fifth Discipline* to describe organizations that value knowledge, education, and employee training. They also learn from their competition, industry trends, and other sources, and they develop systems to support continued growth and development in order to remain competitive.

listening   An active, learned process consisting of four phases—receiving/hearing the message, attending, comprehending/assigning meaning, and responding.

listening gap   The difference in the speed at which the brain can comprehend communication and the speed at which the average adult speaks in the United States.

M

media blending   Technology that allows a service provider to communicate with a customer via telephone while at the same time displaying information to the customer over the computer.

memory   The ability to gain, store, retain, and recall information in the brain for later application. Short-term memory stores small bits of information (7 items, plus or minus 2) for approximately 20 seconds while long-term memory can store much larger quantities of information for potentially unlimited duration.

mentees   Typically less experienced recipients of the efforts of mentors.

mentors   Individuals who dedicate time and effort to befriend and assist others. In an organization, they are typically people with a lot of knowledge, experience, skills, and initiative, and have a large personal and professional network established.

message   A communication delivered through speech or signals, or in writing.

miscellaneous cues   Refers to factors used to send messages that impact a customer's perception or feelings about a service provider or organization. Examples are personal habits, etiquette, and manners.

mission   The direction or focus of an organization that supports day-to-day interactions with customers.

mobility or motion impairments   Physical limitations that some people have, requiring accommodation or special consideration to allow access to products or services.

modesty   Refers to the way that cultures view propriety of dress and conduct.

moment of truth   A phrase popularized by Scandinavian Airlines System President Jan Carlzon in his popular 1987 book of the same name. It is defined as any instance when a customer comes into contact with any element or representative of an organization.

monochronic   Refers to the perception of time as being a central focus with deadlines being a crucial element of societal norms.

N

needs   Motivators or drivers that cause customers to seek out specific types of products or services. These may be marketing-driven, based on advertising they have seen, or may tie directly to Abraham Maslow's hierarchy of needs theory.

noise   Refers to physiological or psychological factors (physical characteristics, level of attention, message clarity, loudness of message, or environmental factors) that interfere with the accurate reception of information.

nonverbal feedback   Messages sent to someone through other than spoken means. Examples are gestures, appearance, and facial expressions.

nonverbal messages   Consist of such things as movements, gestures, body positions, vocal qualities, and a variety of unspoken signals sent by people, often in conjunction with verbal messages.

North American Free Trade Agreement (NAFTA)   A trade agreement entered into by the United States, Canada, and Mexico to help, among other things, eliminate barriers to trade, promote conditions of fair trade across borders, increase investment opportunities, and promote and protect intellectual property rights.

O

objections   Reasons given by customers for not wanting to purchase a product or service during an interaction with a salesperson or service provider (e.g., "I don't need one," "I can't afford it," or "I already have one").

offshoring   Refers to the relocation of business services from one country to another (e.g., services, production, and manufacturing).

online information fulfillment system   Technology that allows a customer to access an organization's Web site and click on desired information without having to interact with a service provider.

open-end questions   Typically start with words like who, when, what, how, and why and are used to engage others in conversation or to gain input and ideas.

organizational culture   Includes an element of an organization that a customer encounters.

outsourcing   Refers to the practice of contracting with third-party companies or vendors outside the organization (usually in another country) to deliver products and services to customers or produce products.

ownership of property   Refers to how people of a given culture view property.

P

paralanguage   Consists of voice qualities (e.g., pitch, rate, tone, or other vocal qualities) or noises and vocalizations (e.g., "Hmmm" or "Ahhh") made as someone speaks, which let a speaker know that his or her message is being listened to and followed.

paraphrase   The practice of a message receiver giving back in his own words what he believes a sender said.

pauses   A verbal technique of delaying response in order to allow time to process information received, think of a response, or gain attention.

perception checking   The process of clarifying a nonverbal cue that was received by stating what behavior was observed, giving one or two possible interpretations, then asking the message sender for clarification.

perceptions   How someone views an item, situation, or others.

personal factors affecting stress   Refers to issues that someone has related to family, finances, or other elements of life that can create pressure or frustration.

personal obstacles   Factors that can limit performance or success in life. Examples are disabilities, lack of education, and biases.

pet peeves   Refers to factors, people, or situations that personally irritate or frustrate a service provider and which, left unchecked, can create a breakdown in effective service.

pitch   Refers to the change in tone of the voice as one speaks. This quality is also called inflection and adds vocal variety and punctuation to verbal messages.

Planning Process Model   Five-step process for creating contingency or backup plans to better serve customers when problems arise or things do not go as expected.

Platinum Rule   Term coined by speaker and author Tony Alessandra related to going beyond the step of treating customers the way you want to be treated, to the next level of treating them the way they would like to be treated.

podcasts or podcasting   A word that is a derivative of Apple® Computer's iPod® media player and the term broadcasting. Through podcasts, Web sites can offer direct download or streaming of their content (e.g., music or video files) to customers or Web site users.

polychronic   Refers to the perception of time as a fluid commodity that does not interfere with relationships and elements of happiness.

posture   Refers to how one sits or stands in order to project various nonverbal messages.

predictive dialing system   Technology that automatically places outgoing calls and delivers incoming calls to the next available service representative in a call center.

primary behavior pattern   Refers to a person's preferred style of dealing with others.

prioritizing time   Relates to how someone decides the importance of various tasks and the order in which they are dealt with.

problem solving   The system of identifying issues, determining alternatives for dealing with them, then selecting and monitoring a strategy for resolution.

Problem-Solving Model   The process used by a service provider to assist customers in determining and selecting appropriate solutions to their issues, concerns, or needs.

process improvement   Refers to the process of continually evaluating products and services to ensure that maximum effectiveness, efficiency, and potential are being obtained from them.

product   Something produced or an output by an individual or organization. In the service environment, products are created to satisfy customer needs or wants.

prohibitions   Local, state, or federal regulations that prevent a service provider from satisfying a customer's request even though the provider would normally do so.

proxemics   Relates to the invisible barrier surrounding people in which they feel comfortable interacting with others. This zone varies depending on the level of relationship a person has with someone else.

psychological distracters   Refers to mental factors that can cause a shift in focus in interacting with others. Examples are state of health and personal issues.

R

rapport   The silent bond built between two people as a result of sharing of common interests and issues and demonstration of a win-win, I care attitude.

rate of speech   Refers to the number of words spoken per minute. Some research studies have found that the average rate of speech for adults in Western cultures is approximately 125–150 words per minute (wpm).

rational style   One of four behavioral groups characterized by being quiet, reflective, task-focused, and systematic.

receiver   One of the two primary elements of a two-way conversation. Gathers the sender's message and decides how to react to it.

recognition   A process that occurs in thinking when a previously experienced pattern, event, process, image, or object that is stored in memory is encountered again.

relationship management   The process of continually monitoring interactions with a customer in order to strengthen ties and retain the customer.

relationship-rating points   Values mentally assigned by customers to a service provider and his or her organization. They are based on a number of factors starting with initial impressions and subsequently by the quality and level of service provided.

relationship-rating point scale   The mental rating system that customers apply to service and service providers. Ratings range from *exemplary* to *unsatisfactory*, with average being assigned when service occurs as expected.

respect for elders   A value held by people from many cultures.

responding   Refers to sending back verbal and nonverbal messages to a message originator.

road rage   A term used to describe the practice of a driver or passenger in a vehicle verbally and/or physically assaulting others as a result of the frustrations experienced while driving (e.g., driver failing to signal, cutting into a lane abruptly, or tailgating).

rude or inconsiderate customers   People who seem to take pleasure in being obstinate and contrary when dealing with service providers and who seem to have their own agenda without concern for the feelings of others.

RUMBA   An acronym for five criteria (realistic, understandable, measurable, believable, and attainable) used to establish and measure employee performance goals.

S

screen pop-ups   Small screen images that are programmed to appear on someone's computer monitor when a Web site is accessed.

seamless service   Service which is done in a manner that seems effortless and natural to the customer. Processes and systems are fully functional, effective, and efficient. Service representatives are well-trained and proficient in delivering service, and there is no inconvenience to the customer.

semantics   The scientific study of relationships between signs, symbols, and words and their meaning. The way words are used or stressed often affects their perceived meaning.

sender   One of the two primary elements of a two-way conversation. Originates messages to a receiver.

service breakdowns   Situations when customers have expectations of a certain type or level of service that are not met by a service provider.

service culture   A service environment made up of various factors, including the values, beliefs, norms, rituals and practices of a group or organization.

service delivery systems   The mechanisms or strategies used by an organization to provide service to customers.

service economy   A term used to describe the trend in which businesses have shifted from primarily production and manufacturing to more service delivery. As part of this evolution, many organizations have developed specifically to provide services to customers.

service industry   A term used to describe businesses and organizations that are engaged primarily in service delivery. Service sector is a more accurate term, since many organizations provide some form of service to their customers even though they are primarily engaged in research, development, and manufacture of products.

service measurement   Techniques used by organizations to determine how customers perceive the value of services and products received.

service options   Alternatives offered by service providers when an original request by a customer cannot be honored because of such restrictions as governmental statutory regulations, nonavailability of products, or inability to perform as requested.

service philosophy   The approach that an organization takes to providing service and addressing the needs of customers.

service recovery   The process of righting a wrong or correcting something that has gone wrong involving provision of a product or service to a customer. The concept involves not only replacing defective products, but also going the extra step of providing compensation for the customer's inconvenience.

service sector   Refers to organizations and individuals involved in delivering service as a primary product.

setting priorities   The process of deciding which factors or elements have greater importance and placing them in a hierarchy.

silence   Technique used to gain attention when speaking, to allow thought, or to process information received.

Small Business Administration (SBA)   United States governmental agency established to assist small business owners.

small talk   Dialogue used to enhance relationships, show civility, and build rapport.

spamming or spam   An abusive use of various electronic messaging systems and technology to send unsolicited and indiscriminant bulk messages to people (also used with instant messaging, Web search engines, blogs, and other formats).

spatial cues   Nonverbal messages sent on the basis of how close or far someone stands from another person.

stereotype   Generalization made about an individual or group and not based on reality. Similar people are often lumped together for ease in categorizing them.

strategies for preventing dissatisfaction   Techniques used to prevent a breakdown in needs fulfillment when you are dealing with customers.

strategies for reclaiming time   Techniques used to eliminate time wasters and to become more effective and efficient.

stressors   Factors in a person's life that cause them to react positively or negatively to a situation that caused the pressure. (*See also* fight or flight syndrome.)

T

talkative customers Customers exhibiting extroverted behavior who are very people-oriented.

Technical Assistance Research Program (TARP) Worldwide An Arlington, Virginia, based firm specializing in customer service research studies for call centers and many other industries.

Telecommunications Device for the Deaf (TDD) or Telephone Typewriter (TTY) A typewriter-type device used by people with hearing disabilities for typing messages back and forth via telephone lines.

Telecommunications Relay Service (TRS) Through such services, specially trained operators act as intermediaries between people who are deaf, hard-of-hearing, speech disabled, or deaf and blind and standard telephone users.

telecommuting A trend seen in many congested metropolitan areas and government offices. To reduce traffic and pollution and to save resources (e.g., rent, telephone, and technology systems) many organizations allow employees to set up home offices and from there electronically communicate and forward information to their corporate offices.

Telephone Typewriter system (TTY) A typewriter-type device used by people with hearing disabilities for typing messages back and forth via telephone lines. [Also known as Telecommunications Device for the Deaf (TDD).]

telephone management Strategies for the effective use of the telephone and associated equipment in communicating.

thought speed The rate at which the human brain processes information.

time allocation Amount of attention given to a person or project.

time management The systematic practice of categorizing daily activities, identifying and eliminating factors that interfere with efficiency, and developing effective strategies for getting the most out of the time available.

time management and technology Refers to the ability to use technology to improve effectiveness and efficiency in a service environment.

time management face-to-face Techniques for increasing time efficiency when dealing with customers.

time management on the run Strategies for using downtime effectively to accomplish small tasks or be creative.

time perception The manner in which time is viewed as being either polychronic or monochronic.

time reality Acceptance of the fact that each person has only a finite amount of time each day to accomplish tasks and to enhance its usage.

time wasters Events, people, items, and other factors that create unnecessary loss of time.

total quality management (TQM) and continuous quality improvement (CQI) A systematic approach to identifying and quantifying best practices in an organization and/or industry in order to make improvements in effectiveness and efficiency.

touch point Any instance in which a service provider or organization (e.g., face to face, in writing, through technology) comes in contact with a customer; it is an opportunity to influence customer loyalty and enhance the customer relationship.

trust Key element in cementing interpersonal relationships.

two-way communication An active process in which two individuals apply all the elements of interpersonal communication (e.g., listening, feedback, positive language) in order to effectively exchange information and ideas.

U

underpromise and overdeliver A service strategy in which service providers strive for excellent customer service and satisfaction by doing more than they say they will for the customer or exceeding customer expectations.

V

values Long-term appraisals of the worth of an idea, person, place, thing, or practice held by individuals, groups, or cultures. They affect attitudes and behavior.

verbal feedback The response given to a sender's message that allows both the sender and receiver to know that a message was received correctly.

verbal fillers Verbal sounds, words, or utterances that break silence but add little to a conversation. Examples are uh, um, ah, and you know.

vision disabilities Condition resulting from reduced or lost visual acuity or ability.

vocal cues Qualities of the voice that send powerful nonverbal messages. Examples are rate, pitch, volume, and tone.

voice mail management System for creating outgoing messages and leaving messages on an answering system effectively.

voice quality Refers to the sound of one's voice. Terms often attributed to voice quality are raspy, nasal, hoarse, and gravelly.

voice response unit (VRU) System that allows customers to call 24 hours a day, 7 days a week by keying a series of numbers on the telephone keypad in order to get information or answers to questions.

volume Refers to loudness or softness of the voice when speaking.

W

wants Things that customers typically desire but do not necessarily need.

what customers want Things that customers typically desire but do not necessarily need.

wiki   A form of server software that allows nontechnical personnel to create and edit Web site pages using any Web browser and without complex programming knowledge.

win-win situation   An outcome to a disagreement in which both parties walk away feeling that they got what they wanted or needed.

workplace violence   A trend that has developed and escalated in the past decade. Spawned by many changes in the workplace, shifting societal values and beliefs, and a variety of other factors, violence is blossoming in the workplace.

Y

Y2K bug   The term applied to a programming error made in many software packages that would cause a computer to fail to recognize the year 2000 at midnight on December 31, 1999. In instances where the oversight occurred, computers would cease to function at that hour. Billions of dollars were spent to correct the error worldwide.

younger customers   Subjective term referring to anyone younger than the service provider. Sometimes used to describe members of generation X (born to baby boomers) or later.

Chapter 1

1. www.amica.com/about_us/company_history/history.html.
2. M. Toosi, "Consumer Spending: An Engine for U.S. Job Growth," Monthly Labor Review, U.S. Department of Labor, Bureau of Labor Statistics, Washington, DC, November 2002, p. 12.
3. U.S. Bureau of Labor Statistics, "Employment Outlook: 2008–18," Monthly Labor Review, November 2009. www.bls.gov/opub/mlr/2009/11/art1full.pdf.
4. Ibid.
5. U.S. Bureau of Labor Statistics, "Employment Projections: 2008–2018 Summary." www.bls.gov/news.release/ecopro.nr0.htm.
6. U.S. Bureau of Labor Statistics, "American Time Use Survey Summary–2008 Results." www.bls.gov/news.release/atus.nr0.htm.
7. "Four in Five Americans Made Cuts to Personal Spending Due to Economy." www.harrisinteractive.com/harris_poll/pubs/Harris_Poll_2009_08_19.pdf.
8. "Tomorrow's Jobs," U.S. Bureau of Labor Statistics. www.bls.gov/oco/oco2003.htm.
9. Bureau of Labor Statistics, "Labor Force Demographic Data, Civilian Noninstitutional Population (2008–2018)." www.bls.gov/emp/ep_data_labor_force.htm.
10. U.S. Census Bureau, "2007 Internet and Computer Use Supplement to the Current Population Survey." www.census.gov/Press-Release/www/releases/archives/communication_industries/013849.html.
11. U.S. Bureau of Labor Statistics, "Civilian Labor Force by Age, Sex, Race, and Ethnicity, 1988, 1998, 2008 and Projected 2018." www.bls.gov/emp/ep_table_301.pdf.
12. U.S. Bureau of Labor Statistics, "Current Population Survey, Usual Weekly Earnings of Wage and Salary Workers, Third Quarter 2009." www.bls.gov/news.release/pdf/wkyeng.pdf.
13. Bureau of Labor Statistics, Foreign-Born Workers: Labor Force Characteristics in 2008." www.bls.gov/news.release/pdf/forbrn.pdf.
14. U.S. Census, "Retail Trade Sales—Total and E-Commerce by Kind of Business: 2007." www.census.gov/compendia/statab/2010/tables/10s1021.pdf.
15. U.S. Bureau of Labor Statistics, "Employee Tenure in 2008." www.bls.gov/news.release/pdf/tenure.pdf
16. A Stew of Small Biz Stats. www.businessweek.com/smallbiz/content/may2006/sb20050502.489185.htm.

Chapter 2

1. "A Crash Course in Outsourcing," Harvard Management Update, Vol. 8, No. 11, November 2003.

Chapter 3

1. Statistics about Business Size (including Small Business), U.S. Census Bureau. www.census.gov/epcd/www/smallbus.html.

Chapter 4

1. Julius Fast, Body Language, Pocket Books, New York, 1960.
2. Albert Mehrabian, Silent Messages: Implicit Communication of Emotions and Attitudes, 2nd ed., Wadsworth Publishing, Belmont, CA, 1981, pp. 75–80.
3. Mann, J, The Difference: Discovering the Hidden Ways We Silence Girls: Finding Alternatives That Can Give Them a Voice, Werner Roohr, New York, NY (1996).
4. National Geographic Society, www.nationalgeographic.com.

Chapter 5

1. National Sleep Foundation, "Fatigue and Excessive Sleepiness." www.sleepfoundation.org/article/sleep-related-problems/excessive-sleepiness-and-sleep.
2. National Sleep Foundation. Sleep Drive and Your Body Clock. www.sleepfoundation.org/article/sleep-topics/sleep-drive-and-your-body-clock.

Chapter 6

1. Desmond Morris, Bodytalk: The Meaning of Human Gestures, Crown Trade Paperbacks, New York, 1994, pp. 118–119, 130–131.
2. Ibid., p.142.

Chapter 7

1. www.heinz.com/our-company/ethics-and-compliance.aspx
2. www.heinz.com/media/ourcompany/Code_of_conduct.pdf

Chapter 8

1. Tony Alessandra and Michael J. O'Connor, The Platinum Rule, Warner Books, New York, 1996.
2. American Indian Policy Center, www.airpi.org/research/tdlead.html.
3. Chickasaw Nation home page, www.chickasaw.net/site06/heritage/250_965.htm.
4. www.harrisinteractive.com/harris_poll/index.asp?PID=146.
5. "Foreign-Born Workers: Labor Force Characteristics in 2008." United States Department of Labor, Bureau of Labor Statistics. March 26, 2009, www.bls.gov/news.release/pdf/forbrn.pdf

6. National Geographic Society, Washington, DC, http://nationalgeographic.com.

7. Matthew W. Brault, "Americans with Disabilities 2005: Household Economic Studies." Issued December 2008, www.census.gov/prod/2008pubs/p70-117.pdf

8. National Institute on Deafness and Other Communication Disorders, www.nidcd.nih.gov/health/statistics/quick.htm.

9. National Center for Health Statistics, "National Health Interview Survey," 2006, www.cdc.gov/nchs/nhis.htm.

10. Matthew W. Bault, "Review of Changes to the Measurement of Disability in the 2008 American Community Survey (September 22, 2009)," U.S. Census Bureau, www.census.gov/hhes/www/disability/2008ACS_disability.pdf.

11. "65+ in the United States: 2005," U.S. Census Bureau, www.census.gov/prod/2006pubs/p23-209.pdf.

Chapter 9

1. Manufacturing/Durable Goods; E-Business. August 18, 2009. The American Customer Satisfaction Index, Second Quarter 2009; www.theacsi.org/index.php?option=com_content&task=view&id=196&Itemid=207.

2. Quarterly Retail E-Commerce Sales 2nd Quarter 2009, U.S. Census Bureau www.census.gov/retail/mrts/www/data/html/09Q2.html.

3. Annualized Wireless Industry Survey Results—December 1985 to June 2009. http://files.ctia.org/pdf/CTIA_Survey_Midyear_2009_Graphics.pdf

4. Telephone Subscribership in the United States. Alexander Belinfante, Industry Analysis and Technology Division Wireline Competition Bureau, Federal Communications Commission. www.fcc.gov/Daily_Releases/Daily_Business/2009/db0604/DOC-291222A1.pdf.

5. Teens, Cell Phones and Texting: Text Messaging Becomes Centerpiece Communication, Amanda Lenhart. Pew Internet & American Life Project, April 20, 2010. http://pewresearch.org/pubs/1572/teens-cell-phones-text-messages.

6. Pratt, Joanne, *E-Biz.com: Strategies for Small Business Success*, Office of Advocacy of the U.S. Small Business Administration. www.sba.gov/advo/research/rs220tot.pdf.

Chapter 10

1. Lowenstein, M., "Customer WOM Power: How Product and Service Experiences Impact Customers' Downstream Communication and Loyalty Behavior, and How Online and Offline Sources of Product/Service Information Impact Customer Actions." Harris Interactive. www.harrisinteractive.com/partner/whitepapers.asp#loyalty.

2. Consumer Word of Mouth Changes Buying Habits 60% of the Time. www.tarp.com/news_wom_poll.html.

3. The American Customer Satisfaction Index.

4. Humphrey Taylor, "Why Some Companies Are Trusted and Others Are Not: Personal Experience and Knowledge of Company More Important Than Glitz." June 20, 2001, www.harrisinteractive.com.

5. The Harris Poll® No. 53, June 12, 2007, Consumer Concern Over Product Recalls High. www.harrisinteractive.com/harris_poll/index.asp?PID=769.

6. Lost Customers Are Ripe for Win-back, www.customersat.com/News/PressRelease_68.asp.

7. The Face of Loyalty Programs: Who Has What Cards in Their Wallet, August 2006, www.maritzresearch.com/release.asp?rc=297&p=2&T=P.

8. J.D. Power and Associates 2009 North America Hotel Guest Satisfaction Index Study www.jdpower.com/corporate/news/releases/pressrelease.aspx?ID=2009133.

9. Channel/Partner Loyalty Management. Harris Interactive. www.harrisinteractive.com/services/loyaltyCPLM.asp.

10. Churn Management and Winback, Harris Interactive. www.harrisinteractive.com/services/loyaltyCMW.asp.

11. www.marriott.com/hotel-rates/pop-up.mi.

12. The Small Business Economy: A Report to the President (2009), Small Business Administration, Office of Advocacy Washington, DC. www.sba.gov/advo/research/sb_econ2009.pdf.

13. TARP Worldwide Customer Mine blog. http://blog.tarp.com/?m=20081109.

Bibliography

Aguilar, Leslie, and Linda Stokes. *Multicultural Customer Service: Providing Outstanding Service Across Cultures.* New York: McGraw-Hill/Irwin, 1996.

Alessandra, Tony, and Michael J. O'Connor. *The Platinum Rule: Discover the Four Basic Business Personalities and How They Can Lead You to Success.* New York: Grand Central Publishing, 1998.

Andersen, Peter A. *The Complete Idiot's Guide to Body Language.* New York: Penguin Group, 2004.

Anderson, Kristin, and Carol Kerr. *Customer Relationship Management.* New York: McGraw-Hill, 2002.

Anderson, Kristin, and Ron Zemke. *Knock Their Socks Off Answers.* New York: AMACOM, 1995.

Arredondo, Lani. *Communicating Effectively.* New York: McGraw-Hill, 2000.

Axtell, Roger E. *Gestures: The Do's and Taboos of Body Language Around the World.* New York: Wiley, 1991.

Berko, Roy M., Lawrence B. Rosenfeld, and Larry A. Samovar. *Connecting: A Culture-Sensitive Approach to Interpersonal Communication Competency.* 2nd ed. Fort Worth, TX: Harcourt Brace, 1997.

Bosworth, Michael T., and John R. Holland. *Customer Centric Selling.* New York: McGraw-Hill, 2004.

Bowman, Judith. *Don't Take the Last Donut: New Rules of Business Etiquette.* Franklin Lakes, NJ: Career Press, 2007.

Calero, Henry H. *The Power of Nonverbal Communication: How You Act Is More Important Than What You Say.* Los Angeles: Silver Lake Publishing, 2005.

Capodagli, Bill, and Lynn Jackson. *The Disney Way: Harnessing the Management Secrets of Disney in Your Company.* New York: McGraw-Hill, 2007.

Disney Institute. *Be Our Guest: Perfecting the Art of Customer Service.* New York: Disney Editions, 2001.

Ford, Lisa, David McNair, and Bill Perry. *Exceptional Customer Service: Going Beyond Your Good Service to Exceed the Customer's Expectation.* Avon, MA: Adams Media, 2001.

Gee, Val, and Jeff Gee. *Super Service: Seven Keys to Delivering Great Customer Service.* New York: McGraw-Hill, 1999.

Lebon, Paul. *Escape Voicemail Hell: Boost Your Productivity by Making Voicemail Work for You.* Highland Village, TX: Parleau, 2000.

Lucas, Robert W. *How to Be a Great Call Center Representative.* Watertown, MA: American Management Association, 2001.

National Restaurant Association. *Customer Service Competency Guide.* Upper Saddle River, NJ: Prentice Hall, 2007.

Pease, Allan, and Barbara Pease. *The Definitive Book of Body Language.* New York: Bantam Dell, 2004.

Quinlan, Kathryn A. *Customer Service Representative.* Mankato, MN: Capstone Press, 1999.

Richardson, Will. *Blogs, Wikis, Podcasts and Other Powerful Tools for Classrooms.* Thousand Oaks, CA: Corwin Press, 2006.

Satterwhite, Marilyn, and Judith Olson-Sutton. *Business Communication at Work.* New York: Glencoe/McGraw-Hill, 2000.

Sterne, Jim. *Customer Service on the Internet: Building Relationships, Increasing Loyalty, and Staying Competitive,* 2nd ed. New York: Wiley, 2000.

Stinnett, Bill. *Think Like Your Customer: A Winning Strategy to Maximize Sales by Understanding How and Why Your Customers Buy.* New York: McGraw-Hill, 2005.

Swift, Ronald S. *Accelerating Customer Relationships: Using CRM and Relationship Technologies.* Upper Saddle River, NJ: Prentice Hall, 2001.

Timm, Paul R., and Christopher G. Jones. *Technology and Customer Service: Profitable Relationship Building.* Upper Saddle River, NJ: Pearson Education, 2005.

Wainwright, Gordon R. *Teach Yourself Body Language.* Chicago: Contemporary Books, 2003.

Zemke, Ron, and Chip Bell. *Service Magic: The Art of Amazing Your Customers.* Dearborn, MI: Dearborn Trade Publishing, 2003.

Zemke, Ron, Claire Raines, and Bob Filipczak. *Generations at Work: Managing the Clash of Veterans, Boomers, Xers, and Nexters in Your Workplace.* New York: AMACOM, 2000.

Zemke, Ron, and John A. Woods. *Best Practices in Customer Service.* New York: AMACOM, 1998.

Zimmerman, Scott, Ronald Finklestein, and Tony Alessandra. *The Platinum Rule for Small Business Mastery.* New York: Morgan James Publishing, 2007.

Credits

Chapter 1

p. 2: Courtesy Larry Wilson; p. 5: Courtesy Amica Mutual Insurance Co.; p. 8: © Corbis; p. 12: © Comstock/Getty RF; p. 18: © Tim McGuire/Corbis; p. 22: © Chuck Savage/Corbis.

Chapter 2

p. 39: Courtesy Ben & Jerry's; p. 51: © BananaStock/PunchStock RF; p. 58: © Digital Vision/Getty RF; p. 62: © The McGraw-Hill Companies, Inc./Erica S. Leeds; p. 66: © Getty RF.

Chapter 3

p. 76: © Bob Daemmrich/PhotoEdit, Inc.; p. 79: © AP Photo/ The Cleaner, Mike Lawrence; p. 82: © Jeff Greenberg/PhotoEdit, Inc.; p. 90: © Stock Byte/Punch Stock RF; p. 98(top left): © Getty Images; p. 98(top middle): © Getty RF; p. 98(top right): © Lon C. Diehl/PhotoEdit, Inc.; p. 98(middle left): © David Urbina Photography/PhotoEdit, Inc.; p. 98(middle center): © Digital Stock RF; p. 98(middle right): © Corbis RF; p. 98(bottom left): © Clayton Sharrard/PhotoEdit, Inc.; p. 98 (bottom right): © IMS Communications Ltd./Capstone Design RF.

Chapter 4

p. 114: © The McGraw-Hill Companies, Inc./Jill Braaten, photographer; p. 119: © Helen King/Corbis; p. 123: © Comstock/ Punchstock RF; p. 128: © Photodisc/Getty RF; p. 138: © Bob Daemmrich/PhotoEdit, Inc.

Chapter 5

p. 150: © Thony Belizaire/AFP/Getty Images; p. 157: © Spencer Grant/PhotoEdit, Inc.; p. 160: © Godshoot/PictureQuest RF; p. 164: © Monkey Business Images/Cutcaster RF; p. 170: © Comstock/Getty RF.

Chapter 6

p. 182: Courtesy Guardian Pest Control Management Inc.; p. 185: © Photodisc/Getty RF; p. 198: © John Henley/Corbis; p. 207(left): © BananaStock/Jupiter Images RF; p. 207(right): © Digital Vision/Getty RF.

Chapter 7

p. 215: © The McGraw-Hill Companies, Inc./Pamela Carley, photographer; p. 221: © Phil Martin/PhotoEdit, Inc.; p. 223: © Getty RF; p. 225: © Getty RF.

Chapter 8

p. 252: © The McGraw-Hill Companies/Pamela Carley, photographer; p. 256: © Stewart Cohen/Pam Ostrow/Blend Images/ Corbis; p. 277: © Digital Vision/Getty RF.

Chapter 9

p. 287: Courtesy Google; p. 294(both): © BananaStock RF; p. 310: © Image Source/Getty RF; p. 315: © Getty Images.

Chapter 10

p. 332: Courtesy Stoner, Inc.; p. 335: © Don Emmert/AFP/ Getty Images; p. 344: © Joey Foley/Getty Images for Payless ShoeSource; p. 356: © JLP/Jose L. Pelaez/Corbis; p. 359: © Getty Images.

Index